TO FIGHT ALOUD IS VERY BRAVE

American Poetry and the Civil War

Faith Barrett

UNIVERSITY OF MASSACHUSETTS PRESS
Amherst and Boston

Printed in the United States of America

ISBN 978-1-55849-963-8 (pbk); 962-1 (hardcover)

Designed by Sally Nichols
Set in Goudy Old Style
Printed and bound by Thomson-Shore, Inc.

Library of Congress Cataloging-in-Publication Data

Barrett, Faith, 1965–
To fight aloud is very brave : American poetry and the Civil War / Faith Barrett.
p. cm.
Includes bibliographical references and index.
ISBN 978-1-55849-963-8 (pbk. : alk. paper) — ISBN 978-1-55849-962-1 (library cloth : alk. paper) 1. United States—History—Civil War, 1861–1985—Literature and the war. 2. American poetry—19th century—History and criticism. 3. War poetry, American—History and criticism. 4. Patriotic poetry, American—History and criticism. I. Title.
PS310.C585B37 2012
811'.409358737—dc23
2012030820

British Library Cataloguing in Publication data are available.

TO FIGHT ALOUD IS VERY BRAVE

For Eve and for Karen
With thanks and with all my love

To fight aloud, is very brave –
But *gallanter*, I know
Who charge within the bosom
The Cavalry of Wo –

Who win, and nations do not see –
Who fall – and none observe –
Whose dying eyes, no Country
Regards with patriot love –

We trust, in plumed procession
For such, the Angels go –
Rank after Rank, with even feet –
And Uniforms of snow.

Emily Dickinson

CONTENTS

ILLUSTRATIONS

ACKNOWLEDGMENTS

It gives me great pleasure to thank the many colleagues and friends who supported me in my work on this project. I could not have completed this book without the advice, encouragement, and invaluable critical responses provided by Paula Bennett, Cristanne Miller, and Elizabeth Young. For their extraordinary generosity as mentors and the inspiration of their fine scholarship, I am deeply grateful. The members of my writing group in northeastern Wisconsin—Monica Rico, Melanie Boyd, and Deirdre Flynn—read the entire manuscript in draft; their comments improved this work immeasurably. My Milwaukee-area Americanists group—Angela Sorby, Sarah Wadsworth, and Amy Blair—were extraordinarily helpful and attentive readers of the manuscript as well. The members of my nineteenth-century women writers group (WWGSD) provided crucial moral support and helpful critical readings in the later stages; warm thanks to Desiree Henderson, Jennifer Putzi, and Theresa Strouth Gaul, with particular thanks to Alex Socarides and Elizabeth Stockton, who read multiple drafts of some chapters. Elizabeth Dillon, Eliza Richards, Don Dingledine, David McGlynn, Jennifer Geigel Mikulay, and Elizabeth Robinson all provided sound advice and critical intervention at crucial moments. Mary Loeffelholz, Martha Nell Smith, Elizabeth Renker, Douglas Robillard, and Tenney Nathanson provided insightful commentary on earlier versions of these chapters. I am grateful to the scholars who read my manuscript both for the University of Massachusetts Press and for my tenure file; their comments proved invaluable in the final stages of revising. Bruce Wilcox of the University of Massachusetts Press has been generous and supportive of this project throughout my years of work on it. The genesis for this book was a chapter of the dissertation I wrote at UC Berkeley under the guidance of Nancy Ruttenburg, Susan Schweik, and Sam Otter. I am particularly grateful to Sam Otter both for his generous encouragement of my work and for the inspiring model he provides in his scholarship and teaching in the field of American studies.

A fellowship from the American Antiquarian Society enabled me to work with their wonderful holdings and their extraordinarily generous and collegial staff. My particular thanks to Caroline Sloat, Elizabeth Pope, Megan Bocian, Jaclyn Donovan, Georgia Barnhill, and Joanne Chaison. My thanks also to the scholars who were at AAS during my fellowship month and who read and responded to my work on soldiers' poetry: Philip Gura, Jennifer Anderson, Nancy Schumacher, Robert Bonner, Edward Larkin, Katja Kanzler and Gesa McEnthun. For the financial support I received from the National Endowment for the Humanities as part of the "We the People" initiative, I am deeply grateful. A generous fellowship I received from the Huntington Library enabled me to work extensively with soldiers' papers there. The College of Letters, Arts, and Sciences at Cal Poly Pomona provided me with invaluable release-time from teaching as well as travel stipends in support of this project. I am grateful to the graduate students who took my Civil War culture courses at Cal Poly for the stimulating discussions of those seminars. Provost David Burrows of Lawrence University supported this project in ways both large and small. Generous travel funds from Lawrence enabled me to do extensive archival work at the Library of Congress, the Newberry Library, the Jones Library in Amherst, special collections at Amherst College, and the Houghton Library at Harvard. I am grateful to the staff at these archives for their assistance. My particular thanks to Tevis Kimball, curator of Special Collections at the Jones Library. A number of electronic archives proved invaluable to my work on this project: the Lester S. Levy collection of sheet music at Johns Hopkins University, the Making of America collections of nineteenth-century periodicals available through the University of Michigan and the Cornell University libraries, and the Documenting the American South collection at the University of North Carolina. The friendly and patient staff of the library at Lawrence University have provided timely support and assistance since I first arrived on campus; my particular thanks to Antoinette Powell, who provided help both with nineteenth-century sheet music and with nineteenth-century periodicals. Several student researchers at Lawrence assisted me in my work: my thanks to Elizabeth Breese, Julia Callandar, Cherisse Hall, and Alison Vere Halen. Lawrence staff members Joanne Johnson and Lori Rose provided invaluable administrative support throughout this project.

For the fellowship and good company of Milwaukee Friends Meeting, I am deeply grateful. Special thanks are due to Kathy Dahlk, Mary Lord, Peg Remsen, Rebecca North, Roger Hansen, and John Payton. Karen Hoffmann and Maxa Ott were unfailingly supportive and encouraging of my work on this project, in ways too numerous to count, from start to finish. I hope I will have future occasion to return in some measure the support, encouragement, and friendship so many have generously offered me.

The following material was previously published in a different form. Part of chapter 4 appeared as "Addresses to a Divided Nation: Images of War in Emily Dickinson and Walt Whitman," *Arizona Quarterly* 61.4 (Winter 2005) and is included by permission of the Regents of the University of Arizona. Another part of chapter 4 appeared as "'Drums off the Phantom Battlements': Dickinson's War Poems in Discursive Context," *Emily Dickinson Companion*, edited by Mary Loeffelholz and Martha Nell Smith (Oxford: Blackwell, 2008). Finally part of chapter 6 appeared as "'They answered him aloud': Popular Voice and Nationalist Discourse in Melville's *Battle-Pieces*," *Leviathan: A Journal of Melville Studies* 9 (2007).

TO FIGHT ALOUD
IS VERY BRAVE

INTRODUCTION

The Rhetoric of Voice in Civil War Poetry

"Mine eyes have seen the glory of the coming of the Lord" writes Julia Ward Howe in the opening lines of her career-making "Battle Hymn of the Republic." Beginning with a solitary speaker's declaration of her prophetic vision of the future of the nation, the piece builds to a dramatic climax in the fifth and final stanza which enacts rhetorically the forging of the collective of Union supporters: "As he died to make men holy, let us die to make men free." In moving from the singular "I" to the collective "us," Howe's "Battle Hymn" exemplifies the sense of political purpose that guided many American poets as they attempted to define the relationship between the individual and the nation during the Civil War years. Yet while scholars often point to Howe as a prototypical patriotic poet of the war, they frequently overlook the complexity and ambivalence of her many poetic stances. For example, in "The Lyric I," included in her 1857 collection *Words for the Hour,* Howe explores the challenges facing a woman poet who writes work that is both politically engaged and aesthetically complex. The "lyric I" of the title splinters into multiple irreconcilable I's, as the poem considers how to negotiate the relationship between domestic, political, and aesthetic stances. While scholars have been quick to see in Howe's "Battle Hymn" a decision to endorse a patriotic "we," a closer look at Howe's work from the Civil War era reveals a writer who was profoundly ambivalent about the relationship between singular and collective stances in her poetry. Indeed it is Howe's probing exploration of the relationship between the lyric "I" and the collective "we"—rather than an unabashed endorsement of nationalist stances—that marks her work as exemplary of the poetry of this period. The multiple perspectives within Howe's body of work—and within individual poems—reveal that the lyric self and the collective voices of nationalism are not diametrically opposed in Civil War–era poetry: rather they are related positions on a continuous spectrum of potential stances.

This spectrum of potential stances—the versatility of poetic voice—prompted a remarkable outpouring of poetry by men and women from all walks of life during the American Civil War.[1] The war called on Americans to make decisions about their familial, regional, and national allegiances; this demand that each individual define his or her own position in relation to the construct of the nation coincided with rising rates of literacy and with pedagogical methods and print media that promoted the cultural centrality of poetry. In the Civil War era, Americans on both sides of the conflict believed that poetry had a vital role to play in developing and disseminating the ideologies of national identity. How did Civil War–era poets create for themselves a rhetorical platform from which they could address their immediate circle of family and friends, and the nations of the Confederacy, the Union, and the United States? How did their poetry respond to the ways that the war destabilized the constructs of "family," "community," and "nation"? These are two of the central questions this study will pursue.

To Fight Aloud Is Very Brave considers the work of leading white male writers, unpublished soldier-poets, and women and African American poets who have either been overlooked or who have yet to be studied in relation to the war. Reading across this spectrum, my analysis reveals a remarkable shift in the ways that poets address their local and national audiences. During the war, a growing number of writers and readers began to recognize poetry as an extraordinarily versatile means of expression. As the mourning of individuals and families coincided with the mourning of states and nations, the national crisis of the war led to a blurring of the boundaries between "civic" and "private" stances. In the flexible genre of poetry, writers could test out a range of different potential stances, speaking in the first-person singular or the first-person plural for the collectives of local groups, groups of soldiers, or a whole region—or shifting deftly between and among these positions, not only between poems but also within one text. Quickly read, and also potentially quickly written, printed, and distributed, poetry became the central literary site for this exploration of the changing relationship between self and nation. Two significant historical developments worked to support the versatility of poetry. First, with the proliferation of new and more affordable methods of publishing, circulating, and receiving poetry, both amateur and professional writers began to rely on poetry to address audiences they could not previously have reached; boundaries between once distinct kinds of audiences thus became increasingly fluid. Second, popular song and poetry became more closely connected, and this mingling of oral and textual forms of circulation lent to poetry the ideological flexibility of song.

Thus new modes of circulation worked to collapse both the boundary between poetry and song and public–private boundaries, generating newly imaginable forms of community and a proliferation of new audiences in both the North and the South; even as poets wrote poems and songs that forged a collective "we" of Union or Confederate supporters, new modes of circulation and new reading audiences led to a proliferation of conflicting and mutually exclusive "we's" in Civil War–era poetry. As a growing number of writers sought to define their relationship to the nation, they offered a proliferating array of definitions in a dynamic process that worked to both constitute and subdivide national audiences. The American Civil War was not just "a *literary* war," to borrow the phrase Paul Fussell applies to World War I; rather the Civil War was more specifically a *poetry*-fueled war.[2]

Nineteenth-century Americans understood poetry as a crucial means of engagement with political discourses. Yet Civil War poetry often fared poorly in the hands of twentieth-century scholars precisely because its political commitments are writ so large. In *Patriotic Gore*, Edmund Wilson dismisses much of the poetry of the Civil War as "versified journalism"; Wilson's view also reflects the New Critical consensus that the Civil War—and indeed the nineteenth century—produced little poetry of lasting literary value, apart from the work of Whitman and Dickinson.[3] At the start of the twenty-first century, Wilson's critique remains surprisingly influential in scholarly circles, as is made evident by the wealth of American studies approaches to popular fiction and prose and the comparatively few scholarly analyses of nineteenth-century popular poetry. Writing in the aftermath of two world wars, mid-twentieth-century critics celebrated twentieth-century modernist poets for their commitment to an aesthetic of fragmentation, irony, and indeterminacy. Turning back to the nineteenth century, these same scholars tended to admire mainly Whitman and Dickinson, anointing them as forebears of modernism and abstracting their work both from its immediate political context and from the extraordinary poetic dialogue of their own times. This critical maneuver had the effect of flattening the richness and complexity of the poetic conversations of this era even as it also tended to overstate the distinctiveness of Whitman's and Dickinson's achievement. New Criticism thus put into place a binary opposition between a nineteenth-century poetry that was seen as having serious aesthetic limitations and a modernist poetry that was seen as having aesthetic merit. This opposition made the critical neglect of nineteenth-century poetry seem like a reasoned decision even as it also foregrounded poetry as the generic site for expression of timeless and eternal aesthetic values. While some Civil War–era poetry lacks the aesthetic ambition that twentieth-century scholars valued most highly, this body of work nonetheless offers a remarkable variety of stances and voices and a far greater range of experiment than critics have previously acknowledged. Moreover, to analyze American Civil War culture without attending to the poetry of this period is to ignore the most influential and vital discursive conversation taking place in the divided nation at that time.

Recent scholarship in the field of American studies has done much to redress the critical neglect of nineteenth-century poetry. Groundbreaking studies by Paula Bennett, Mary Loeffelholz, Eliza Richards, and Angela Sorby have argued for the richness and vitality of this body of work.[4] To date, however, there has been no book-length study of Civil War poetry, and there has been no work on poetry written by soldiers. Scholarly interest in literature of the Civil War is reflected in Timothy Sweet's study of Whitman and Melville, Elizabeth Young's analysis of Civil War–era prose by women, Alice Fahs's account of popular literature of the war, Lisa Long's study of the treatment and representation of the body in the Civil War era, Kathleen Diffley's analysis of popular Civil War fiction, and Shirley Samuels's work on visual and literary representations of the nations of the Union and Confederacy.[5] None of these studies, however, offers an extended analysis of the full range of Civil War poetry. My book builds on this groundbreaking scholarship by examining that range.

Like Virginia Jackson's *Dickinson's Misery*, my study suggests that we need to rethink the way that we read nineteenth-century American poetry through the generic lens of the lyric.[6] My analysis thus spans the high/low and modernist/non-modernist divides that shaped earlier critical approaches to the poetry of this period: I will argue that the origins of the modernist poets' commitment to skepticism, irony, and fragmentation can be found not only in Whitman's and Dickinson's poetics but rather across the full range of American Civil War poetry. Reading poetry from the Civil War era in particular offers us new ways of understanding nineteenth-century poetry more broadly; and we risk misreading modernist poetry in profound ways if we fail to understand its broader roots in the nineteenth century. In his dismissal of Civil War poetry, Edmund Wilson reaffirms the generic opposition between nationalist declamatory verse—which he finds lots of—and introspective private poetry—which he has difficulty finding. Reading across the full spectrum of Civil War–era work quickly unsettles this opposition, however, as individual writers—and even individual poems—shift flexibly from the declamatory postures of nationalism to moments of introspection, skepticism, or self-disclosure.

Reading both canonical and noncanonical writers, I examine the ways that nineteenth-century poets write to and for one another in an ongoing conversation about the political commitments of poetry. Reading poems in relation to popular song, journalism, political essays, and visual representations of battlefields (particularly images from magazines and newspapers), I situate these writers' stances in relation to their nineteenth-century discursive contexts. Building on the insightful work of Paula Bennett and Mary Loeffelholz, both of whom foreground the role that nineteenth-century women poets play in determining the kinds of cultural work that poetry does, I argue that women writers and writers of color play a leading role in establishing the centrality of poetry during the war years. For these writers, the stakes will be particularly high as they map out the relationship between the personal "I" and a collective "we."

Though this is in part a recovery project that seeks to renew interest in the work of neglected nineteenth-century poets, it also responds to current critical debates about the relationship between popular literature and nationalism in nineteenth-century America. Meredith McGill's important study of the culture of reprinting in the antebellum era challenges scholars to reconsider the material practices of printing and reprinting that shaped American conceptions of authorship and publication.[7] McGill argues that the development of the literary marketplace results in a proliferation of possible audiences and the emergence of new categories for authorial identity, categories that could potentially include not only middle-class white women but also escaped or freed slaves. Building on McGill's analysis, I will argue that during the Civil War, the highly flexible genre of poetry is particularly well suited to encourage a proliferation of audiences and authorial identities. Like Milette Shamir's *Inexpressible Privacy*, my study attends to the contested and rapidly changing relationship between the private self and public sphere, unsettling the oppositions that have frequently shaped scholarly approaches to these cultural categories.[8] Christopher Castiglia's *Interior States* revises earlier scholars' more stable accounts of nineteenth-century nationalism, suggesting that the interiorization of the social in antebellum America resulted in a multiplicity of divided interiors that resist assimilation into a unified national whole.[9] All three of these works have shaped my approach to the fluid and multiple versions of the nation that Civil War–era poets propose.

Some preliminary historical context on the growth of new forms of print circulation, on the permeable boundary between poetry and song, and on the changing relationship between public and private stances in the Civil War era will help to explain how poetry became a central site for discussion of the construct of the nation. The Civil War coincided with an era of rapid expansion in the print media, as innovations in printing and transportation technologies enabled publishers to produce more newspapers and magazines more quickly and more cheaply and to distribute them both farther and faster via the growing railroad network. Northern readers were the most direct beneficiaries of these developments: as Alice Fahs notes in her innovative study of popular Civil War literature, Northern magazines and publishers had a far wider reach than any Southern publishing house ever achieved.[10] Wartime shortages of paper, ink, and printing presses posed daunting challenges for Southern publications; while the war prompted an extraordinary outpouring of nationalist literary production by white Southerners, the South lacked both the industrial infrastructure and the raw materials necessary to disseminate this body of work widely. The most popular of the wartime Southern periodicals, the *Southern Illustrated News*, was reputed to print as many as 20,000 copies of some numbers; in 1864 *Southern Field and Fireside* advertised that it had "13,000 subscribers."[11] These figures are impressive in relation to the obstacles the publishers faced in bringing an issue to the Southern public; they pale, however, in comparison to the circulation of the Northern publications with which these magazines were aiming to compete.

In the North, new and less expensive printing techniques combined with an increase in education and literacy rates led to robust increases in magazine and newspaper readership. Two of the most successful Northern publications exemplify this kind of growth. In 1857, *Frank Leslie's Illustrated Newspaper* reported a circulation of 100,000; by 1860, that number had increased to 164,000.[12] Though the paper experienced a precipitous drop in subscriptions in the last year of the war due to a rise in its production costs, its popularity rebounded in the 1870s.[13] At the end of 1861, *Harper's Weekly* claimed a circulation of 120,000; by 1872, that figure had risen to 160,000.[14] As Fahs notes, illustrated weeklies like these experienced a dramatic rise in readership at the outset of the war.[15] More affordable printing techniques also spurred an increase in the printing and distribution of broadsides, pamphlets, and pocket-sized books, which were distributed in both the North and South at recruitment events, departure ceremonies for local military units, and celebrations for returning troops.[16] With the growth of public education programs, particularly in the Northern states, these printed materials reached readers from a range of different socioeconomic backgrounds.[17]

Both Northern and Southern magazines and newspapers of this era regularly used poetry as featured material—and as a way to fill out their columns of type. Moreover, nineteenth-century American schoolrooms made reading, memorization, and recitation of poetry a central aspect of pedagogy.[18] Most American readers encountered poetry on a weekly if not a daily basis; and while poetry readership may have been shaped in the schoolroom, it was by no means limited to that environment. Many literate men and women of the Civil War era would have at least tried their hand at writing a few lines of poetry, penning some verses for a Valentine or for a friend's keepsake album.[19] The growth in periodical readership during this time combined with the history-making events of the war itself to fan the flames of poetic ambition for many writers.[20] In the North and to a somewhat lesser extent in the South, a range of new magazines and newspapers published an eclectic mix of journalism, fiction, editorials, and poetry; amateur poets and poets who had once written for a specific kind of reader could now begin to write for multiple intersecting audiences.[21] Twentieth-century conceptions of "high literary" and "popular" poetry are particularly inadequate to describe the complexity of American Civil War poetry since the magazines and newspapers in which this poetry first appeared sought to engage as broad a readership as possible.[22] In the North, Julia Ward Howe's "Battle Hymn" was distributed as sheet music and was sung by Union soldiers on the march; she also published the poem as a text in the prestigious and exclusive *Atlantic Monthly*, however. In the South, one of the leading lights of antebellum literary culture, Henry Timrod, published poems in the weekly *Southern Illustrated News*, though he might well have been reluctant to appear in the pages of a "story paper" before the founding of the Confederacy. Writers on both sides of the Mason-Dixon line felt a strong obligation to define their relationship to the nations they supported by means of their writing. As these examples suggest, the war prompted poets to address audiences that might not previously have interested them; it also enabled poets to address audiences they had not previously been able to reach. Even as poets began to constitute new audiences by means of their stances of address, however, those same stances resulted in a proliferation of distinct factional audiences; Civil War–era poetry thus works to constitute the "imagined community" of the nation—to borrow Anderson's phrase—even as it also produces a destabilizing array of smaller audience-communities.[23]

The expansion of print media in the Civil War era combined with the wide-ranging public awareness that the war represented a crucial turning point in American history: what resulted was not only an increase in amateur authorship but also a simultaneous interest in collecting and circulating poetry (as well as letters, stories, and photographs) among family and friends.[24] Professionally edited compilations such as Leslie's *Pictorial History* and G. P. Putnam's still more comprehensive *Rebellion Record* gave amateur scrapbookers a model for how to assemble their own personal collections of poems, songs, stories, and illustrations of the war; these items might be clipped from newspapers and magazines or handwritten, as they had been since earlier in the nineteenth century.[25] Soldiers sent journals, poems, and letters home with the sense that their lived experience of the war might well have meaning for readers outside of their immediate family circle; but civilians also recorded their responses to wartime developments by means of poems, journals, albums, and scrapbooks. In some cases they constructed albums and scrapbooks in the hope that soldiers now far from home might be able to peruse them later on; in other cases, they made these books as a record of their own impressions of wartime experience.[26] As Alice Fahs notes, the ambitious thoroughness of the *Rebellion Record* implicitly argued that "every aspect of the war was important and worthy of recording."[27] Compilers of personal scrapbooks could shape their own version of the war's events, foregrounding the poems, songs, and other materials that best represented their own experience.

Editing scrapbooks and albums gave readers a powerful sense of personal connection to the poems they chose to include. Scrapbooking practices may also have led to an increased interest in producing self-published volumes of poetry. In the years after the war, soldiers who were amateur poets sometimes sought the broader audience that print publication would offer their work; some collected their poems into handmade books, a form of self-publication that was widely practiced in mid-to-late nineteenth-century America. Just as Dickinson bound her poems into the now famous fascicles and Melville opted to self-publish volumes of poetry late in his life, so too did amateur poets of the Civil War era seek to self-publish, either in handwritten books or, for the more affluent, in self-funded print editions. Poetry played a crucial role in the scrapbooks and self-published books of this era because of the relative ease and speed with which poems could be written, copied and/or printed and circulated. The brevity of short poems and the ease of excerpting longer pieces made the genre of poetry both easily portable and highly economical either for handwritten or print replication. As the practice of scrapbooking suggests, many readers developed an intimate and deeply felt relationship to the poetry produced during the war years, finding in both nationally published and informally circulated work expression of their innermost feelings of loss, displacement, or sorrow. The capacious flexibility of poetic voice—combined with the fact that poems could be easily circulated, memorized, and read aloud—offered readers from a range of backgrounds the sense that the poet spoke to or for them. Collecting war poems and often reading them aloud to family and friends, scrapbook editors could encounter again and again poetic voices that expressed their own emotional experience of the war.

The intensity of readers' personal connection to poetry was heightened, as I will go on to suggest in chapter one, by the hand-in-glove relationship that developed between poetry and popular song in this era. The permeability of the boundary between poetry and song offered amateur and professional writers alike both rapid and inexpensive means of circulating their work and an extraordinary degree of ideological flexibility in their texts, as writers revised and responded to earlier versions of song lyrics. During the war years, recruitment events, farewell ceremonies for departing units of soldiers, and celebrations for their return all included singing and recitation of poems; Civil War–era newspapers abound in accounts of soldiers singing while on the march, in camp, or in military hospitals.[28] Poets wrote lyrics, composers wrote music, and publishers rushed to get sheet music and songsters into the hands of soldiers and civilians. Songwriters and publishers soon learned that sheet music and songsters would sell briskly in wartime; writers and publishers also recognized the power of song to forge alliances within disparate groups of singers, readers, and listeners.

Because the genre of poetry hovered on the boundary between text and voice then—both metaphorically on the page and also culturally in nineteenth-century America—a central concern of this study will be close examination of what I will call voice-effects in the texts under consideration. The apostrophe, the exclamation, first- and second-person pronouns and the dialogic postures they imply, the play between first-person singular and first-person plural stances, and the songlike techniques of repetition and refrain: all of these voice-effects make explicit poetry's dual status as written and spoken word.[29] Moreover, these rhetorical techniques bring to the surface of the texts the personal and political stakes for each writer in addressing his or her contemporaries: close examination of the rhetorical maneuver of the apostrophe, for example, or the tension between the writerly "I" and the collective national "we" does much to illuminate a writer's relationship to the audience she addresses. While Emily Dickinson usually avoids the dramatic posture of the apostrophe to the nation, Whitman uses the apostrophe to try to hold the nation together in one of his antebellum poems. As a white middle-class woman writer, Julia Ward Howe frequently relies on dramatic voice-effects—apostrophes to leading male reformers, stances in which she speaks in the first-person in the voice of a soldier or slave—in order to shore up the authority of her writerly voice; by contrast the black poet Frances Harper, a talented and sought-after public speaker, rarely uses dramatic voice-effects, knowing that she will recite her poems from the lecture platform herself. Both Howe and Harper use phrase repetition and refrains to underline the political messages of their protest poems. A detailed analysis of poetic voice-effects also points up the frequency with which poetry echoes the gestures and stances of song in this era.

Important in their own right, new developments in the publication and dissemination of poetry and the increasingly close ties between poetry and song also set the stage for the most significant change in Civil War–era poetry: namely, the new permeability between "civic" and "private" stances. This is a shift that shapes the concerns of all of the writers I will consider here and one that has particularly far-reaching consequences for American poets' relationship with their audiences. When an elegy meditates on the death of a son in slavery or in battle, it can speak not just for one bereaved family, but for whole communities, unifying disparate groups in a collective posture of grief. It is this flexibility of speaking positions that Edmund Wilson overlooks in his dismissal of Civil War poetry. Wilson writes: "It is a striking phenomenon of the period that the declamatory versification of public events should have completely rendered inaudible, should have driven into virtual hiding, the more personal kind of self-expression which has nothing to do with politics or battles, which was not concocted for any market, and which, reflecting the idiosyncrasies of the writer, was likely to take on an unconventional form."[30] Wilson argues that there is not enough poetry of introspection, but as I will go on to suggest, the permeable boundary between public and private in this body of work means that poets writing at all levels of expertise and experience move back and forth between writing from the self and writing to and for the nation. Even in the work of amateur soldier-poets, the nationalist "we" is disrupted or unsettled by the persistence of the individual speaker; even in the work of introspective writers like Dickinson and Melville, the commitments of the nationalist "we" are apparent. Thus when the reclusive Emily Dickinson writes an elegy to honor the sacrifice of a young family friend who died in the battle of New Bern, she engages with the conventions of the sentimental elegy in order to express the shock and sadness felt not only by her own family but by many in Amherst. She addresses not only her immediate Amherst community: it was widely known in the town that the older Dickinson daughter wrote poetry, and Dickinson may have circulated some of her soldier elegies among family and friends. By extension Dickinson addresses also the Union for which young Frazar Stearns died.

Changing parameters in public and private stances thus offer previously marginalized writers new kinds of rhetorical authority and new audiences, as women and African Americans write poems that speak to the larger purposes of military campaigns that are planned and led by white men. The black poet Frances Harper, for example, addresses the "men of the north" both during the war and in its aftermath, urging them to continue the struggle for justice for African Americans. A Southern black poet, George Moses Horton, will rely on his experience writing love poems for young white Southern men to write poems that speak to and for white Union soldiers, even as these same poems also express the melancholy of an emancipated slave who is about to leave his Southern homeland for good. The flexibility of poetic stances in this era foregrounds the powerful ideological ties that link sacrifices on the battlefield to sacrifices on the homefront. Like many other poets of this era, the Confederate writer Henry Timrod depicts "two armies," one of the soldiers fighting at the front and one of the women doing the support work necessary to sustain combat. The imaginative versatility of poetry makes it possible for writers to create speakers whose voices resist the limits of individual racial or gender communities: thus, for example, male poets can use sentimental postures to represent the grieving wife left at home while female poets can write poems in which speakers boldly call on men to join up and head to the front.

Both male and female poets draw from the repertoire of romanticism—evoking a lost pastoral splendor, for example—to represent gory battlefield scenes. Using the heightened dramatic postures of the solitary romantic speaker's perspective on nature, poets figure the American nation as a landscape drenched in blood, an image that becomes one of the most potent and dominant tropes of Civil War–era poetry. Such romantic landscapes make explicit the multiple public and private layers of American life in wartime, as poets draw images from the local garden, the family farm or homestead, or a nearby woods to represent either imagined or actual battlefield landscapes: thus the local boundaries of the family farm or nearby woods are superimposed onto the contested national boundaries of the Union or the Confederacy. For Northern as for Southern writers—both amateur and professional—the pressing question of the war years becomes: how can a writer address the nation when that nation itself is divided? Because of its versatility and capaciousness, poetry becomes one of the preferred genres that writers turn to in seeking to position themselves in relation to the new audiences created by the national crisis.

As this book will suggest, poetry enjoys a privileged position in Civil War culture because it draws on the rhetorical power of both textual and oral discourses; throughout the Civil War era, poetry circulated by means of both of these discursive networks simultaneously. Twentieth-century critical approaches to the lyric poem have, however, frequently privileged the definition of poetry provided by John Stuart Mill in an essay first published in 1833.[31] With its emphasis on the solitary poet speaker and the secrecy of compact between this speaker and the poem's solitary reader, Mill's model represents the scene of the lyric address in isolation from the social and historical context that produces the poem, emphasizing instead the poem's status as a fictive utterance, a staged performance of poetic voice. "Poetry," Mill writes, "is feeling confessing itself to itself, in moments of solitude."[32] Using Mill's definition as a model, twentieth-century scholars working on nineteenth-century lyric poetry have sometimes argued for a time-stalling model of the lyric stance, suggesting that the lyric speaker arrests time in order to express "emotion recollected in tranquility."[33] Such a reading model privileges poetry that offers a tersely proto-modernist expression of seemingly personal feeling, unconfined by its immediate political context.

But poetry in Civil War–era America is much richer and more varied than this limiting critical lens suggests. In a culture where poems were routinely published in newspapers and magazines and read, sung, and recited aloud both in public and in private settings, Mill's model of the solitary poet stepping out of time to soliloquize would seem to have only limited relevance.[34] As I will argue throughout this study, the poetry of the Civil War era does not step out of time—even Dickinson's riddling and hermetic poems do not. On the contrary, as I will suggest in analyzing Julia Ward Howe's "Battle Hymn," poetry lends itself to rapid composition and circulation, and many Civil War–era writers titled their poems "Words for the Hour." Dickinson's extraordinary output of poetry during the Civil War years is only one example of the lightning speed at which many writers produced new work in this era.[35] As many contemporary commentators noted, the American Civil War was the first war in which large numbers of soldiers could be transported to and from the front via the rail system and the first in which rapid and frequent updates from the front could be sent via telegraph; the speed with which poems could be written, printed, and, in many cases, sung, corresponds to this accelerated pace of action and communication. While poetry often looks back with nostalgia to a lost pastoral world, it is also the genre of instantaneity—or at least of contemporaneity—during the Civil War years.

As a prologue to my study of Civil War poetry, my first chapter offers readings of three representative songs of this era: Dan Emmett's "I Wish I Was in Dixie's Land," the Sorrow Song "Let My People Go," and Howe's "Battle Hymn of the Republic." Tracing the rapid circulation and the variant versions of these songs, I show how the permeable boundary between poetry and song worked to increase both the breadth of audiences and the flexibility of first-person and collective stances in these closely related genres. Turning next to a group of writers whose poetry was clearly strongly shaped by song, my second chapter examines the work of a group of amateur soldier-poets, both Northern and Southern, arguing that these men employ poetry as a means of defining the "nation," "home," and "family" for which they are fighting. While soldier-poets frequently rely on nationalist stances, tensions between the collective "we" of military experience and the personal "I" of the poetic speaker often undermine the conventional patriotic meanings of nation and family, underlining the extent to which soldiers reinvent these constructs for their own rhetorical purposes. In my third chapter, I discuss two professional women poets, both of whom had published volumes of poetry prior to the war. Reading the work of Julia Ward Howe and Frances Watkins Harper, I examine each woman's conflicted relationship to the personal lyric I and to the poetic stances of political protest. While Howe achieves widespread recognition for the nationalist "we" she forges in her "Battle Hymn," both in her antebellum poetry and in her Civil War–era work she continues to question the efficacy of nationalist stances. For her part, Frances Harper uses activist stances to forge a unified "we" of abolitionists and an accusatory "you" to address the failings of white Northerners; shifts and slippage within these unifying collective pronouns, however, betray the persistence of Harper's personal I—and her personal stake—in the poems.

My fourth chapter examines the poetry of Emily Dickinson, using parallel readings of her canonical counterpart, Walt Whitman, to contextualize an analysis of her address to the nation. It is a critical commonplace that Whitman addresses the nation confidently while Dickinson avoids political stances. In response to this view, I counter that Dickinson's war poetry does address the nation, though it often does so skeptically or obliquely; reading Dickinson's soldier-elegies in the context of the popular poetry and the journalism she is responding to, I argue that she alternates between skeptical and patriotic nationalist stances in her wartime work. My fifth chapter looks at two Southern poets who opposed slavery, Sarah Piatt and George Moses Horton, reading their poetics in relation to the normative Confederate example of Henry Timrod. Sarah Piatt embeds her political critiques of Southern romanticism in multivalent and elusive dialogic structures so that the genteel familial "we" of Victorian domesticity is split into the fractured and conflicted self of a singular feminine "I." Relying on multiple aesthetic stances to draw in a wide range of readers, George Moses Horton revises the stances of conventional Southern romanticism by positing a black speaker for the romantic lyric self; in representing that speaker as estranged from the Southern homeland he loves, Horton expands the boundaries of the Southern lyric "I," giving voice to the complex mix of emotions many black Southerners must have felt in the aftermath of the war. In my sixth and final chapter, I examine Herman Melville's *Battle-Pieces*, situating Melville's war poetry in the context of the popular songs, journalism, and the high romantic poetry he takes as his inspiration. Like those of the nation he seeks to address, Melville's allegiances are painfully divided: he expresses both a nostalgic faith in the powers of nationalist poetic voice and a profound skepticism about the possibility that poetry might work to reunite a divided nation. Echoing the skepticism of both some soldier poets and some of his female contemporaries, Melville thus foregrounds the changes to come in modernist poetry, where aesthetic unities and patriotic pieties alike will be fractured by the disintegration of the lyric speaker as the moral center of the poem.

My analysis of this range of Civil War work suggests that these writers regard poetry as a form of engagement with the ideologies of the nation; these poets suggest that the war was fought not only with weapons but also with what Sarah Piatt calls the "fierce words of war."[36] The poetry of this period clearly reflects the fact that people's identities were profoundly changed by the Civil War. Still more important, however, this book argues that the war changed the way that American poets addressed their audiences and that poetry changed the way that Americans understood the construct of the nation. The poetry of the Civil War era fuels a dynamic exchange among its writers and readers: in that exchange, regional and national audiences are both constituted and ultimately further fragmented by writers' complex and multilayered stances of address. Even as writers explore the unifying possibilities offered by nationalist poetic voice, the networks in which poetry circulates result in a proliferating array of smaller audience-communities. For writers, poetic voice offers the freedoms of its capaciousness, including the flexibility of shifting from a nationalist "we" to an individual "I." For the nations of the Confederacy and the Union, however, poetry is both an extraordinarily powerful tool for building collective identity and an extraordinarily effective means of creating division through dissent.

CHAPTER ONE

SHAPING COMMUNITIES THROUGH POPULAR SONG

During the early years of the Civil War, three American songs became essential anthems for the communities that adopted them, and each of these songs helped define and affirm the bonds that constituted those communities. These three songs were Dan Emmett's "I Wish I Was in Dixie's Land," the Sorrow Song "Let My People Go: A Song of the 'Contrabands'" (now better known under the title "Go Down, Moses"), and Julia Ward Howe's "Battle Hymn of the Republic," a variant version of the popular soldiers' song "John Brown's Body." Underlining the powerful legacy of Civil War culture, all three songs continue to shape conflicting versions of American identity today. Describing the ways that language works to establish the "imagined community" of the nation, Benedict Anderson emphasizes the centrality of poetry and song to that dynamic process, noting that the singing of the national anthem, for example, allows participants an experience of "contemporaneous community"; collective singing of anthems links disparate participants through an experience of simultaneity and selflessness that Anderson calls "unisonance."[1] Given the centrality of singing to American public rituals of the nineteenth century—songs were routinely and collectively sung in church, before and after lectures, and as part of school-based ceremonies—it is no surprise that songs played such a central role in defining and disseminating Civil War–era ideologies. While analysis of the full range of popular song of the Civil War period lies beyond the scope of this project, an examination of the writing and revision of these three representative songs will foreground the parallels between the circulation of song and the circulation of poetry during the war. Readings of these three songs will thus serve as a prologue to my analysis of Civil War poetry, underlining the extraordinary ideological flexibility that both song and poetry offered writers, singers, readers, and listeners in this era. Reading the three songs alongside one another reveals how their skillful layering of pronouns maximizes the number of readers and listeners who can identify with the national constituencies the lyrics propose.

In performing, a singer inhabits a song physically, drawing breath and calling notes and words out of his or her body; the memorizing and reciting of poetry requires an analogous process of physically inhabiting a text and making it one's own. What these two closely related genres offer then is a physical experience of connection to a text. Because of its comparative brevity, its emotional intensity, and also its sonic components, the genre of poetry lends itself particularly readily to this experience of shared feeling. While reading a poem aloud or singing a song can be a powerful experience for an individual, the intensity of that experience is often heightened when the recitation or singing is collective. Many of the poets this project will consider are clearly invested in writing the kind of poems that could create a powerful experience of shared community. Popular song played a crucial role in reshaping poetry's audiences, offering writers proliferating avenues for reaching wartime readers. Poems written to be performed or sung in public resist easy categorization as "literary," "popular," or "political" texts because of the broad range of audiences they were able to reach. In forging communities out of those audiences, such poems worked to smooth over or conceal underlying differences that threatened to turn the experience of unisonance into dissonance; the highly permeable boundary between poetry and song enabled both genres to perform this unifying function.

The three songs I will consider all speak to the issues of race and regional allegiance that propelled the nation toward war. Moreover, these songs also foreground the fluid ease with which preexisting compositions—either the music or the lyrics to a song—could be reappropriated for different political purposes, a frequent occurrence in popular song writing of this era. Proliferating variant versions of song lyrics resulted in what might be called a pentimento effect: traces of the earlier version of the song would remain in the singer's or listener's memory as he or she sang or heard the variant version, shaping the song's underlying ideological commitments. The permeable boundary between poetry and song worked to sustain this effect by enabling multiple lyrics to be written for the same popular tunes. The genre of the popular song thus lends itself particularly readily both to call-and-response dialogic exchange and to ideological revision; while this effect is generally more subtle in poetry that has no connection to music, a poem that is densely layered with allusions to earlier poems can also revise and talk back to its predecessors.

Dan Emmett's "Dixie" offers a particularly striking instance of this kind of reappropriation: though "Dixie" would eventually be taken up as a Southern anthem by the Confederacy, it was originally composed in 1859 by Dan Emmett, a white minstrel born in Ohio who performed in blackface.[2] Emmett wrote "Dixie" in New York City as the finale for a performance of Dan Bryant's minstrels, and a sheet music version of Emmett's song was published in New York in 1860.[3] Minstrel performances of the piece—like all blackface performance—relied on crude racist stereotypes of black characters; Emmett's lyrics imitate Southern black dialect. The first Southern performance of the piece occurred in New Orleans in that same year, with the result that by 1860, the song was enormously popular with white audiences in both the North and South.[4] It was a particular favorite of Abraham Lincoln, who first heard it performed at a minstrel show in Chicago in 1860. Lincoln is reported to have requested that "Dixie" be performed for him not long after the fall of Richmond.[5]

As music historian Hans Nathan notes, Dan Emmett had a particular talent for loading heated political content into songs that provoked the release of laughter in his white audiences.[6] Nathan notes that the figure of the African American longing for his lost Southern home was an established type in blackface minstrelsy by the early 1850s.[7] Emmett's innovation was to bring the song perilously close to explicit description of the nation's current political divisions and then to control the risk of that content through the racist laughter evoked in white audiences by the figure of the blackface speaker. Echoing in its chorus the call and response of traditional African American singing, the song presents as its central character a stereotyped black speaker who looks back with longing at the Southern homeland he has lost:

[VERSE 1]

I wish I was in de land ob cotton,
Old times dar am not forgotten;
Look away! Look away! Look away! Dixie Land.
In Dixie Land whar I was born in,
Early on one frosty mornin,
Look away! Look away! Look away! Dixie Land.[8]

This first verse focuses on Southern regional pride and the Southern nostalgia for an idyllic agrarian past, two sentiments that would become cornerstones of Confederate nationalist ideology. These lines also emphasize that the speaker was born in the South, a birthplace from which he has now been displaced.

Verses two and three unfold an oblique narrative about the impending civil conflict by representing the tension between the speaker's mistress and her new husband. Here the politically uneasy union of North and South is represented as a marriage based on misplaced trust, manipulation, and the thinly veiled threat of violence. The "Old Missus," a figure for the conciliatory factions in the North, is credulous, eager for matrimony, and unable to see the menace beneath William's "gay" manner:

[VERSE 2]

Old Missus marry "Will-de-weaber,"
Willium was a gay deceaber;
Look away! Look away! Look away! Dixie Land.
But when he put his arm around 'er,
He smiled as fierce as a 'forty-pound'er.
Look away! Look away! Look away! Dixie Land.

[VERSE 3]

His face was sharp as a butcher's cleaber;
But dat did not seem to greab'er;
Look away! Look away! Look away! Dixie Land.
Old Missus acted de foolish part,
And died for a man dat broke her heart.
Look away! Look away! Look away! Dixie Land.

In representing William, the lyrics point toward the rise of Southern regional pride and the martial ardor that was an integral part of that pride. William's "gay" façade is belied by his "fierce" smile, which the lyrics liken to a forty-pound cannon.[9] Though his face is as "sharp as a butcher's cleaber," the undeterred mistress proceeds with the planned marriage, a decision that results in her death. Reversing the conventional gender associations that link the South to the feminine and the North to the masculine, the lyrics suggest that the uncomfortable political compromises of the 1850s may well lead to the demise of the unified nation.

The last two verses of the song defuse the tension of this implication, however, by moving away from the narrative of the failed marriage and pointing toward a range of disparate narrative and imagistic possibilities:

[Verse 4]

> Now here's a health to the next old Missus,
> And all de galls dat want to kiss us;
> Look away! Look away! Look away! Dixie Land.
> But if you want to drive 'way sorrow
> Come an hear dis song tomorrow.
> Look away! Look away! Look away! Dixie Land.

[Verse 5]

> Dar's buckwheat cakes and 'Ingen' batter,
> Makes you fat or a little fatter;
> Look away! Look away! Look away! Dixie Land.
> Den hoe it down and scratch your grabble,
> To Dixie land I'm bound to trabble.
> Look away! Look away! Look away! Dixie Land.

The speaker's toast to "the next old Missus" implies that white Northern politicians will continue to be manipulated by white Southerners, but the quick turn to the topic of "all de galls dat want to kiss us" disrupts this implication with the threat of miscegenation. Pointing all but explicitly to the ways in which the song works to divert its listeners from the looming political crisis on the horizon, the speaker urges his listeners not to worry: "But if you want to drive 'way sorrow,/Come an hear dis song to-morrow." The song's final verse alludes ironically to the poverty and hunger that mark the lives of slaves, implying that the South is a land overflowing with pancake batter where slaves and poor farmers eke out a meager living by "scratching [their] grabble," a reference that seems to suggest both masturbation and hardscrabble farming. Emmett here punctures the image of an Edenic sunny South as a land of plenty.

Heightening the irony of this image of deprivation is the speaker's insistent determination to return to his Southern homeland: "To Dixie land I'm bound to trabble." In the chorus, the speaker backs up that determination with the declaration that he is willing to die for the right to return to that homeland:

> Den I wish I was in Dixie, Hooray! Hooray!
> In Dixie Land, I'll took my stand,
> To lib an die in Dixie,
> Away, Away, Away down south in Dixie,
> Away, Away, Away down south in Dixie.

Throughout the verses, the repetition of the phrase "Look away! Look away!" calls on all exiles to look back with longing at the homelands they have left behind; at the same time, however, the phrase "look away" points implicitly to the ways that whites in both the North and the South have tried to ignore or "look away" from the violence inherent to slavery and from the impending political conflict caused by slavery. The militarism central to Southern regional pride is voiced in the song's chorus by the black speaker: "In Dixie Land, I'll took my stand, To lib and die in Dixie." In order to defuse the threat of an armed black uprising against Southern whites, the lyrics use an ungainly imitation of black dialect: "I'll take my stand" becomes "I'll took my stand," a hybrid tense that is neither past nor future. And while Emmett wrote the song as a "walk-around," the finale in which all performers on the stage would participate, the lyrics also diminish the threat of black violence by insisting on the singular rather than the collective pronoun: "I'll took my stand." Even as this phrasing defuses the threat of black violence against whites, however, Emmett also defuses the threat of a white Southern uprising against the North by putting the words "I'll took my stand" in the mouth of a black speaker, whose belligerence is part of a comic and racist stereotyped pose. Though the speaker repeatedly laments his displacement from his Southern home, the song offers no explanation for the causes of that displacement, eliding both the violence and the suffering within the institution of slavery.

On the eve of the war, both Northern and Southern whites were clearly amused and entertained by the cartoon image of a poor black speaker who looks back with longing to the home he has lost. In the months leading up to secession, however, Southern loyalists in the nation's capital would have "Dixie" performed to express their displeasure at Lincoln's election. Jefferson Davis had "Dixie" played at his inauguration in February 1861, and by the second year of the war the song was both sung and understood as an anthem of the Confederacy. Historian Bell Irvin Wiley argues that "Dixie" was the most popular of the patriotic songs sung by Confederate soldiers.[10] Alternate versions of "Dixie" proliferated in both the North and the South during the war: in many of these variants, the repeated phrase "away, away" urged men off to battle while the crucial line "I'll took my stand" articulated a commitment of military support for the defense of the Union or the Confederacy.

When Confederate soldiers sang "Dixie," they often changed the singular pronoun of the song's refrain to a collective that emphasized Confederate unity. One of the best known Confederate versions, by Arkansas journalist Albert Pike, was titled "Southrons, hear your country call you!"; Pike's version was first published in the Natchez *Courier* and later included in William Shepperson's 1862 *War Songs of the South.* The first verse and the chorus are representative of the martial patriotic fervor of the song as a whole:

[Verse 1]

Southrons, hear your country call you
Up! lest worse than death befall you
To arms! to arms! to arms! in Dixie!
Lo! all the beacon fires are lighted,
Lo! all the hearts now be united!
To arms! to arms! to arms! in Dixie!

Chorus:
Advance the flag of Dixie!
Hurrah! hurrah!
For Dixie's land we'll take our stand,

And live or die for Dixie!
To arms! to arms!
And conquer peace for Dixie!
To arms! to arms!
And conquer peace for Dixie![11]

Strongly echoing Emmett's phrasing, Pike's chorus uses standard white English and the first-person plural to articulate a Confederate rallying cry: "For Dixie's land we'll take our stand, / and live or die for Dixie!" This declaration is in fact the only phrasing that Pike preserves from Emmett's lyrics; all of Pike's verses are rallying cries for the Confederate cause. Pike replaces the ironically evasive "Look away! Look away!" with an insistent and explicit "To arms! to arms!." The comically defiant blackface speaker of Emmett's "walk-around" has become a militant white Confederate supporter, one who is willing to die for the newly created Southern nation. The ideological slipperiness of Emmett's version—which seems to mock the foolishness of both Northern whites and Southern blacks—is in Pike's version reified into the ideological clarity of Confederate nationalism; historians suggest that Pike's version was the most popular Southern variant among Confederate soldiers.[12]

Revising and fixing the original song's meaning, the two song-poems set to the tune of "Dixie" that Shepperson includes in his *War Songs of the South* both replace Emmett's lyrics' emphasis on the black speaker's bodily desires with white Southern patriotic fervor and a call to arms; in so doing these versions also elevate the song from a bawdy minstrel tune to a more lofty nationalist anthem. The inclusion of Emmett's original lyrics in the *Jack Morgan Songster*, a 60-page paper-bound volume published in North Carolina in 1864, nonetheless suggests that Emmett's version of the song remained popular in the South during the war years.[13] Shepperson's decision to include the two Confederate versions of "Dixie" in his more expensively produced 216-page leather-bound volume underlines the ease with which a popular song could be transformed into a more literary one, even as it was adapted to express emphatically nationalist allegiances. Given the enormous popularity of Emmett's version of "Dixie," white Southerners who sang loftier Confederate variants during the war years undoubtedly did so with Emmett's lyrics echoing in their minds: Pike's images of valiant white Southerners striving to found a new nation could easily be laid over Emmett's image of a blackface speaker longing for his lost Southern home. Pike's lyrics thus forge a unified white Confederate community by layering the collective "we" of Confederate nationalism over the solitary "I" of Emmett's blackface buffoon. For white Southern singers and listeners, the two different versions of the song could thus support each other's symbolic investments, an overlapping of commitments that no doubt worked to increase the popularity of both versions in the South: white racial superiority thus worked to sustain the ardor of white Confederate nationalism.

While white Confederates took up and revised Emmett's "Dixie," white Northern abolitionists published and circulated the African American spiritual "Let My People Go: A Song of the 'Contrabands'" as a rallying cry for militant Northern support of emancipation. When escaped slaves began to seek protection behind Union lines at Fortress Monroe starting in May 1861, they performed this and other spirituals to galvanize support for emancipation among white Union soldiers and white envoys from the American Missionary Association and other Northern Christian organizations.[14] While "Dixie" was used to assert the right of white Southerners to defend a Southern homeland, "Let My People Go" asserted the right of blacks to escape the violence and oppression of the slave system endemic to the South.[15] In answer to Dan Emmett's comic portrait of the hapless slave grieving for the loss of his Southern home, "Let My People Go" articulated the determination of African Americans to escape white Southern oppression and to travel, like the Jews of the Old Testament, in search of a new homeland. Reverend Lewis Lockwood, a delegate from the American Missionary Association, was one of the first Northerners to report on his experience of hearing black spirituals performed in the political context of the war. When Lockwood first arrived at Fortress Monroe in early September of 1861, he told a group of African Americans assembled for a prayer meeting that he had come to serve as their chaplain under the auspices of the American Missionary Association. The group welcomed him and thanked him for the offered support. Their performance of "Let My People Go" made a particularly powerful impression on him, an impression he described in a report published in the *National Anti-Slavery Standard* in October. Lockwood's transcription of the complete lyrics of "Let My People Go" appeared in both the *New York Tribune* and the *National Anti-Slavery Standard* in early December, 1861; a sheet music version was published just two weeks later. Music historian Dena Epstein suggests that this was the first time an African American spiritual was published with its complete text and as sheet music.[16]

Two key aspects of the song's presentation in published form underline the ways that Northern white abolitionists hoped to use it to muster support for abolition. Emphasizing for white Northern audiences the dignity of the song's portrait of slaves' suffering, Lockwood's version of the lyrics used standard English rather than Southern regional dialect, a decision that implicitly underlined blacks' capacity for self-improvement through education.[17] Moreover, published versions of the song appeared under the full title "Let My People Go: A Song of the 'Contrabands'."[18] The publishers' decision to add the explanatory secondary title underlined their support for emancipation: the term "contraband" was first used in May 1861 at Fortress Monroe by Union General Benjamin Butler, who argued that slaves who escaped to Union lines could be considered "contraband of war" and should therefore be allowed to remain free. Long before African Americans were officially authorized to serve in the Union Army, Butler was one of the first Union generals to use black labor behind the lines to support the work of white Union troops. Though it reiterated the idea that blacks were property, the term "contraband" was also associated with the idea of blacks' military service and remained popular among white Northern abolitionists.

Intervening in the wartime ideological discourses about both abolition and nationalism, the song's lyrics foreground the argument that blacks have a God-given right to freedom and to a homeland:

[Verse 1]

When Israel was in Egypt's land,
O let my people go!
Oppressed so hard they could not stand,
O let my people go!

[Verse 2]

Thus saith the Lord bold Moses said,
O let my people go!
If not, I'll smite your first born dead,
O let my people go![19]

Though the letter that accompanied the lyrics suggested that the song had "been sung for at least fifteen or twenty years in Virginia and Maryland," the African Americans who performed the song at Fortress Monroe very likely understood how powerfully its lyrics would resonate with white Northern abolitionists once war had broken out. Echoing the New England Puritans' reading of the Old Testament, which emphasized God's covenant with his chosen people, the song's lyrics articulated the theological convictions of many Northern white abolitionists who supported the idea of linking the war to the emancipation of slaves; invoking the image of a God of wrath guiding his people to the promised land, the lyrics also articulated the rage and longing of many escaped slaves who were willing to fight for the Union and for their freedom but who were initially relegated to menial labor and service duties behind the front lines. In verse six, the reference to Moses and Aaron leading "the armies" points explicitly to the immediate context of war; verses seven through twelve develop an extended image of the divided waters of the Red Sea, an image that implies that God has divided the American nation in order to bring about the liberation of slaves.

Yet if the image of the divided waters suggests that God supports a war that will end slavery, the dividing of pronouns in the song's lyrics ultimately disrupts both black and white listeners' ability to identify with the song's speakers. While rewritten versions of "Dixie" allowed Confederate soldiers to declare their collective allegiance to their Southern homeland ("For Dixie's land, we'll take our stand"), "Let My People Go" does not offer such ready access to Benedict Anderson's experience of "unisonance": the voice that speaks in the vast majority of the verses is the voice of God, and that voice repeatedly utters an imperative to all Americans to bring an end to slavery. As performed by black singers at Fortress Monroe and later by white supporters of abolition in the Northeast, that speaking position lends the authority of God to arguments for abolition. But when the voice of God declares in verse fifteen "Your foe shall not before you stand," the identity of that "foe" is not easily defined in the political context of the Civil War since there are Southern whites who don't support slavery and Northern whites who don't support emancipation. The conflicting allegiances of race, class, and region work to unsettle any comfortable stances of identification with these lyrics. For example, distancing black performers from the enslaved people the song describes, the lyrics repeatedly refer to God's chosen people with a third-person "they." In the song's climactic seventeenth and eighteenth verses when pronouns do finally shift to include a first-person human "we," these shifts are temporary and do not offer stable possibilities for collective identification. Verse seventeen attempts to forge a "we" that combines slaves with all devout Christians:

> O let us all from bondage flee,
> O let my people go!
> And let us all in Christ be free,
> O let my people go!

Likening the bondage of sin to the bondage of slavery, these lines propose a unified "we" of black and white Christians. In the next verse, however, references to slavery seem to become more literal, narrowing to include primarily black slaves:

> We need not always weep and mourn,
> O let my people go!
> And wear these Slavery chains forlorn,
> O let my people go!

Further unsettling the human "we," the refrain spoken in the voice of God—"O let my people go!"—repeatedly interrupts that collective voice. While Pike's version of "Dixie" builds to a chorus that offers Confederate soldiers a unified martial "we," in its final stanzas "Let My People Go" oscillates between a shifting "we" that may or may not include both blacks and whites and the imperative voice of God. The splitting of voices within the song is already writ large in the song's full title with the phrase "Let My People Go" spoken by God and the phrase of the secondary title, "A Song of the 'Contrabands,'" spoken by the explanatory voice of Northern white abolitionists. With its proliferation of voices and stances, "Let My People Go" does not readily lend itself to the kinds of unifying political appropriations that variant versions of "Dixie" made possible.

Just as the song's lyrics destabilize the possibilities for a collective "we," so too does its musical form work against those possibilities. Epstein notes that the song was performed at Henry Ward Beecher's Brooklyn church, was available for sale at the Anti-Slavery office in Philadelphia, and was included in an 1862 collection of abolitionist songs, yet she ultimately concludes that the song "made little impression outside antislavery circles."[20] Given the divisiveness of the slavery issue in 1862 and given the clarity of the lyrics' abolitionist message, it is not surprising that the song did not circulate more widely. Further, while Epstein pins the blame for the song's limited popularity on the musical arrangement included in the first sheet music edition, still other aspects of its musical form would have limited its ability to achieve popular success. Unlike the tunes of Emmett's lively and upbeat "Dixie" or the popular marching song "John Brown's Body," "Let My People Go" is written in a minor key; unlike "Dixie," "Let My People Go" calls for a slow dignified tempo. In the context of African American worship practices, the repetitiveness of the song's lyrics and music would have signaled the strength of the worshippers' faith and their resolve to fight for freedom and abolition; yet this repetition also implicitly underlines the enormous challenges faced by those struggling to endure the violence and oppression of the slave system and the many setbacks and adversities faced by those who attempted to escape. "Let My People Go" is not so much an anthem that celebrates the triumph of emancipation as it is a hymn that articulates African Americans' unwavering determination to achieve freedom against all odds. Though the song is explicitly a call to arms for the cause of emancipation, its repetitive lyrics and musical structure implicitly mourn the horrors of slavery.

While the wartime influence of "Let My People Go" was limited to select abolitionist circles in the Northeast, the influence and impact of Julia Ward Howe's career-making "Battle Hymn of the Republic" quickly surpassed those circles. Where the divided pronouns of "Let My People Go" implicitly signal the divisions between blacks and whites in the North and within the abolitionist community, Howe's "Battle Hymn" builds to a triumphant "we" in its final verse, the rhetorical climax of the lyrics. And just as Albert Pike relies on the popularity of Dan Emmett's "Dixie" to support his Confederate anthem, so too does Julia Ward Howe rely on the success of "John Brown's Body" to disseminate her "Battle Hymn of the Republic." While Pike uses the "I" of Emmett's exiled blackface speaker to forge a Confederate "we," Howe layers the unified "we" of the Union over the more distanced third-person stances of "John Brown's Body." With its prophetic voice of biblical authority, its imagery of harvest and apocalypse, its stirring martial rhetoric, and its appropriation of an already popular song tune, Howe's "Battle Hymn" catapulted her to a level of public recognition that had previously proved elusive. And while the lyrics of "Let My People Go" limited that song's audience to supporters of abolition, Howe's more elliptical references to slavery in her "Battle Hymn" ensured that her song would be performed and circulated by Northerners with a range of perspectives on the issue of emancipation; many white Union soldiers who sang Howe's "Battle Hymn" may well have understood the phrase "Let us die to make men free" as referring not to emancipation but rather to the democratic freedoms to which they believed white Americans were entitled.

The story of the song's composition foregrounds Howe's process of revision in writing her "Battle Hymn." On a visit to Washington, DC, in November 1861, Howe and a group of companions had ridden out to see a review of troops that had to be cancelled when Confederate forces threatened Union positions. Caught among the columns of Union troops headed back to the city, Howe and her friends sang "John Brown's Body," to the cheers of the soldiers walking near them; James Freeman Clarke, who was one of the party, urged Howe to write better words for the tune which was so popular among the Union troops. The next morning, waking before dawn in the Willard Hotel, Howe scrawled out the words for all the verses in the darkness. "The Battle Hymn of the Republic" received prominent positioning as the opening piece in the February 1862 issue of the *Atlantic Monthly*. The piece quickly gained popularity with Union soldiers as well, a process that was facilitated by its inclusion in Union Army songbooks not long after its appearance in the *Atlantic*.[21] The success of Howe's version—both with a literary readership and with the broader public—underlines the ease with which a single song or poem could function as a literary and a popular text simultaneously.

While Pike's rewriting of Dan Emmett's "Dixie" never achieved the career-making acclaim that Howe's "Battle Hymn" received, what both songs shared was their pentimento effect, the residual layers of meaning left by earlier versions of the lyrics. Before turning to an analysis of Howe's "Battle Hymn" then, I want to offer a discussion of the popular soldiers' song "John Brown's Body," in order to consider how its lyrics worked to influence and shape Howe's version. Offering a prime example of the hall-of-mirrors-like proliferation of variant versions of popular songs, the soldiers' song "John Brown's Body" was itself a rewritten version of a widely sung evangelical camp meeting hymn of the 1850s, "Say, Brothers, Will You Meet Us?"[22] While multiple variants of "John Brown's Body" circulated in sheet music and broadside form during the war years, most versions of the lyrics begin with the graphic image of Brown's decaying body before moving on to represent Brown's symbolic transformation into "a soldier in the army of the lord."[23] The version published by the Oliver Ditson company in Boston in 1861 is a representative example:

VERSE 1

> John Brown's body lies a mould'ring in the grave,
> John Brown's body lies a mould'ring in the grave,
> John Brown's body lies a mould'ring in the grave,
> His soul is marching on!

Chorus

> Glory! Glory Hallelujah! Glory! Glory! Glory Hallelujah!
> Glory! Glory Hallelujah! His soul is marching on.

VERSE 2

> The stars of Heaven are looking kindly down,
> The stars of Heaven are looking kindly down,
> The stars of Heaven are looking kindly down,
> On the grave of old John Brown!

VERSE 3

> He's gone to be a soldier in the army of the Lord!
> He's gone to be a soldier in the army of the Lord!
> He's gone to be a soldier in the army of the Lord!
> His soul is marching on!

VERSE 4

> John Brown's knapsack is strapped upon his back,
> John Brown's knapsack is strapped upon his back,
> John Brown's knapsack is strapped upon his back,
> His soul is marching on!

VERSE 5

His pet lambs will meet him on the way,
His pet lambs will meet him on the way,
His pet lambs will meet him on the way,
And they'll 'go marching on.

VERSE 6

They will hang Jeff Davis to a tree,
They will hang Jeff Davis to a tree,
They will hang Jeff Davis to a tree,
As they march along.

Music scholars suggest that the song's lyrics were originally composed by members of a Massachusetts unit that included a sergeant whose name was also John Brown. According to this account, the lyrics were written in joking reference to the fact that the two men—the Massachusetts soldier and the radical abolitionist—coincidentally had the same name.[24] This context would make sense of the ways in which the lyrics foreground not Brown's raid on Harpers Ferry or the cause of abolition but rather the realities and the rough humor of army life: the insistent repetition of the image of Brown's decaying body signals the soldiers' collective masculine bravado in the face of mortality as they march off to fight. Read in this context, the song is not a celebration of the abolitionist's heroism but rather an ironic reflection on the death of a Union soldier with a common name. This is in effect the ghastly joke at the heart of the song: unlike the abolitionist whose execution made his name a household word throughout the nation, the soldier runs the risk of "mouldering" in an unmarked grave after dying on the battlefield. Thus when singers strike up the chorus of "Glory Hallelujah!" after the song's first verse, that chorus has an edge of wry or ironic humor, as the singers celebrate the transformation of the soldier's rotting body into the exalted soul. While the lyrics suggest that Christian martyrdom will compensate for the anonymity of the individual soldier's death, they also gesture toward the possibility that war results in the meaninglessness of nameless bodies mouldering in nameless graves.

As the song was taken up across the North, supporters of abolition certainly understood the lyrics as celebrating the abolitionist John Brown's heroism and endorsing the idea that the war was being fought to end slavery; the chorus of "Glory Hallelujah" offers strong echoes of Emerson's statement that Brown's death would "make the gallows glorious like the cross."[25] Yet given the widespread popularity of the song and the relatively low numbers of Union soldiers who saw themselves as fighting to end slavery, it is very likely that large numbers of soldiers who sang it did not particularly endorse the view that the abolitionist Brown was a hero.[26] Bell Irvin Wiley calls "John Brown's Body" "the favorite going-away song" for Union army units headed South and the most popular song in Union camps.[27] In his multivolume compendium of Civil War journalism, the *Rebellion Record*, Frank Moore cites a number of accounts of crowds being swept up in the ardor of a performance of "John Brown's Body." In a piece from the *New York Independent* written in the first year of the war, the writer describes with astonishment how New Yorkers joined in the singing when a newly formed regiment from Massachusetts marched down the city streets with "John Brown's Body" on their lips: "It was a notable fact that while the regiment united as with one voice singing this song, thousands of private citizens, young and old, on the sidewalks and in crowded doorways and windows, joined in the chorus."[28] New York would be the scene of vicious anti-black and anti-abolition draft riots in the summer of 1863, and yet in 1861 civilian New Yorkers eagerly joined the chorus when the Massachusetts regiment marched by. Two images from the May 4, 1861 issue of *Harper's Weekly* convey the enthusiasm of the New York crowds that turned out to send off the Union troops in the early months of the war. One shows New York's Seventh Regiment marching down Broadway past cheering onlookers (fig. 1), while a second shows Boston regiments boarding Jersey City trains headed to Washington, again surrounded by cheering crowds (fig. 2). Clearly the experience of "unisonance" that singing "John Brown's Body" offered Massachusetts soldiers and New Yorkers alike was not that of a shared commitment to ending slavery but rather that of a shared, if fleeting, fervor for the cause of the Union. New Yorkers joining Massachusetts soldiers in this song in 1861 may have been helped in their enthusiasm by the song's detached pronouns: nowhere in the 1861 Ditson version do the lyrics articulate a collective "we." Though "John Brown's Body" is a marching song, it refers to abolitionists and soldiers alike with a distanced third person, first a singular "he" and then a collective "they."

While the lyrics do not foreground the abolitionist John Brown's life and actions, what they do emphasize is the argument that God supports

1. "The Seventh Regiment Marching down Broadway to Embark for the War," magazine illustration, 1861

the Union position in the war: Union soldiers who die on the battlefield are Christian martyrs in the song's network of symbols: "His soul is marching on!" In the song's symbolic logic, this martyrdom compensates for the anonymity of the soldier's individual death. By closing with an image of the hanging of Confederate President Jefferson Davis, the lyrics offer soldiers a particularized image of revenge; moreover, the song's final verse replaces Brown's hanging—which is not represented—with an image of Davis's execution, which is. And just as the song was appropriated by Northern abolitionists as an anthem for the cause of abolition, so too could it again be reappropriated for the cause of the Union Army: a widely circulated alternate version of the lyrics replaced Brown's name with that of Colonel Elmer Ephraim Ellsworth, a young Union officer who was shot by a Confederate supporter in May 1861 and who quickly became an icon of martyred youth in the North. Sheet music versions of the song often included both Brown's name and Ellsworth's as alternate possibilities.

In rewriting "John Brown's Body" then, Julia Ward Howe superimposes a unified "we" onto the third-person pronouns of these earlier versions. Though Howe admired John Brown's willingness to take action in support of his convictions, even decades after the war she writes of the Harpers

2. "The Boston Regiments Embarking for Washington in the Jersey City Cars," magazine illustration, 1861

Ferry Raid, "none of us could exactly approve an act so revolutionary in its character."[29] In writing new words for the popular song then, she omits any explicit reference to Brown, offering instead a first-person speaker who speaks with prophetic authority of the violence to come; in effect, Howe makes Brown himself the poem's speaker, without making that substitution explicit. Echoing the prophetic tone of Brown's remarks after his capture, in the first verse Howe's speaker describes how a God of wrath will purify the nation by drenching the American landscape in blood:

> Mine eyes have seen the glory of the coming of the Lord:
> He is trampling out the vintage where the grapes of wrath are stored;
> He hath loosed the fateful lightning of his terrible swift sword:
> His truth is marching on.[30]

This opening verse adds literary and biblical weight to the plainspoken imagery of the note Brown handed to a guard on the morning of his execution: "I John Brown am now quite *certain* that the crimes of this *guilty, land: will* never be purged *away;* but with Blood."[31] Even as Howe has her speaker mimic Brown's voice, however, she also wants to invent a speaker whose voice and perspective transcend the limits of Brown's.

When James Freeman Clarke urges Howe to write better lyrics for the tune, he implicitly expresses his discomfort with the popular song's emphasis on embodiment: its graphic image of the decaying body, the wry humor with which the chorus responds to that death. And while Howe wants to revise the graphic embodiment and the wry humor out of her version, these elements nonetheless persist in her "Battle Hymn" because of the traces of the original "John Brown's Body" that remain in listeners' and singers' minds. The words of the chorus ("Glory! Glory Hallelujah!") are all but identical in the two songs, underlining these traces.[32] In rewriting the song then, Howe wants the soldiers' stance of nonchalant bravado in the face of death; what she doesn't want, however, is the song's emphasis on the mouldering body or the doubt that image implicitly casts on the possibility of the soldier's martyrdom. Her solution to this problem is to position God on the side of the Union still more emphatically than the popular song does: Howe's song is loftier and more literary in part because it is loaded up with literary and biblical imagery. In verses two and three, Howe's speaker makes explicit the many signs of divine presence in Union camps and on battlefields:

> I have seen Him in the watch-fires of a hundred circling camps;
> They have builded Him an altar in the evening dews and damps;
> I can read His righteous sentence by the dim and flaring lamps.
> His day is marching on.

I have read a fiery gospel, writ in burnished rows of steel:
"As ye deal with my contemners, so with you my grace shall deal;
Let the Hero, born of woman, crush the serpent with his heel,
Since God is marching on."

In "John Brown's Body," a remote God smiles benignly and passively on Brown's actions: the "stars of Heaven" look "kindly" on John Brown's grave. Howe's "Battle Hymn," however, invokes the second coming, makes Christ a speaker in the abolition debate, and ultimately argues that Christ is an active participant on Civil War battlefields.

Representing battle as the day of judgment, verse four suggests that God himself will separate the wheat from the chaff ("He is sifting out the hearts of men"), a task preliminary to the work of unifying the righteous of the nation. Verses four and five build on one another then to establish the collective "we" of the Union Army and its Northern supporters:

He has sounded forth the trumpet that shall never call retreat;
He is sifting out the hearts of men before his judgment-seat:
Oh! be swift, my soul, to answer Him! be jubilant, my feet!
Our God is marching on.

In the beauty of the lilies Christ was born across the sea,
With a glory in his bosom that transfigures you and me:
As he died to make men holy, let us die to make men free,
While God is marching on.

The rhetorical tension in the text reaches its climax as the authoritative "I" addresses an imperative first to the self in stanza four ("be swift, my soul") and finally to a collective "us" in stanza five: "let us die to make men free." Enacting syntactically the joining together of the disparate elements of Northern population, the "you and me" of stanza five have been "transfigure[d]"—though the intervention of Christ himself—into a unified "us," the collective of the Union.

Blending explicit images of a God of wrath with implicit references to John Brown, Howe's "Battle Hymn" thus includes both residual echoes of the graphic image of the abolitionist Brown's embodiment and the image of his immaterial apotheosis through her version's lofty lyrics. Because Howe chooses a popular soldiers' song as her tune, she is able to write in the first person in the voice of a soldier.[33] The rhetorical power of Howe's "Battle Hymn" lies in the prophetic authoritative voice that she establishes in this piece; the prophetic authority of that voice is sustained in part by the pentimento effect which allows Howe to forge a unified "we" from the disparate voices of John Brown, Union soldiers, and white Northern civilians who have a range of perspectives on the war and emancipation. Tacitly recognizing the extraordinary power of that unified voice, in her "Reminiscences" Howe acknowledges the sense of accomplishment she felt after finishing the piece: returning to bed after writing out the words in the early morning hours, she fell back to sleep thinking, "I like this better than most things that I have written."[34]

Yet while Howe's "Battle Hymn" achieves popular success because of the unified "we" she forges in it, traces of the writerly "I" also persist in the text, signaling Howe's struggle to reconcile her political commitments, the demands of her family life, and her desire to make her name as a poet.[35] The story of the piece's composition offers evidence of the traces of this writerly I in the "Battle Hymn's" speaker. In her "Reminiscences," Howe notes that the habit of writing in the pre-dawn hours was one she had acquired during her years of raising children. She adds that when she composed poems in the dark, she had to make sure to recopy them that same day while she could still remember the words well enough to decipher them.[36] In the "Battle Hymn" this scene of composition is written into the text itself, particularly in the references to reading, sight, light, and darkness that abound in stanzas two and three:

> I have seen Him in the watch-fires of a hundred circling camps;
> They have builded Him an altar in the evening dews and damps;
> I can read His righteous sentence by the dim and flaring lamps.
> His day is marching on.
>
> I have read a fiery gospel, writ in burnished rows of steel:
> "As ye deal with my contemners, so with you my grace shall deal;
> Let the Hero, born of woman, crush the serpent with his heel,
> Since God is marching on.

Even as these two stanzas point toward Howe's visit to the Union camps in the fall of 1861, they also evoke the predawn scene in which she transcribes the words that came to her in a single burst of inspiration: stanza two makes reference to reading God's "righteous sentence" by the "dim and flaring lamps," while stanza three represents the gospel as a "fiery" text whose letters need no illumination. In Howe's "Battle Hymn," then, the I that speaks to and for the nation is permeated by the personal I of the woman writer who seeks a meaningful way to contribute to the war effort. In her "Reminiscences," Howe describes how discouraged she felt that her husband was too old and her sons too young for military service: she could not send the "Hero, born of woman" off to war. She suggests that the "Battle Hymn" was divinely inspired and enabled her to contribute through an alternative means: "because of my sincere desire, a word was given me to say, which did strengthen the hearts of those who fought in the field and of those who languished in the prisons."[37] Ultimately then, Howe's "Battle Hymn" creates the extraordinary rhetorical power of its speaker's voice by combining the collective voices of soldiers, the radical voice of John Brown, and the genteel feminine Christian literary voice of its author.

As my analysis of these three songs suggests, it is in part the echo-laden power of the pentimento effect that leads to the extraordinary outpouring of poetry during the war years. Drawing rhetorical power from those poems written to be sung and performed, poets who write for the page will respond to the imagery of all three of these songs—particularly the "Battle Hymn" and "Dixie"—throughout the war years. Even poets whom we now classify as "literary" writers—Dickinson and Melville, for example—will respond to popular poems and songs with remarkable frequency in their Civil War work. Moreover, the crucial play of pronouns in these song lyrics signals what is at stake for Civil War poets as they position themselves in relation to the divided nation: the first-person blackface speaker in the chorus of Dan Emmett's "Dixie" becomes a patriotic collective of white Confederate soldiers in Pike's revision, while the collective "we" in Howe's "Battle Hymn" is layered onto the collective of soldiers' voices established by the lyrics of "John Brown's Body." Shifts and divisions within the pronouns of "Go Down, Moses" reflect the multiple constituencies the lyrics describe and address even as they also limit the possibilities for broader collective identification.

Howe's "Battle Hymn" is woven into the fabric of American culture, still sung in churches and schools and on public occasions where its rhetorical grandeur is called for. Many Americans can recite its martial lyrics from memory, and many Americans would quickly link the patriotic ardor of the phrase "let us die to make men free" to the nineteenth-century abolitionist movement. Just beneath the patriotic fervor of the song's collective "we," however, lie traces of Howe's singular and feminine writerly "I," the personal I of the woman poet who scrawled out the lyrics in a hotel room in the early morning hours because she was accustomed to writing while her children were still asleep. The chapters that follow, then, will trace the connections between collective patriotic stances and personal singular ones, considering how each stance works to shape and delimit the other. Because of the centrality of singing to military life, soldier-poets will echo with particular frequency the meter, rhyme, and imagistic repertoire of popular song. While soldier-poets will often write poems that echo patriotic marching songs and that proclaim the nationalist causes for which they are fighting, their poems too will be shaped by the frustrations, ambivalence, and particular experience of the personal "I." Responding to their experience of military training, combat, and their postwar identities as veterans, soldier-poets will foreground in their writings both the range of conflicting nationalist perspectives inside the military and the disparities between official ideologies and soldiers' reasons for joining in the fight.

CHAPTER TWO

"WE ARE HERE AT OUR COUNTRY'S CALL"

Nationalist Commitments and Personal Stances in Union and Confederate Soldiers' Poems

On a rainy Decoration Day in May 1869, George Bryant Woods was one of a number of invited speakers who stood before the monument for fallen soldiers in his hometown of Barre, Massachusetts. As an eighteen-year-old, Woods had served for six months as a private in the Eighth Massachusetts Battery before returning to his civilian job as a journalist and newspaper editor. His speech offers memories of other young Barre men who enlisted in the war's early years and describes their combat service. At Antietam, in the midst of artillery fire, Woods finds a Barre friend who is fighting with the Twenty-First Massachusetts Infantry and, with the soldier's hunger for news from home, eagerly reads the friend's recent copy of the *Barre Gazette* until the Twenty-First receives its orders to advance. Among the men moving forward in that line, Woods recognizes another face from the Barre school he had attended just a few years before. Describing the encounter, Woods points toward the kinds of literary models of heroism that shape young men's decisions as they moved from the schoolroom to the enlistment office to the battlefield:

> I noticed especially the bright young face and gallant bearing of a young lieutenant, only lately risen from the ranks, who had been a schoolmate of my own, when he came up from the Plain to attend the High School. We had declaimed "The Charge of the Light

> Brigade" for the stage of the Town House in those boyish days, little thinking we should ever know the real meaning of war. He was at the further end of the line; so I could not speak to him; but he smiled and touched his cap as he tightened his belt and slung his sword. Then he led his company up to the precipice, into the jaws of death; and in five minutes he was down; and we read on the monument today the name of Henry Holbrook.[1]

Woods's childhood memory of reciting Tennyson's ringing dactyls at the town hall with Holbrook underlines the ways in which poetry worked to define and confirm the bonds of community and nation in nineteenth-century America: in a Massachusetts town in the late 1850s, a time of growing tensions between North and South, a group of boys on the verge of becoming men declaimed "The Charge of the Light Brigade" for an assembled audience of parents and townspeople.[2] Though Woods notes the boys had little idea that they would "ever know the real meaning of war," the choice of poems underlines a patriotic military ideal for which the boys are implicitly being urged to strive: proving allegiance to one's country by obeying the orders of commanding officers, proving allegiance to one's country by risking one's life in war. The public recitation of the poem confirms for the Barre audience that a new generation of young men will be willing to fight and die for the idea of the nation.[3] Echoes of Tennyson's poem in Woods's Decoration Day eulogy for Holbrook signal that poetry is still working to support that idea of nation-building in the war's aftermath.

Moreover, these echoes of Tennyson's phrasing also suggest that many who fought in the Civil War and many who wrote about it perceived the actions of its soldiers through the lens of this poem, which celebrates the courage of the nameless British cavalrymen even as it also questions the wisdom of the officers who ordered the ill-fated charge.[4] Woods sees in Tennyson's poem both a model for masculine heroism and a model for the literary representation of that heroism.[5] Tennyson's popular ballad shapes the wartime writings both of now canonical writers like Emily Dickinson and Herman Melville and of the many soldiers who turned to poetry as a means of representing their experience. The ubiquitousness of echoes of "The Charge of the Light Brigade" throughout the literature of the Civil War underlines the crucial role that poetry played in shaping wartime ideologies.

While Woods's memory of reciting Tennyson underlines the centrality of poetry to those ideologies, it also points toward the fact that soldiers in the camps and hospitals had ready access to poetry: in newspapers, magazines, broadsides, and songsters, soldiers read poems responding to every aspect of the war.[6] Not surprisingly, many felt called upon to write their own poems, using poetry to legitimate their identity as soldiers—to confirm that they were present at particular battles in particular places—and to articulate their familial and national allegiances, even as the constructs of family and nation were being profoundly shaken by the war.[7] Poetry is a genre in which individual heroic deeds can be recorded and celebrated; it is also a versatile and adaptable medium for responding to government policies and to nationalist ideologies. Poetry was regularly read aloud and recited at recruitment meetings, at the send-offs given by local communities for their departing soldiers, at celebrations welcoming groups of soldiers home, and at Decoration Day ceremonies. Many soldiers composed poetry or recopied poems and songs by fellow soldiers into their journals and letters, and regimental newspapers—published by and for soldiers—frequently included poems as well. Understandably, the poems that circulated in this historic context were perceived as having an impact in Washington, in Richmond, and on battlefields.[8] Making literal the close ties between poetry and scenes of battle, newspapers published numerous anecdotes about poems found in the pockets of dead soldiers, sometimes attributing the poems to the men who carried them, sometimes acknowledging that men carried published poems they found meaningful into battle. Analysis of Northern and Southern soldiers' writings confirms that soldier-poets see both reading and writing poetry as a means of taking part in a larger conversation about what it means to support the Confederacy or the Union.

While many Civil War soldiers' poems endorse conventionally patriotic definitions of the Confederacy and the Union, others threaten to resist or at least destabilize conventional definitions of "nation," "home," and "family." In negotiating the complex ties between a poet-speaker's personal "I" and the vital collective "we" of military experience, many soldier-poets are clearly pulled in different directions by conflicting aesthetic and political aims. Drawn to the genre of poetry at least in part because of the omnipresence of song in military life, many soldiers write both songs and poems, and most rely on regular metrical and rhyme schemes, using poetic form to frame strongly held nationalist convictions. In these soldier-poets' pieces, however, failed gestures of formal or aesthetic closure—awkward rhymes or unexpected swerves in the speaker's stances—often unsettle conventional nationalist ideologies. Thus while soldier-poets often define the nation they are fighting to defend, those definitions are far more ambivalent and polyvocal than we might at first expect them to be. Many cultural historians have argued persuasively that relatively few soldiers believed they were fighting to abolish or defend slavery, particularly in the early years of the war; the relative paucity of references to slavery and racial difference in this body of work is therefore not surprising. What is perhaps surprising, however, is the amount of attention these poets give to gender roles and gender difference. While soldier-poets' nationalist commitments are influenced by their relationship to their male and female readers, soldiers' poetry foregrounds models of masculinity and femininity that are being rapidly reshaped by the Civil War. Indeed in the work of the soldier-poets examined here, representations of gender expectations and gender roles seem to distinguish Northern from Southern poets more readily than nationalist commitments do; more specifically, the Union soldier-poets I will consider resist conventionally patriotic depictions of Northern femininity in some surprising ways.

In reading the work of a group of soldier-poets, I aim to revise some of the critical assumptions that have shaped twentieth-century scholars' neglect of Civil War poetry. Civil War scholars have been particularly reluctant to unsettle the hierarchical positions of professional versus amateur writers when the work being produced is poetry. While scholars eagerly read the journals, diaries, letters, and essays of nonprofessional writers of the war era, they step gingerly around the work of amateur poets, fearing perhaps the jarring missed rhyme or infelicitous excesses of imagery or meter.[9] The tacit assumption seems to be that soldiers' poetry will not be able to transcend the limitations Wilson finds in the broader spectrum of war poetry: if Melville's and Lowell's wartime poetry can be dismissed as "patriotic journalism," how much more likely is it that amateur soldier-poets will fall prey to the easy clichés of nationalist ardor and sentimental postures of grieving?[10] This critical dismissal, however, does not do justice to the complexity and range of the poetry produced by Civil War soldiers.

The four poets whom I will discuss in depth in this chapter all produced a substantial body of war-related poetry (ranging from ten poems to 250); these were men for whom the writing of poetry seems to have been, at least for a time during the war years, a routine pursuit.[11] In their journals and other writings, soldier-poets tend to use the terms "song" and "poem" interchangeably; in the analysis that follows, I have relied on the soldiers' own generic terms for their pieces. Three of these writers embedded their poetry in letters and/or journals and notebooks that were subsequently preserved by family members and descendants; the fourth writer sent his lavishly penned and illustrated manuscript to President Theodore Roosevelt, accompanying the manuscript with an explanatory letter, commenting both on the audience he hoped to reach and the reasons he chose to write poetry. The availability of these rich parallel contexts enables me to examine in depth the ways that these poets positioned themselves in relation to a range of audiences. All four men were of fairly modest means in the antebellum era; in all probability, none of them had received a college education prior to the war. The three Union soldiers all worked as teachers either before or after the war, and the Confederate soldier became a preacher after the war's end; all four were thus men for whom reading and writing were important skills. All three Union poets were from the Midwest (two from Iowa and one from Michigan), an intriguing detail that suggests that both public education and class mobility in the Midwest may have been particularly encouraging to poetic ambition. References to slavery and racial difference are few and far between in this body of work (only two of the four—both Union soldiers—make explicit mention of the enslavement of African Americans), underlining the Union versus States' Rights debate that many soldiers believed they were fighting for, particularly in the early years of the war.

These case studies are sufficiently representative to allow me to trace some dominant and conflicting themes in soldiers' definitions of the nation; they are also sufficiently representative to allow consideration of why poetry and songs were favorite genres for so many soldiers. While this body of work does not have the stylistic polish or aesthetic complexity that twentieth- and twenty-first-century readers tend to prize in poetry, it does offer arresting and unexpected moments: one soldier's terse list of unanswered questions in which he tries to imagine how his wife imagines his life at the front, another soldier's suggestion that women can and do imagine the exhilarating pleasures of combat, and still another soldier's blunt and angry rejection of the heroic stories used to fire up young men's military ardor. Both these exceptional moments and the more predictable nationalist commitments on display in this body of work enrich our appreciation of the ways that these men approached the task of writing poetry, underlining the extent to which they saw military service and poetry not as two discrete activities, but rather as a dialogic process in which military experience might shape poetry and poetry might shape soldiers' emotions and actions, both in camp and on the field of battle.

Before turning to the work of the four soldier-poets, I want to provide a context for these case studies by offering an overview of the ways that a broader range of soldier-poets position themselves in relation to their audiences; I will also offer an overview of the ideological purposes editors posit for the poetry and song collections circulating in military camps and hospitals. The range of thematic and formal choices in soldiers' poetry testifies to the vitality of their participation in the poetic conversation the war prompted. Soldiers write poems that represent the pleasures and terrors of combat, poems that focus on the immediate aftermath of battle, comic poems that poke fun at the rigors of military life, elegies for fallen comrades, poems that recreate soldiers' dreams of home, poems that imagine life after the war, love poems for wives and sweethearts, poems that imagine the war from women's perspectives, and patriotic nationalist song-poems for their units to sing while on the march or while at sea. Drawing on many of these standard themes and adding some of his own, Obadiah Ethelbert Baker of the Second Iowa Cavalry writes two hundred and fifty poems during and after the war years, including numerous ballads about cavalry charges and the brief verses addressed to his wife that he uses to close out entries in his wartime journals. Sextus Goddard, who served with the Fifty-Third Massachusetts Infantry, writes a call-to-arms poem with an elaborate metrical pattern that his brother Lucius prints as a pamphlet back in his home state. While serving with the Thirty-Seventh Massachusetts, Edwin Oberlin Wentworth, also a printer by trade, starts a regimental newspaper called *The Reveille*, soliciting a wide range of poetry for its pages and possibly writing some poetry himself. Robert Leslie Wiles, a Creek Indian who was imprisoned on suspicion of having Confederate loyalties and who later served with the Eleventh Missouri Cavalry, passes his off-duty hours in the military by writing love poems and acrostics for young women of his acquaintance. Serving in the Confederate Navy, A. L. Drayton transcribes the songs sung by sailors on his ship in the evening. Writing in March 1864, Confederate General Alexander Welch Reynolds writes three cleverly rhymed quatrains to decline politely a dinner invitation from a Mrs. Hardee.

As this list of examples begins to suggest, soldier-poets positioned themselves in relation to a shifting array of audiences, including first the addressees of family and friends back home but also the audience of their fellow soldiers; many went on to revise their wartime poems, hoping to reach an even broader circle of readership. While Reynolds writes his witty poem for Mrs. Hardee, he writes knowing that a poem by a Confederate general might well be recopied and circulated with pride among family and friends and then carefully preserved in the years after the war. Though Baker writes many brief and deeply personal verses to his wife during the war years, when he begins to prepare fair copies and typed versions of his war poems in the 1880s and '90s—with an eye toward eventual publication—the poems that he prepares in clean copies are for the most part longer historically shaped narratives of battles and soldiers' reunions. Like Baker, Jasper Jay Stone wrote an extensive body of poetry during and after the war years and aspired to see his name in print. An instructor of penmanship after the war, Stone wrote a manuscript of nearly 200 pages of poems about his service with the Thirty-Fifth Iowa Volunteers. Inspired to finish the project by an announcement that President Theodore Roosevelt was collecting war songs, Stone sends Roosevelt a letter of introduction and the completed manuscript. After hailing Roosevelt as "the most conspicuous hero of 'The Spanish American War,'" Stone acknowledges the limitations of his work even as he hopes that his experience as a soldier will make his poems worthy of a wider American audience: "It is not much, but it comes from one who is proud of the fact that he gave to his country in his boyhood all that life held in store for him: —health, manhood, hope, ambition, and fair promise of success in life: from one who desires to see the American people rise to that supreme plane of liberty and enlightenment which his fallen comrades earned for them by the sacrifice of their lives."[12] Though Stone's manuscript did not bring him the recognition he had hoped for, it nonetheless stands as a remarkable testament to a desire many soldier-poets shared: to define their identities as soldiers, to shape their understanding of their experience of the war, to affirm their loyalty to the nation they fought for, and to reach toward the possibility of a national audience for their poems.

Just as soldiers sought to define their national allegiances in the poems they wrote, so too did editors of wartime magazines and collections of poetry and songs intend their publications to inspire, disseminate, and affirm nationalist commitments. Though some of these publications were designed specifically for sale or distribution to soldiers, still others were designed for multiple markets, including not only the armies, but also churches, schools, and the family parlor. The editors of the *Southern Literary Messenger* clearly hoped to have many Confederate soldiers among their subscribers. In January 1863, the *Messenger*'s pages included a fictional letter from a loyal Confederate soldier urging other Southerners to purchase gift subscriptions and perhaps also to subscribe themselves: "Sirs, —Enclosed you will find $3 (three dollars) for the *S. L. Messenger*— a Christmas gift to a young Lady, by a Soldier. How many young men, of the South, will follow my example, in presenting this valuable work to the noble, angelic sympathizers of the Southern soldier."[13] The letter implies that the *Messenger*'s pages provide vital encouragement to Southern soldiers, to the loyal women who wait for their return, and more broadly to the new nation of the Confederacy. The advertisement also implicitly likens buying a subscription to the *Messenger* to joining the Confederate Army: "How many young men, of the South, will follow my example?" the soldier asks. Comparisons that link literary activity to bravery on the battlefield abound in editors' notes and prefaces. In 1862, William Shepperson, a correspondent for the *Richmond Dispatch*, compiled and published a substantial body of Southern-authored poems and songs for *War Songs of the South*. Linking poetic inspiration directly to the violence of combat, he began his preface by declaring that "Southern independence has struck the lyre as well as the unsheathed sword," proudly hailing the birth of the Confederate nation and the birth of its independent literature in one breath.[14] As an epigraph to the volume, he, like other editors both North and South, chose a quotation from the Scottish political theorist Andrew Fletcher: "I knew a very wise man [. . . who] believed that if a man were permitted to make all the ballads, he need not care who should make the laws of a nation." Editing an 1864 volume of his own *Camp Songs for the Soldier*, Union General William Hayward used the same sentiment in simplified form for his epigraph: "Let me write songs of a Nation, I care not who makes its Laws."[15] As the repeated use of the Fletcher quote makes clear, editors on both sides of the Mason-Dixon line understood the extraordinary cultural power of popular song and its twin genre poetry to forge unified national communities out of disparate factions of readers, singers, and listeners.

In their 1864 compilation *Soldiers' and Sailors' Patriotic Songs*, the Loyal Publication Society of New York printed as a preface the Society's "Declaratory Resolution," a resolution that makes the editors' aims of undermining the Confederacy and strengthening the Union explicit. Like William Shepperson, these editors closely link the power of the poem or song with the violence of combat. All of their publications, the editors note, are intended to "stimulate a broad national patriotism, and to aid in the suppression of the Rebellion by the extinction of its causes, and in the preservation of the integrity of the Nation, by counteracting the efforts of the advocates of a disgraceful and disintegrating Peace."[16] Citing a favorable review of their volume, the Northern editors of the 1862 *Army and Navy Melodies: A Collection of Hymns and Tunes*, both ministers, make explicit the ideological link between piety, song, and nationalism, noting that the Civil War "is the Lord's war, and these stirring, sacred melodies have just the right martial ring to strengthen the hearts" of "the army of the Lord."[17] The preface by the Reverends Dadmun and Fuller also makes explicit another goal of many of these collections, that of linking soldiers at the front with friends and family at home through a shared set of songs, thereby affirming the bonds that made soldiers' and families' sacrifices meaningful: "If this volume supplies in any degree the social and religious needs of those who are striving in the national defence, and is found acceptable in our vestries, schools, and homes where these brave men are remembered, and their names cherished, the highest hopes of both the Editors will be fully answered." Working to ensure that those on the homefront and those on the battlefields are singing the same song—both literally and figuratively—Dadmun and Fuller believe that their songster will help readers and listeners continue to understand and believe in the higher purpose of the war's bloodshed.

Though the scarcity of paper becomes a constraint on Southern publications and keeps both collections and prefaces brief, the editors of the 1864 *Southern Zion's Songster*, a collection of hymns "Designed for Sabbath Schools, Prayer, and Social Meetings, and the Camps" implicitly echo this idea of the interconnectedness of piety and nationalism for Confederate loyalists; a terse preface expresses their sense of urgency about publishing their volume, insisting that these hymns are "much needed, at this juncture."[18] As an epigraph to his *War Songs for Freemen*, Northern editor Francis Child draws a quote from British theologian Frederick William Robertson: "Poetry has distinguished—as, in spite of all mercenary and feeble sophistry, men ever will distinguish—war from mere bloodshed. It has distinguished the higher feelings which lie beneath its revolting features."[19] Child thus implies that his compilation of poems and songs will help to identify the "higher feelings" of war, making meaning out of bloodshed for Northern readers. As these examples suggest, editors emphasize three interrelated purposes for their publications: first, to promote and sustain nationalist loyalties; second, to link soldiers at the front with their families at home; and third, to find purpose and meaning in the war's violence. Such editorial goals would no doubt have seemed idealistic—if not unrealistic—to many soldiers serving in the field. The work of the four soldier-poets I will examine here suggests that these utopian collective "we's" of the nation, the family, and the military unit are fractured again and again by the soldier-poet's personal "I" and by the complexity of the individual soldier's experience of war.

Personal and Collective Stances in the Work of Obadiah Ethelbert Baker

Obadiah Ethelbert Baker's substantial body of Civil War poetry offers invaluable insight into the kinds of poetry soldier-poets admired and how Union poets imagined they might contribute to an American poetic tradition. Born in Eden, New York, Baker moved to Iowa as a young man and taught school there for three years before enlisting in the Second Iowa Cavalry Volunteers in March 1862. Leaving behind a young wife whom he had married just a year and a half earlier, Baker would see combat in several states before receiving his honorable discharge in April 1865. He would also spend many months in military hospitals, a circumstance that may in part explain his extraordinary productivity as a writer: during the war years, Baker wrote thirteen volumes of diaries, regularly interspersing poems among his entries. Between 1859 and the 1920s, he wrote about two hundred and fifty poems; of these, about seventy-five reflect on his wartime experience. Though Baker returned to Iowa at the war's end, working again as a teacher, he moved his family to California in the 1870s, propelled by the quest for better employment and also by the chronic health troubles he suffered from after his military service. In the 1870s and '80s, Baker made fair copies of several of his wartime journals and began making notes for a prose memoir of his war experiences; he also submitted a number of his poems—probably including some of his war poems—to California newspapers in hopes of seeing them in print. The many war poems that Baker composed in the 1880s and 1890s suggest that he looked back on his military service as a defining moment in his life. As a civilian, he struggled to provide financial stability for his wife and children; as a veteran of the Union Army, however, he could legitimately claim that he had helped secure the victory that reestablished the United States.

Because Baker embeds many of his war poems in his Civil War journals, his writings are particularly suggestive in what they reveal about soldier-poets' relationships to their audiences. Like the work of most soldier-poets, Baker's poems are strongly shaped by the gender positions of the writer and his addressee. In those poems he addresses to his wife Melissa, Baker emphasizes the distance that separates Northern women's lives from the excitement, the suffering, and the horrors of the soldier's life; he also complains from time to time about the boredom, fears, and hardships of that life. He closes a poem he writes to her on November 30, 1862, with a particularly angry and despairing outburst: "O God! When will this strife be o'er?/When will we learn to war no more?."[20] By contrast in his longer battle poems, which seem to address a broader audience, Baker emphasizes the heroism and glory of combat, often endorsing the nationalist ideologies that give meaning to the war's violence. His poetry underlines the extent to which becoming a soldier was for many young men of this era a rite of passage on the way to manhood and to a more clearly defined sense of masculinity.[21] The title of Baker's 1863 poem "My Army Birth" emphasizes that he understood his military experience as a fundamental reshaping of his identity.

Baker usually addresses journal entries to his wife Melissa—an unusual epistolary stance for a wartime journal writer—and he frequently closes out journal entries with brief poems addressed to her. He sends individual volumes to her on a regular basis, and she in turns regularly sends him her journals and poems of her own composition. For Baker, this writerly exchange is clearly both sustaining and inspiring. Writing poetry becomes a crucial means of maintaining close ties with a wife whom he had married only a year and a half before; since Baker had written poetry before the war, continuing to write poetry is also a way of maintaining his identity as a schoolteacher/poet—in his own and his wife's estimation—even during the culturally disorienting experience of military service. In the brief poems he uses to close out journal entries, he often imagines the war from his wife's perspective, representing her affection for him as a force that will sustain him in combat. Imagining the war from her vantage point gives him the freedom to escape the pressures of army life, if only in his poetry; this vantage point also allows Baker to represent himself in heroic terms without sounding self-aggrandizing.

Baker closes a journal entry from January 1863 with a particularly evocative series of questions in verse, questions that underline the distance that separates him from his wife:

> Do you often think of me, dear wife?
> Am I dearer than all else in life?
> Do you dream of me in the stilly night?
> Do you see me mingle in the fight?
> Do you hear the cannon's mighty roar?
> Do you see men fall to rise no more?[22]

Echoing the interrogative phrasing of the marriage vows ("Do you?" "I do"), the poem reveals Baker's anxiety about the impact separation will have on their relationship. His decision to build the poem out of a list of unanswered questions points toward the dialogic nature of his writing process, yet the language that he uses to describe his wife's vision of his participation in combat—as he imagines that she imagines it—underlines her remoteness from the battlefield, the distance that separates her "stilly night" from the "cannon's mighty roar"; the sequence of questions suggests that he believes combat is unimaginable to women and to all who have not seen it. The verbs "mingle" and "fall" sound bloodless and passive, and the battle seems to occur in choreographed slow motion, even as the last line points obliquely toward the possibility of his own death. The questions mingle a sense of masculine pride in his experience as a soldier with a desire to protect his young wife from the knowledge of combat's horrors. The tension that runs throughout the poem is the possibility that the answer to all of these questions might be "No, I don't think of you."[23]

The terseness of the questions underlines Baker's sense of isolation—his awareness that his wartime experience has separated him in profound ways from his wife. The spare directness of the unanswered questions also makes it difficult to categorize this poem as offering a sentimental vision of combat. Countering the critical stereotype that soldiers' poetry usually endorses the patriotic ideal of the faithful loving wife at home, Baker's poem foregrounds the painful rift that combat experience creates between soldiers and their families.

While the correspondence with his wife provides Baker with an initial purpose for writing, most of his longer poems about combat do not specifically address her. Typescript versions of these longer poems that Baker prepared in later decades suggest that he hoped these pieces—some of which he composed during the war—would reach a wider audience. In many of his longer war poems, he speaks to the conflict of regional loyalties that divides the nation. While Baker uses the brief verses for Melissa to create an imagined and intimate link between himself and his absent wife, his longer battle poems affirm the bonds of comradeship between different groups of soldiers and ally his experience to that of soldiers in the field—even when Baker writes from a military hospital or years after the war. In some of his earliest wartime writings, Baker joins Union and Confederate soldiers into an alliance of men who have seen combat, showing a remarkable willingness to forgive the Confederate soldiers whom he had been fighting just days before.[24] After taking part in the battle of Corinth, Mississippi, in October 1862 and after visiting a field hospital in which he saw gravely wounded Confederate soldiers, Baker describes these experiences in detail in his journal. His poem "After the Battle: The Dirge" draws extensively on the imagery and the descriptions of the journal entry; Baker may have written the poem in the days and weeks after the battle, during one of his extensive stays in a military hospital in 1863 or '64 or after the war's end. Regardless of its date of composition, "After the Battle" makes clear that the literary tradition of representing military heroism in poetry offers Baker a means of making sense of his combat experience. As a poem that represents the aftermath of battle, it clearly responds to a conventional framework used by many poets of this era. Indeed, the lofty, rhythmic language of the October 5 journal entry that immediately precedes the poem suggests that Baker quickly begins to use a literary voice to express—and perhaps also to try to contain—the horror of what he has seen: "O it was awful, and cannot be described; nor can it ever be forgotten by its participants. It would have been glorious; it would have been magnificent, had one not known the lives it was costing: O how many a wife was deprived of a devoted husband; how many a mother, of a dutiful son; how many a father of the prop, and staff of his old age."[25]

In the poem that draws from this entry, Baker replaces the exclamatory "O" of lamentation in the prose with the high literary "O" of the apostrophe, a shift that seems to signal that he has gained still more aesthetic mastery over the horror of what he has witnessed. Like many Civil War poets, Baker opens his poem about the aftermath of battle with an address to the heavenly bodies above:

O shine alike, sun, moon, and stars,
    O'er graves of Blue and Grey;
And may you all sweet vigils keep
    Till Resurrection day.
No more the well-known drum will beat,
    For these the Blue and Grey;
No more the fife and bugle sound
    Will call them where they lay.

No more these many fallen braves,
    Shall in the battle meet;
No more will speed to battle line
    With willing, hurrying feet;
No more at roll-call or parade,
    With comrades will they fly
No more in dreams their loved ones meet
    And waking heave a sigh.

Here Baker writes of the conflict he took part in using a distancing elegiac stance, one that quickly elevates all of the conflict's participants—both Union and Confederate—to heroic status and one that imagines a speedy resolution to the present political crisis. The speaker's opening apostrophe confidently imagines postwar reconciliation between North and South as "sun, moon, and stars" look on with approval. With the grammatically ambiguous use of "alike," Baker's first two lines refuse to differentiate between Union and Confederate graves ("O shine alike, sun, moon, and stars, / O'er graves of Blue and Grey"), imagining the reunited Union as a nation of veterans, a nation founded on masculine ideals of military heroism. The list of familiar sights and sounds of camp and battlefield in stanzas one and two suggests that the shared experiences of Northern and Southern soldiers during the war years will make respect and reconciliation possible in the war's aftermath. The soldierly reconciliation on which this national reunification depends will be supported by the affection, stories, and tears supplied by women, as the penultimate stanza suggests: "The sister, though she weepeth sore, / For him her brother dear / Will tell of deeds of valor done / Though telling brings the tear."

In the poem's last two stanzas, however, the speaker's confident linking of Union and Confederate soldiers begins to unravel as the penultimate stanza celebrates the deeds of Union soldiers only: "Our countrymen never will forget / Deeds done here by the Blue." The collective "countrymen" would now seem to refer to Northerners only. The contradictions in the speaker's perspective on Confederate soldiers come to the surface in the poem's final stanza:

> I praise the bravery of the Grey.
> It deserved a better cause;
> But may the Lord each one forgive.
> As also does our laws:
> Then farewell, no ill I bear you.
> Ye who did wear the Grey;
> But to the wearer of the Blue
> Hallow'd ground where you lay.

In this final stanza, the speaker represents secession and support for the Confederate nation as errors that both God and the legal system must forgive. While the awkward rhyme scheme and the ungainly inversion ("As also does our laws") may reflect the limits of Baker's abilities as a poet, these verbal stumbles also suggest that he feels some discomfort with this ideal of forgiveness. While stanza one suggests that both Confederate and Union soldiers might hope to ascend to God on "Resurrection Day," in the final stanza only Union soldiers' graves are considered "hallow'd ground." Though Baker begins his poem with a commitment to reconciliation that will reunite the Union, by the poem's end his speaker's stance has become more ambivalent.

While "After the Battle: The Dirge" focuses on the aftermath of the battle and of the war, in still another poem about the Battle of Corinth, Baker offers a day-by-day account of the battle's events in the form of a narrative ballad. Written in forty-two stanzas of eight lines each, "Battle of Corinth" begins with a celebratory opening stanza with the meter and rhyme scheme of a marching song:

> 'Twas the third day of October,
> In eighteen sixty-two,
> That Price and Van Dorn encountered,
> The Union boys in blue.
> Oh! our leader was brave Rosencranz,
> Not many souls were we,
> But under such a leadership,
> Victory did we see.

In echoing a marching song, the opening stanza signals the heightened sense of unity and comraderie Union soldiers would have experienced after the victory. The second stanza insists on the vividness of the speaker's recollections:

> It was at the town of Corinth,
> In Mississippi State,
> And these scenes I do live over,
> Which now I will relate.
> I see the scattering oak trees,
> Which o'er this landscape grew.
> Ah! yes, they all come back to me,
> So real, and so new.

Insisting on the accuracy of his memory, Baker speaks of the battle as if it had occurred in the distant elegiac past. If he wrote the poem in the decades after the war, this distanced stance makes logical sense. If he wrote the poem not long after the battle, however, such a stance would have the advantage of distancing him abruptly from combat and its terrors. Like "After the Battle: The Dirge," "Battle of Corinth" removes its speaker to a position of safety outside the temporal zone of the war. This distanced temporal perspective also has the effect of making recent events seem to be already the stuff of heroic legend—a legendary battle in which the speaker himself participated.

Midway through the poem, Baker's speaker considers what role God may have played in protecting Union troops:

> Did God watch o'er this little band?
> I'm sure I cannot tell.
> Though near one hour we were exposed,
> None by their missiles fell.
> A charmed life we seemed to live,
> Amongst this leaden hail,
> And we were shielded more secure,
> Than in a coat of mail. (Stanza 16)

Though the speaker hesitates to assert explicitly that God protected his unit ("I'm sure I cannot tell"), the stanza as a whole seems to support this idea. Moreover, the poem's final stanza takes a much stronger stand, insists that God was instrumental to the victory, and calls several times for cheers for the Union troops, combining these celebratory cheers with the reference to God's authority in a strong gesture of ideological and aesthetic closure:

> We give three cheers for Davis' men,
> Who from the battle's shock,
> Helped turn the key of victory,
> Which God did here unlock.

Baker frequently concludes his war poems with such strong gestures of national and ideological closure.

Yet though the poem opens with a celebration of Union victory and ends by positioning God on the side of the Union, what happens in the body of the poem is considerably more complicated. Midway through the poem, describing the horror of mutilated bodies on the field, Baker shifts to an uncharacteristic first-person plural speaker and refuses to describe the carnage further:

> Oh! what a fearful mangling here,
> Is made by shot and shell,

The horrors of Death Valley now,
  We will no longer tell. (stanza 27)

The shift to a collective "we" implicitly underlines the gap that divides soldiers from civilians, suggesting both that soldiers are a unified community and that they are unwilling to describe to civilians the horrors that they have seen. Moreover, throughout the poem, the accumulation of details about troop positions and battle plans makes the narrative of events difficult to follow: Baker struggles to construct a lucid chronology out of the wealth of detail at his disposal. Shifting restlessly from the past to the present tense and back again, Baker probably wants the present tense to heighten the poem's drama; overall, however, these shifts have the effect of destabilizing a speaker who knows too much to settle comfortably into any one temporal position. While the awkwardness of the speaker's shifts in position results in part from Baker's limitations as a poet, the poem's ungainliness also conveys how psychically overwhelming the experience of combat is: how difficult it is for any one soldier to write a clear chronological narrative of events, how difficult it would be for him to settle into one stable position from which he might observe and describe the battle, how impossible it is for a noncombatant to understand what the soldier has seen and done.

This swerve to detail becomes perhaps even more striking in some of the war poems he wrote in later decades. In "The Charge at Monterey," a page-long piece that was probably written in the 1880s or 1890s, Baker begins by promising a narrative of the cavalry charge:

I'm carried back again today
  To fields of sixty-two,
I'm carried down to Tennessee,
  Those fields look bright and new.

Where memory leads him, however, is not finally to the heart of the battle, which is evoked in several broad strokes midway through the poem, but rather to the horse he rode that day:

My horse was shot, my noble steed,
  The best I ever strode.
The king of all our mounts was he,
  A daisy on the road.

In drill he knew all the commands,
And did not need a goad.

The terse phrase "my horse was shot" partially elides the battle's violence by refusing to state what happened to Baker himself: since Baker's horse was mortally shot in the midst of battle while Baker was mounted, Baker himself only narrowly escaped serious injury. Blocking off that possibility and its terrors, however, the poem swerves abruptly away from the scene of battle, back to drill, away from the heroism of men toward the intelligence and bravery of his horse. A man of only modest means in civilian life, Baker clearly takes great pride in the fact that he had such a fine horse for the battle. Because the horse died in the charge, Baker's account of the battle becomes an elegy for this extraordinary animal. While this kind of idiosyncratic detail registers Baker's presence on the battlefield, such details also underline again that the individual soldier's perspective on the conflict must inevitably be decentered and therefore must also derail any easy assumptions about the unified patriotic "we" of military experience.

A fragmentary poem from 1889 entitled "The Charge" begins by offering powerful echoes of Tennyson's "Charge of the Light Brigade," particularly in its second stanza:

And once I rode with eighty men
Death's jaws were open wide.
We met five thousand of the foe.
Rode we the battles tide.

The poem's final stanza, however, focuses not on the battle's outcome, but rather on Baker's feelings of anxiety and uncertainty as he rides forward:

One prayer upon my lips arose,
As we charged upon the foe;
It was for those I'd left at home,
The end I did not know.

It is as if inserting a first-person speaker into the framework of Tennyson's poem—which adheres throughout to the third-person plural—derails that famous poem's celebration of the cavalry's heroism. Though many of Baker's postwar poems end with celebratory affirmations of the Union victory, the endings of "The Charge at Monterey" and "The Charge" suggest that Baker can more readily affirm his identity as a Union veteran through recollection of specific details of his personal experience of the war: the collective "we" of military service gives way to a more personal and specific "I." Moreover, in the final stanza of "The Charge," the thought of the young wife he has left at home seems not to sustain and support the poem's soldier-speaker—as the conventional patriotic military argument would suggest. Rather the "prayer" for those "left at home" seems to leave the speaker suspended in an unresolved limbo of doubt and fear: "The end I did not know." Thus while Baker often uses declarations of his support for the Union as gestures of closure in his poems, swerves to personal details work against these larger ideological gestures of closure. Baker wants to emphasize his membership in the collective of Union soldiers, but his poems slide again and again toward the details of his individual wartime experience—and the fears, frustrations, doubts, and joys that made up that experience.

Confederate Commitments and Gendered Stances in the Work of George Washington Hall

While Northern soldier-poets often aim to position themselves—like Baker—as spokesmen for a reunited nation of veterans, Southern soldier-poets seek to confirm the birth of a new nation by helping to invent its literature. Their work thus endorses the metaphoric link between poetry and war offered by William Shepperson in his preface to *War Songs of the South:* "Southern independence has struck the lyre as well as the unsheathed sword."[26] While Baker's poems and journals are partially shaped by the initial purpose of writing to his wife, my second case study, George Washington Hall, relies on a different rhetorical model, drawing extensively from the genre of the conversion narrative, linking his spiritual rebirth to the birth of the Confederacy, and interspersing nationalist and devout poems among his journal entries. Born in Alabama, Hall enlisted in the Fourteenth Georgia Volunteers in May 1861 at the age of twenty, serving for the entire war and spending one year in a Union prison. Deeply religious and strongly devoted to the Confederacy, Hall had a conversion experience in April 1863, just before the two-year anniversary of his enlistment, at a time when waves of revivals were sweeping through the Confederate camps.[27] After the war, Hall returned to his family, then in Florida, married, and became a Baptist minister; working in both Georgia and Florida, he served as a minister for the rest of his life. Within the three volumes of handwritten journals he left behind, Hall includes sixteen poems, all of which were written or transcribed between April 1862 and May 1863. Later volumes of his war journals include no poetry, suggesting perhaps that he had less time for or interest in writing poetry in the war's later years. Though the journal does not specify the authorship of the poems, textual evidence suggests that Hall wrote many if not all of them himself. While he makes reference to writing regular letters home, he seems to have used both his journals and the included poems for different purposes—partly as an account of his spiritual struggles and partly as a record of the history of his Georgia regiment. Of the sixteen poems he includes in the journals, eight are identified as songs; these may have been sung in camp or on the march by soldiers in his unit. Even the eight poems that are not identified as songs, however, show the strong influence of popular song form both in the relative brevity of their lines and in their regular meter and rhyme schemes.

Though Hall makes no reference to a sweetheart or fiancée left behind, like Baker and like many other soldiers he writes poems that imagine scenes of combat from the perspective of women who await the soldiers' return. In a three-stanza poem called "My Soldier," dated August 1862, Hall's female speaker imagines her beloved soldier first on his watch dreaming of home, secondly stricken with a severe fever far from home, and thirdly rushing bravely into combat. Like his Union counterpart Obadiah Baker, Hall uses a series of questions to underline the gap that separates women at home from men at the front. Yet the detail and complexity of these questions suggest that Hall is willing to grant his female speaker a far more vivid and thorough understanding of the horrors of combat than Baker is willing to imagine for his wife. Hall begins each stanza with a sequence of questions in which the female speaker tries to imagine what the soldier is doing, and each stanza ends with her calling on God to protect him. In the poem's second stanza, the speaker imagines that the soldier lies gravely ill:

> Is he lying sorely stricken
> Fever scorched on lip and brow
> Murmuring faintly names of dear ones
> Dear ones all unanswering now
> Shrieking out each ghastly vision

Dark with dread or mad with pain
Visions such as haunt the chambers
Of the sick bewildered brain
God have pity on my darling
Give those sad beseeching eyes
Slumbers such as used to bless them
Morning such as used to rise.[28]

As I suggested in analyzing the poem in which Baker tries to imagine his wife's perspective on combat, poems in which soldiers imagine a woman's perspective on the conflict allow them to escape imaginatively from the stresses of combat. Such poems also allow soldiers to represent themselves in sentimental postures of vulnerability without having to speak in the first person from such a position. In the case of Hall's poem, such a posture allows him to put prayers for his own well-being into the mouth of a character other than his own first-person speaker. In stanza two, the female speaker's imagining of the soldier's delirious fever also allows Hall to gesture toward the terrors of combat without ever having to admit that he has felt fear on the battlefield. The phrase "Visions such as haunt the chambers/Of the sick bewildered brain" points obliquely toward the soldier's recurring traumatic memories of combat.

Like many other Southern writers, Hall represents Confederate women and men as playing mutually sustaining roles in the prosecution of the war. He frequently argues that Confederate soldiers are fighting to protect the honor of Southern women; this argument certainly reflects the fact that most of the war's battles took place on Southern territory—therefore closer to the homes of Southern soldiers—yet more important, Hall's reliance on this argument underlines its centrality to Southern nationalist ideologies.[29] "My Soldier" foregrounds the Southern code of masculine heroism—which is endorsed and inspired by a feminine speaker—in its third and final stanza:

Is my darling daring nobly
Where the battle thunders peal
Fiery eyed and gallant hearted
Darling onward steel to steel
Or with front of stern defiance
Does he breast the foemans sway

Standing where the headlong billows
Break and sink in scattered spray
God protect him, God preserve him
Or from earths poor faint existences
Raise him to heavens perfect health.

In this stanza, the punning eye-rhyme of "darling" and "daring" emphasizes that Southern women urge men into combat and that Southern men feel impelled to fight in order to protect Southern women.[30] The "darling" in line four—which may or may not be an error for "daring"—suggests that the female speaker commands her lover with the imperative "Darling, onward!," an imperative that suggests women fully understand the exhilaration of going into combat. The feverish terrors of stanza two have been superseded by the adrenalin-loaded thrill of the charge. In its final two lines, the poem shifts abruptly away from its otherwise regular stanza, meter, and rhyme scheme. This abrupt swerve away from formal closure—which may indicate that the poem is unfinished—also signals the difficulty that Hall has in reconciling his profound spiritual commitments with his military ones—in this poem at least. Reading like a swerve toward prose, the last two lines heighten the urgency of the speaker's plea that God protect the soldier, again perhaps signaling fear on Hall's part. The lines omit any direct reference to the possibility of the soldier's death, moving abruptly to the hope of his ascent to heaven. The date attached to the poem—August 1862—is significant insofar as we know that Hall was in the hospital with a severe illness at this time and feeling the separation from his family acutely. Writing the poem in the voice of an imaginary female beloved may have been a less painful choice for him than writing the poem in the voice of his mother, whom he mentions often and with great affection in the journals, particularly during the time of his illness.

Hall's "My Soldier" relies on a metrical pattern that is also used in an enormously popular song from this era, "The Vacant Chair," with text by Henry S. Washburn and music by George F. Root. Hall's reliance on this pattern underlines that the generic boundary between song and poem is particularly permeable in his work. Moreover, since Washburn's text imagines the empty chair left at the family table by a fallen soldier and Hall's poem imagines what an absent (and possibly dead) soldier might be doing, the echoes of the song's metrical pattern in Hall's poem may be more than coincidental. While "The Vacant Chair" offers a sentimental model for how a grieving family should respond to the loss of their son, Hall's poem breaks with that model in significant ways. In its three verses, "The Vacant Chair" traces the trajectory of the family's mourning: they gather together and remember the departed soldier ("We shall meet, but we shall miss him"), they remind themselves that he died for a noble cause (He "[upheld] our country's honor, In the strength of manhood's might"), and ultimately they mourn by his grave in harmony with nature, joining their singing voices to "the dirges from the pine and cypress."[31] Stanza one of Hall's "My Soldier" begins by following the sentimental formula for representing the distance between soldiers and their loved ones, picturing the soldier remembering "the home where happy faces/Beamed with such a lovely light." In stanza two, however, the description of the gravely ill soldier grappling with the memory of what he has seen in combat and "Shrieking out each ghastly vision" pushes the poem away from a conventional sentimental scene toward a more graphically realistic depiction of life in an army hospital. And while "The Vacant Chair" carefully preserves the distance that protects the family from comprehension of the war's violence, stanza three of Hall's poem has his female speaker vividly imagining the exhilarating adrenalin rush of entering combat. Though Hall is clearly responding to sentimental narratives of how a family ought to grieve, he rings significant changes on this formula by lessening the imaginative distance that separates the soldier from the women left at home.

As "My Soldier" makes clear, for Hall, the soldier-poet's task of helping to found the Southern nation is inseparable from the idea that the war is being fought to defend the honor of Southern women; most of Hall's poems touch on this idea. In an elegy he writes in July 1862 for an unnamed soldier, "To one brave young spirit who gave his life in his Country's cause," Hall represents not only the thrill of going into combat, but also the passionate Confederate nationalism that spurs the soldier forward—and the desire to protect mother and sister that is inseparable from that nationalism:

> Thy daring spirit led thee on
> To battle for thy country's good
> To save thy mother from a wrong
> Thy Sisters from a tyrants mood.

Though not himself in a cavalry unit, Hall makes the soldier a dashing and heroic figure by representing him as riding into battle on horseback. The nine-stanza elegy is formulaic rather than specific, insisting throughout on the gallant bravery of the soldier and the righteousness of the cause for which he is fighting, and ending with the assertion that he died as a Christian martyr for the cause of Southern freedom:

> Rest martyred soldier, rest in peace
> Beneath the flower enameled sod
> Thy form in Holy wood now sleeps
> Thy soul we trust is with thy God

While Baker represents the graves of both Union and Confederate soldiers as part of his vision of national reunion, Hall focuses on a Confederate soldier only, endorsing the argument that the war has made possible the founding of the Confederacy. Since the speaker's stance in the poem makes Hall's national allegiances clear, he has no reason to specify which side his soldier is on.

A shorter more rhythmically emphatic piece from that same month, July 1862, underlines the idea that Hall has no interest in celebrating the heroism of Union soldiers.[32] The opening stanza of "After Battle—A War Song" dismisses that possibility:

> On yesterday, untrodden lay,
> The fields now tramp'd and gory,
> We met the foe, we laid them low,
> Bereft of life and glory.

Stanza four points toward the eternal life that awaits the martyred Confederate soldiers, as their deeds are celebrated in poetry:

> Though dead, they live, who freedom give
> In death, to unborn ages;
> Their names enrolled, in glittering gold,
> Shall grace our history's pages.

While Baker's "After the Battle" begins with an attempt to unite both armies as a reconciled nation of veterans, Hall's piece remains exclusively focused on the cause of Confederate nation-building.

In Hall's poems as in the work of many Southern Confederate poets, the South is figured as feminine.[33] This figuring of the South as feminine has the effect of emphasizing or heightening the gender positions of other masculine and feminine characters in the poems, emphasizing soldiers' manliness and bravery and emphasizing both women's beauty and the inspiration that beauty offers to Confederate soldiers. In a poem called "When the War Is Over," Hall imagines a summer evening in which a young woman promises herself in marriage to a young man, the poem's first-person speaker. Pressed by him to name the hour when she would be willing to marry him, she replies, "Not soon, but when the war is over, love." The third and final stanza begins with the bride-to-be stating explicitly that the young man must—for now—marry himself to the Confederacy:

> Thy country is thy bride till she shall stand
> Stand proudly mid the nations of the earth
> Till gentle peace come smiling o'er the land
> And direful woes give place to joy and mirth
> Strike till the presence of the dastard foe
> Our hopes of happiness no longer mars
> And if no more I'll see thee here below
> I'll meet thee in the world beyond the stars

The bride in stanza one already suggests an allegorical figure for the South, with her "leafy bower," her "gentle sigh," and the "small white hand" she offers the young man.

This delicate feminine image of the Southern belle who awaits the soldier's return is complemented by the emphatic masculinity of the collective "we" of the soldiers depicted in still another Hall poem, "The Soldier's Song." The second stanza begins:

> We are here at our country's call, boys
> We will stay till our work is done
> Till the final blow is struck, boys
> And our independence won.

Emphasizing the close relationship between the "call" of the nation and the response of the "boys" who volunteer for the fight, the poem also underlines both the strength of the bond between the men and how young they are: repeating the apostrophe to the "boys" at the end of every other line, Hall writes a rousing call to arms, urging young men to show both their courage and their commitment to the Confederacy.

If we read Hall's figures for the Southern nation back in relation to Baker's representation of the reunited States, we can see that feminine desires and feminine figures play a much more central role in supporting Hall's vision of Southern masculine heroism. While Obadiah Baker figures the reunited Union as a masculine collective of veterans, sustained and supported by a background of women's tears and stories, George Washington Hall figures the birth of the Southern nation in terms of a happy marriage—first the happy marriage of the young soldier to his beloved Confederacy and second the happy marriage of the young soldier to a Southern belle, a happy marriage that will take place only if Confederate forces succeed on the battlefield. The fact that Baker more or less divides his body of poetry into two separate genres—short poems marked by stance of address to his wife and long battle poems that are intended for a broader audience—underlines a crucial difference in the ways that gender works to support nationalist ideologies for Northern and Southern soldiers. While Hall's female characters are imaginary or allegorical figures, they are everywhere present in his poetry; the battle poems cannot be categorized separately from the poems that represent marriage and family ties between Southern men and women. And while some of Baker's poems seek to protect his wife from full knowledge of combat's horrors, Hall's poetry implies that Southern women are intimately aware of both the pleasures and the horrors of combat.

Yet while the representation of women's relationship to combat distinguishes the Southern from the Northern soldier-poet, what poems by these two men share is a strong commitment to nationalist ideological closure. Though Baker's poems sometimes switch verb tenses or swerve toward personal detail and away from wide-angle views of battles, his longer battle poems nonetheless frequently end with ringing endorsements of Union patriotism or celebratory praise of the Union victory. Tense shifts and thematic swerves work against the poems' commitments to closure, but these shifts and swerves do not fundamentally destabilize Baker's commitment to representing the war's violence as necessary to reestablish a unified nation. Hall's conviction in the justice of the Confederate cause is even stronger than Baker's commitment to the Union, and this conviction manifests itself in Hall's poems with endings that offer paeans to the Confederacy and to those who lost their lives helping to give birth to the Confederate nation. In Baker's work and even more clearly in Hall's, poems conclude with confident declarations of nationalist commitments; their poetry is fundamentally structured by their insistence that the war was being fought for a worthy cause. Reading Baker's and Hall's poetry in relation to that of other soldier-poets and also in relation to social historians' analyses of why men fought in the Civil War suggests that their nationalist commitments are representative of the wartime views of many Union and Confederate soldiers.[34]

Political Dissent and Formal Disruption in the Work of Lyman Holford

By way of contrast, however, I want to turn to one soldier-poet whose war poetry offers a counterexample to the strong gestures of nationalist closure displayed by Baker and Hall. A member of the Sixteenth Wisconsin Volunteers, Lyman Holford wrote three volumes of pocket-sized diaries during his years of military service, including two poems in his first volume, eight in his second, and none in the third. Wounded above the knee in the early stages of the battle of Gettysburg, Holford spends several weeks in Union Army hospitals in July and August 1863. Bored and at loose ends, he writes out the eight poems in his second journal during this time: "As there is nothing of interest to note down, I have taken to filling up my book with scraps of poetry."[35] While Holford doesn't identify himself as the poems' author, the length of the pieces and their fragmentary state suggest that he himself probably composed them. Beyond his brief statement that he is writing poetry to fill the time, the journals give no indication as to what kind of audience, if any, he might have imagined his work could reach. A farmer before the war, Holford returned to Wisconsin and worked as a teacher after his discharge from the Union Army in July 1864.

Most of Holford's pieces focus on romance, courtship, or nature, and many are light-hearted song-poems. A poem written apparently written in the immediate aftermath of Gettysburg offers a striking contrast with these other pieces, however. Though Holford often titles his pieces and usually relies on sedate and regular meters and rhyme schemes, the untitled and apparently unfinished seven-page poem he writes not long after

Gettysburg is written in ringing, energetic trochees with a rhyme scheme that is irregular, though dense with internal rhyme and echoic repetition. In combination with the trochaic meter, the poem's relatively short lines drive its energy and movement forward, conveying the speed and exhilaration of participating in combat. The poem begins:

> Oh! the music of the battle;
> The excitement and confusion,
> And the chomping of the bridles
> Of the wild and eager horses,
> Eager, wild to join the battle,
> And the rushing of the chariots,
> And the twaggling [?] of the trumpets

With references to music, horses, chariots, and trumpets, Holford begins by representing battle as literary and heroic. The poem's syntax—which offers a pile-up of suspended progressive verb forms and postpones the subject-verb pairing a declarative sentence would require—conveys the excitement and confusion of entering combat. Just a few lines later, however, Holford has shifted from the excitement of battle to its horrors:

> Oh! the horrors of the battle;
> 'Mid the howling, fury, wailing,
> Of the conquering, wounded, dying,
> And the cursings, groanings, pleadings,
> With the pale and ghastly riders

In these lines, the tumbling accumulation of verbs conveys the disorientation of combat, the inability to distinguish individuals or friend from foe. Holford represents battle in apocalyptic terms, though God seems remote from the Day of Judgment he describes:

> Onward rolls the surge infuriate [?]
> Onward rolls the tide of battle
> Like the flames among the branches
> Like ten thousand furious demons

While the first page of Holford's poem uses meter and syntax to convey how overwhelming the sights and sounds of combat are to participants, the six remaining pages rely on the same meter and similar syntactic patterns to convey the idea that the battle's aftermath is equally overwhelming to those who walk the battlefields, to those who bury the dead, and to friends and family mourning their losses.

Holford's poem is relentlessly dark and bitter, both in its representation of Confederate soldiers and in its response to the ideals of nationalism and military heroism used to gain recruits for the Union army. The next two pages of the poem turn toward Gothic imagery, with vultures, ravens, tombs, graveyards, and a blood-drinking "grey wolf," this last one of many bitter references to Confederate soldiers as "blood-nursed tyrants."[36] By page four, Holford's omniscient speaker has turned to the conventional task of describing the last words of the dying soldier.[37] Drawing on literary conventions in widespread use at this time, Holford adds a dark and original twist to these patterns. Conveying his final messages to a fellow soldier who is a childhood friend, Holford's dying soldier wants his friend to give different messages to the various friends and relatives he has left behind. The message he wants delivered to his classmates displays the soldier's acute disillusionment with the ideals of masculine heroism:

> "Tell my schoolmates when you greet them,
> That I never more shall meet them:
> Point them back to when we pondered
> Over Greek and Roman glory,
> How our hearts grew warm within us,
> As we read the glowing story;
> Tell them fame is but a shadow,
> Earthly hopes are false and fleeting
> Singing sands that lure them, cheating,
> Fickle as inconstant aspen
> Earthly pleasures, toil and trouble,
> Wealth as rotten straw or stubble,
> Happiness an empty bubble,
> That will perish in the grasping."

Holford here uses a tighter scheme of end rhymes and the unexpected syntactic closure of a complete imperative sentence to foreground the cynical despair at the heart of the soldier's message to his classmates, themselves potential recruits for the army. Tales of "Greek and Roman glory," Holford suggests, lead young men to enlist and seek their own fame; such fame Holford dismisses as nothing more than "a shadow." The young recruits' "earthly hopes" of achieving such fame are "singing sands that lure them, cheating." Indeed, the dying soldier dismisses not only military glory but all "earthly pleasures," including "wealth" and "happiness," as illusory and unattainable aims. Holford's speaker bitterly warns his schoolmates not to believe the patriotic model of young boys reading about and hoping to emulate epic tales of glory.

When, on the fifth page of the poem, the dying soldier offers the conventional pro-Union nationalist and Christian sentiments as messages for his father, his mother, and his wife, the jarring swerve from disillusionment to conventional patriotic pieties is so abrupt as to make clear that those pieties are offered not because the soldier really believes in them, but rather because he sees them as the only possible means of consoling his mourning family. The series of brief imperatives Holford uses heightens the emptiness of the ideologies his grieving family must rely on:

> "Tell my father when you greet him
> That I died to save my country,
> Tell my mother God is wisest,
> [. . .]
> Tell her not to weep or worry,
> For her son was always loyal,
> And he died to save his country.

Reading the sentimental trope of the dying soldier, Alice Fahs argues that such poems often represent both the soldier and his imagined listener on the homefront as "similarly emotive and sympathetic," thereby imagining close emotional ties between the soldier and his loved ones.[38] Representing his dying soldier as cynically pragmatic and his mourning family as hopelessly ignorant of war's realities, Holford exposes these emotional ties as illusory ones. Though Holford's dying soldier hopes that he will be reunited with his wife in the afterlife ("Tell her [. . .] I hope with joy to meet her,/When the day of life is ended."), this is a fleeting moment of hope in what is otherwise a relentlessly dark poem.

Underlining the inadequacy of the conventional forms of consolation offered to bereaved families, in the poem's final two pages, the speaker turns in anger on the collective of noncombatant readers, accusing civilians of ignoring the sufferings of soldiers and refusing to assist them:

Go, ye idle, cursed complainers,
Who complain at *home* of trouble;
Think upon the soldier's sorrow,
Wounded, bleeding, for his country
[. . .]
Cast a thought and truly pity,
Weary, weak and wakeful pickets.
As they tread their rounds in silence,
Keeping up this country's honor,
Guarding you from foul oppression,
Keeping you a home of pleasure—

In this section, Holford's poem emphasizes the vast divide that separates the soldier's life of boredom and suffering from the lives of the "idle complainers" who give no thought to those defending their "home of pleasure." After indicting his readers for their hypocrisy with a divisive and accusatory "ye" ("Go, ye idle, cursed complainers"), the speaker concludes the poem by calling on his Northern readers to join him in cursing the "rebellious people" who support the Confederacy, those "godless traitors." The syntax in this final section of the poem again becomes suspended and complex; the accumulation of verbal clauses heightens the sense of rage in the speaker's call for revenge. In his closing image, an embittered and pitiless speaker hopes that "the widows of the traitors" will be forever weeping for husbands who will not return, weeping for the Confederate dead whom he bluntly calls "murderers" in the poem's last line.

As this analysis suggests, Lyman Holford's poem undermines both the ideals of military heroism and the ideals of patriotic nationalism—ideals that serve as a structural foundation in Baker's and Hall's poetry. While these ideologies work to contain the horrors of war in Baker's and Hall's poems, Holford's poem does not aim for emotional or formal closure. Rather the poem pushes strongly toward the irregular formal patterns and the jagged ironies we typically associate not with American Civil War poetry but rather with the beginnings of modernism, with British poetry of the First World War, for example. Within the pages of his journal, immediately after the seven-page war poem I have been discussing, Holford switches his theme abruptly, writing a four-page tragi-comic poem about the misadventures a young man has when he goes sleighing with a young woman. Though "When I Was Out A-Sleighing" is ostensibly a peacetime narrative of courtship at home, the tale is a comically violent one as the speaker and his companion are pelted with snowballs by mischievous boys and flung from the sleigh in a series of accidents. Ultimately, the rented sleigh is wrecked in a crash, and the speaker has both a crying young woman and an unexpected debt on his hands in return for his seemingly harmless desire to go sleighing. The poem gives voice to some of the anger Holford expresses in his untitled war poem against civilians whose lives unfold peacefully far from the front; the text represents courtship as a ritual fraught with physical, financial, and emotional complications. For a reader paging through the journal, this abrupt shift in topic—from a scene of combat to a courtship ritual gone awry—only has the effect of underlining the uncontained disillusionment in the preceding war poem.

Moreover, just as Baker seems to make a clear generic distinction between the brief verses addressed to his wife and his longer heroic battle poems, so too does Holford divide his poems into two discrete categories: poems about romantic love (nine of his ten poems) and his single long poem about combat. Cordoning women off from the experience of war's violence, Holford's war poem foregrounds the powerful bonds of masculine comradeship that war establishes between and among men who fight together. Indeed if the embittered and cynical speaker of Holford's war poem seems to believe in anything at all, it is that men must tell other men the truth about war's horrors. The dying soldier offers his loved ones a terse but comforting narrative of the soldier's heroic martyrdom for the cause of the nation. When speaking to his male friends, however, he must tell a fuller and truer story: that war leads to gory carnage and that there is little patriotic or personal meaning that can be drawn from it. The lack of formal closure in Holford's long combat poem corresponds to the speaker's restless bitterness about the empty platitudes of patriotic ideologies.

Postwar Anger and Reconciliation in the Work of Jasper Jay Stone

While Holford's war poem offers an example of a soldier-poet questioning nationalist and military ideologies in the midst of the war, the work of Jasper Jay Stone offers insight into soldier-poets' questions about these ideologies in the decades after the war. In the extensive introductory remarks Stone includes when he compiles his poems into a finished manuscript in 1908, he weighs in at length on the ideals of nationalism and patriotism and the ways that poetry can support those ideals. David Blight describes the wave of public interest in the war that made publishing Civil War memoirs and recollections a lucrative commercial undertaking after 1880; Stone's introductions and prefaces underline his desire to contribute to this outpouring of soldiers' writings, thereby helping to shape the national memory of the war.[39] Three of Stone's poems also protest the poverty and neglect that afflict the veteran in the war's aftermath, signaling his partial disillusionment with that national memory.[40] After serving as a private in the Thirty-Fifth Iowa Volunteers, Stone handwrote and elaborately illustrated a manuscript of nearly 200 pages of poetry in the early years of the twentieth century, including also some poems that he wrote during his time as a soldier. Though he worked as a calligrapher and penmanship instructor after the war, Stone's time in the military left him disabled; he mentions partial paralysis of his writing arm. In the letter that he writes to Theodore Roosevelt in 1908 in which he introduces himself and his work, Stone notes that he has "toiled and struggled" with his manuscript for twenty-five years in hopes that it "*might, sometime*, reach the *world*" (emphasis in original) (fig. 3).[41] Though Stone is modest about his poetic abilities, he suggests that his experience as a soldier and the ill health he has suffered as a result of his years of military service have both strengthened his dedication to this writing task. While he imagines Roosevelt to be his immediate audience, Stone clearly hopes that his work will receive wider recognition through Roosevelt's promotion of it as part of an anthology of war poems. Both in the letter to Roosevelt and in the volume's various prefaces, Stone emphasizes the dissemination of patriotic ideals as a central purpose for his writing. To Roosevelt, Stone writes that he "desires to see the American people rise to that supreme plane of liberty and enlightenment which his fallen comrades earned for them, by the sacrifice of their lives."

Like Obadiah Baker who, in the decades after the war, also wrote war poetry and carefully revised his wartime poems, Stone writes poetry after the war's end to affirm his identity as a veteran and a soldier; clearly Stone's years of military service were central to his sense of self. His pride in his military service contrasts sharply with the brief references he makes to his postwar life which is marked by "disease and poverty, and lack of education and proper environments."[42] Like Baker, Stone was displaced from his Iowa home by financial pressures and health troubles after the

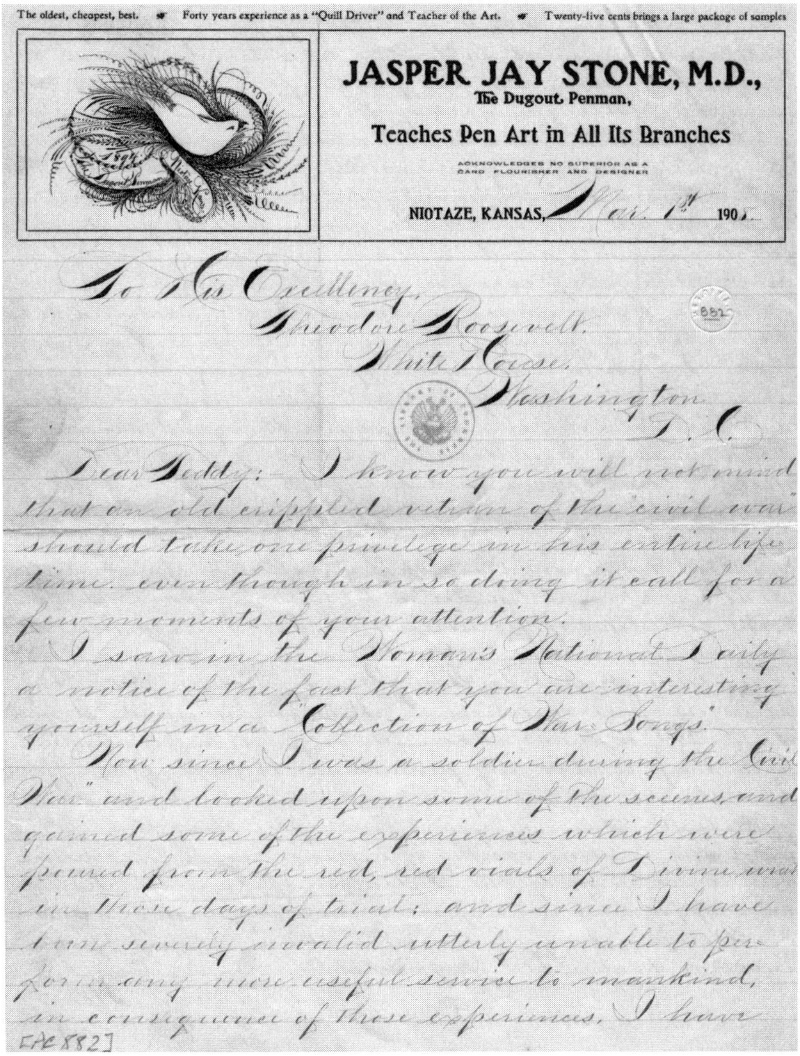

The oldest, cheapest, best. Forty years experience as a "Quill Driver" and Teacher of the Art. Twenty-five cents brings a large package of samples

JASPER JAY STONE, M.D.,
The Dugout Penman,
Teaches Pen Art in All Its Branches
ACKNOWLEDGES NO SUPERIOR AS A CARD FLOURISHER AND DESIGNER

NIOTAZE, KANSAS, Mar. 1st 1908

To His Excellency,
Theodore Roosevelt.
White House,
Washington
D. C.

Dear Teddy: I know you will not mind that an old crippled veteran of the "civil war" should take one privilege in his entire life time. even though in so doing it call for a few moments of your attention.

I saw in the Woman's National Daily a notice of the fact that you are interesting yourself in a "Collection of War Songs."

Now since I was a soldier during the "Civil War" and looked upon some of the scenes, and gained some of the experiences which were poured from the red, red vials of Divine wrath in those days of trial: and since I have been severely invalid utterly unable to perform any more useful service to mankind, in consequence of those experiences, I have

3. Jasper Jay Stone's letter to President Theodore Roosevelt, March 1, 1908

war; in recreating idyllic memories of military comradeship, both men attempt to reestablish the bonds of the small-town life that they knew in childhood.[43] For Stone in particular, the bonds of small-town life played a crucial role in his decision to enlist: in the "Prologue" to one of the long poems in his manuscript, he calls on his reader to "suppose" all the "young heroes" in his poems "to be schoolmates from the same school," all of whom were "educated, trained, and disciplined under the watchful eye of the same schoolmaster," a schoolmaster who joins up with his young pupils in order to continue serving as their teacher and guide.[44] Though Stone does not give his soldiers or battles specific names, he insists that the "scenes and characters described" are "all real."[45] For Stone then, schoolroom models of patriotism and heroism are literally brought to the battlefield in the person of the beloved schoolmaster.

In his "Bequeathment," the opening statement in which he dedicates the manuscript to his comrades in arms, Stone emphasizes his fervent hope that the work will be well received by an audience of his fellow soldiers. If it is warmly received by the comrades with whom he "camped and marched and battled [. . .] for the preservation of the Union," then he will "have renewed occasion to feel that his comradeship with the grand old Thirty-Fifth Iowa has not been utterly in vain."[46] Poetry, in other words, will renew his faith in the nationalist ideals for which they fought even as it will also recreate the intense bonds of soldierly comradeship. The idea of addressing his fellow soldiers strongly motivates his writing: he insists, somewhat anxiously, that he has "the faith to believe that the ties of army comradeship will endure when all else fails," before going on to hope that his volume of poetry might "win for [him] an humble place in the ranks of the survivors of the old regiment."[47] Stone uses poetry then to write his way back into the army, not only to reimagine the bonds of comradeship but also to legitimate his claim to being a veteran. The rhetorical urgency of the "Bequeathment" results from his anxiety about the legitimacy of that claim. Insisting that he did nothing particularly noteworthy during his combat service, he wants his comrades to find in his poems evidence that he "was there" (emphasis in original).[48] Reiterating his hope that the poems might meet with success, Stone concludes by saying that such recognition would repay him for the years of "helpless invalidism" he has endured since the war's end. Poetry—and the success of his manuscript in particular—might help to compensate for the suffering the war has caused him.

Just as an undercurrent of anxiety about his worth as a soldier runs throughout Stone's "Bequeathment," so too are his war poems shot through with ambivalence about whether or not the outcome of the war was worth its terrible cost. This ambivalence is perhaps most evident in his postwar poems: of the three poems that protest the neglect and poverty in which many veterans live, the first, "Reminiscentia," offers the darkest account of violent memories that haunt the veteran. Yet even Stone's wartime poetry betrays some uncertainty about the war's costs. Like Obadiah Baker and many other popular poets of his day, Stone takes up the conventional task of writing an "After the Battle" poem with its ritualized opening apostrophe to the heavens; though Stone probably edited and revised those poems he composed during wartime, the note that he places after this poem suggests that he composed it on April 10, 1864, just one day after the Thirty-Fifth Iowa took part in the Battle of Pleasant Hill in Louisiana. Like Baker's "After the Battle," Stone's poem of the same title relies on ballad form, alternating lines of eight and six syllables; his use of ballad form again underlines the extent to which soldiers wrote poetry in relation to the songs they had in their heads. In "After the Battle," Stone offers a collective elegy for the Union war dead. While Baker's "After the Battle" tries to mourn for both Confederate and Union dead, Stone's poem remains exclusively focused on the Union dead and the question of what might be gained by the sacrifice of their lives:

> Shine on, shine on, oh stars of heaven!
>   Shine o'er the battle plain;
> Where Death's destroying angel hath
>   Today reaped heavy gain.
>
> Our Nation's bravest sons lie strown [*sic*]
>   At foot of Freedom's shrine:
> And she hath claimed them for her own,
>   And given them peace divine.
>
> Shine on, shine on, oh stars of heaven!
>   Shine consecration o'er this plain;
> That sacrifice so nobly given,
>   May not be all in vain.

Our Nation will rejoice today,
For victory gathered here:
Tomorrow, all her laurels fade
In bitter scalding tears.

Shine on, shine one, oh stars of heaven!
Shine thro' the rolling years;
In witness that our nation hath
Reaped glory with her tears.[49]

Though Stone's second stanza insists that the Union's "bravest sons" have died to save Freedom and have thereby gained "peace divine," his third stanza seems less confident, calling on the stars to consecrate the battlefield so that this sacrifice "may not be all in vain." Reflecting on the vicissitudes of war, stanza four notes that the Nation's rejoicing for the victory will soon give way to "bitter scalding tears" as her "laurels fade." The fifth and final stanza attempts to close off the uncertainties of this cycle by moving forward into the postwar future ("Shine on, shine on, oh stars of heaven! / Shine thro' the rolling years"). Yet while Stone uses a temporal shift into the future to will peace and unity to the nation, the poem offers no guarantee that the stars will be able to consecrate the battlefield. In calling on the stars to guarantee that the war is being fought for a just cause, the speaker hovers precariously on the brink of moral uncertainty.

Still another poem Stone wrote during the war offers an equally ambivalent depiction of the larger meaning of soldiers' wartime deaths. In "Relief at Last," written in "Convalescent Camp" in Vicksburg, Mississippi, on October 25, 1863, Stone depicts a soldier's final moments of suffering by means of a high romantic scene: the soldier is a solitary walker, a feverish and wounded sentry, who drinks from and contemplates the rushing waters of a natural fountain. Stone here offers a response to Ethelinda Beers's enormously popular poem "The Picket-Guard," which depicts the sudden and unnoticed death of a foot soldier as he thinks of his family while doing his picket duty; like many sentry poems from the war years, Stone's poem closely parallels Beers's poem by emphasizing the idyllic natural setting in which the sentry dies, the thoughts of home and family that cross his mind just before his death, and the quiet and isolated nature of that death.[50] Yet while Beers's poem offers an extended account of the soldier's thoughts of home, Stone shortens those thoughts to three brief lines, offering instead an extended development of the nature imagery that Beers only sketches in lightly.[51] As the sentry walks his assigned beat, he waits for "relief," a word that gestures toward the possibility of a replacement sentry, medical assistance, God's intervention or, at the very least, the solace offered by a beautiful natural setting. The poem is at once extremely conventional—with its regular rhyme and meter and its high romantic repertoire of imagery—and surprisingly original in the way it stages a collision between that romantic nature repertoire and the soldier's "gory fate."[52] Drawing on an image in widespread use in Civil War poetry—an image that responds to the historical realities of some of the war's bloodiest battles—Stone represents the fountain's waters as stained by the soldier's blood, an image that underlines the interconnectedness of the human and natural worlds: "Still the sentry's blood kept staining / All those waters once so bright."[53] Echoing the repetition of the cycles of night and day, the repetition dictated by the poem's formal framework underlines the repetition of the soldier's movements and gestures: again and again he walks his rounds, again and again he drinks from the fountain. But while the water that gushes from the natural spring is inexhaustible, the sentry's flowing blood signals the ebbing of his life. Meanwhile, nature looks on impassively, as the stars and the moon make their appointed rounds in the sky, mirroring military actions but not intervening in any way in the soldier's fate. Cycles in nature are represented as eternal and unchanging, like the ever-flowing waters of the fountain:

> One by one, the stars in grandeur
>   Wheel their sentry beats on high
> The silver moon above the mountains
>   Rolls the grand rounds above the sky.[54]

While in stanza eight the speaker declares that only the "runing whippoorwill" breaks the night's silence, by stanza nine the "moan" of the dying sentry breaks the night's stillness as well.[55] Nature's cycles will continue indefinitely, but the individual sentry's life will not.

Stone builds drama in the poem's final stanzas through repetition of "no relief," a crucial phrase that encapsulates the ambivalent moral perspective of the poem as a whole. Stanza twelve emphasizes both the isolation and the loyalty of the dying soldier: "No relief comes; hours drag slowly: / Silent, patient doth he wait."[56] While the poem's final stanza

4. An illustrated page of Jasper Jay Stone's unpublished poetry manuscript

concludes that "relief" has come, the meaning of "relief" remains ambiguous in these closing lines:

> Now his gun leans on his bosom;
>   Clutched there in his right hand fast;
> And his left to his torn temple
>   Pressed:—relief has come at last.[57]

"Relief" clearly signifies death, but—again echoing Beers's poem—Stone's poem makes no attempt to attribute a higher redemptive meaning to that death. Though the closing stanza emphasizes the soldier's loyalty and heroism—he dies clutching his gun in one hand and his wounded face with the other—it does not reiterate the nationalist ideals that the soldier fought to uphold; nor does it suggest that God played any role in the soldier's life and death. The soldier's death provides narrative closure for the poem, but the poem does not end with a strong gesture of patriotic closure.

As if unsettled by the ambiguous ending of his own poem, however, Stone offers a much stronger gesture of ideological closure in the elaborately illustrated end-page that follows the poem. Beneath a stylized drawing of a dove, surrounded by ornamental flourishes with a motif of leaves and feathers, Stone pens the words "God's relief has come at last" (fig. 4).[58] This echoic "afterword" sentence in the illustrated end-page provides a moral certainty that the body of the poem refuses to offer; the afterword confidently states that God has sanctioned the soldier's death or has at least offered the "relief" of an end to suffering and safe passage to heaven. The afterword thus also implies that God supports the Union position in the war.

This pattern of reifying interpretation by abruptly resolving ambiguities within the poems becomes even more pronounced in Stone's postwar poetry, where his speakers oscillate between positions of deep despair about the war's costs and declarations of patriotic nationalism. One of the longest and most complex poems of the manuscript, "Moon Runes or the Sentry's Vision," written in 1894, offers a vision of war as apocalypse, representing combat as a chaotic hell on earth. The poem alternates between offering praise for soldiers' heroism and representing battlefield deaths as the caprice of fate; events on the battlefield are manipulated, Stone suggests cynically, by a gore-seeking prankster named Death, who mocks men for sacrificing their lives for the sake of the "magic word [. . .] 'Liberty.' "[59] What drives men to fight, Stone argues, is their desire to take "Sweet Glory for their bride."[60] Stone emphasizes the cruel moral paradox that men must forfeit their lives to prove their bravery: "Oh, cruel fate! oh, cruel human needs! / That man alone by blood and crime / May rise to proud heroic deeds."[61] Meditating on the rise and fall of nations across the centuries, Stone suggests that war's violence is inescapable: "Man's highest hopes and holiest schemes / Must be sustained by blood and war."[62] Yet though Stone's vision of the war is profoundly dark and pessimistic in the body of the poem, in its final pages he reaffirms the nationalist principles for which the Union fought. Though he suggests that the quest for Glory drove both Northern and Southern soldiers, he repeatedly calls the Southern cause "Treason," and, in the last few pages of the poem, affirms that God supported the Union position: "Ah yes, Secession's boastful pride / Went down before God's awful hand."[63] Immediately after this assertion of Union pride, however, Stone distances his speaker from these arguments—in part—by reminding readers that everything that has come thus far in the poem is only the sentry's "half-remembered dream:"

> The vision faded as it came
> In trembling pulses to the last:
> Till it seemed some half-remembered dream:
> Some troubled nightmare of the past.[64]

Emphasizing the feverish and perhaps distorted nature of the sentry's recollections, Stone drops a softening veil over the despair and disillusionment that the poem expresses by having his central character fall into a mysterious "trance." With these lines, he pushes the war's troubling and unanswered ethical questions back into the distant "half-remembered" past.

Though the speaker again ponders the larger meaning of the war in the last few pages of the poem, ultimately he seems to suggest that the war—as represented by the sentry's terrifying dream of it—is a mystery beyond human understanding ("Howe'er this may be, I cannot say"), a mystery that is controlled by God's "Love Divine" for the human world. Thus, while the poem's speaker has moments of moral uncertainty about the war's costs, the ending Stone writes for the piece strongly endorses the idea of Union national pride and God's support for the reunited nation. The final stanza seems to close off the poem's probing questions and ambiguities with an abruptness that betrays Stone's uneasiness with this gesture of argumentative closure. Moreover, the "Prologue" to the poem that follows "Moon Runes" and which—somewhat oddly—reflects at length on the preceding poem's meaning, emphatically reaffirms these closing arguments. As if to erase any possible uncertainty in the reader's mind about Stone's view of the war's costs, this "Prologue" returns with obsessive zeal to the subject of patriotism and the ways in which poetry might support and disseminate it. Flattening out all of the moral complexity of "Moon Runes," Stone insists that his primary aim as a poet is "to teach patriotism"; he dismisses Southern nationalist pride as "mere local enthusiasm or sectional pride," insisting that a "universal patriotism" is what the reunited nation must strive for.[65] In rejecting the idea that men will "throw themselves before the cannon's mouth" merely out of "passion or self-interest"—an argument he develops in some detail in "Moon Runes," particularly when he suggests that soldiers on both sides of the conflict long to take "Glory" as their bride—Stone's anxious insistence on his nationalist patriotism suggests that he is uneasy with the contradictions that abound in his poems. Just as the afterword on the end-page fixes the meaning of "Relief at Last," so too does the "Prologue" that follows "Moon Runes" attempt to reify the meaning of the far more complex poem that precedes it. Ordering the poems was clearly a key concern for Stone: the three poems that protest mistreatment of veterans are situated in the middle of the volume, preceded and followed by poems that emphasize the ideals of nationalist patriotism.

The fervor of Stone's patriotic ardor in the late nineteenth century reflects the rise of the collective American fascination with the Civil War, a fascination that results in the widespread observance of large-scale rituals on Decoration Day and the many veterans' reunions that took place in both the North and the South. Stone and Baker both hoped that this collective national fascination with the war and its veterans would help them find an audience for their poetry in the final decades of the nineteenth century. Both clearly hoped to use poetry as a way of connecting themselves to a national audience; both clearly also use poetry as a way to lessen their sense of isolation, recreating in their poems the bonds of military comradeship they experienced as young men and that ultimately came to define their adult sense of self. Emphasis on masculine bonds of comradeship is particularly prominent in Stone's work. Unlike Baker, Hall, and Holford, Stone imagines in his poetry an almost exclusively masculine world; his few and fleeting references to women are either abstract (the soldier's desire to take "Glory" as his bride) or generic (an occasional reference to mothers and sisters left behind). While Baker, Hall, and Holford represent family ties as a powerful force in the soldier's life, Stone effectively replaces family ties with military ones, following the dedication of "Moon Runes" to his father with a preface that implicitly dedicates the poem to his schoolmaster and schoolmates. Also striking in Stone's work is the contrast between his emphasis on the strength of bonds of comradeship (he believes "that the ties of army comradeship will endure when all else fails"[66]) and the number of solitary isolated soldiers he represents in his manuscript: from the sentry who dies alone and unnoticed in "Relief at Last" to the sentry for whom memories of the war are a heavy burden in "Moon Runes," the soldier in Stone's work is a solitary figure burdened with harrowing memories of combat.

In his many dedications, prefaces, and prologues, Stone struggles anxiously to affix a patriotic nationalist meaning to these memories. His prose writings make clear, however, that he looks forward to a future era of more perfect patriotism, an ideal that doesn't yet exist. His letter to Roosevelt implies that this nationalist ideal is one that is ever receding into an all-but-unattainable future: he "desires to see the American people rise to that supreme plane of liberty and enlightenment which his fallen comrades earned for them, by the sacrifice of their lives." Like all of the soldiers I have examined in this chapter, Stone argues in his poems that the cause of "liberty" impelled men onto the battlefield. Though Stone's "Prologue" dismisses the Southern desire for liberty as fanatical "sectional pride," in "Moon Runes" he offers a more complex argument, suggesting that an elusive ideal of "Liberty" drove both Union and Confederate soldiers to fight.[67]

As David Blight has argued persuasively, the narratives of reconciliation that dominated American public discourse about the war in the 1880s and 1890s simplified the war's range of causes, focusing on where and how the war was fought and downplaying the role that race and slavery played in leading the country into civil conflict.[68] These poems by Baker, Hall, Holford, and Stone largely confirm the work of social historians who have argued that Union and Confederate soldiers fought in the war for a complex array of loyalties to nation, region, home, and family. McPherson notes that relatively few Northern soldiers claimed to be fighting to end the institution of slavery.[69] Of the Union and Confederate poets I've examined in this chapter, neither Hall nor Holford makes any direct reference to the emancipation of black slaves; while Hall regularly refers to "slavery," the reference invariably points to the threat of Northern control of the Confederacy. Both Baker and Stone point to ending slavery as a desired outcome of the war. Baker does so explicitly several times both in his wartime and in his postwar writings; in Stone's work, however, anti-slavery references are both rare and relatively oblique. In an 1862 poem entitled "Farewell" that describes the soldier's departure for war, Stone describes the Union soldier's purpose in the following terms:

We go a blessed
    Peace to win
And wipe away
    Our Nation's sin.[70]

In keeping with the majority of white veterans' war narratives of the 1880s and 1890s, however, Stone makes no references to emancipation or to the plight of black veterans in his postwar poems. Obadiah Baker's support for abolition reaches a kind of dramatic crescendo in his postwar poetry. In a piece called "The Death of Lincoln"—which probably dates from the 1880s or later—Baker notes:

The freeing of so many slaves,
From slavery's cursed ban,
Was the greatest, grandest duty done
By any mortal man.

And in a poem titled "August 3rd, 1886" Baker offers an elegiac description of a postwar parade of the Grand Army of the Republic, again including a fleeting reference to emancipation: "John Brown's form rises anew/'Mongst the noble boys in blue." In striking contrast with Baker's and Stone's extended accounts of their loyalty to the construct of a reunited Union, however, the brevity and paucity of these references makes clear that the emancipation of black slaves was not a primary motivating factor for either man's decision to enlist in the Union army.

Analysis of poems by Baker, Hall, Holford, and Stone makes clear that both Union and Confederate soldiers struggled—with varying degrees of success and commitment—to justify the war's costs by arguing for the construct of the Union or Confederate nation. Just as George Bryant Woods echoes Tennyson to unite his Barre listeners as a community mourning a young soldier's death, so too do Baker, Hall, Holford, and Stone use their poetry to ally and unite the different constituencies that stand in for their ideal of the nation. Allegiances to family, home, local community, and to the community-based bonds of military comradeship played a crucial role in shaping each soldier's sense of that ideal. I have suggested that Confederate soldiers' poems seem to link women much more closely and directly to the violence of combat than Union soldiers do, signaling the mutually supportive relationship between masculine and feminine roles in Confederate nationalist ideologies. I have suggested also that Union soldier-poets seem either to emphasize Northern women's distance from battlefields or—in the case of Stone—barely represent women at all, a distance that unsettles the conventional patriotic argument that Northern men are fighting to preserve the invaluable freedoms of the family and the home.

Tellingly, both Northern and Southern soldiers' poetry rarely figures families (either husbands and wives or parents and sons) as a unified "we"; rather the collective "we" is reserved for representing the powerful bonds of homosocial comradeship in the military. Again and again, however, that collective and patriotic "we" is undermined by unassimilable aspects of the soldier's individual experience of the war: the sudden swerve away from the collective military effort toward focusing on one's own horse, the fear of entering combat, the terrors of traumatic memory after combat, or anger at the platitudes about heroism offered to young boys by their teachers. The personal I of the poetic-speaker unsettles or at the very least decenters the collective "we" of military experience, a decentering that is made evident in the ways these poems often resist formal closure, breaking out of the regular metrical and rhyme schemes of the traditional marching song or war ballad. This resistance to formal closure signals also a resistance to conventional nationalist pieties. While tensions between individual and collective experience may be particularly difficult to sidestep in the genre of poetry—a genre where a personal "I" would be expected at least occasionally—this inevitability may also explain the extraordinary popularity of the genre of poetry with soldiers: readily accommodating both polyvocality and swerves in position and perspective, the capaciousness of poetry allows the amateur soldier-poet to experiment with both kinds of voices, alternating between a personal "I" and a collective "we" without having to fix or reify his position in either stance.

These sudden shifts between the personal "I" and the collective "we" in soldier-poets' work signal the wide range of possible stances for the address to the nation that professional writers will explore in their work as well, though professional writers may accomplish such shifts in more nuanced or subtle fashion. Writing at a remove from the field of combat, professional writers will also rely on the versatility of poetic voice to address their immediate circle of family and friends, their community, and the larger construct of the nation, building, dividing, and reconfiguring their chosen audiences over the course of the war. In reimagining the relationship between public and private stances, these writers will also expand the range of speaking positions available to American poets, offering both new definitions of the American nation and new models for American poetic voice.

CHAPTER THREE

THE LYRIC I AND THE POETICS OF PROTEST

Julia Ward Howe and Frances Harper

For amateur soldier-poets, the genre of poetry offers the flexibility of changing perspectives, moving swiftly between the nationalist "we" of the military collective and the decentered "I" of individual experience. Soldier-poets can represent combat or can argue—with the authority of their wartime experience—that it defies representation. They can imagine women's relationships to battlefield violence—or they can suggest that women are too far removed from the field of combat to be able to understand the soldier's experience. While poetry offers nineteenth-century women writers extraordinary freedoms—the freedom to speak in the first person in the voice of a soldier or a slave, for example—a professional woman writer who speaks in the voice of a soldier or seeks to forge a unified "we" of Union supporters must find a means of anchoring the authority of her imaginative stance. Poetry allows women writers the imaginative freedom to assume roles they could never assume in life, thereby suspending provisionally the complex boundaries that divide public and private spheres and that separate one racial community from another; for this very reason, the stakes are high for the professional woman writer as she seeks to establish the authority of the speaking stances in her poems.

Both the women writers I consider in this chapter had already established professional reputations as poets prior to the Civil War. Yet both Julia Ward Howe and Frances Harper would find in the crisis of the Civil War a renewed sense of writerly purpose—and expanding access to new audiences. Both Howe and Harper were deeply committed to the possibility of using poetry as a vehicle for political intervention at the national level; both earned extraordinary public acclaim by marshaling the power of poetry written for public performance, using regular meter and rhyme schemes to make their protest poems particularly accessible and memorable.

In her antebellum poetry, Julia Ward Howe proposes a utopian ideal in which poetry can work to build unified communities. In keeping with this ideal, as she moves from her more lyrical antebellum work to her more explicitly political Civil War–era poems, Howe makes a deliberate decision to write a more direct and accessible kind of poetry. It is this decision that enables her to write her career-making "Battle Hymn," a poem that meets Howe's utopian goal by layering multiple voices on top of one another, thereby forging a unified nationalist "we." In spite of the success of her "Battle Hymn," however, Howe's Civil War–era work does not celebrate the capacious versatility of poetry's voices for the woman writer; rather the wide range of her poetic experiments with voice-effects—including the apostrophe, the imperative, the use of dramatic first-person speakers, and the direct address to the reader—underlines her frustration with the limited roles open to middle-class white women in wartime. This frustration with the limitations imposed on women emphasizes in turn her skepticism about the efficacy of nationalist stances in poetry. These two strands of frustration and skepticism run as parallel undercurrents throughout Howe's second and third volumes of poetry. Across the range of her Civil War–era work, she alternates between endorsing the efficacy of nationalist stances and expressing doubt about them. Howe cannot consistently believe in the efficacy of the nationalist "we" because she is so acutely aware of the ways that gender roles divide the nation.

For her part, Frances Watkins Harper uses the political authority she has earned in her career as a public speaker to anchor the authority of the speakers in her poetry. She is thus far less inclined than Howe to use dramatic voice-effects, to write in the first person, or to write in the voice of the soldier or the slave. In Harper's late war and postwar poetry, however, both the unified "we" of abolition supporters and the accusatory "you" directed at Northern whites are sometimes shaped by traces of a personal "I," traces that underline the frustrations Harper faced as a educated free black woman who had devoted her adult life to the cause of abolition. In considering poems by Howe and Harper, this analysis will focus on the often complex relationship between the personal "I" and the unifying "we" each writer relies on in positioning herself in relation to the Union.

Julia Ward Howe: The Lyric I and Stances of Reform

Though Julia Ward Howe first achieved widespread public acclaim with the February 1862 publication of "A Battle Hymn of the Republic," she had already published her first volume of poetry, *Passion Flowers*, eight years earlier. Against the strong objections of her husband, Howe published both a play and a second collection of poems, *Words for the Hour*, in 1857.[1] By the time this second collection appeared, she was clearly deeply engaged in thinking through the possibilities that poetry offered for political engagement: *Words for the Hour* is the first of her volumes to include a carefully calibrated mix of poems that engage directly with current national policy issues, poems that take up more abstract intellectual or philosophical questions, and poems that focus on the pleasures and perils of friendship, motherhood, and romantic love.[2] *Words for the Hour* can thus be read as a transitional work for Howe: it bridges the gap between the more exclusively lyric and genteel poems of her first collection, *Passion Flowers* (1854), and the outspoken reform stances of some of her 1866 collection, *Later Lyrics*, the volume in which her "Battle Hymn of the Republic" appeared. By 1857, Howe knows her audience well enough to know that the careful balance of *Words for the Hour* is more likely to gain her publication and a reading audience than would a collection that included only politically explicit poems, sentimental poems about motherhood, or poems that make their intellectual ambitions explicit. In *Later Lyrics*, she carefully balances a group called "Poems of the War" and another called "Poems of the Street" with a substantial number of poems that position themselves in the Victorian sphere of domesticity—though Howe's response to that sphere is often ironic, subversive, and deeply conflicted. Invested as she is in writing a politically engaged poetry that addresses issues of public policy, Howe nonetheless understands that her access to the Northeastern publishing establishment depends in part on her performance of upper middle-class genteel femininity.

Howe takes up the question of the conflicting public and private identities of the woman poet most explicitly in the opening poem of *Words for the Hour*, a piece entitled "The Lyric I" which serves as a kind of preface to the rest of the collection. Though "The Lyric I" precedes the war by four years, the poem is a kind of ars poetica for Howe's entire body of work; it is the poem in which she wrestles most explicitly with the competing pressures of her writerly ambitions, her family obligations, and her desire to participate by means of her poetry in the work of political reform. "The Lyric I" is also the poem in which she lays out most explicitly her hopes and fears about poetry's utopian capacity for unifying groups of listeners and readers. Punning on the relationship between the poet's eye and the first-person pronoun "I," "The Lyric I" offers a critical examination of the possible stances of the woman poet's I, contrasting the stances of the lyric I, the "empiric" I, the I of the protest poem, and the I that does domestic work.

Foregrounding images of sight and vision, the poem also responds obliquely to Howe's husband's much acclaimed work with the blind at the Perkins Institute.[3] Williams and other Howe biographers emphasize the tensions and conflicts in Julia's marriage to Samuel Gridley Howe, a physician who was eighteen years her senior; already famous at the time of his marriage both for his heroism in the Greek Revolution and for his work with the blind, Samuel opposed his wife's ambition to have her own career as a writer and reformer. While Howe herself complained of eye trouble throughout her life, in "The Lyric I" in particular, the centrality of metaphors for sight and vision suggests that she is here exploring possible responses to her ongoing argument with her husband about the appropriate social roles for women. In "The Lyric I," Julia Ward Howe takes up the question of how she herself might participate in the work of reform, considering whether or not poetry might provide her with a means of participation.[4] The eleven densely laden stanzas of "The Lyric I" reveal her nuanced understanding of the pressures and challenges faced both by the reformer and by the woman poet:

THE LYRIC I

Have pity on the lyric I,
The poet's eye that finely rolls,
And holds convertible domain
From burning Cancer to the poles.

Not of itself th'incendiant spark
That sets men's thoughts to smoke and blaze;
It is a spirit fire-glass,
That kindles with concentred rays.

It hath a weary work to do,
Fifth of all sounds that sing or sigh,
Third of the great things I O U,
It speeds, the monographic I.

Its pain and evil I have seen
Where heart and manhood withering lie,
And said: "Good friend, you cannot heal,
Till you consent to lose this I."

Empiric if our notions be,
Or with Hegelian learning wise,
Or set on simplest common sense,
There is a difference in our I—s.

The philosophic I, is not
The I that any man may meet
On errands of familiar use,
Or held to greetings in the street.

The I that cannot choose but stand
Great rights and wrongings to assert,
Is not the I that wastes the meal,
And leaves hiatus in the shirt.

* * *

Nor must the sorrows of my song
Stand for the household weights I bear,
Who thankful every morn return
To tasks beloved of thought and prayer.

Nor such as share my working sphere,
Plagued with my music to the soul,
For Giant foes that shut the world
With false and tyrannous control.

Eyes may be sad at prison bars
To whom the sun is glad and free;
And placid depths of Being show
The storm-clouds of Humanity.

And as one emblematic cup
From lip to lip doth fervent move,
So make my poet vase a boon
For all who weep, and think, and love.[5]

Howe opens the poem with an ironic gesture, calling on her readers to pity the plight of the "lyric I." In a collection that includes poems that protest the plight of enslaved African Americans and that lament the sufferings of Charles Sumner beaten on the floor of the Senate by a cane-wielding supporter of slavery, a plea for pity for the poet's "lyric I" can only come with considerable irony attached. The first four stanzas of the poem map out the powers, the struggles, and the limitations of that "I." Linking the pronoun "I" to the poet's vision, stanza one links the turning of the poet's eye to the spinning of the globe, suggesting that the poet believes his "domain" expands to include the whole world, "from burning Cancer to the poles"; the poet, these lines suggest, has the power to "convert" readers or listeners. Comparing "the lyric I" to a chain reaction, Howe suggests that poetry cannot directly move men to action: "Not of itself th'incendiant spark/That sets men's thoughts to smoke and blaze." Rather poetry will, like a magnifying glass, concentrate and thereby "kindle" thoughts men already have to blazing passion, as the glass can concentrate rays of light.

Shifting from the realm of the visual to the realm of sound, stanza three puns on the status of the "lyric I" by underlining the ubiquity of the vowel "I," which has "weary work to do" in helping to constitute so many words. The "lyric I" keeps busy with his romantic singing and sighing ("Fifth of all sounds that sing or sigh"). Here Howe begins to suggest the extent to which the "monographic I" can become a trap of narcissism for the poet who believes his self-based poetic vision to be essential to representation of the world. Line three of Howe's third stanza points to the problematic relationship between self and other that the "lyric I" constructs: "Third of the great things I O U." As in her opening line, which calls on readers to pity the weary lyric I, here too Howe mocks the lyric poet's sense that his work is essential to others, that readers eagerly await the lyric poet's performance of self, a performance that he feels he owes his readers.

Howe makes her critique of the narcissism of the I explicit in the fourth stanza, suggesting that the corruptive I "wither[s]" both "heart and manhood":

> Its pain and evil have I seen
> Where heart and manhood withering lie,
> And said: "Good friend, you cannot heal,
> Till you consent to lose this I."

Positioning her own poetic I as a witness to the corrosive egotism of the I, the speaker boldly calls on her addressee to "lose this I" that he may heal himself. Howe here implicitly offers a critique of the ways in which the ego's narcissism drives the reformer's zeal for helping others. Simultaneously, she calls for a new kind of poetry, one that would posit a different kind of relationship between "I" and "U," between self and other. Always canny in the way she uses gendered and ungendered pronouns, in this stanza Howe comes as close as she will get to linking explicitly the "lyric I" and the masculine position, the "withering" of "manhood." Part of the wit of this poem consists in the way that Howe's proposals for alternative poetic speakers gradually add up to a critique of the masculine position from a distinctly feminine one; stanza five insists "There is a difference in our I—s." Particularly in the first half of the poem, Howe conceals the urgency of this critique through satiric wordplay and a witty, bantering tone. Stanza five suggests that the speaker, like her masculine counterpart, would have access to "empiric" observation, "Hegelian learning," or "common sense." Stanzas six and seven, however, carefully delineate the positions of distinct poetic I's, contrasting "the philosophic I" with the I who runs errands, the I of the protest poem with the poetic I of the woman who has household labor to do—and who does it badly, wasting "the meal" and abandoning the half-ironed shirt. Resisting obvious gender associations, however, Howe refuses to align the philosophic I or the I of the protest poem with the masculine position, leaving these possibilities open for the woman writer as well. Thus the gendered critique made explicit in stanza four becomes an implicit undercurrent in the second half of the poem.

Stanza seven insists that the I of the protest poem cannot be the I who performs household labor:

> The I that cannot choose but stand
> Great rights and wrongings to assert,
> Is not the I that wastes the meal,
> And leaves hiatus in the shirt.

This stanza marks a shift from the bantering tone of the poem's first half to a darker more frustrated stance. While stanza four chides the masculine poet for the narcissism of his lyric I, in stanza eight the speaker chides herself for allowing the sadness of her domestic life to seep into her poetry:

> Nor must the sorrows of my song
> Stand for the household weights I bear
> Who thankful every morn return
> To tasks beloved of thought and prayer

The speaker struggles to keep separate selves that are in practice inextricable from one another. The elliptical style of the poem here offers some suggestive ambiguities. When the speaker describes herself returning to "tasks beloved of thought and prayer," the phrase seems to point toward both the household labor she performs as a wife and mother and the work she does as a writer, work that allows her to escape that household labor temporarily. Stanza nine hovers in this place of ambiguity, an ambiguity heightened by the elision of its main verb. Is the speaker's "working sphere" the sphere of home and family? Or is it the sphere of literary publication? Is she saying she must not "plague" her family members with her poetry, even as her poems protest society's injustices? Or is she saying she must not plague her fellow reformers with her poetic "music"? Though stanza ten points toward the issue of prison reform and how a poet might represent the prisoner's fate, the stanza also gestures toward the double life of the woman poet who is a mother and wife, the writer who struggles with her own sense of domestic imprisonment, whose "placid depths" do not entirely conceal the "storm-clouds" within.

The poem closes with the speaker hoping that her poetry might be like that "emblematic cup"—perhaps the chalice of the Eucharist, perhaps the shared cup of a ceremonial toast—that passes from "lip to lip." She hopes that her poetry might work to unite as one collective community a disparate group of readers and listeners, "all who weep, and think, and love," a community she refuses to separate into public or private, masculine or feminine, rich or poor. Howe closes the poem by imagining that poetry might work to link these disparate groups together in a shared experience of reading, speaking, and listening, a shared experience she evokes with the phrase "lip to lip" with all its implications of physical intimacy. This shared experience of mutual and "fervent" intimacy appears in marked contrast to the "withering" of "heart and manhood" that results from the poetry of the "lyric I" in the fourth stanza.

Yet while the poem reaches a sort of provisional closure with this utopian image of poetry uniting disparate readers and listeners, in the ten preceding stanzas Howe reaches no clear argumentative conclusion about which poetic I might be most effective in creating such a community of readers. Though the poem mocks and rejects the model of the self-focused "lyric I," a speaking position the poem links with male poets, having rejected that I, the speaker goes on to represent the ways in which her own loyalties are thoroughly divided among an array of mutually exclusive possibilities—possibilities in which the experience of the writerly self seeps inevitably into the poetic I. After exposing the limits of "the lyric I," Howe cannot settle on a viable alternative; she can only hope that her poetry will somehow succeed in uniting an audience in spite of the conflicting allegiances of her poems' speakers. And those conflicting allegiances are writ large in the array of speakers Howe offers in her poetry collections. Published as the opening poem in *Words for the Hour*, "The Lyric I" underlines the challenges a woman poet faces both in trying to escape the trap of the narcissistic I and in trying to speak to and for poetry's disparate audiences. In the poems that follow in *Words for the Hour* and in *Later Lyrics*, Howe addresses these challenges by assuming and appropriating a range of speaking positions. In assuming these varied stances and identities, however, these poems for the most part strike compromises—compromises that "The Lyric I" suggests are problematic. The prologue poem to *Words for the Hour* thus signals her awareness of the limitations of the speaking positions she will experiment with across her body of work.

In both *Words for the Hour* and *Later Lyrics*, Howe places a group of explicitly political poems at the volume's outset, before moving on to poems that focus primarily on domestic, romantic, and touristic settings. These opening political poems respond to issues of public debate, including abolition, soldiers' perspectives on war, women's relationship to the work of reform, and women's relationship to war. The placement of these poems at the outset of each volume signals the strength of Howe's desire to write a politically engaged poetry; in *Later Lyrics*, the leading position of the group of war poems may also have been designed to attract readers who knew Howe as the author of the "Battle Hymn." In reading a selection of these politically engaged poems, I will focus in particular on Howe's representation of the voices of abolitionist speakers, the voices of soldiers, and women's relationship to the war.

In a group of poems in *Words for the Hour*, Howe responds to abolitionist oratory of the 1850s, focusing particularly on Frederick Douglass and Charles Sumner. In two of these poems, Howe's speaker uses a sequence of imperatives to represent the power of each man's voice. In "Slave Eloquence," she argues that Douglass's body alone is sufficient to offer silent testimony to the sufferings endured under slavery. In "An Hour in the Senate," she protests Preston Brooks's brutal attack on Sumner, suggesting that after his recovery Sumner will be still more able to speak for the suffering slave; again describing the slave's eloquent body as "agonized and dumb," Howe suggests that a recovered Sumner will be able to speak for the mute slave in a "universal speech," one that will move even the "coldness of our distant sympathies" (*WH* 28).

In "Slave Eloquence" and "An Hour in the Senate," Howe uses a dramatic apostrophe to address each orator, positing a poetic speaker who can speak to and for the former slave and the wounded senator. In both poems, Howe effectively borrows the rhetorical platform of a famous male orator in order to create an authoritative rhetorical platform for her poetic speaker; presenting herself as a go-between between the male orator and the poetic speaker's reading audience, Howe's speaker introduces each orator to her readers. Voice-effects such as the apostrophe and dramatic imperatives foreground the voice of the poem's speaker, thereby echoing or doubling the voice of the orator each poem describes. Just as she will later address the already established audience for "John Brown's Body" with her "Battle Hymn of the Republic," in these two earlier abolitionist poems the imagined audience whom the famous orator addresses becomes a stand-in for the audience who will read Howe's poetry. In these poems, Howe pursues what is clearly an urgent question for her: who can claim the authority to speak for the suffering slave? Howe's conflict with her husband over her decision to publish her poetry undoubtedly raised the stakes for her, as she explored possibilities for intervening in the abolition debate by means of poetry. Her decision to write abolitionist poems that pay respect to two of the leading abolitionist orators of her day—one of whom, Charles Sumner, is a close friend of her husband's—is part of a broader strategy she uses in both *Words for the Hour* and *Later Lyrics:* Howe frequently relies on stances of imitation and homage to create a rhetorical platform from which her speakers can address the nation.[6]

"Slave Eloquence" establishes its speaker's authority through a series of probing rhetorical questions and dramatic imperatives: the speaker metaphorically directs Douglass's oratorical performance, first querying "Why shouldst thou speak?", then commanding him to stand without speaking, and finally acknowledging Douglass's desire to speak, permitting him to address the audience the poem imagines for him. In the poem's first four stanzas, Howe suggests that Douglass's body alone will testify to the injustice of slavery, eliminating the need for speech (*WH* 25). Representing his body as a moving and powerful piece of sculpture, she suggests that the humanity of that body will remind the audience that African Americans have been betrayed by whites, their fellow men. Stanza three explicitly likens the marks of suffering on Douglass's body to the marks of Christ's suffering, suggesting that the suffering body can express more than the voice ever could:

> Stand, like the prophet's Christ, so grief-possest
> That silence shall afflict us more than sound;
> Express in marble passion, motionless,
> The anguish of the fratricidal wound. (*WH* 25)

In stanzas four through eight, the speaker authorizes Douglass to speak, "to ease the throbbing fullness of thy heart" (WH 26), a phrase that suggests a sexual release, before going on to praise his speech for its "modest gesture" and "manly phrase." Though stanza five declares that Douglass is attempting to speak "the white man's language," a phrase that seems to limit Douglass to a position of racial inferiority, the stanzas that follow suggest that Douglass's speech uses biblical and legal arguments to powerful effect. The poem concludes with the speaker reasserting her original argument:

> Speaking, he kept the measure of our wish.
> But we had deemed him eloquent, unheard,
> For, looking on the wronged and rescued man,
> His presence pleaded stronger than his word. (*WH* 26)

This closing gesture's repetition of the idea that Douglass's body alone can articulate the injustice of slavery undermines the arguments advanced in stanzas five through eight about Douglass's extraordinary performance as a speaker. In limiting Douglass to a mute physical performance of slavery's injustice, Howe's poem reiterates the racist assumption that whites are better able to speak for the slave than the slave himself. And yet in a volume in which Howe so anxiously asserts her own right to "speak" in public as a woman poet, "Slave Eloquence" seems to point toward her own struggles to master the "white man's language" as much as it does to Douglass's. The mute body of the black man on display at the start of the poem points elliptically to the unseen body of the woman poet who uses poetry rather than oratory to reach her audience. In praising Douglass's restraint—his refusal to "stoop to curses impotent"—Howe seems to enjoin herself to imitate Douglass's moderate speech. When her speaker commands Douglass to "ease the throbbing fulness of [his] heart," the phrase suggests that Howe too feels an intense physical desire to speak, a desire that can be met only through the release that language offers. While the speaker's dramatic imperatives to Douglass exercise a metaphorical control over his speaking and his silence, the poem's vivid representation of Douglass's desire to speak underlines the strength of the speaker's own desire to speak and of her identification with Douglass's position as an outsider in the world of the "white man's language."

Like "Slave Eloquence," Howe's "An Hour in the Senate" uses apostrophes and imperatives to establish the authority of its speaker and to heighten the drama of its scene of oratory. The poem describes the angry and heated exchanges that preceded Brooks's attack on Sumner, imagining both the defiance and the "impudence" of the Southern defense of slavery. The poem evokes the brutality of the physical attack on Sumner only obliquely through its description of the violence of Southern speech, a description that unfolds in stanzas one through six. In the second half of the poem, the speaker voices a series of imperatives that enjoin Sumner to rise and respond; these imperatives also implicitly hope for his full and speedy recovery from his injuries. The speaker articulates these imperatives in stanzas seven through nine:

> Yet, rise to answer, chafing in thy chair,
> With soul indignant stirred, and flushing brow.
> Thou art God's candidate—speak soothly now,
> Let every word anticipate a prayer.
>
> Gather in thine outstretched hands that strive
> To help thy pleading, agonized and dumb;
> Bear up the hearts whose silent sorrows come
> For utterance, to the voice that thou canst give.
>
> Theirs is an eloquence that cannot reach
> The coldness of our distant sympathies,
> Then, pluck them bleeding for the country's eyes,
> Speed with the wings of universal speech. (*WH* 28)

In this sequence of imperatives, Howe imagines the utopian possibility of a "universal speech" that a great speaker like Sumner can achieve. While "Slave Eloquence" declared that Douglass need only stand before his audience and let his body testify, "An Hour in the Senate" limits all slaves to a position of mute physical "pleading, agonized and dumb:" "An Hour in the Senate" underlines that Sumner's speech will be sustained by the "outstretched hands" of blacks who bring to him their "silent sorrows" so that he can give "voice" to them. The awkward mix of metaphors in stanza nine, however, suggests that Howe cannot entirely resolve the contradiction between representing blacks' "eloquence" and representing them as "agonized and dumb": when line three of stanza nine calls on Sumner to "pluck them bleeding for the country's eyes," the antecedent of "them" is ambiguous at best. The adjective "bleeding" suggests that "them" refers to the "hearts" of the suffering slaves, in which case Sumner might "pluck" these "hearts" to reach the "coldness of our distant sympathies," a first-person collective of white listeners. Still both the ambiguity of the pronoun references and the awkward slippage between metaphors of sight and sound and flight in the last two lines of stanza nine work to undermine the confidence of the speaker's call for "universal speech": "Then, pluck them bleeding for the country's eyes, / Speed with the wings of universal speech." The strangely intransitive imperative "Speed with the wings of universal speech" seems to elide awkwardly whatever message Sumner will be "speeding"; the metaphor comes unmoored, obscuring where Sumner's speech is speeding from or to.

Read in relation to the arguments advanced in "The Lyric I," the awkward metaphoric constructions of stanza nine signal Howe's ambivalence not only about the possibility of blacks' speaking for themselves on the issue of abolition but also about the utopian possibility of the "universal speech" for which her speaker calls. As noted earlier, "The Lyric I" concludes with the speaker hoping that her poetry might unite her disparate readers and listeners in a shared communion. In analogous fashion, the speaker of "An Hour in the Senate" hopes that Sumner's powerful oratory will work to link the "distant sympathies" of white Northerners with the "pleading, agonized and dumb" of the suffering slaves. Yet just as "The Lyric I" suggests that the woman poet might face particular challenges in making of her poetry "one emblematic cup," so too does "Slave Eloquence" underline the ways in which blacks—and by implication women—face extraordinary limitations when speaking in a public forum. In "An Hour in the Senate," the utopian ideal of "universal speech" is undermined by the instability of the poem's metaphors; the slipperiness of Howe's metaphors betrays her lack of confidence in the utopian ideal of this white male-authored speech. More broadly then, the explicitly political poems in *Words for the Hour* suggest that Howe is plagued both by doubts about the possibility of the woman poet gaining access to a "universal speech" and by doubts about any writer's ability to use poetry as an "emblematic cup" that might unify his or her readers and listeners.

Her postwar volume *Later Lyrics* offers a still darker account of the possibilities for a wartime dialogue about abolition between blacks and whites. Simultaneously, however, the success of her "Battle Hymn" seems to have emboldened Howe to write a poem spoken in the first person by a slave. Where *Words for the Hour* represented blacks' eloquence as "agonized and dumb," *Later Lyrics* includes a poem spoken confidently by an anonymous male slave. In both her earlier and later abolitionist poems,

Howe tends to rely on the authority of a male character or speaker to bolster the rhetorical authority of her poem; unlike other white female abolitionist writers of her day, Howe avoids conventional sentimental-feminist abolitionist stances and chooses not to foreground the experience of women and mothers under slavery. This decision may reflect not only a deliberate strategy of relying on male authority figures to bolster her speakers' authority but also perhaps Howe's ambivalence about the demands of motherhood and domestic labor in her own life; her reluctance to write about the slave's experience of motherhood is particularly striking, however, in view of the many poems about white mothers and children that she includes in her collections.

Where the earlier poems were invested in thinking through the theoretical challenges of articulating the slaves' lived experience to Northern white audiences, this later poem "The Question" is committed to relaying clearly and directly to Northern white audiences a crucial message about why abolition should be linked to the outcome of the war. Howe's decision to write a poem in the first person in the voice of a slave corresponds to a decision—evident in many of the politically engaged poems written after the success of the "Battle Hymn"—to simplify imagery and formal commitments in order to foreground the poem's political message. Protesting the continuation of slavery through conventional abolitionist imagery and emphatically regular schemes for rhyme and meter, "The Question" presents a series of questions posed by a Southern male slave to a white "Master," a representative of white Northern men:

THE QUESTION

Tell me, Master, am I free?
From the prison land I come,
From a mocked humanity,
From the fable of a home;

From the shambles, where my wife
With my baby at her breast,
Faded from my narrow life,
Rudely bartered, ill-possest.

Will you keep me, for my faith,
From the hound that scents my track,

From the riotous, drunken breath,
From the murder at my back?

Masters, ye are fighting long;
Well your trumpet-blast we know;
Are ye come to right a wrong?
Do we call you friend or foe?

God must come, for whom we pray,
Knowing his deliverance true;
Shall our men be left to say
He must work it free of you?

Fetters of a burning chain
Held the spirit of our braves;
Waiting for the nobler strain,
Silence told him *we* were slaves.[7]

Pressing the white "Master" for a response, the slave speaker asks about the meaning of the war: is the war being fought to end slavery? Will a Northern victory bring about emancipation? In the poem's final two stanzas, the speaker declares that God will eventually end slavery if white men don't succeed in doing so. When the white "Master" addressed offers no answer to the slave-speaker's question, the slaves know what that silence means both to God and to themselves: "Silence told him we were slaves." The Master's inability to speak guarantees that the slaves will continue as slaves. While the abolitionist poems in *Words for the Hour* praised Sumner's extraordinary ability to speak for blacks and represented slaves themselves as limited in their capacity for speech, in this later abolitionist poem Howe uses a black speaker to emphasize whites' failure to speak—their failure to link the war to the cause of abolition—and the disastrous consequences of that failure. Significantly, Howe represents the way that Northern whites have failed Southern slaves during wartime as a keeping silent, a refusal to speak. Abandoning any theoretical discussion of the possibility of a "universal speech," she instead relies on metaphoric and formal clarity both to broaden her audience and to endorse the poem's explicitly stated political message.

In Howe's abolitionist poems, as in her poems about the soldiers' perspective on war, the urgency of her desire to write and speak in the voices of multiple characters—and perhaps particularly in the voices of male characters—is clearly evident. Just as many of her abolitionist poems use stances of imitation and homage to establish the authority of her poems' speakers, so do many of her soldier poems draw on the same techniques. In "Balaklava," a poem included in *Words for the Hour,* Howe writes a poetic reworking of Tennyson's "Charge of the Light Brigade," a poem much admired by Americans. Testing out a first-person plural for the soldiers in the second stanza—"Traced all in fire we saw our way"—Howe reverts thereafter to the safer third-person plural that Tennyson uses throughout his poem, keeping her pronouns consistent in all the remaining stanzas (*WH* 35). In *Later Lyrics,* however, Howe draws on the confidence she gained with the success of "Battle Hymn" to include two poems with first-person soldier-speakers. As with her "Battle Hymn," which used echoes of "John Brown's Body" to allow her access to the first-person position of the soldiers, the two soldier-poems Howe includes in *Later Lyrics* rely on already established genres of war poems: with "Harvard Student's Song," Howe echoes the tradition of the college student's war song, and with "Left Behind," she responds to sentimental popular songs that commemorate soldiers' battlefield deaths. Though only the first of these poems identifies itself as a song, both poems have the regular rhyme and meter schemes one would expect to find in a song. In both poems, Howe experiments with a collective "we" for the soldiers' perspective. "Harvard Student's Song" establishes that collective "we" by gliding gradually from the general collective of white Northerners ("Remember ye how hearts indignant bounded/When our first dead came back from Baltimore?") to a "we" that seems limited to the cohort of Harvard students who watch their classmates go off to the war, ultimately deciding to join up themselves:

> Look back no more! our time has come, my brothers!
> In Fate's high roll our names are written too:
> We fill the mournful gaps left bare by others,
> The ranks where Fear has never broken through. (LL 30)

Howe's allegiance to Harvard in particular may be a product of her marriage: Samuel Gridley Howe pursued his medical studies there. Though Howe did not herself attend college, the "we" that she forges in the poem allows her to speak not only in the voice of a soldier but also in the voice of a Harvard student.

In "Left Behind," Howe experiments still more boldly with a singular first-person soldier-speaker. Like the abolitionist poem "The Question," "Left Behind" uses regular rhyme and meter and conventional imagery to drive home directly its central message—in this case the idea that soldiers die willingly, glad to have taken part in the camaraderie of the military and glad also to have sacrificed their lives for a cause they believe in. In the clarity and simplicity of this message, Howe echoes sentimental ballads of the era that endorse the view that soldiers have not died in vain. The poem's final stanza implies that slain soldiers will ascend to heaven, martyrs for a righteous cause:

> My soul rises up on the wings of the slain,
> A triumph thrills through me that quiets the pain:
> If it were yet to do, I would do it again!
> Farewell, comrades, farewell! (*LL* 32)

Throughout *Later Lyrics* with its wide range of poetic speakers, a reader senses Howe's impatience with the narrow range of roles available to middle-class women during wartime. In "Left Behind," the soldier-speaker, mortally wounded on the field of battle, addresses his comrades who have gone before him as he fell in the line of the charge. As Howe's "Reminiscences" make clear, however, she too felt "left behind" by the possibilities the war offered men for participation in the great moral and political struggle of her lifetime: she describes her "feeling of discouragement" as she approached Washington on her wartime visit there in the fall of 1861, noting that her husband is too old to serve and her sons too young. "I could not leave my nursery to follow the march of our armies," she adds.[8] Only with the success of her "Battle Hymn" is she relieved of the burden of this sense of her own uselessness.

As I suggested in chapter one, however, even Howe's "Battle Hymn" reveals traces of her frustration with the limits placed on middle-class white women's roles. Images of light and darkness in the "Battle Hymn" echo the scene of Howe scrawling out the lyrics in the early morning darkness in a room at the Willard Hotel; these traces of the scene of the poem's composition implicitly point toward Howe's habit of early morning writing, underlining the challenges she faced in juggling the demands of parenting young children while pursuing her career as a writer. Indeed the tone of righteous anger that Howe uses in her "Battle Hymn" implicitly reflects her indignation at the limited roles available to white middle-class women. In one of the most striking and original of the war poems in *Later Lyrics*, Howe takes up the topic of women's roles explicitly, bitterly emphasizing the narrowness of upper middle-class women's lives and experience during the Civil War. "The Jeweller's Shop in War-Time" presents a conversation between a female speaker and a young bride-to-be as they contemplate a jeweler's wares. Though this is a dramatic poem laden with gothic imagery, it's also a poem that situates its speaker in the upper middle-class Northeastern society to which Howe herself belonged. Both the diction and the imagery are high literary. Howe uses both to evoke the elaborate social rituals that comprise the narrow confines of these women's lives:

THE JEWELLER'S SHOP IN WAR-TIME

Past these counters wilt thou lead me,
Notes of luxury to read me
In the pearly shows and golden
That to outward boast embolden?
Watchful sit the shapes of sorrow.
Say: the Black Death comes to-morrow.

Bride, the altar-gifts are waiting
The permission of thy mating;
Heart and purse make brief unclasping
From the daily miser-grasping.
Fill the cup! away with sorrow!
Will the Black Death come to-morrow?

Lo! he lies in bloody heather,
'Neath the burning summer weather:
Not a drop his dry lip wetteth;
Dryer yet his sad eye setteth.
Rend thy bridal robes for sorrow:
Doth the Black Death wait the morrow?

See! the silver vessels goodly
Hands of hirelings stir not rudely;
Gems that deck the board's white wearing,
In a house of noble bearing;

Legendary urns of sorrow:
Death attends the feast to-morrow!

See! the rings of wild desire—
Dreamy opal; diamond fire;
Emerald, green as summer grasses
Lit of sun that never passes;
Jets, the dim delights of sorrow,
That the Black Death Buys, the morrow.

Chalice see and salver ghostly
That affright the gazer mostly;
Stirrup-cup that awes and blesses,
Cordial drop of last distresses;
Pearl of hope dissolved in sorrow,
Dear where Death is due the morrow.

Take me rather when the hours
Write their journal fair in flowers;
Where our sweet joys die and darken
With the firmament to hearken.
Soft in silence sinks our sorrow;
Resurrection comes to-morrow.

Life ye tear to shred and flitter,
Joying in the costly glitter
To rehearse each art-abortion
That consumes a widow's portion.
Lavish feast makes secret sorrow;
Pinch at heart brings Death to-morrow!

Take me where sweet doctrine, hoarded,
Stays the ravage, ill-afforded;
Wisdom's store, divinely pleasured,
Hero heart-beat, poet-measured.
Song that lightens out of sorrow
Shields from every Death to-morrow. (*LL* 36–38)

As the women tour the shop, each object they see foretells the eventual death of the bride's beloved, who seems to be a soldier. The poem underlines the absurdity of shopping for silver and jewels while men are dying of wounds on Southern battlefields. It mocks the ritual of toasting the bride-to-be when her fiancé is off to war: "Fill the cup! away with sorrow!" With its slow rhythms and its dramatic refrain ("The Black Death comes tomorrow"), the poem's sounds enact the women's entrapment in a world of costly luxury, consumption, and ceremony, a world in which they are utterly disconnected from the men who die on battlefields and powerless to save them.

While "The Lyric I" represented poetry as a cup that might be passed "lip to lip," thereby building a utopian community of readers, in "The Jeweller's Shop" recurring images of toasts not given and cups not shared suggest the breakdown of community or the impossibility of building community in wartime. The imagined wedding toast is mocked by the image of the soldier, dying of his wounds and of thirst under a blazing Southern sun:

> Lo! he lies in bloody heather,
> 'Neath the burning summer weather:
> Not a drop his dry lip wetteth.
> Dryer yet his sad eye setteth.

Seen in relation to the soldier's death, wedding cups and bowls become "legendary urns of sorrow." The "wild desire" connoted by precious gems—the opal, the diamond, the emerald—is destined never to be fulfilled. The "stirrup-cup" only reminds the viewers of the dying man's "last distresses." And it is not only the communion between husband and wife that the war disrupts. The engagement's tragic outcome works to destabilize the community that surrounds them, emptying the many communal rituals of marriage of their meaning: "Chalice see and salver ghostly/That affright the gazer mostly."

In the poem's final two stanzas, Howe turns to the question of whether or not art—and perhaps also poetry—might work to mitigate the tragedy of the young soldier's death or to alleviate the solitude of the young woman left widowed. In the penultimate stanza, the most biting in the poem, Howe suggests that life offers few prospects for happiness in marriage and that the lavish celebrations of a wedding must inevitably be followed by heartbreak and sorrow:

Life ye tear to shred and flitter,
Joying in the costly glitter
To rehearse each art-abortion
That consumes a widow's portion.
Lavish feast makes secret sorrow;
Pinch at heart brings Death to-morrow!

The arresting phrase "art-abortion" suggests that the artistry of the wedding silver and wedding jewels will be of little worth when the marriage itself is aborted by the young man's death; the phrase evokes not only the children the couple will not have but also the ruin of the young woman's life in the aftermath of her beloved's death. The stanza suggests that the costliness of the wedding gifts will do little to alleviate the widow's poverty and despair. With its shock effect, the phrase "art-abortion" implies that war is fundamentally destructive to the artist's purposes—a striking implication given that Howe's national reputation as a poet was built on her wartime work. These lines also point obliquely toward Howe's sense of entrapment in her own unhappy marriage: read in this light, the phrase "art-abortion" might refer to the ways that her husband's opposition to her career as a writer thwarted her aspirations. The world of genteel domestic luxury the poem describes is one that Howe herself knew well; the poem casts a critical eye on women's consumerism even as it also emphasizes that only a narrow range of social roles are open to middle-class women—in wartime or in peacetime.

Only in the poem's final stanza does Howe offer some alternative to the paralyzing social rituals her poem so bitterly dismantles and even this alternative seems provisional at best:

Take me where sweet doctrine, hoarded,
Stays the ravage, ill-afforded;
Wisdom's store, divinely-pleasured,
Hero heart-beat, poet-measured.
Song that lightens out of sorrow
Shields from every Death to-morrow.

In this last stanza, Howe calls for a "sweet doctrine"—perhaps Christian faith, perhaps a hero-making poetry—that might alleviate the "ravage" of the bride's loss. "Wisdom's store," she suggests, might help both the bride and the speaker to bear this tragedy. As represented (or "measured") by the poet, the young man's life might become a "hero heart-beat." The poet's "song"—perhaps a song like Howe's own "Harvard Student's Song" or her "Left Behind"—might "lighten" their "sorrow." In the final line, however, this lightening is revealed to be only a temporary shield "from every Death." Poetry is here represented as a "sweet doctrine" that can make heroes out of dying soldiers; but this doctrine is evoked only fleetingly and only in the poem's final stanza. It accomplishes nothing beyond delaying the confrontation with death and loss until "to-morrow." The consolations it offers seem provisional at best—particularly in comparison with the striking realism of the stanza that describes the soldier's death ("Not a drop his dry lip wetteth; / Dryer yet his sad eye setteth."). In "The Jeweller's Shop in War-Time," Howe invents a speaker whose voice closely approximates her own: from this stance, she rages against the limits imposed upon women's lives even as she also suggests that the forms of community poetry can build are provisional and elusive at best.

Throughout her eclectic body of poetry, then, Julia Ward Howe considers how the engaged woman poet might best respond to the political crises of her day: how might a woman poet address the nation on the subject of slavery, of the war, and of woman's relationship to it? In "The Lyric I," Howe hopes that a woman poet might be able to write a kind of poetry that could conjoin its readers, unifying them in support of a particular reform cause. The woman poet's keener awareness of the risks of the "lyric I" and of the male reformer's zeal might enable her to overcome those risks in her own poetry. In her attempt to create that "emblematic cup," Howe experiments with different speaking positions across her body of work. Considering who might best speak for the suffering slave, she begins by suggesting that the gifted white abolitionist orator might be best suited for this role, but ultimately her identification with the ways in which blacks are excluded from public speech and her doubts about the possibility of a "universal speech" undermine this suggestion. By the time of her postwar volume, *Later Lyrics*, Howe has abandoned theoretical discussion of a "universal speech" in favor of more direct and more explicitly persuasive engaged stances; in this volume, she includes poems that speak in the first person in the voices of slaves and soldiers, as well as the "Battle Hymn" with its collective multilayered "we."

Yet if *Later Lyrics* shows us a Howe who is more willing to write explicitly political poems, the eclectic range of this collection also shows us a Howe who sometimes has misgivings about the confident authoritative "we" of her "Battle Hymn," with its prophetic voice of divine authority. While the "Battle Hymn" marks a turning point in the public reception of Howe's work, the range of these later war poems suggests that Howe was ambivalent about the rhetoric of this unifying "we." Though "Battle Hymn" is the final poem in the "Poems of the War" section, it is immediately preceded by two much darker poems: "The Jeweller's Shop in War-Time," a poem that foregrounds Howe's frustration with the limited roles open to women in wartime, and "The Battle-Eucharist," a poem that foregrounds the vast divide that separates the human world from the divine. If "A Jeweller's Shop in War-Time" implies that the "emblematic" and community-building cup of poetry may be nothing more than an elusive utopian vision, "The Battle-Eucharist" makes still more explicit Howe's crisis of confidence in the possibilities that poetry offers for reunifying communities in the aftermath of war.[9] While Howe's "Battle Hymn of the Republic" unites Northern supporters of the Union into a triumphant "we" with a God of vengeance supporting their position, the speaker in her "Battle-Eucharist" calls out to a distant Christ to descend to earth to help human beings endure the sorrows brought on by the war. While "Battle Hymn of the Republic" announces Christ's second coming as a victory for the Union, the speaker of "The Battle-Eucharist" beseeches a more remote Christ: "Remain with us, O Lord! Remain." The speaker of Howe's "Battle Hymn" boldly addresses the nation with a prophetic and authoritative first-person, offering herself as an intermediary between God and the Union; by contrast, the first-person speaker of "The Battle-Eucharist" anxiously calls on Christ to intervene in human affairs in order to wrest meaning from the "surpassing pain" and "woe" of the war. Though Howe ends the war poems section of *Later Lyrics* with "Battle Hymn of the Republic," the doubts and anxieties expressed in "The Battle-Eucharist" echo in a reader's ears as she reads the far more confident and much more familiar "Battle Hymn." While the latter poem proclaims the war to be God's will and insists that God is on the side of the Union, the former anxiously calls on Christ to sustain the goals and ideals of the Union; the urgent plea of "The Battle-Eucharist" points toward the violence to come in the Reconstruction era. While the crisis of the Civil War catapulted

Julia Ward Howe to public recognition as the author of one of the Union's leading anthems, the war also foregrounded Howe's frustrations with the limitations placed on middle-class women's lives and the ways that gender roles inevitably worked both to divide the Union and to exclude women from full participation in the collective "we" of the nation; the enduring power of her "Battle Hymn" notwithstanding, the Civil War profoundly shook Howe's confidence in the power of poetic voice to unify the nation.

Frances Watkins Harper: The Poet-Preacher and the Address to the Nation

While Julia Ward Howe masters the rhetorical maneuver of the impassioned nationalist "we" with her "Battle Hymn," the onset of the war gives Frances Ellen Watkins Harper an even stronger sense of purpose in using the abolitionist "we" that she had already been working with in her poetry for many years. In reading Julia Ward Howe, I suggested that her wartime poetry displays a restlessness of perspective, as she creates speakers who can speak for abolitionists, slaves, and soldiers, using a range of voice-effects. By contrast, Frances Harper—already an accomplished and well-known speaker on the abolitionist lecture circuit—employs a much more limited range of voice-effects in her poems, sometimes using an exclamation or an apostrophe but only occasionally using the first person in her poems, only rarely speaking in the voice of a slave or a white character. In contrasting Harper's narrower range of voice-effects with Howe's broader array, I will suggest that Harper's work as a public speaker plays a crucial role in shaping the rhetorical stances in her poems: Harper did not need to use dramatic voice-effects to heighten the authority of her poet-speakers because she often recited her poems in person. The relative lack of voice-effects in Harper's work underlines the quiet confidence with which she approached the task of writing poetry by the time the war began; Harper's successful career as a public speaker offered a solid foundation for her efforts as a poet.

Many scholars have commented on the simplicity and directness of Harper's ballads; beneath their surface simplicity, however, Harper's protest poems reveal some of the conflicting allegiances of her position as a free black educated woman addressing a mixed audience of blacks and whites. Just as a personal "I" permeates Julia Ward Howe's abolitionist and wartime poems, so too does a personal "I" permeate Frances Harper's poetry—though in much less obvious ways. Even as Harper creates speakers who assume stances of prophetic authority in addressing the nation, the personal "I" of the African American woman activist inevitably shapes the ambivalence of some of Harper's speakers as they seek to address the American nation. In her Civil War–era poetry, Harper calls for a community of whites and blacks unified by their opposition to racism and slavery; by layering distinct voices to forge that "we," Harper seeks to make a rhetorical place for blacks within the community of the American nation. In their layering of multiple voices and pronoun positions, however, those Harper poems that seek to forge that American "we" also trace the fault lines that threaten to divide the nation, separating black and white opponents of slavery, white readers from black poets, and Southern slaves from free-born African Americans.

A brief discussion of Harper's career as a speaker and as a writer will help to illuminate the relationship between the personal "I" and the collective "we" in her poetry. Though Harper had compiled her first volume of poetry at the age of twenty, no copies of this collection have been found; her first widely circulated volume, *Poems on Miscellaneous Subjects*, was published in 1854 when she was twenty-nine. In that same year, she met with still another form of professional success when she was offered a position as a traveling lecturer by the Maine Anti-Slavery Society. By the time the war broke out, Harper had sold more than ten thousand copies of her *Poems* and had been working for several years as a public speaker; she had also published essays, letters, and poems in abolitionist papers. Though she began to write poetry as a teenager, the fact that she enjoyed success as a speaker in her twenties no doubt shaped the kinds of poems she wrote thereafter; her stances as a speaker and as a poet became mutually influential and interdependent. Harper frequently performed or recited her poems when she lectured, and many of her antebellum abolitionist poems rely on regular meter and rhyme schemes as well as clear and direct narratives to relay a persuasive political message to a broad range of listeners and readers. These strong formal commitments indicate that Harper was as interested in reaching listeners as she was readers.

In the years after the war when she scaled back on her public speaking commitments and had more time for writing, Harper began to experiment with long poetic forms, writing *Moses: A Story of the Nile*, as well as her remarkable Aunt Chloe sequence, a group of dialect poems set in the rural South and spoken in the first person in the voice of an emancipated slave in her sixties.[10] Demonstrating her versatility as a writer, she also wrote a novel, *Iola Leroy* (1892), focusing on the challenges faced by a Southern-born mixed-race woman, before, during, and after the Civil War. Though it is her short abolitionist protest poems that are now most often anthologized, Harper's work has considerable range both formally and thematically. As Frances Foster points out, "Harper's poetry was never exclusively devoted to topics of race and slavery"; in *Poems on Miscellaneous Subjects*, she notes, only a third of the poems make explicit reference to slavery.[11] One benefit of reading Howe and Harper comparatively is that this comparison makes evident the extent to which formal and thematic versatility was an asset to women poets in the Civil War era: like Howe, Harper writes in multiple literary and poetic genres. Over the course of long careers of writing and activism, both women write complex long poems that place considerable demands on their readers, but both also achieve widespread recognition for pieces that are more readily accessible and memorizable—indeed even singable. In their own time, their renown as writers depended in large part on the popularity of these readily accessible pieces.

Scholars have been unanimous in classifying Harper's work as popular. While an early generation used the category to suggest that Harper was merely a minor poet, more recently feminist scholars have noted the political centrality of popular stances in nineteenth-century literature of reform. These scholars argue for the recovery of Harper's work, making a persuasive case that study of Harper's poetry will offer key insights into black women's participation in the abolition movement and other reform causes, as well as contributing to our understanding of the development of African American literature.[12] Still another way in which reading Harper's work can be helpful is that this examination will enable scholars to develop a more nuanced understanding of what the term "popular" means as applied to Harper's varied body of work, signaling the ways in which our use of the term in the nineteenth-century context is still limited by twentieth-century critical frameworks. Because Harper wrote many of her formally conventional poems for public performance, their categorization as "popular" would seem to be almost inevitable. As I will suggest, however, Harper finds in the genre of poetry an extraordinary perspectival flexibility; like Howe she uses the medium of poetry as means of layering multiple voices, a layering that belies the surface simplicity of these pieces. Reading Harper's war poetry, I will first consider examples of some of her speaking voices, including a poem in the voice of divine authority and poems in the first person in the voices of black and white speakers. Second I will turn to poems addressed to white speakers and writers and poems addressed to various constituencies of the American nation, considering how Harper positions her poet-speaker in relation to a range of white addressees.

A frequent choice in Harper's Civil War–era work is the voice of divine authority: Harper's Christian faith and her work on the abolitionist lecture circuit both serve as guarantors for the rhetorical authority of this prophetic voice. Like Howe's "Battle Hymn," Harper's "Retribution" offers the authority of biblical narrative and imagery to argue that God has visited a day of reckoning on the United States for the national sin of slavery. Again like Howe's "Battle Hymn," "Retribution" treats both race and abolition obliquely. Though the nation's "guilt" is implicitly the crime of slavery, the poem does not explicitly call for abolition. The poem's refusal to make explicit the nature of the nation's crime only boosts its speaker's authority: the crime is so obvious as to require no direct mention. The rhetorical context in which the poem was delivered or sung would have made that message clear:

Judgment slumbered. God in mercy
  Stayed his strong avenging hand;
Sent them priests and sent them prophets,
  But they would not understand.

Judgment lingered; men, grown bolder,
  Gloried in their shame and guilt;
And the blood of God's poor children
  Was as water freely spilt.

Then arose a cry to heaven,
  Deep and startling, sad and wild,
Sadder than the wail of Egypt,
  Mourning for the first-born child.

For the sighing of the needy
  God at length did bare his hand,
And the footsteps of his judgments
  Echoed through the guilty land.

Oh! the terror, grief and anguish;
  Oh! the bitter, fearful, strife,
When the judgments of Jehovah
  Pressed upon the nation's life.

And the land did reel and tremble
  'Neath the terror of his frown,
For its guilt lay heavy on it,
  Pressing like an iron crown.

As a warning to the nations,
  Bathed in blood and swathed in fire,
Lay the once oppressing nation,
  Smitten by God's fearful ire.[13]

First published in book form in 1871, "Retribution" may have appeared in a newspaper during the war. While Howe's "Battle Hymn" uses a first-person speaker to relay her vision of God's judgment, Harper omits first-person pronouns altogether, thereby sidestepping—for white audiences—the dilemma of a black woman writer creating a divine prophetic voice—while nonetheless also claiming that authority. While the Howe poem explicitly makes the speaker an intermediary between God and the human world, the Harper piece offers instead a series of boldly declarative statements that trace the narrative of God's intervention into American history. While Howe's poem builds to a climactic and unifying first-person plural ("Let us die to make men free"), Harper's poem uses a more distanced and more accusatory "they" to refer to American whites, a pronoun choice that allies the poem's speaker with the voice of God. Reading Harper's poetry in relation to her Evangelical Unitarianism, Carla Peterson argues that Harper uses the voice of the "poet-preacher," a voice that conjoins rational and emotionally based arguments to move listeners to social action; Harper's formal education at her uncle's school, the conviction of her faith, and her years of experience of addressing audiences from a lecture platform would all have given her the confidence to write in the authoritative voice of the poet-preacher, as she does in "Retribution."[14] The omission of the first-person pronoun from the poem, in combination with the presence of Harper herself delivering the poem from a lecture platform, would adroitly both elide and assert the speaker's authority; in analogous fashion, the conventional form of the poem—its regular meter and rhyme scheme—works to normalize the speaker's authority, concealing the boldness of the speaker's prophetic voice within the structure of literary tradition. Indeed, as Peterson suggests, Harper's protest poetry routinely relies on conventional forms to control the force of her radical stances.[15] Harper's decision to use a marching-style trochaic meter in "Retribution" heightens the speaker's rhetorical authority by suggesting the presence of a collective of marchers or of Christian worshippers singing or chanting the poem.

Set either in the midst of war or in the war's aftermath, "Retribution" offers an apocalyptic vision of the violence visited on the nation by both slavery and warfare. Stanza three describes a strangely disembodied, anonymous "cry" that rises to heaven, an image that conflates the cry of the suffering slave with the cry of the white soldier dying in battle. In the poem's last two stanzas, Harper offers an arresting image that replaces the body of the suffering slave with the body of the bleeding nation, aligning that nation with the body of Christ:[16]

> And the land did reel and tremble
> 'Neath the terror of his frown
> For its guilt lay heavy on it
> Pressing like an iron crown.
>
> As a warning to the nations,
> Bathed in blood and swathed in fire,
> Lay the once oppressing nation,
> Smitten by God's fearful ire. (190)

Struck down, the body of the nation hovers between life and death with no possibility for redemption. If Harper wrote this poem during the war, the darkness of its imagery reflects the horror of the war's bloodshed and its sectional and racist strife; if she wrote the poem in the war's aftermath, it suggests that the war did little to resolve the sectional conflict or to address the violence of racism against Southern blacks. And though the poem includes no explicit apostrophe to the nation, in the last four stanzas the insistent repetition of phrases that emphasize the nation's collective guilt ("the guilty land," "the nation's life," "the land did reel and tremble," "as a warning to the nations," and "the once oppressing nation") builds to a climax of rhetorical urgency. "What shall become of the nation?" Harper's sibylline speaker asks, but the piece ends without any narrative resolution, and this lack of closure only heightens the urgency of the speaker's question.

The prophetic voice of authority that Harper relies on in "Retribution" is a dramatic posture, one that is arguably quite close to her speaking stance as an orator on the lecture platform and one that Harper relies on frequently in her poetry. As I have suggested, however, Harper is remarkably resistant to inhabiting the speaking positions of slaves in her poetry; she is even more resistant to speaking in an autobiographical first person, preferring instead the authoritative stance of the reform orator who foregrounds the experience of the voiceless oppressed. Harper had extensive contact with slaves and fugitives both through her childhood in Baltimore and through her network of associates working for the Underground Railroad; had she wished to write first-person poems about slaves' experience, she certainly had access to plenty of sources. Her reluctance to write poetry in the first person clearly corresponds to contemporary accounts of the soft-spoken dignity of her oral performances: descriptions of Harper's speaking style emphasize not only its persuasive force, but also its modesty and femininity. In *The Underground Railroad*, William Still cites a postwar *Portland Daily Press* report on one of Harper's lectures: "Mrs. Harper has a splendid articulation, uses chaste, pure language, has a pleasant voice."[17] Still cites also an 1871 review from the Mobile *Register*: "Her voice was remarkable—as sweet as any woman's voice we ever heard, and so clear and distinct."[18] In a review for the *Independent*, Grace Greenwood emphasizes the gentility of Harper's performance: "Her form is delicate, her hands daintily small. She stands quietly beside her desk, and speaks without notes, with gestures few and fitting. Her manner is marked by dignity and composure."[19] Carla Peterson suggests that contemporary accounts of Harper's oral performances "constitute attempts to decorporealize Watkins Harper by emphasizing the quietness of her body, the chastity of her language, and the purity of her voice."[20] Such descriptions, Peterson argues, result in "a complex compromise between presence and absence," a compromise that elides the black female body even as it presents "the voice as pure melody" and "a negation of presence."[21] Harper's reluctance to assume first-person stances in her poems corresponds to the presence-absence of her body on the lecture platform: even as she modestly avoids speaking in the first person in her poems, as a lecturer Harper nonetheless confidently speaks as a representative of her race and sex.

A poem called "The Fugitive's Wife" offers a notable exception to the principle that Harper's poetry avoids first-person stances. Spoken in the first person by a slave who is a mother to young children, this ballad presents the conventional abolitionist argument that slavery destroys the African American family. Harper rings her own changes on this formula by offering nuanced portraits of the drama's two central characters: the husband who can no longer bear the sufferings of life under slavery and the loyal wife and faithful mother, who urges her husband to seek freedom for himself but who remains behind to care for their children. Harper here uses her first-person female speaker to offer analysis of the difference between the husband's and the wife's experience of slavery. In the fifth stanza, the female speaker argues that slavery is fundamentally destructive to her husband's sense of masculine identity:

> He vainly strove to cast aside
> The tears that fell like rain:—
> Too frail, indeed, is manly pride,
> To strive with grief and pain. (72)

Only in stanza six does the husband make explicit his intention to escape: "Again he clasped me to his breast/And said that we must part." Well before this point, however, the wife has already successfully read his body and understood his desire for freedom, as stanza three explains:

> And in his eyes a gloomy night
> Of anguish and despair;—
> I gazed upon their troubled light
> To read the meaning there.

When the speaker concludes the poem by urging him to seek his freedom, the urgency of her plea to her husband is dramatically heightened by the fact that she is the first-person speaker of the poem:

> "Bear not," I cried, "unto your grave,
> The yoke you've borne from birth;
> No longer live a helpless slave,
> The meanest thing on earth!" (73)

The poem underlines then the two forms of self-sacrifice that constitute the black woman's heroism: she urges her husband—the "one thing" that "cheer[d] [her] lowly cot"—to seek his freedom, and she remains a slave for the sake of her young children. "The Fugitive's Wife" thus argues that slavery is damaging not only to black masculinity but also to the multiple forms of familial love which—the poem emphasizes—blacks feel just as strongly as whites. It is the first-person speaker of the poem that allows Harper to represent these many layers of complex emotional allegiance. Moreover, at the same time, in the poem's climactic final stanza, Harper layers the authority of her own orator's voice over that of the fugitive's wife. Endorsing the wife's voice, it is the poet-preacher Harper who urges the husband in particular and oppressed slaves more broadly to seek their freedom: "'Bear not,' I cried, 'unto your grave, / The yoke you've borne from birth'" (73).[22]

While "The Fugitive's Wife" ultimately uses the poet-preacher's stance to endorse that of its first-person slave speaker, in another of those few poems where Harper speaks in the voice of a slave, the alternation of first- and third-person pronouns signals more strongly Harper's ambivalence about assuming a dramatic first-person stance. In this poem, Harper again employs a complex layering of different speaking voices. "The Slave Mother: A Tale of the Ohio" tells the story of the fugitive slave Margaret Garner's attempt to kill her children in order to liberate them from slavery.[23] The poem begins in the first-person perspective of the slave mother but shifts to the perspective of an omniscient sympathetic speaker just at the crucial moment when the mother decides to kill the children. Stanzas eleven through thirteen alternate swiftly between these two perspectives, foregrounding the ways that Harper's female body speaking on the lecture platform does and does not double for the body of the slave mother who is one of the poem's speakers:

Then, said the mournful mother,
    If Ohio cannot save,
I will do a deed for freedom,
    She shall find each child a grave.

I will save my precious children
    From their darkly threatened doom,
I will hew their path to freedom
    Through the portals of the tomb

A moment in the sunlight,
    She held a glimmering knife,
The next moment she had bathed it
    In the crimson fount of life. (85)

As Paula Bennett suggests, Harper was acutely aware of the ways in which she was both inside and outside of the black community for whom she spoke; in "The Slave Mother," that somewhat precarious inside-outside position is signaled by the alternation of pronouns.[24] If pronoun slippage in the middle of the poem signals Harper's ambivalence about first-person stances, however, by the penultimate stanza, Harper again uses her orator's voice to endorse and support the position of the slave mother. Here the perspectives of the poet-preacher and Margaret Garner the slave mother are blended into one, as Harper uses a first-person singular possessive pronoun to put pressure on the idea of blacks' relationship to the nation: "Sends this deed of fearful daring/Through my country's heart no thrill?" (86). The allegiance to nation suggested by the phrase "my country" then allows Harper to build to the poem's rhetorical climax, a moment when she explicitly addresses the white men of the United States: "Will ye not, as men and Christians,/On the side of freedom stand?" (86). Analyzing Harper's representation of the female slave's body, Michael Bennett argues that Harper "believed that the violated private body of the slave needed the public protection not only of the family but also of the metaphorical families of race and nation"; Bennett goes on to suggest that Harper "recognizes that the only lasting protection of the body of the slave comes not from ties of family and race but from integration into the nation's body."[25] In "The Slave Mother: A Tale of the Ohio," Harper uses a sequence of shifting first-person stances, layering her own public voice onto the private voice of Margaret Garner in order to build to a rhetorically forceful direct address to the American nation.

While Julia Ward Howe's abolitionist poems focus on the male slave and on male orators, using the authority of male orators to shore up Howe's authority as a poet, Frances Harper's abolitionist poems rely on what Jane Tompkins has called "sentimental power," focusing on the perspectives of women, mothers, and children on slavery. In her poems about Douglass and Sumner, Howe foregrounds the bodies of these male speakers in place of her own body, which will not be on the lecture platform. By contrast, Harper writes knowing that she herself will recite or sing many of her poems in person; she therefore needs no bodily proxy for her own performance. In her responses to white writers and speakers, however, Harper like Howe sometimes borrows the authority of better-known writers to affirm her own. Among the first poems Harper published were three tributes to Harriet Beecher Stowe, a major touchstone for most abolitionist writers of the nineteenth century; those poems included "To Mrs. Harriet Beecher Stowe," "Eliza Harris," and "Eva's Farewell." In "Eliza Harris," Harper effectively reclaims for the black community a story that Stowe appropriated from the community of black women in her writing of *Uncle Tom's Cabin;* by retelling the story, however, Harper also pays homage to Stowe's novel. In "Eva's Farewell," Harper writes in the first person in the voice of Eva, imagining her farewell to her father and her ascent to heaven. Harper can speak in the voice of a white character both because the speaker is a female child and because the poem is implicitly an endorsement of Stowe's portrait of her child character.

Moreover, like Julia Ward Howe, Harper also writes a tribute poem for Charles Sumner. First published as part of a letter in the *National Anti-Slavery Standard* in July 1860, Harper's "Lines to Charles Sumner" uses regular meter and rhyme scheme to lend solemnity and dignity to her words of thanks:

> Thank God that thou hast spoken
>   Words earnest, true and brave,
> The lightning of thy lips did smite
>   The fetters of the slave.
>
> I thought the shadows deepened,
>   Round the pathway of the slave,

As one by one his faithful friends
Were dropping in the grave.

When other hands grew feeble,
   And loosed their hold on life,
Thy words rang like a clarion
   For freedom's noble strife.

Thy words were not soft echoes,
   Thy tones no syren song;
They fell as battle-axes
   Upon our giant wrong. (173)

An immediately striking difference between the Howe and Harper poems is that Harper uses no dramatic imperatives or apostrophes to Sumner. While Howe uses imperatives and apostrophes to augment her own writerly authority—turning up the volume on voice-effects because she is barred as a white middle-class woman from public speaking—Harper has no need of such devices: confident in her own accomplishments as an abolitionist speaker, she addresses Sumner with calm solemnity as one successful orator to another. While Harper does not offer a physical portrait of Sumner, what she does emphasize is the power of his speech: twice in the poem she uses combat metaphors to suggest that language has the power to free the slave from bondage (stanza one: "The lightning of thy lips did smite/The fetters of the slave" and stanza four: "They fell as battle-axes/Upon our giant wrong"). Since Harper herself is an orator, she would seem here to be describing more broadly the power of the orator to effect social and political change, thereby allying Sumner's audiences with her own. While Howe's poem includes a theoretical meditation on the possibility of a "universal speech" and seems to argue that Sumner is ideally suited to speak for the slave, Harper's poem emphasizes Sumner's steadfast loyalty to the cause of abolition at a time when other supporters of the cause were flagging in energy or commitment. The poem concludes with a phrase that joins black and white supporters of abolition together into a unified community: the phrase "our giant wrong" underlines the collective recognition of the injustice of slavery, suggesting that a powerful abolitionist speaker might succeed in unifying such a community.

In many of her antebellum abolitionist poems, Harper uses dramatic gestures of address to unify the disparate white and black communities she hopes to reach. In "Be Active," which first appeared in 1856, she begins by using apostrophes where the race of the addressee is unspecified: she calls on the "sons of freedom," her "brother," and the "Christian father" to save black men, women, and children from slavery (76). Ultimately, the speaker calls on "men of every clime and nation," specifying race through geography and expanding her collective apostrophe to include not only black and white Americans but also abolitionists around the globe (77). Harper supports the abolitionist message with Christian authority in the poem's final stanza:

> Oh! be faithful! Oh! be valiant,
> Trusting not in human night;
> Know that in the darkest conflict,
> God is on the side of right! (77)

The steady trochaic meter of the poem lends solemnity and urgency to the poem's message even as it also uses the weight of Christian singing practices to help forge its unified community of "sons of freedom." Analyzing the cultural function of African American spirituals, Katherine Bassard suggests that this oral tradition enabled African Americans to perform community in such a way that the boundaries between self and other might be renegotiated and a power hierarchy that privileged the interests of whites could be resisted.[26] In "Be Active," the driving trochaic meter, short lines, rhyme scheme, and the urgent repetition of the speaker's address to abolitionists all work to perform community by speaking in one voice for the many different abolitionist constituencies.

In still another abolitionist poem that foregrounds figures of address, Harper seeks not to unify the abolitionist community but rather to divide the white supporters of compromise from whites who are loyal to the cause of abolition. She lashes out against the group of white Ohio politicians and judges who were instrumental in returning Sarah Lucy Bagby, a fugitive slave, to her Virginia owner. Published just on the eve of war in February 1861, "To the Cleveland Union-Savers" is the most biting denunciation of a specific group of individuals anywhere in Harper's body of poetry: Bagby was the last slave to be returned to a Southern state under the terms of the Fugitive Slave law prior to the outbreak of war. With the nation on the brink of collapse in the aftermath of Lincoln's election, Harper employs a stance of rhetorical attack that is far more direct and narrowly focused than that of most of her poetry. She begins by aligning herself explicitly with Bagby in the poem's subtitle: "An Appeal from One of the Fugitive's Own Race" (93). What is perhaps most striking in this poem is the way that Harper uses the dramatic apostrophe "to the Cleveland Union Savers" to underline the dissolution of the Union that was already in progress at the time of the poem's first publication: over the course of the poem, she disassembles the construct of the nation by disassembling the "you" of the "Union-Savers." Mocking the white politicians' proclaimed allegiance to the nation of the Union, she uses the accusatory phrase "your Union" three times in the eleven-stanza poem. The aural doubling of "you" and "Union" heightens the accusatory tone of the phrase, emphasizing that the so-called Union now includes only a shrinking constituency of cowardly whites so eager for political compromise that they will bend over backwards to uphold a law about to be overthrown by the onset of war. The fourth stanza compares the white politicians to practitioners of human sacrifice, a metaphor that Harper extends and develops throughout the poem:

> On your Union's bloody altar
> Was your helpless victim laid;
> Mercy, truth, and justice shuddered,
> But your hands would give no aid. (94)

In the final stanza, Harper changes the altar metaphor to a foundation metaphor, underlining that neither the "you" of the men addressed nor the "Union" itself will survive the impending conflict:

> And your guilty, sin-cursed Union
> Shall be shaken to its base,
> Till ye learn that simple justice
> Is the right of every race. (94)

These final accusatory lines suggest that the "you" of the "Union" must inevitably be destroyed since the nation's legal systems have excluded the possibility of a collective "we" that would include both blacks and whites.

While the antebellum poem "To the Cleveland Union-Savers" uses an accusatory "you" to denounce the ways that compromise has destroyed the nation, "An Appeal to the American People," which first appeared in book form in 1871, separates the "you" of white Northerners from the "we" of the blacks who supported the Union. The poem's intricate network of shifting pronouns presses white Northerners to continue to fight for justice for blacks even as it also underlines subtle distinctions between the different constituencies Harper here addresses. Though the poem may have appeared in a newspaper prior to its 1871 publication, narrative details in the piece suggest it was written in the war's aftermath. The poem's title, "An Appeal to the American People," explicitly underlines the gap that separates black and white Americans, stressing the extent to which blacks were dispossessed of the rights of national citizenship. The first stanza establishes an opposition between the collective "you" of white Northerners and the collective "we" of freeborn blacks who have struggled for emancipation and fought side by side with whites in the war:

> When a dark and fearful strife
> Raged around the nation's life,
> And the traitor plunged his steel
> Where your quivering hearts could feel,
> When your cause did need a friend,
> We were faithful to the end. (167)

These lines implicitly underline the idea that blacks supported the Union even when the Union did not yet support emancipation: the speaker labels the cause of the Union "your cause." The sequence of stanzas two, three, and four draws an analogy between free blacks' loyalty to the white cause of the Union and free blacks' loyalty to the cause of fugitive slaves:

> When we stood with bated breath,
> Facing fiery storms of death,
> And the war-cloud, red with wrath,
> Fiercely swept around our path,
> Did our hearts with terror quail?
> Or our courage ever fail?
>
> When the captive, wanting bread,
> Sought our poor and lowly shed,
> And the blood-hounds missed his way,

Did we e'er his path betray?
Filled we not his heart with trust
As we shared with him our crust?

With your soldiers, side by side,
Helped we turn the battle's tide,
Till o'er ocean, stream and shore,
Waved the rebel flag no more,
And above the rescued sod
Praises rose to freedom's God. (Stanzas 2–4, 167)

Just as free blacks earned the trust of fugitive slaves, so too, Harper argues, have they earned the trust of the white soldiers they fought beside. Stanza three draws a subtle distinction between free blacks and blacks who are fugitives from slavery; these lines clearly mark the differences in education and experience that separate free Northern blacks from previously enslaved Southern blacks, resisting the idea that blacks are one homogeneous group. Stanzas two and four both underline the heroism of black soldiers' under fire. In stanza four, Harper plays adroitly on the multiple meanings that the word "freedom" took on in the context of wartime ideology:

With your soldiers, side by side,
Helped we turn the battle's tide,
Till o'er ocean, stream and shore,
Waved the rebel flag no more,
And above the rescued sod
Praises rose to freedom's God. (167)

Stanza four's final couplet underlines the difference between Northern whites' visions of democratic "freedom" and blacks' call for "freedom" in the form of abolition. Perhaps the most striking aspect of the poem is that the "we" it voices is always the "we" of free blacks; whenever that "we" could potentially include a collective of blacks and whites working together, Harper carefully reasserts the distinction between "we" and "you," as she does, for example, in the first line of stanza four: "With your soldiers, side by side,/Helped we turn the battle's tide." Harper here gives

5. Unidentified African American soldier in Union uniform with wife and two daughters, photograph

voice to the mixture of pride, courage, frustration, and resignation felt by the black soldiers who served in the Union Army, a mixture of emotions that is evident in a group photograph of a black soldier and his family (fig. 5).

This refusal to bring the nation together in a collective "we" emphasizes that both during and after the war the country was deeply riven by racist, sectional, and partisan conflict. Harper effectively uses these pronoun divisions to put pressure on her white audience, underlining the idea that Northern whites owe a debt of loyalty to free blacks; she also uses the pronoun divisions to express the frustration that middle-class blacks must have felt as they watched the promises of the Emancipation Proclamation and the Fifteenth Amendment being dismantled in the postwar era. In the fifth of the poem's seven stanzas, Harper introduces a third player, "the traitor" whose "knife" threatens the life of the nation:

But to-day the traitor stands
With the crimson on his hands
Scowling 'neath his brow of hate,
On our weak and desolate,
With the blood-rust on the knife
Aiméd at the nation's life. (168)

No unified national "we" can be posited so long as the "you" addressed strikes compromises with the traitorous white South. The fractured pronouns of "An Appeal to the American People" disclose the anger that Harper must have felt after working side by side with white reform leaders for decades. Restrained by the conventional parameters of meter and rhyme, Harper's stance of protest articulates not only the frustrations of free Northern blacks who have been active in the struggle for abolition but also her personal frustration with the conciliatory compromises that followed the war's end. As Carla Peterson argues, Harper's poetry expresses deeply held personal convictions even when it uses conventional poetic forms to confine and restrain personal feeling.[27] "An Appeal to the American People" suggests that in the war's aftermath Harper understands the address to the nation as a utopian stance, a stance that cannot yet conjoin or unify the deeply divided country Harper nonetheless seeks to address in her poetry.

A versatile and accomplished poet, keenly aware of the range of different audiences she aims to reach, Frances Harper understands that poetry, like oratory, can work to unify—if only temporarily—powerful political communities. In the stances she assumes in her Civil War poetry, Harper aims to unite blacks and whites in their opposition to slavery and in their support for the war as a war of emancipation. Simultaneously asserting and eliding the authority of her black female body on the lecture platform, Harper writes many of her poems for her own public performances, aiming to reach a wide range of listeners with her stirring yet formally conventional ballads. She effaces a personal "I" in order to speak for the collective of enslaved African Americans; she also usually resists speaking in the first person in the voice of the slave. Yet because her work relies on the moral authority of her voice as poet-preacher on the lecture platform, it also reveals traces of her personal investment in the causes she devoted her life to; shifts and slippage in Harper's pronoun choices reveal traces of the personal "I" in her poems, disclosing also her conflicting allegiances as a free black educated woman dedicated to the struggle for African American rights. Harper's commitment to addressing the American nation results in the complex and shifting array of personal pronouns she uses in her poetry; it is her powerful commitment to including African Americans within the American nation that results in the fissures and divisions within that pronoun array; Harper's divided pronoun stances thus signal the challenges that will face the American nation after the war in bridging the divides not only of regional loyalty but also of gender and race.

CHAPTER FOUR

ADDRESSES TO A DIVIDED NATION

Emily Dickinson, Walt Whitman, and the Place of the Lyric I

"War feels to me an oblique place," Emily Dickinson writes in a letter to Thomas Wentworth Higginson in February 1863, three months after Higginson traveled to South Carolina to take command of a black regiment (JL 280).[1] Scholars who examine Dickinson's poetry often cite this passage as an example of Dickinson's ambivalent relationship toward the Civil War in particular and toward expressing political commitments more generally. We expect Dickinson, as one of the first American modernists, to position herself at a skeptical and oblique angle in relation to the war and its ideologies. We look for Dickinson to posit a lyric "I" in her poetry and to avoid the collective stance of the nationalist "we." Reading Dickinson, we expect to encounter a writer who lives in internal domestic exile, addressing the crisis of the Union and other political events of her day only indirectly if at all. In this same letter, however, Dickinson also offers a far more conventional statement about the war and its risks: echoing the concerns of many women on the homefront writing to friends and relatives in the military, she worries aloud about Higginson's safety and tells him that she prays for him and for other soldiers in church: "though not reared to prayer – when service is had in Church, for Our Arms, I include yourself" (JL 280). Significantly the phrase "Our Arms" includes not only Higginson and other soldiers, but also Dickinson herself in the collective body of Union supporters in Amherst. As Dickinson's letter to Higginson suggests, Dickinson's wartime poetry offers both skeptical commentary on military ideologies and expressions of concern or grief about soldiers who are in peril or who have lost their lives, expressions that sometime echo sentimental depictions of soldiers as Christian martyrs or of soldiers rejoining their dead mothers in the afterlife. Unlike Frances Watkins Harper, whose protest poetry foregrounds the collective "we" and all but effaces a personal "I," Dickinson only rarely uses the first-person plural in her war-related writings; like Julia Ward Howe, however, Dickinson wrestles with the place of the feminine I in her wartime work.

Because of the wide variety of stances Dickinson draws on in responding to the war and because of her refusal to publish via the conventional print means, we need to attend with particular care to the rhetorical contexts in which she produces individual texts. In reading the much cited letter to Higginson, for example, we need to consider the extent to which Dickinson plays a role Higginson would by now expect of her: her reclusiveness and her eccentricity, both coded as part of her diminutive femininity in the correspondence with him, contrast with his bravely engaged public masculinity, his decision to serve as an officer and to lead one of the first black regiments. In emphasizing that her own rapport to the conflict is an "oblique" and thus a sheltered one, Dickinson may well be telling Higginson what she imagines he wants to hear. Indeed, Dickinson here echoes the common refrain of Northern soldier-poets who insist that Northern women are too far removed from combat to imagine or understand its horrors. By praying for Higginson's safety, Dickinson joins the collective of Union supporters in Amherst and assumes the role of the faithful woman on the homefront, keeping her loved ones alive with hopes and prayers and letters. Just as Julia Ward Howe balances poems about abolition with poems about Victorian motherhood in her collections, so too will Dickinson balance radical and sentimental stances in her wartime poems and letters in order to meet the expectations of the family and friends who read her work. Repositioning Dickinson's wartime poetry in relation to that of her female contemporaries foregrounds the concerns these women share in establishing a relationship between the individual "I" and the collective "we" of nationalist ideologies.

While analysis of Dickinson's wartime writings will serve as the main focus of this chapter, parallel readings of Walt Whitman—the other great formal innovator of this era and the other nineteenth-century American poet with high canonical status—will serve to contextualize my analysis of Dickinson's addresses to the nation. It is a critical commonplace that

Whitman is a public poet and Emily Dickinson a private one: while Whitman's "I" addresses the whole nation, in Dickinson's poems the positing of the poetic speaker seems to require a privacy of address that excludes the outside world. Such a reading, however, neglects the tensions that underlie Whitman's inclusive apostrophes and his expansive "I's" and "we's"; it also neglects the ways in which Dickinson deliberately, though sometimes skeptically, addresses the collective of the nation. Dickinson's poems, I will suggest, do address the American nation; simultaneously, however, she also offers an exhaustive analysis of the challenges a woman writer faces in using that rhetorical platform. Dickinson's speaker often undercuts her own position; readers have thus only recently begun to recognize the range of her critical engagement with nineteenth-century political debates. Redrawing the boundaries between public and private stances, Dickinson's poetry exemplifies the ways that women writers can address new audiences in the Civil War era.

From the twentieth-century perspective, Whitman's status as the great poet of the Civil War is well established. His decision to publish a discrete volume of war poems, *Drum-Taps*, in 1865 testifies to his desire to become America's bard in a time of national crisis; the extensive critical attention this text received in the twentieth century confirms the scholarly consensus that Whitman is the leading poet of the war. Dickinson scholars have, however, only recently begun to examine her engagement with wartime discourses. Following the publication of Thomas Johnson's edition of Dickinson's complete poems in 1955, many of the first generation of Dickinson scholars argued that she had little interest in the historical and political events that unfolded around her.[2] In his biography of Dickinson, the first definitive scholarly account of her life, Richard Sewall notes that "a few random remarks comprise her total comment on the Civil War." More specifically, Sewall writes that Dickinson's work says "nothing about issues, about slavery or the Union, nothing specific about victory or defeat or any of the heroes on either side."[3] In recent decades, however, new approaches to Dickinson's life and work have emphasized the strength of her engagement with the literary, social, and political communities that surrounded her; Shira Wolosky's *Emily Dickinson: A Voice of War* and several recent articles explore the range of Dickinson's responses to the Civil War, calling for a reconsideration of her supposed silence on this subject.[4] As Richard Sewall notes, Dickinson clearly resists assuming fixed ideological or nationalist positions in her poems; yet the two or three dozen poems in which Dickinson responds directly to the war suggest that her resistance to assuming fixed ideological positions might be a critical rejoinder to those discourses rather than a refusal to engage with them. While scholars who have read Dickinson's poetry in relation to the war have often emphasized her radical and innovative questioning of the nationalist ideologies that fueled the conflict, this argument flattens the complexity and range both of popular responses to these ideologies and of Dickinson's own response to them.[5] In reading a group of Dickinson's Civil War poems, I will suggest that her stances both question these ideologies and endorse them.

While Dickinson's poems sometimes take a skeptical view of the address to the nation, Whitman adopts this platform enthusiastically, self-consciously styling himself as America's bard. In order to understand Dickinson's suspicions about address, we need also to consider Whitman's enthusiasm for it.[6] Comparative readings of Dickinson and Whitman will serve to illuminate the ways that twentieth-century New Criticism worked both to canonize Whitman and to underline his status as the leading poet of the Civil War while that same critical approach worked both to canonize Dickinson and to read her work as radically disengaged from the political sphere. These comparative readings will set the stage for a reconsideration of Dickinson's wide-ranging engagement with the nationalist and military ideologies of the Civil War era.

Letters to America: Dickinson and Whitman

In reading Dickinson and Whitman's addresses to the nation, I will return to John Stuart Mill's model for the scene of the lyric address in order to argue that Dickinson's and Whitman's aesthetic projects foreground the limitations of that romantic model for American Civil War–era poetry. Mill's definition will serve particularly well for this purpose not only because it continues to serve as a central model in contemporary critical discussions of the lyric but also because it emphasizes both the poetic speaker's relationship to his or her audience and the relationship between voice and text in poetry. It is in part the centrality of Mill's model that leads twentieth-century scholars to overlook or misunderstand the extent of Dickinson's engagement with the Civil War: Mill's definition points up the contrast between lyric poetry and oratory that at first appears so prominent when we juxtapose Dickinson's seemingly private and hermetic poetic stances with Whitman's seemingly public and outspoken ones. "Poetry and eloquence," Mill writes, "are both alike the expression or utterance of feeling. But if we may be excused the antithesis, we should say that eloquence is heard, poetry is overheard."[7] What separates poetry from oratory in Mill's scheme is the kind of reader or listener each creates: in the case of poetry, both the reader and the speaker are supposed to agree tacitly to ignore the fact that the poem is not a spontaneous verbal outcry, but rather a written text. The contract between speaker and reader stipulates that the reader will "eavesdrop" on the speaker's private soliloquy. It is precisely by ignoring the reader that the poet achieves his or her goal of engaging the reader's attention.[8] The orator by contrast makes his persuasive aims—and his claims on the audience's attention—explicit.[9]

Whitman and Dickinson will both critique Mill's model for the romantic scene of address—not through their innovative and proto-modernist poetic stances but rather through their embeddedness in nineteenth-century poetic practices. Because Whitman's work obsessively addresses the reader and because his speaker makes explicit his persuasive aims, he rejects Mill's definition of poetry. Examining the relationship between poetry and oratory, Whitman argues that these two rhetorical stances are closely allied; his position is strongly supported by the range of poetry the Civil War produced, including, for example, not only Howe's "Battle Hymn" and her other politically persuasive pieces, but also much of Frances Harper's wartime work.[10] When Dickinson addresses the nation, she too implicitly critiques Mill's model for the scene of the lyric address; she does so, however, not by linking poetry and oratory but rather by pointing insistently to the gap that separates poetic voice from poetic text and to the fictional character of the soliloquy on which Mill's romantic model depends. In pointing to the fiction of this one-sided soliloquy, Dickinson will suggest that women writers must adopt oblique and adroit stances in order to reach their intended audiences in wartime.

In "This is my letter to the World" (F 519), a poem deceptively simple on its surface, Dickinson offers an incisive analysis both of the limitations of the romantic scene of address for any writer and of the challenges that the woman poet in particular faces in seeking to address a wartime audience. In two brief stanzas, the speaker seems to touch directly on Mill's model for the lyric speaker's position and Dickinson's own decisions as a writer:

> This is my letter to the World
> That never wrote to Me –
> The simple News that Nature told –
> With tender Majesty
>
> Her Message is committed
> To Hands I cannot see –
> For love of Her – Sweet – countrymen –
> Judge tenderly – of Me (F 519)[11]

Boldly declaring the poem to be a "letter to the World," Dickinson begins by disrupting the romantic staging of voice and making textuality evident; indeed, the poem as a whole would seem to emphasize the oxymoronic status of the poem as "written utterance." Emphasizing the frequency with which poems were read aloud in nineteenth-century America, the opening line already points to the fictional nature of the scene of address by juxtaposing the deictic "this" with the idea of a poem as a "letter to the World"; the deictic foregrounds the idea of the presence and voice of the speaker even as the "letter" points to the speaker's absence and the text of the poem on the page. Moreover, in the poem, Dickinson also presents the scene of address as one marked by triangulation: the speaker suggests that her "letter to the World" is in fact nothing more than "The simple News that Nature told," a phrase that occurs in apposition to the "letter." According to these lines then, the speaker does not deliver his or her own message; rather he or she is merely an insignificant go-between, relaying to the "World" the "simple News" told to him or her by "Nature."

Although the first line declares the poem to be the speaker's "letter to the World," by the second stanza the poem has become "Her Message," a message from Nature, and this message, the speaker explains, has been "committed/To Hands I cannot see –." The unseen "Hands" might be those of God or those of the "Sweet – countrymen –" who are subsequently addressed. In either case, the speaker has lost control over the "committ[ing]" of the message; the speaker has been shut out of the circuit of address. The concluding lines of the poem undercut the emphasis on the poem as text with what is for Dickinson a highly uncharacteristic moment of address. The speaker calls on her "Sweet – countrymen – "

to "Judge tenderly – of [Her]," not out of love for the speaker, but out of love for Nature, who is, the speaker insists, the actual source of the poem. Dickinson's poem points to the limitations of the romantic scene of the lyric address by offering a parodic retelling of its basic elements: the hapless poet-speaker can do nothing more than breathe out his or her effusions about nature, all the while trying to ignore his or her unresponsive audience and fearing the harsh critical judgments that may subsequently come.

Yet while we can read the poem as a critique of the romantic scene of address for writers of either sex, if we keep in mind that the poem was written in the midst of the Civil War, it also becomes possible to read it as a commentary on the particular difficulties a woman poet faces in addressing her "countrymen" in wartime. Such a reading is supported by the poem's position in fascicle 24, a packet that includes two poems that make explicit reference to the war: "When I was small, a woman died" (F 518) and "It feels a shame to be Alive –" (F 524), two poems I will turn to later in this chapter. As we have seen, Mill declares that the skill of the genteel poet consists in his being able to conceal the fact that he desires or expects to have a listener/reader; but a nineteenth-century woman poet who conceals her claims on her audience too effectively may well have no audience at all. Indeed, Dickinson's withdrawal from the world in her own life also presents a parodic version of Mill's account of the romantic scene of address—particularly if we consider those accounts of her preferring not to receive guests directly, but rather remaining in an adjacent room to overhear conversations. Dickinson was herself an eavesdropper, and poems like "This is my letter to the World" thematize the fact that other readers will "eavesdrop" on the scenes of address presented in her poems.

"This is my letter to the World" offers a trenchant analysis of the challenges of the scene of address for the woman poet, implicitly thematizing Dickinson's literal and historical refusal to send her "letter to the World" by means of conventional print publication. The deictic "this" of the opening line thus refers implicitly to her entire body of work. Moreover, in its play on the relationship between the presence of the text and the absence of the speaker's voice, the poem's first line both presents and elides the body of its genteel white female speaker who is forbidden by gender norms from reciting her poem in a public forum and therefore must deliver it by means of the text. "This is my letter to the World/" the speaker declares, "That never wrote to me," and the second line points both to the lack of reciprocity in the scene of the lyric address and to the frustrations of a woman writer who may not hear back from the editors or "the World" to whom she addresses her work.

In the lines that follow, the speaker describes herself as nothing more than an intermediary between "Nature" and the "World," which is of course the conventional position of the romantic poet in the tradition of Wordsworth. Yet the gesture might also be read as one of feminine, self-deprecating modesty: the speaker declares her letter to be nothing more than "the simple News that Nature told." The lines effectively erase the female speaker's agency as a writer, making her merely a messenger. And what could be more appropriate for a genteel woman poet during a time of war and bloodshed, a time when the actual "News" was rarely "simple"—than to serve as a conduit for the transcendent "tender Majesty" of "Nature"? In the second stanza of the poem, then, this link between the speaker and Nature is made still stronger by means of feminine pronouns that make the speaker Nature's double. "Her Message" replaces the speaker's "letter," and "For love of Her," the speaker pleads with her "countrymen" to "judge" her "tenderly." The second stanza thus also juxtaposes the position of Nature/the speaker (both gendered feminine) with the position of the audience, the "countrymen," a masculine collective.[12] When the speaker declares that she has lost control of her "letter" ("Her Message is committed/To Hands I cannot see –"), she seems in part to allude to the loss of control over her own words that would attend print publication—just as Dickinson effectively lost control of those few of her poems that appeared in print during her lifetime. One thinks, for example, of Karen Dandurand's account of the 1864 publication of three Dickinson poems in a newspaper raising funds for the Union army—and of the subsequent reprinting of these poems in other newspapers, as was common practice in nineteenth-century America. The poems that Dickinson allowed Richard Storrs to publish in the *Drum Beat* are universally about the "simple News that Nature told."[13] Reprinted in a number of different Northern publications, Dickinson's poems reached additional audiences beyond those of Storrs's *Drum Beat*.

Ultimately "This is my letter to the World" suggests that addressing a national audience is a particularly fraught undertaking for the woman writer because that audience must inevitably fragment when it is addressed by a female speaker. In the poem—as in Dickinson's own experience of print publication—the delivery of the letter to the public results in the subdividing of "the World" into the many unseen hands that hold the text. The address to the nation fails to fix or stabilize that audience. Rather at precisely the juncture when the poem first posits an "I," the audience for the poem's speaker fractures: "Her Message is committed/To Hands I cannot see – ." Just as the speaker loses control of the text as she hands it over, so also does the text fail to hold the nation together as a unified group of readers: the "Sweet countrymen" whom the speaker addresses become individuated, anonymous, and distanced from the speaker. While Howe's "Battle Hymn" succeeds in unifying the Union—at least temporarily—by means of a "we" that layers the voices of John Brown, of Union soldiers, and of the poem's genteel female author, Dickinson's "This is my letter" strips the woman writer's voice down to the solitary genteel "I," underlining the inadequacy of the lyric self for the task of unifying the nation. Dickinson here wrestles with the same issue that Howe takes up—and cannot completely resolve for herself—in "The Lyric I": the range of stances available to the feminine I in addressing the nation. The fragmenting of the addressed nation in Dickinson's "This is my letter" is analogous to the fragmenting of the North into discrete and opposing factions in Frances Harper's "An Appeal to the American People": in both poems that fragmentation results from the persistence of the female writer's personal "I". In "This is my letter to the World" then, Dickinson's speaker assumes an ironic stance toward the many perils a woman writer faces in addressing her "Sweet – countrymen –": she writes knowing she cannot anticipate a reply; she effaces her own position as a woman writer, figuring herself instead as a mere intermediary between a feminine Nature and the masculine World of readers; she acknowledges that her letter has been "committed" to a proliferation of recipients whom she cannot see; and she worries about the critical judgments that will be passed on her work.

Yet the frustration and anxiety that this reading implies cannot entirely account for the clever wit—or the undertone of quiet victory—that sustains Dickinson's poem. The poem's opening couplet also implicitly contrasts the lack of reciprocity in the world of literary publishing with the alternative opportunities for intellectual and literary exchange offered by nineteenth-century epistolary communities; though the "World" never "wrote" to the poem's speaker, many friends, family members, and editors did write to Dickinson, asking for her poems and commenting on them. Working largely outside the establishment of print publication, Dickinson—like many other unpublished nineteenth-century writers—built a community of readers to whom she could send her work. Thus even as the poem foregrounds its speaker's reclusiveness and isolation, it also points toward the letter-writing practices that offered Dickinson a substantial readership outside of the conventional means of print publication. We know that Dickinson circulated hundreds of her poems among family and friends through her correspondence, and if we assume that some of these poems were sent to a wider group of readers by their intended recipients, as was common practice with correspondence at this time, then hundreds of Dickinson's unpublished poems could have been read by hundreds of readers, as copies of the texts were "committed" to more and more unseen "Hands."[14] "This is my letter to the World," the speaker declares, announcing in celebratory fashion the existence of an impressive body of work that she will deliver not by conventional print publication but rather by means of letters and other informal modes of circulation. As the declarative stance of the poem's first line suggests, Dickinson can and will address her "Sweet countrymen" even in wartime; she will do so, however, in an oblique and sometimes circuitous fashion, sometimes representing battlefield landscapes through a lens of decorative natural imagery, sometimes exaggerating her speaker's genteel femininity in order to soften the edges of her political critiques. Dickinson's decision not to publish via conventional print means will also offer her rhetorical freedoms that neither Julia Ward Howe nor Frances Watkins Harper can afford: while tensions between a personal "I" and a nationalist "we" lie beneath the surfaces of Howe's and Harper's poems, Dickinson can examine the tensions and contradictions between these different stances explicitly in her poems because she is freed from the obligation of meeting a public's demand for consistent political positions. Freed from the obligation of persuading her readers, Dickinson can also reverse her own position from one poem to the next, endorsing romantic imagery in one battlefield poem and critiquing it in the next, for example.

While the speaker in Dickinson's "This is my letter" coyly figures herself as a self-effacing messenger who has lost control over the transmission of her own textual/epistolary message, Whitman's poems frequently present a speaker who argues, like an orator, for the powers of the human voice—even as he is at times overcome by the power of his own poetic cries. While Dickinson's poem insistently points to its own dual status as text and as the staging of a voice, Whitman's poems frequently seek to foreground voice above all else. Examples of the direct address to the nation abound in Whitman, but in its excesses the poem "Apostroph" presents a particularly striking example of all that he hopes to accomplish in his poetics of address. The fact that the poem appeared in only the 1860 version of *Leaves of Grass* (though eleven of its lines do appear in the 1867 edition) signals Whitman's ambivalence about the heightened rhetorical stances of the piece. "Apostroph" consists essentially of an extraordinarily inclusive list of dramatic addresses to various persons, groups, individuals, objects, and abstractions, each line beginning either with the "O" of romantic apostrophe ("O mater! O fils") or with the "O" of dramatic exclamation ("O I heard, and yet hear, angry thunder").[15] Though the poem can unfold only in the suspended temporality of its own apostrophes and dramatic exclamations, it nonetheless maps out a narrative in the present-tense immediacy of the speaker's cries: the speaker calls on various groups to awake (2:290, lines 1–12), witnesses a shipwreck (lines 12–15), worries aloud that the whole world might be "a sham, a sell" (line 16), praises "America" and "freedom" as the only "real" thing (lines 17–18), addresses and praises first the North and then the South (lines 21–23; 35–37), declares the union "impossible to dissever" (line 53), and finally, in the last five lines, both anticipates his own death and calls on the "poets to come" to fulfill his visions for America.

If we read the poem as a whole in light of the last five lines, its drama seems to consist in the speaker's postponing his own death for as long as possible by means of his own poetic exclamations. "O present! I return while yet I may to you!" the speaker cries, and the line emphasizes the tenacity with which the speaker clings to the suspended present tenses of apostrophic time throughout the poem (line 64). Likewise the poem reads as an attempt to hold in abeyance the threat of the dividing of the nation: "O Libertad! O compact! O union impossible to dissever!" (line 53). By means of the address to the nation, the poem aims to hold the nation together. This utopian project of unifying the nation is inseparable from Whitman's aim of using poetic voice to unite signifiers with signifieds, a goal that is clearly evident in "Apostroph."[16] Whitman's poetics thus leads him to privilege voice—with the promise of presence that it offers—over writing, which threatens to insert the reader into symbolic hierarchies that the poet insistently rejects as oppressive and authoritative.[17] Not surprisingly, Whitman's poetics also explicitly privileges oratory because he values both the immediacy of the orator's voice and the possibility of the efficacy of that voice in the political present. With its heated verbal flourishes, "Apostroph" imitates the dramatic style of revivalist preaching that Whitman admired throughout his life, the emotional fervor of the acting he saw on New York stages in the 1830s and '40s, and the oratory of the lyceum and the political arena, oratory that was a lifelong interest for him.[18] Echoing contemporary performance culture in its stances of address, the poem emphatically insists on establishing a dialogic and participatory relationship with its audience. In "Apostroph" then, Whitman's speaker is not the solitary poet of Mill's model, but rather an American poet addressing a turbulent American crowd; the poem represents the cacophony of the political and reform oratory that immediately precedes the war.

Yet while the poem aims to conjure up the groups addressed and the scenes the speaker exclaims over, the sheer quantity of exclamations in the poem lends the speaker's voice a tone of frenzied anxiety: anxiety about the inefficacy of language, anxiety about the difficulties of addressing another person in a poem, and perhaps most pressingly anxiety about a nation divided from and within itself.[19] It is no coincidence that Whitman's poetry moves increasingly away from explorations of address in the aftermath of the Civil War.[20] In his wartime poetry, Whitman must confront head-on the philosophical dilemma that his exploration of the apostrophe leads to: namely, the impossibility of encountering the other—and representing the other's suffering—through poetic address. In "Apostroph," the tension between naming and loss, between union and division, both propels the poem forward and keeps the speaker suspended in a state of feverish chatter. The proliferation of addressed groups and abstractions only points to the speaker's fear of loss: the incantatory repetition of the poetic "O" which conjures up the sound of the speaker's voice simultaneously suggests the null or zero of the loss of each person or thing named.[21] "O Libertad! O compact! O union impossible to dissever!" the speaker cries. Writing in 1860, however, Whitman is well aware that these three abstractions no longer apply to the condition of the United States.

If we juxtapose Whitman's "Apostroph" with Dickinson's "This is my letter to the World," certain contrasts and shared concerns in their explorations of address become apparent. In these poems, the two poets' respective positions are clearly inflected—in a self-consciously exaggerated fashion—by gender. With feminine modesty, Dickinson's speaker represents her relationship to her readers as demure, genteel, indirect, and epistolary; she hesitates to enter the fray of the print publishing marketplace. With a coyness layered with irony, she also hesitates to write about the war, preferring instead simply to relay "The simple News that Nature told—." Whitman effectively addresses a masculine figure for himself when he calls on the "bearded roughs" to awake and become "bards" (line 10). He calls on them to step up in manly fashion and speak directly to a national audience; he also addresses "muscle and pluck," calling for masculine strength and the power of masculine voices to hold the nation together (line 30). Yet while the speakers take opposing gender positions, what ultimately links these two poems is the argument each offers about the challenges of addressing the divided nation. In its insistent catalogue of apostrophes, Whitman's poem, like Dickinson's "This is my letter to the World," points to the inevitable fragmentation of the national audience. Calling out to a nation soon to be sundered, Whitman's speaker tries to invent the kind of poetry and the kind of audience that might avert such a catastrophe: "O union impossible to dissever!." But the "bearded roughs" whom he calls on to become "bards" will soon have little time for reading, writing, and public speaking and will instead have to use their "muscle and pluck" in a bloody war (lines 10 and 30).

The speaker of "This is my letter to the World" promises to address the divided nation only obliquely, demurely, and in a roundabout fashion; she will not address her "Sweet – countrymen" with an explicit apostrophe again. What she will do, however, is serve as a go-between between her "countrymen" and "Nature"; and that "Nature," as Dickinson sees it during the years of the Civil War, is often a bloody and violent place. Distrustful of the authoritative posture that the apostrophe requires—and equally distrustful of the institutions of print publication—Dickinson proceeds to address the nation by indirection.[22] Yet the poems that she writes about battlefield violence and suffering during the Civil War must necessarily be read as addresses to her fellow Americans.

Whitman, however, will take a very different approach to the dilemmas of addressing a nation at war. Though few of his Civil War poems will use the apostrophe quite so insistently as this one, Whitman's speaker nonetheless persists in using direct addresses to his audience in his representations of war: styling himself as the bard who will chronicle the war for the nation, he attempts to reunite a war-torn country with poetry. When his attempt to hold the Union together with apostrophes fails, Whitman turns his hand to the related task of linking those at home with those on the front lines, linking the observers of the war with the soldiers fighting and dying in it.

Landscapes of War: Dickinson and Whitman

For Dickinson and Whitman, the task of writing poetry in a time of war leads to a crisis of faith in the stances and imagery of the romantic lyric poem. Both writers present themselves as intermediaries who can represent the violence of war to those not on the front lines; both envision poetry as a place where one might bear witness to the suffering of others. At the same time, however, both rigorously examine the philosophical dilemmas of the intermediary's position and the attendant dilemmas of representing the violence of war. In their Civil War poetry, Dickinson and Whitman experiment with representing panoramic views of battle, writing poems that might be called "landscapes of war." In these poems—which showcase the contemporary fascination with panoramic vistas in literature, painting, and photography—both poets also grapple with the difficulties of representing the enormous scale of modern warfare. Responding to daguerrotypes of battlefields (and the widely disseminated engravings of them that appeared in print), the harmonious images of nature in the Hudson River school paintings, and the epic visions of luminist painters, Dickinson's and Whitman's battlefield landscapes point to the limitations of the pastoral tradition in both poetry and painting of the nineteenth century, underlining the ways that the construct of American identity has been writ large onto the fiction of a harmonious and unified American landscape.[23]

In view of their different approaches to the address to the nation, it is not surprising that Whitman and Dickinson offer two distinct perspectives on the uses of romanticism in representing war. Just as Whitman persists in addressing the nation even as that nation is on the brink of dissolution, so too will he aim to bind the nation together again through his depiction of the war's violence. Although Whitman feels he has a moral obligation to render in poetry as accurately as he can the horror of the suffering he has witnessed, he also believes he has a moral commitment to represent that suffering in a way that justifies the war's violence. Faced with the conflict of these obligations, Whitman most often chooses to argue that the loss of life serves the purpose of redeeming and reuniting the nation. While Whitman clearly found a renewed sense of purpose—both personally and as a writer—in the nursing work he did in Civil War hospitals, the language of his war poems is marked by the tension between his loyalty to the construct of the nation and his devotion to the experience of individual suffering soldiers.[24] In Whitman's work, the pastoral mode becomes an essential part of the poet's strategy for reuniting the wholeness of the nation; and if at times the horror of the violence the speaker must represent threatens to destabilize that pastoral structure, the poems nonetheless usually insist on the moral certainties that the recuperative force of the pastoral provides.[25]

In Dickinson's work by contrast, the speaker's ambivalence about the rhetorical platform of the address to the nation corresponds to a very different approach to wartime violence. In "This is my letter to the World" (F 519), Dickinson's speaker insists that her work conveys nothing but "the simple News that Nature told"; this feminine self-effacing modesty becomes a strategic rhetorical maneuver when it is read in relation to Dickinson's battlefield landscapes. Seamlessly mingling romantic landscape and carnage, Dickinson treats the war obliquely in these poems. This strategy, however, is not merely an instance of a female writer adroitly veiling her choice of a political topic; rather, by representing the horror of war through landscape description, Dickinson also points insistently toward the limitations of the romantic lexicon. While Whitman portrays suffering as part of the heroism necessary to reunite a nation, Dickinson represents death and violence as events that may profoundly separate the witness from the suffering individual and the poet-speaker from her audience. In her battlefield landscapes, Dickinson suggests that romantic poetry is inadequate to the task of representing the vast scale of suffering in modern war.[26]

Dickinson's "They dropped like Flakes –" (F 545) and "The name – of it – is 'Autumn' –" (F 465) both employ descriptions of pastoral scenes in order to evoke the horrors of war. They do so, however, with very different effects. "They dropped like Flakes –" represents a battlefield massacre by means of metaphors for nature's harmonious cycles; deliberately rejecting these kinds of metaphoric links; "The name – of it – is 'Autumn' – " represents natural cycles themselves as inherently violent and destructive. In "They dropped like Flakes –," which was probably written midway through the war, Dickinson's speaker begins by likening soldiers falling in battle to falling flakes of snow. In the first stanza, the poem then goes on to change the central metaphor two more times, comparing the falling men to shooting stars and falling rose petals:

> They dropped like Flakes –
> They dropped like stars –
> Like Petals from a Rose –
> When suddenly across the June –
> A Wind with fingers – goes – (F 545)

In her search for the most apt nature metaphor for falling soldiers, the speaker maintains a genteel tone of composure. Each new metaphor is layered carefully over its predecessor. Echoing newspaper accounts that sometimes emphasized the neat rows in which advancing soldiers fell in combat, the visual image of successive lines of falling men is dance-like, almost balletic. The proliferation of metaphors and the rapidity with which each replaces the one that came before suggests both the speed with which the dying men fall and the speed with which fresh soldiers step in to replace the dead. The stanza suggests both that an infinite number of soldiers will die and that death is an extraordinarily passive process. The sequence of images—from the falling snows of winter to the falling "Petals" of June—suggests that the rapid accumulation of dead bodies is as inevitable as the rapid changing of the seasons. The images used to describe the men—the snow, the stars, the petals—all belong to the conventional poetic repertoire for landscape description; yet the vision that they present—of death on a massive scale in the context of modern warfare—is an unsettling match for this repertoire.

Although the conventional metaphors seem to collide with the poem's content, this collision is not powerful enough to disrupt the soothing, dreamlike effect of the poetic imagery. The overall effect of the first stanza is to represent death as part of the cycles and events of the natural world, even though the sheer numbers of deaths involved would seem to undermine such a claim.[27] The falling soldiers are in harmony with the natural landscape that surrounds them. Only in the second stanza does the speaker begin to address death as loss, and even here the vision of death is a redemptive, relatively reassuring one:

> They perished in the seamless Grass –
> No eye could find the place –
> But God can summon every face
> On his Repealless – List. (F 545)

In an image that evokes both the endless vista of the prairie and the smaller cultivated fields of the Northeast, the individual dead are here represented as blending into the "Seamless Grass –" and thus blending harmoniously into the landscape itself. The blades of grass emphasize the abundance of dead bodies, even as they suggest that each dead man is identical to the next; individual deaths are subsumed into the totality of death on a massive scale. The final two lines of the poem, however, present a God who records and maintains individuality in his tally of the dead. Unlike the human "eye"—the one fleeting trace of the poet-speaker's "I" in the poem—God can "summon every face." While the word "Repealless" underlines the irrevocable nature of death, the verb "repeal" emphasizes the idea of being "called back" to or redeemed by God: once one's name has been entered on the list of the dead, that entry can never be revoked or annulled. The poem here points toward the lists of the dead—and the lists of the drafted—that routinely appeared in the newspapers, linking those lists with the lists of the saved and converted from revival meetings, the lists of God's chosen. Significantly, the speaker in this poem seems removed from the perils of the battlefield; the soldiers are evoked through a reiterated "they." Throughout the poem, the speaker's position as witness to the scene seems both authoritative and secure; there is no risk that she herself will be among the fallen.

Where "They dropped like Flakes –" succeeds in making human death seem a part of nature's cycles, the poem "The name – of it – is 'Autumn' –" (F 465), which may date from the fall of 1862, makes natural cycles the site of bloody carnage.[28] If "They dropped like flakes" rewrites death on the battlefield as a natural event, "The name – of it – is 'Autumn' –" rewrites the change of nature's seasons as the scene of a massacre. The poem first appeared (under the title "Autumn") in *Youth's Companion* in September 1892, where it was presumably read as a description of an autumnal landscape. However, if the poem was composed in the fall of 1862, it was written during the same time in which the battle of Antietam took place, with its massive toll of 23,000 dead and wounded; the word "Autumn" in the opening line points aurally to the name of this battle. The poem describes a landscape transformed not by the color of blood, but by blood itself:

> The name – of it – is "Autumn" –
> The hue – of it – is Blood –
> An Artery – opon the Hill –
> A Vein – along the Road –
>
> Great Globules – in the Alleys –
> And Oh, the Shower of Stain –
> When Winds – upset the Basin –
> And spill the Scarlet Rain –
>
> It sprinkles Bonnets – far below –
> It gathers ruddy Pools –
> Then – eddies like a Rose – away –
> Opon Vermillion Wheels – (F 465)

Where "They dropped like Flakes – " erases the gore of death with its array of romantic metaphors, in "The name – of it – is 'Autumn'–" conventional poetic metaphors repeatedly go awry and always in gory fashion. The opening line of the poem suggests that we ought to read the "Blood" as a metaphor for the "hue" of the autumn landscape, but the details that accumulate around this central metaphor make such a reading untenable. Ultimately, the "Blood" that the poem offers as a metaphor can only be read as literal blood. To describe a landscape in relation to the human body is to follow the English romantic tradition; yet to make the "Artery" and "Vein" a central part of such comparisons is to emphasize the fragility of the human body and thus the violence that underpins these metaphors. Where "They dropped like Flakes –" links death "Seamless[ly]" with the snow, the "Stars" and the "Grass," "The name – of it – is 'Autumn'–" points to the violence erased by the other poem's metaphors. There is no blood in "They dropped like Flakes –" and nothing but blood in "The name – of it – is 'Autumn'–."

In comparing a battlefield to a fall landscape, "The name – of it – is 'Autumn'–" strongly echoes the many popular poems of the Civil War era that rely on this metaphor. The poems that Dickinson's "The name – of it – is 'Autumn'–" responds to include Whittier's "The Battle Autumn of 1862," Julia Ward Howe's "Battle Hymn of the Republic," and perhaps also W. L. Gage's "The Crimson Tree," which appeared in the *Springfield Republican* in October 1862.[29] What Dickinson's poem shares with these poems is its investment in representing a battlefield by means of pastoral imagery. In these poems, New England writers also redraw the boundaries between the personal and the public by layering a local autumnal New England landscape—perhaps a neighboring field or farm—onto the contested national landscapes of Southern battlefields. What separates Dickinson's poem from its popular counterparts, however, is Dickinson's refusal to read battlefield bloodshed as a cycle of redemptive suffering for the nation that is endorsed by God. When Howe evokes the wave of color and blood that issues from the autumn harvest in the first stanza of her poem ("He is trampling out the vintage where the grapes of wrath are stored"), the blood imagery is inseparable from the idea that God supports the Union position, that God endorses the power of bloodshed to rejuvenate and reunify the nation. Likewise in Whittier's poem, the female figure of Nature, closely allied with the Divine, waits patiently for the seasonal harvest of good that will follow the war's carnage: "For all the tears of blood we sow,/She waits the rich return." Gage's "The Crimson Tree" echoes Howe's and Whittier's poems in emphasizing the argument that God is the Maker both of the beautiful autumn landscape and of the "crimsoned waters" and "crimsoned sod" that result from the war. The poem presents a speaker who wanders through the autumn woods, contemplating the beauty and the sadness of the fall colors, his eye particularly drawn to one tree, an image that points strongly toward the crucifixion:

As I looked, I saw the color of blood,
One tree with crimson dye
Reached up above the colored flood,
And touched the gentled sky.

Yet 'twas a hue from God's own hand,
His touch had set it there

While Gage's poem threatens—like Dickinson's—to represent the landscape as flooded with gore, it controls this risk through a refrain that reiterates the idea that God's agency is at work in all worldly events: "Its Maker and Builder is God." In "The name – of it – is 'Autumn'–," Dickinson's refusal to represent God's role in the conflict becomes a refusal to ascribe Christian or nationalist meaning to wartime suffering and bloodshed.

Still another element of Dickinson's poem that distinguishes it from its popular counterparts is her acknowledgment that the war did not only take place in timeless pastoral settings. "They dropped like Flakes – ," like the Whittier and Gage poems, describes a battlefield solely in terms of a rural landscape; "The name – of it – is 'Autumn'–," however, ranges from the battlefield on "Hill" and "Road" to the "Alleys" of the cities and towns—where fighting also took place—to the "Basin" of blood in the war hospital and the "Vermillion Wheels" of the trains and ambulance wagons that bore the dead and wounded away from the scene of the fighting. Dickinson situates her poem in the immediate and historically specific setting of the modern warfare taking place on Southern battlefields. The movement that each stanza describes is the movement of blood, first implicitly through the "Artery" and "Vein," then explicitly with the "Shower of Stain" and the verbs "spill," "sprinkles," "gathers," and "eddies." Stanzas one and three are built around an emphatic use of the pronoun "it"—which is set off by dashes in stanza one and which starts the first two lines of stanza three; though the first line of the poem establishes "Autumn" as a referent for "it," the pronoun might also refer to "war" which remains unnamed in the poem. While the poem includes words that belong to the conventional repertoire for describing the natural world—the "Hill," the "Shower," the "Winds," the "Rain," the "Pools" and the "Rose," for example—the poem consistently disrupts the workings of these images. For example, the strongly alliterative phrase that opens stanza two—"Great Globules"—jars the poem's imagery with its sudden and graphic specificity about the quality of the blood. The dramatic "Oh" in this stanza's second line ("And Oh, the Shower of Stain –") mocks the use of the exclamation in lyric poetry, even as it also fleetingly implies that the speaker is a direct eyewitness to this scene of horror: the "Oh" here might be read as an ironic echo of a cry of pain.

In the final stanza, then, the poem's two metaphoric registers—which might be called the genteel-poetic and the medical—collide with each other decisively:

> It sprinkles Bonnets - far below -
> It gathers ruddy Pools -
> Then - eddies like a Rose - away -
> Opon Vermillion Wheels -

As part of the conventional poetic register, the word "Bonnets" also introduces a feminine figure—by way of metonymy—into the poem. The two meanings of "sprinkle" allow for two alternate readings of "Bonnets." In the first possibility, it is "Autumn" that scatters red "Bonnets" or leaves across the landscape; in this reading, the "Bonnets" have replaced the "Globules" as the central noun of the poem's grammar. In the second possible reading, the "Bonnets" are themselves "sprinkled" or stained with the drops or "Globules" of blood shed in the war. Taken symbolically, either possible reading suggests that women too have been touched by the war's violence. The poem then goes on to conclude with a climactic moment of metaphoric disjunction. In the third line of this stanza, Dickinson's speaker introduces a simile—for the first time—in a poem that has otherwise relied on unstated metaphorical links; the speaker insists that the blood "eddies *like* a Rose" (my emphasis). Yet the explicit statement of the metaphoric link only serves to underline the disconnection of the metaphor's two parts: the simile compares blood to the conventional "Rose," a comparison that seems deliberately and jarringly unsuccessful. While the spilling blood might well "edd[y]," it is more difficult to imagine an "edd[ying]" Rose. The poem's metaphoric structure founders, and this collapse would ultimately seem to point to the impossibility of rendering such a scene in genteel romantic imagery.

While "They dropped like Flakes" erases the bloodshed of the war and endorses the idea of a redemptive God who will save the fallen, "The name – of it – is 'Autumn'–" emphatically rejects the possibility of such an erasure or of Christian redemption for soldiers; "The name – of it – is 'Autumn'–" emphasizes that romantic imagery is inadequate to the task of representing war's violence. While the closing image of "The name – of it – is 'Autumn'–" suggests that the red leaves will vanish as quickly as they appeared, scattered by autumn winds, the persistence of the word "blood" in the poem belies that image of vanishing: the landscape has been indelibly stained. Moreover, "The name – of it – is 'Autumn'–" underlines the proximity of women ("Bonnets") to battlefields (a factually accurate detail for many Southern women), implicitly suggesting that women writers are not too removed from the war to represent it. Read in counterpoint to one another then, these two Dickinson poems would seem to suggest that conventional romantic metaphors—if not the genre of the romantic lyric poem itself—are inadequate for the task of representing modern war. Exposing the pastoral and ultimately Christian vision of "They dropped like Flakes" as fraudulent and deceptive, "The name – of it – is 'Autumn' –" suggests both that the bloodshed of war has no redemptive nationalist purpose and that the language of romantic poetry is inadequate to represent that bloodshed.

Reading Whitman's *Drum-Taps*, Timothy Sweet argues that the pastoral mode performs significant symbolic work in relation to the representation of violence, providing "a powerful, typifying structure of recuperation."[30] In the poetry of the war years, Whitman's poetics of the pastoral works to erase the political complexity of the dead bodies on the battlefield in order "to legitimate the outcome of the war and provide a vision of the future."[31] Perhaps the most obvious example of this strategy of legitimation in *Drum-Taps* is the poem "Pensive on Her Dead Gazing," which offers the symbolic figure of the "Mother of All," walking the battlefields and mourning the dead even as she calls on the earth to reabsorb and thus to recover their bodies. After the opening frame structure of the first four lines, in which the speaker describes overhearing the Mother's soliloquy, the remaining thirteen lines of the poem are devoted to the Mother's words. The figure's posture is dramatic and her speech high literary:

> Absorb them well O my earth, she cried, I charge you lose not my sons, lose not an atom [. . .]
>
> My dead absorb or South or North—my young men's bodies absorb, and their precious precious blood [. . .] (2: 527)

In keeping with the complexity and ambition of Whitman's larger aesthetic project, however, an example of a particular stance is often accompanied by a counterexample. The "Mother of All" is a figure of mourning who makes possible the recuperation of the dead through their reintegration into the natural world. In "Come Up from the Fields Father," however, Whitman describes a mother who cannot accept the loss of her son and whose continued mourning thus disrupts the pastoral idyll described in stanzas two and three of the poem. While I agree with Sweet's argument that the pastoral is fundamentally a recuperative mode in Whitman's *Drum-Taps*, in juxtaposing Whitman's battlefield landscapes with Dickinson's I want to attend in particular to passages in Whitman where the recuperative force of the pastoral threatens to collapse, undermining the metaphoric link between wartime bloodshed and nature's cycles of autumnal harvest and spring renewal.

Two short poems from *Drum-Taps* might be read as companion pieces to one another insofar as they depict aestheticized landscape scenes both before and after battle.[32] In both "Cavalry Crossing a Ford" and "Look Down Fair Moon" poetic gestures collide with journalistic description, and the speaker seems caught between these two stances. The result in each poem is an unresolved tension between pastoral symbolism and journalistic detail. As Ed Folsom argues, Whitman's interest in the battlefield photography of Matthew Brady and Alexander Gardner clearly shaped his depiction of battlefield scenes; like these photographers, Whitman updates the aesthetic conventions of the pastoral with a commitment to what Folsom calls "the clutter of reality," the kinds of individual antiheroic details that painters chose not to include but that photographers could not evade.[33] Just as traces of artistic intervention are evident in Brady's and Gardner's seemingly naturalized battlefield landscapes, so too do Whitman's landscape poems reveal the shaping hand of the poet.[34] In "Cavalry Crossing a Ford," which first appeared in 1865, Whitman's speaker offers a picturesque scene—presumably prior to battle—in which soldiers and landscape seem to blend harmoniously:

> A line in long array where they wind betwixt green islands,
> They take a serpentine course, their arms flash in the sun—hark to the musical clank,
> Behold the silvery river, in it the splashing horses loitering stop to drink,
> Behold the brown-faced men, each group, each person a picture, the negligent rest on the saddles,

Some emerge on the opposite bank, others are just entering the
ford—while,
Scarlet and blue and snowy white,
The guidon flags flutter gayly in the wind. (2: 457)

With its panoramic perspective, the poem strongly echoes the balloon and bird's eye views of battlefields that were widely circulated in Civil War–era magazines, showing both topography and the disposition of troops. In its commitment to detail, "Cavalry Crossing a Ford" offers a kind of all-inclusive photographic image of a cavalry unit on the march, making the wide-angle perspective of those photographic commitments explicit in line 4: "each group, each person a picture."[35]

Simultaneously, however, by emphasizing the movement of the soldiers, horses, and water, as well as the colors of the scene, the poem presents precisely the kind of scene that wartime sketch artists could capture but that photographers could not due to the limitations of the technology. The opening line of the poem—"A line in long array where they wind betwixt green islands"—presumably refers to the lines of soldiers, yet might also be read as referring to the river and its winding tributaries. The first three lines of the poem establish emphatic parallels between the movements and sounds of the soldiers and the movements and sounds of the river itself. The men "take a serpentine course." Their weapons, which "flash in the sun," provide a visual complement to the "silvery river"; their "musical clank" mingles pleasantly with the sound of "the splashing horses." The "negligent" ease and confidence of the soldiers seem almost to issue from the natural beauty and vitality of the landscape that surrounds them. The speaker's stance is that of a journalist insofar as the poem offers a detailed description of the scene, yet the harmonious aural and visual blending of the soldiers with the natural world underlines the artistic intervention of the poet-speaker.[36] Moreover, the series of dramatic imperatives to the reader emphasizes that this is a literary presentation of the scene: "hark to the musical clank" (line 2), "Behold the silvery river . . ." (line 3), "Behold the brown-faced men" (line 4). The imperatives have the paradoxical effect of drawing the reader's attention away from the horsemen, toward the speaker who is not merely observing but in fact staging the described scene.

This tension between journalistic realism and artistic intervention comes still more sharply into focus if we read the poem in relation to two wartime drawings by Alfred Waud that are strikingly similar to the poem and that may have influenced Whitman's shaping of this scene. On March 29, 1862, *Harper's Weekly* published a Waud sketch showing McClellan, McDowell, and their staffs escorted, as the caption explains, "by the Fifth Cavalry, Crossing Bull Run at Blackburn's Ford" (fig. 6).[37] Like the Whitman poem, the Waud drawing shows a long line of cavalry wending their way among "islands," taking a "serpentine course," with some horsemen "on the opposite bank" and some "just entering the ford" (2: 457). The sketch also shows horses stopping to drink. If Whitman relied on Waud's sketch in writing his poem, however, he revised or rearranged key details of the scene: not surprisingly, Whitman adds both colors ("green," "brown," "scarlet" and "blue") and sound ("musical clank") to the sketch-artist's black and white image. While Waud focuses on the group of generals and officers in the foreground, including specificity and detail in their facial expressions, Whitman refuses to rank or even to prioritize his soldiers, underlining his ideal of the democratic army and his strong support for the common soldier; no individual portraits come sharply into focus in the Whitman poem. Moreover, Whitman's poem puts considerably more emphasis on the guidon flags than Waud's image does. Ending the poem with the colors of the flags highlights their patriotic symbolism; by listing the colors of the flags only, however, Whitman avoids having to identify the horsemen as either Confederate or Union. And though the poem closes by focusing on the symbolic flags, it refuses to state explicitly a moral about the meaning of war or the role of nationalism. Still another Waud image from *Harper's Weekly*, this one showing a "Rebel Raid into Pennsylvania," offers even stronger parallels to the Whitman poem since it makes little distinction between officers and regular cavalry, including detailed facial portraits of both, and since it includes several horsemen in the "negligent" casual postures Whitman describes (fig. 7).[38] Whether or not Whitman was influenced by the Waud sketches, what the similarities between the sketches and the poem makes clear is that Whitman modeled his approach to battlefield landscapes on that of the groundbreaking wartime photographers and sketch-artists, mingling a journalist's commitment to detail and realism with an aesthetic commitment to the pastoral. And even as Whitman seeks to downplay or minimize the speaker's role in shaping or creating this scene, the poem's many literary gestures (the imperatives to the reader,

6. "Major-General McClellan, Major-General McDowell and Staffs Escorted by the Fifth Cavalry, Crossing Bull Run at Blackburn's Ford," magazine illustration, 1862

7. "The Rebel Raid into Pennsylvania—Stuart's Cavalry on Their Way to the Potomac," magazine illustration, 1862

the aestheticizing of the landscape, the concluding focus on the symbolic flags) work to foreground the poet-speaker's shaping interventions.

In the poem "Look Down Fair Moon," as in "Cavalry Crossing a Ford," genteel poetic imagery collides with gritty journalistic detail. In "Look Down Fair Moon," however, which describes a gruesome nighttime scene in the aftermath of battle, the tension between these two registers is more pronounced and the position of the speaker-observer is as a result less stable. The poem is strikingly brief:

> Look down fair moon and bathe this scene,
> Pour softly down night's nimbus floods on faces ghastly, swollen,
>   purple,
> On the dead on their backs with arms toss'd wide,
> Pour down your unstinted nimbus sacred moon. (2: 519–20)

As Folsom argues, Whitman's depiction of bloated corpses on the battlefield was clearly influenced by Brady's and Gardner's photographs of the dead.[39] Yet in this poem too, as in "Cavalry Crossing a Ford," Whitman chooses to focus on a scene photographic technology could not yet capture: in this case, a battlefield at night. The high literary trope of the address to the moon both opens and closes the poem and thus serves as a framework to contain the horrifying realism of the phrase that is at the poem's core: "faces ghastly, swollen, purple." This reliance on high literary tropes appears elsewhere in *Drum-Taps*, particularly in the poems to the *Sequel* which Whitman added after Lincoln's assassination. Reading Whitman's elegies for Lincoln, Justin Kaplan describes the poet's return to a more conventionally poetic diction as evidence of "a retreat from the idiomatic boldness and emotional directness of [his] earlier work."[40] With its dramatic posture of high literary address, the apostrophe in "Look Down Fair Moon" also represents a stylistic retreat back from the brink of modernism toward the commitments of nineteenth-century romanticism: transfixed by what he sees, the speaker effectively excludes the reader from the scene by dramatically addressing the moon. Whitman has abandoned the easy confidence of the imperatives to the reader that he employed in "Cavalry Crossing a Ford."

Yet though the apostrophe to the moon represents a retreat from Whitman's proto-modernist innovations, in "Look Down Fair Moon" that retreat does not offer the same kind of resolution it provides in the

Lincoln elegies. In "O Captain! My Captain!," for example, Whitman responds to the crisis of Lincoln's death by writing an elegy that reverts to the formal constraints of the lyric tradition both in its metrical regularity and in its repeated use of the apostrophe.[41] The catalogue of poetic techniques employed in "O Captain! My Captain!" has the cumulative effect of erasing the historical specificity of Lincoln's death and inserting the poem into the timeless elegiac tradition of "Lycidas" and "Adonais." The poem thus provides resolution by establishing Lincoln's death as a heroic one through association with the elegiac tradition.

In "Look Down Fair Moon," however, the gesture of the apostrophe seems incommensurate with the scene of carnage that the poem presents. While the speaker calls on the moon to "bathe this scene" with its "unstinted nimbus," the scene that the poem offers is horrifying in its detail and specificity: the "faces" are "ghastly, swollen, purple" and the "dead" are "on their backs with arms toss'd wide." The poem does not capture "night's nimbus floods" softening such a gruesome sight; rather it presents a speaker who, transfixed by the horror before him, calls on the moon to do so. While the speaker in "Cavalry Crossing a Ford" insists on representing a harmonious blending of soldiers with the natural world, in "Look Down Fair Moon," the relationship between the natural world and the battlefield is more ambiguous symbolically. Does the speaker call on the moon to shed a realist light on the horror of wartime slaughter? Or does he call on the moon to cast a romantic aura or nimbus of heroism around each dead man's face? Will nature reveal all the horror of modern war? Or will the moon recreate a redemptive harmony between the human and natural worlds? While the speaker seems to call on the moon to soften the scene ("Pour softly down . . ."), the poem offers no guarantee that the gesture of the apostrophe will be an effective or redemptive one: rather, the drama of the poem lies in its presentation of a speaker who wields the poetic apostrophe without evident success. The brevity of the poem only heightens the drama of this uncertainty.

In these poems then, Dickinson and Whitman examine the possibilities for representing violence by means of images drawn from the natural world. "They dropped like Flakes –" and "Cavalry Crossing a Ford" offer harmonious visions of heroic bodies merging with a vital and redemptive American landscape; in these poems, the speaker's position as witness is secure and authoritative. In "The name – of it – is 'Autumn' – " and "Look

Down Fair Moon," however, this redemptive perspective is revealed to be fraudulent and deceptive. While "Look Down Fair Moon" relies on the high literary apostrophe to control the horror of the faces of the dead, the balance the poem establishes between the literary trope and the gruesome depiction of the dead is a precarious one; the speaker's position is precarious as well. Though the poems in Whitman's *Drum-Taps* frequently rely on pastoral symbolism to imagine reconciliation and harmony after the war, "Look Down Fair Moon" points out that such reconciliation will require the wholesale erasure of the collective memory of violence and death. In "The name – of it – is 'Autumn' – ," Dickinson explicitly rejects the possibility of such an erasure. Simultaneously she suggests that the poetic register of the pastoral is inadequate to represent the horrors of the scene. "Look Down Fair Moon" and "The name – of it – is 'Autumn' – " suggest that the blood that has drenched the American landscape cannot easily be washed away; both poems also suggest that there is no secure outside position from which the war can be witnessed.

In these poems, both writers probe the limits of the lyric speaker's position as witness to suffering; simultaneously through their exploration of the romantic scene of address, Dickinson and Whitman consider the dilemmas an American writer faces in addressing the nation in a time of war. As I have suggested, the speaker's stance in "Look Down Fair Moon" represents a stylistic retreat for Whitman—a retreat from the easy confidence with which his speaker commands the reader in "Cavalry Crossing a Ford." In "Look Down Fair Moon," Whitman reverts to the romantic apostrophe to nature, placing his readers in the position of eavesdroppers as his speaker turns away from the audience. The brevity of the poem speaks both to the speaker's horror at the scene and to Whitman's uneasiness with this speaker's stance. The contrast between "Look Down Fair Moon" and "Cavalry Crossing a Ford" implies that Whitman is conflicted about whether to continue the bold innovation of his direct addresses to the reader or to return to the romantic fiction of the solitary lyric speaker who is seemingly unaware of his audience.

As I have suggested in these comparative readings, it is the judicious balance of patriotic ardor and proto-modernist skepticism in the body of Walt Whitman's war poetry that leads to his critical success in the twentieth century. Whitman styles himself as the national bard of the war, and twentieth-century critics endorse his status in that role, finding in Whitman's war poems both the spare direct language they seek in a precursor to modernism and an unobjectionable celebration of the heroism of Civil War soldiers. If "Apostroph" signals Whitman's anxiety about the impossibility of uniting the nation through the rhetoric of address, it also signals his determination to address the nation in his war poetry; the twentieth-century scholars who first helped to establish Whitman's centrality in the canon tended to overlook the anxiety and to endorse the ambition of his addresses to the nation. In poems like "Look Down Fair Moon" and "Cavalry Crossing a Ford," Whitman relies on the understated language and seemingly detached description that critics would come to value in poets of the First World War and later conflicts. Whitman's reputation as the bard of the war is only confirmed for scholars by the two Lincoln elegies that he wrote—"O Captain, My Captain" and "When Lilacs Last in the Dooryard Bloomed"—two of his most widely anthologized and best loved poems in the twentieth century. The mix of traditional literary devices with the innovative form of free verse that Whitman uses in these two pieces provides scholars with a praiseworthy balance of old and new. Finally Whitman's extensive period of service in the military hospitals gives his war poetry the imprimatur of authenticity: though he did not himself see combat, he had extensive and direct contact with soldiers who did. Whitman's poetic stances, his formal choices, and his wartime activities thus all worked to confirm his status as the national bard of the war.

By contrast, Dickinson's poetic stances, her formal choices, her geographic distance from the war, and her gender all worked to confirm twentieth-century scholars' sense that she had little interest in the war and little to say about it. In reading Dickinson's responses to romanticism in relation to Whitman's, I have argued, however, that her critique of the limits of the romanticism constitutes a pointed rejoinder to wartime ideologies. Dickinson's two battlefield landscape poems offer a sharp critique of the romantic scene of address by sustaining the fiction of a soliloquizing speaker who is rapt in solitary contemplation of nature's wonders. In poems like these, Dickinson relies on romantic imagery to lend a veneer of genteel authenticity to her project: women writers and artists of the nineteenth century are expected to offer decorative or ornamental landscape descriptions. Yet Dickinson's gory but decorative battlefield landscapes satirically undermine the idea that women writers lack the authority or perspective to represent combat. At the same time, these poems suggest that the romantic lexicon—widely used by American poets to endorse the commitments of nationalism during the Civil War—is inadequate to the task of representing battlefield suffering. In these poems, Dickinson points toward the exhaustion of the romantic vision of nature; commenting indirectly on the rise of new weapons technologies that enable armies to inflict massive numbers of casualties in modern combat, Dickinson's work points also toward the inadequacy of first-person expressive lyric stances to bear witness to suffering on this scale. While Dickinson's radical skepticism about the limitations of the lyric poem prefigures the ambivalence of modernist stances, it is that same skepticism that leads scholars trained in New Critical reading methods to overlook the intensity of her engagement with the political discourses of her day. Using these comparative readings of Dickinson's and Whitman's critiques of romanticism as a foundation, I will turn now to an analysis of Dickinson's engagement with the genre of the soldier elegy in order to argue that her work not only critiques but also at times endorses the ideologies of nationalism and Christian martyrdom in battle.

"Drums off the Phantom Battlements": Dickinson's Civil War Elegies

While Emily Dickinson frequently turns to romantic imagery to represent grand battlefield vistas, in meditating on the meaning of individual deaths and losses in the war she draws from a very different set of discursive models, including theological and sentimental arguments about the larger meaning of wartime losses, patriotic nationalist arguments in wide circulation in Civil War–era magazines and newspapers, in popular songs and poems, and in the genre of the Civil War elegy in particular. Trying her hand at the enormously popular genre of the soldier elegy, Dickinson writes a series of poems that may respond to the deaths of young soldiers she knew from Amherst or more broadly to battlefield deaths, a subject that was ubiquitous in the newspapers the Dickinson family read. In reading a group of Dickinson's Civil War elegies, I will consider how she represents the initial shock of grief, how she responds to arguments about Christian martyrdom on the battlefield, and how she represents the culturally central relationship between mothers and their soldier-sons.

Reading Dickinson's elegies comparatively with contemporary newspaper articles, popular songs, and poems, my analysis will attend in particular to the responses Dickinson offers to wartime discourses about the most appropriate ways of mourning soldiers' deaths and about racial tensions within the military.

In a group of poems that seem to respond to the death of Frazar Stearns, son of the president of Amherst College and a friend of her brother Austin, Dickinson explores the stances of the Civil War elegy with a particular sense of urgency. Even scholars who suggest Dickinson took little notice of the war remark on the intensity of her response to this loss.[42] Stearns's death in March 1862 at the age of twenty-one in the Battle of New Bern (North Carolina) corresponds to the time in Dickinson's life that biographers have identified as an era of a life-shattering personal crisis of an undetermined nature.[43] Two letters that she wrote at this time suggest that Stearns's death in particular—and developments in the war more broadly—may have figured as part of this crisis. In a letter to her cousins Louise and Frances Norcross from late March 1862, Dickinson offers a vivid and arresting description of Stearns's death and funeral, and details in the letter make clear that she was reading about the war and Stearns's death in local newspapers:

> . . . 'tis the least that I can do, to tell you of brave Frazer—"killed at Newbern," darlings. His big heart shot away by a "minie ball."
>
> I had read of those—I didn't think that Frazer would carry one to Eden with him. Just as he fell, in his soldier's cap, with his sword at his side, Frazer rode through Amherst. Classmates to the right of him, and classmates to the left of him, to guard his narrow face!
>
> (JL 255)

Dickinson notes that Stearns was killed by a "minie ball," a new kind of bullet, developed in 1848 by the Frenchman Claude Etien Minié and further refined by American weapon makers throughout the 1850s and the early years of the war; her reference to the specific kind of bullet—emphasized by her self-conscious mention of having read about them—punningly underlines the contrast in scale between the dead soldier's "big heart" and the "minie ball" that killed him. Echoing Tennyson's "Charge of the Light Brigade" (1854), Dickinson's description of Stearns riding through Amherst with his classmates to the right and left of him conflates the scene of his departure from Amherst at the time of his enlistment with the scene of his funeral, at which all members of his Amherst class walked in the procession, dressed in mourning. This conflation seems to endorse the view that Stearns both lived and died nobly, and the letter implicitly echoes newspaper depictions of Stearns's bravery and heroism. Concluding her description of the funeral, Dickinson evokes both Stearns's family's grief and their pious acceptance of the loss in a particularly vivid sentence: "And the family bowed their heads, as the reeds the wind shakes" (JL 255).

The shock that the Dickinson family felt at Stearns's death comes still more strongly to the fore in another letter Dickinson wrote, this time to Samuel Bowles, a family friend and the editor of the *Springfield Republican*. The letter is so agitated in its emotion and so oblique in its feints and strategies that one can only conjecture what other incidents—apart from Stearns's death—may have prompted its writing. Johnson suggests that Dickinson uses Austin's name as a cover for her own; in the paragraph concerning Stearns, the references to Austin seem to describe emotions shared by brother and sister:

> Austin is chilled—by Frazer's murder—He says—his Brain keeps saying over "Frazer is killed" –"Frazer is killed," just as Father told it—to Him. Two or three words of lead—that dropped so deep, they keep weighing. (JL 256)

"Two or three words of lead" may suggest a kind of collision of the emotional impact of the news of Stearns's death and that of some other painful sequence of words or an unidentified event in Dickinson's own life. She pleads with Bowles: "Tell Austin –how to get over them!," a plea that is the most urgent moment of distress in the letter. The fatal wounding of Stearns is echoed in the imagery that Dickinson uses to describe her family's response to his death: the "two or three words of lead" wound them just as the lead bullet wounded him. Here, as so often in her work, Dickinson represents language as a wounding and penetrating force; this image may also underline the connection between some other words that have pained her and the phrase "Frazer is killed." Describing Stearns's death as "murder," Dickinson seems to divorce the death from the context of the socially sanctioned killing that takes place in wartime; the shock effect of the word also seems to differentiate Dickinson's private reaction to Stearns's death from the public reaction of his family who "bowed their heads" at his funeral service (JL 255).

In the poem that Johnson links to this letter, "It dont sound so terrible – quite – as it did," the speaker meditates on the shock of losing someone to a sudden violent death and the role of repetition in the survivor's attempt to come to terms with that loss:[44]

> It dont sound so terrible – quite – as it did –
> I run it over – "Dead", Brain – "Dead".
> Put it in Latin – left of my school –
> Seems it dont shriek so – under rule.
>
> Turn it, a little – full in the face
> A Trouble looks bitterest –
> Shift it – just –
> Say "When Tomorrow comes this way –
> I shall have waded down one Day".
>
> I suppose it will interrupt me some
> Till I get accustomed – but then the Tomb
> Like other new Things – shows largest – then –
> And smaller, by Habit –
>
> It's shrewder then
> Put the Thought in advance – a Year –
> How like "a fit" – then –
> Murder – wear! (F 384)

One argument of the poem seems to be that repetition is a necessary part of the cycle of grief, as the speaker tries to persuade herself to recognize the loss that has occurred: "It dont sound so terrible – quite – as it did – / I run it over – 'Dead', Brain – 'Dead'." The phrase "I run it over" suggests the repetitive gestures of ironing or of classroom memorization, an association that is underlined by the first stanza's reference to Latin and "school." These lines suggest that powerful emotion can be disciplined—brought "under rule"—through a numbing repetition that resembles a rote pedagogy. A second and darker argument, however, says that there is no effective way to accustom the self to losses either present or impending, and the dual meanings of the preposition "over" encapsulate the speaker's ambivalent perspective on whether or not a survivor can recover from such a loss. Suggesting both railway and carriage accidents, the phrase "I run it over" points emphatically toward the finality of death (a life is now "over"), and the speaker's position as agent in this sentence suggests her sense of responsibility or guilt that she has survived while the other has not. Simultaneously, the phrase "I run it over" points to the cycle of traumatic recollection and grieving in which the speaker is hopelessly caught as she reviews the details of the death in her mind; this cycle threatens to undermine the pious or patriotic acceptance of loss for which many Civil War elegies and obituaries argued. The closing lines of the poem urge the speaker to anticipate deaths a year in advance so as not to be caught off guard by them ("Put the Thought in advance – a Year –"), even as the speaker tries to imagine how she will feel a year after the loss, hoping that the experience of the loss will by then better "fit" the "Thought" of it.

But the use of the word "Murder" in the poem's final line suggests that even with advance notice or even a year later, the speaker may be no more able to cope with the loss. The noun "fit" may imply that the speaker has adjusted to the person's absence; alternatively, the speaker may still suffer a "fit" or outburst of uncontrollable emotion, the "shriek" that can't be kept "under rule." While Dickinson's use of the word "Murder" divorces the individual's death from the ideological context of war, if we read the poem as a response to the genre of the Civil War elegy, the word "Murder" then serves to reframe collective narratives of wartime loss in order to emphasize the individual specificity of the life that has been lost and the individual specificity of the grief felt by the mourners. Dickinson's resistance to representing this death in relation to the war suggests a refusal to represent death in a way that subsumes the soldier's individuality in a narrative of collective sacrifice for the greater good of the nation. Her refusal to situate the death in the context of war also signals her resistance to the Christian narratives of acceptance and closure offered by the obituaries in local newspapers. A *Hampshire and Franklin Express* piece praises Stearns's family's reaction to the news of his death: "Although coming with such suddenness, they bore it with Christian resignation—feeling that they had entrusted him in the hands of the Almighty, 'who doeth all things well.'"[45] As a minister and a president of Amherst College, Stearns's father would have been expected to respond with faith and humility to such an event. In the intimate space of her poetry, however, Dickinson was under no such obligation. We have no evidence that Dickinson circulated this poem in correspondence.

Reading this poem in relation to her other war poems, however, makes clear that this is just one position on the spectrum of ideological stances she tested out in response to soldiers' deaths in the war. "It dont sound so terrible – quite – as it did – " was completed or copied out in the early 1860s, possibly within months of Stearns's death, and at a time when she was working on other poems that responded still more explicitly to the war. One of these pieces begins with a similar set of images about memory and repetition and takes up the theological arguments often mustered in response to battlefield deaths:

> Over and over, like a Tune –
> The Recollection plays –
> Drums off the Phantom Battlements
> Cornets of Paradise –
>
> Snatches, from Baptized Generations –
> Cadences too grand
> But for the Justified Processions
> At the Lord's Right hand. (F 406)

The returning "Recollection" alluded to in the first stanza's second line may be the memory of Stearns; the imagery of the rest of the poem—which figures death on the battlefield as a glorious procession of the "Justified" to the throne of God—certainly includes strong echoes of the language that local writers used in describing Stearns's heroism and his faith. The Hampshire and Franklin Express account of his funeral excerpted a eulogy that described Stearns's response to the attack on Fort Sumter in terms of a trumpet's call to arms:

> The fall of Fort Sumter, which roused the nation from its fatal slumber startled young Stearns like the sound of a trumpet; and on that dark and portentous Sunday, when so many ministers preached and so many congregations heard the Word under the fearful apprehension that the flag of secession already darkened the capital, the ardent young man thought it no breach of the Sabbath to enroll a company, if needed, for the defense of Washington, and at the head of the list of young patriot warriors stood the name of Frazar A. Stearns.[46]

This mingling of theological with military commitments was, of course, central to Civil War ideologies on both sides of the conflict, and writers in western Massachusetts were particularly emphatic in linking Stearns's Christian faith with his military ardor. The memorial volume that Stearns's father wrote and edited effectively represents his son's death on the battlefield as the final stage in a conversion narrative; through quotes from Stearns's letters, from fellow soldiers, and in his father's words, the volume figures Stearns's death as the will of God and as an instance of Christian martyrdom.

These passages emphatically portray Stearns's relatively brief but much acclaimed military career as a spiritually tranquil and confident time in his life, after the more tumultuous religious struggles of his adolescence, struggles that the volume depicts as a cyclical waxing and waning of his spiritual commitment. An excerpt his father includes from his letters emphasizes that Stearns saw his military service as a religious vocation, a calling that offered a harmonious resolution to his previous struggles with faith: "If God tells me to go and fight, or even *die*, for my country, would you tell me not to go?"[47] The memorial volume foregrounds both the episode of Stearns's baptism as an infant and the early experience of grace that led to his becoming a full member of the church at the age of twelve, details that the poem echoes in its references to "Baptised Generations" and "Justified Processions." The Christian martial "Tune" that is the poem's central image also seems to echo the link that Dickinson establishes in her letter to her Norcross cousins between Stearns's martyrdom and his love of music. Dickinson suggests that when her cousins come to visit the following spring, the women can share their memories of Stearns through music:

> So our part in Frazer is done, but you must come next summer, and we will mind ourselves of this young crusader—too brave that he could fear to die. We will play his tunes—maybe he can hear them. (JL 255)

The repetition that musical performance requires will allow the women to honor the memory of the "young crusader."

In "Over and over, like a Tune –," Dickinson echoes wartime ideologies that represent Christian soldiers' deaths as a triumphant reunion with God. The cyclical pattern of the Christian soldier's waxing and waning belief—implicitly represented in the poem's opening image, "Over and over, like a Tune"—is resolved by his heroic martyrdom, his passage into the realm of the divine. While the poem's first two lines also suggest the survivor's struggle to come to terms with a traumatic loss, the repetition of "over and over" also implies that not one, but many thousands of soldiers will die, and the poem's abundance of plural nouns underlines this image of a vast army. While the poem seems to endorse the view that soldiers are marching in "processions" at God's "Right hand," it also emphasizes the speaker's distance from this otherworldly battlefield, this vision of Judgment Day. Even as the poem offers comfort to those who mourn a soldier's death by framing his death as divinely sanctioned, this shared narrative of collective loss inevitably distances the dead from the living and erases the soldier's individuality. By refusing to specify whether the army is the Union or Confederate force, the poem implicitly makes the point that both sides of the conflict rely on these narratives of martyrdom. If "It dont sound so terrible – quite – as it did –" and "Over and over, like a Tune –" are about Stearns's death, then Dickinson tests two opposing responses to that death: in the former poem, she insists on the soldier's individuality by divorcing his death from the contexts of the war and of religion; in the latter, she makes sense of the death by endorsing the ideology that fallen soldiers were martyrs in a holy war. While that endorsement is at least partially destabilized by the fact that the poem does not specify which army this soldier fought for—or which side God might be on in the war—many poems of the Civil War era did not make their partisan allegiances explicit, relying instead on rhetorical context to identify the writer's positions.[48] Though we have no firm evidence that Dickinson circulated this poem to friends or relatives of Frazar Stearns, if she did so, the context of her family's friendship with the Stearns family and the community's deep sense of loss would have enabled her readers to interpret this poem as endorsement of the view that Stearns died a Christian martyr in a holy war.

In two other poems from this period, Dickinson tests out still other arguments about the larger meaning of individual soldiers' deaths in the war. She may have written these poems in response to the anniversary of Stearns's death, to the deaths of other soldiers she knew, or more broadly to the high death tolls at Antietam or at Chancellorsville. In ways both direct and indirect, these poems suggest that Dickinson was reading widely about the war in newspapers and magazines. In "When I was small, a Woman died –" (F 518), Dickinson represents a mother-son relationship, responding to the frequent focus on mother-son pairings in Civil War literature, if not also to the deaths of a specific historical mother and son.[49] Though some details in the poem do not match Stearns's life story, his mother died during his childhood, a detail that suggests Dickinson may have had him partly in mind in writing the poem:[50]

When I was small, a Woman died –
Today – her Only Boy
Went up from the Potomac –
His face all Victory

To look at her – How slowly
The Seasons must have turned
Till Bullets clipt an Angle
And He passed quickly round –

If pride shall be in Paradise –
Ourself cannot decide –
Of their imperial conduct –
No person testified –

But, proud in Apparition –
That Woman and her Boy
Pass back and forth, before my Brain
As even in the sky –

I'm confident, that Bravoes –
Perpetual break abroad
For Braveries, remote as this
In Yonder Maryland – (F 518)

Like the two poems that seem to respond to Stearns's death, this poem foregrounds images of repetition, including the mother (or perhaps the son) watching the turning of the seasons and waiting and the speaker watching mother and son "pass back and forth before [her] Brain." These images of repetition again point toward the survivor's struggle to cope with the recurring trauma of loss. In its syntactical ambiguity, the second stanza evokes both the mother's and the son's grief simultaneously.

With the mother's death, mother and son are caught in a turning cycle of the seasons, a suspended state of mourning and waiting; according to the poem, the only resolution they can hope for is a reunion through his death. The image of the revolving seasons during their time of separation is reiterated by the circular image of the soldier passing "round" to death after the "Bullets clipt an Angle," a pairing of images conjoining the cyclical or seasonal time of the mother's experience and the linear chronological time associated with the masculine narratives of military heroism.

These images of circling or spiraling movement also suggest that Dickinson was aware of changes in the design of bullets for military use. It was the spin taken on by the minié ball in its trajectory through the spiral grooves in the rifle barrel that made this bullet both more accurate and capable of longer range. The trajectory of the spinning bullet is imagistically transferred to the body of the soldier himself as he spins "round" in death. An 1859 article on "Rifled Guns" in the *Atlantic Monthly* includes a detailed explanation of the ways that American gun-makers had improved on European designs both in the spiral grooving of the rifle barrel and in the conical shape of the bullets, a design first invented by Minié whose name was then associated with later bullets of similar design. Emphasizing the importance of the grooving of the barrel, the article's anonymous author writes: "The ball requires an initial rotary motion sufficient to keep it 'spinning' up to its required range, and is found to gain accuracy by increasing this rotatory speed."[51] Dickinson links the accuracy of the spinning bullet—which takes the young soldier "quickly round" to death—with the repetition of the trauma of the son's loss in the mother's memory. The painfully slow turning of the seasons from the mother's perspective is resolved by the quickly spinning bullet which reunites mother and son in death. Dickinson's arresting image adds a spiral trajectory to the linear tracking of the bullet, so that the bullet—like the young soldier—moves both in a circle and in a straight line. The collision between the cyclical, seasonal time of the mother's experience and the linear trajectory of the son's military career is resolved by an afterlife reunion that effectively removes both characters from the realm of the temporal.

While the poem's fourth stanza returns to images of repetition as the speaker imagines mother and son passing "back and forth, before my Brain," the speaker seems to come to an acceptance of the soldier's death through the imagined reunion of mother and son. Though the speaker struggles with grief—as suggested by the image of mother and son passing "back and forth" repeatedly in her mind—by the poem's final stanza, she seems to have arrived at an interpretation that makes the soldier's death culturally meaningful and purposeful:

> I'm confident, that Bravoes –
> Perpetual break abroad
> For Braveries, remote as this
> In Yonder Maryland –

Like "Over and over, like a Tune," "When I was small, a Woman died –" seems to endorse the view that soldiers are dying in a holy war. The poem ends with the confident assertion that the soldier's bravery will be recognized and celebrated both in the human world and in the afterlife. The poem's investment in endorsing this interpretation seems in large part to depend on the speaker's desire to imagine closure and posthumous happiness for the mother, a reunion "proud in Apparition" between mother and son.[52] The speaker's stance in this stanza signals the strength of Dickinson's own emotional investment in narratives that envisioned happy reunions for families ravaged by the war; she would have known many Amherst families who lost sons or brothers to the conflict.[53]

In still another war poem, Dickinson focuses not on reunions in the afterlife, but rather on the burden of guilt born by the war's survivors. In "It feels a shame to be Alive –," Dickinson considers the sacrifice made by the Civil War dead and questions whether or not the living are worthy of the price that has been paid on their behalf. The newspapers and magazines the Dickinson family subscribed to offered a wealth of information about the war's economic consequences in 1862 and 1863, articles that explained Lincoln's measures for funding the war effort and that listed revenues and debts, gains and losses for both the Union and the Confederacy. In February 1863, an *Atlantic Monthly* article entitled "The Law of Costs" relied on financial metaphors to describe the nation's moral obligations, suggesting that the Union would pay a terrible price for its failure to abolish slavery. "It feels a shame to be Alive –" responds both to recent economic developments in the Union and to the central argument of "The Law of Costs," which suggests that blood sacrifice is necessary to repay the nation's "debt to destiny":[54]

It feels a shame to be Alive –
When Men so brave – are dead –
One envies the Distinguished Dust –
Permitted – such a Head –

The Stone – that tells defending Whom
This Spartan put away
What little of Him we – possessed
In Pawn for Liberty –

The price is great – Sublimely paid –
Do we deserve – a Thing –
That lives – like Dollars – must be piled
Before we may obtain?

Are we that wait – sufficient worth –
That such Enormous Pearl
As life – dissolved be – for Us –
In Battle's – horrid Bowl?

It may be – a Renown to live –
I think the Men who die –
Those unsustained – Saviors –
Present Divinity – (F 524)

The poem opens with the speaker's gesture of self-abasement before the heroism of the soldiers who have sacrificed their lives; this gesture of self-abasement is both depersonalized and generalized by means of the phrase "It feels a shame" which locates this emotion not within one person, but within a larger collective of noncombatants and survivors. Describing the memorial or tomb of the soldiers, stanza two foregrounds the names of those whom they died defending rather than the names of the soldiers themselves; these lines also point toward the economic exigencies that drive the war, declaring that lives have been placed "in Pawn for Liberty –."

As the poem proceeds, Dickinson responds to several developments in the economic crisis that the North faced in 1862–63. In February 1862, Lincoln signed the Legal Tender act which created the first successful paper money system in the United States, a system in which bills were not secured by coin; the paper currency was designed to help the Union meet the rising costs of war. Stanza three's image of "piled" dollars points to the production of "greenbacks," as the bills were often called. In March 1862—the month of Frazar Stearns's death—Lincoln proposed that any state willing to end slavery should be offered compensation for the value of slaves manumitted; he pointed out that the money being spent on the war effort far exceeded the cost of reimbursing slaveholders for freed slaves. In April 1862, this compensation was provided to slave owners in the District of Columbia, with owners receiving $300 per slave. In July 1862, Lincoln signed into law the first real income tax legislation, still another measure designed to provide continuing funding for the war effort. And finally in March 1863, three months after signing the Emancipation Proclamation and a year after Stearns's death, Lincoln authorized the first conscription act in the North, making white men between the ages of twenty and forty-five eligible for the draft unless they could afford $300 for a substitute. The cost of buying a substitute was thus set at the same amount as the financial compensation provided to slave owners in Washington, DC.

In the Dickinson family the conscription act would have registered with particular force, since Austin was thirty-four at the time of its passage and since the act designated men under thirty-five as the group that would be drafted first. In the months following the passage of the conscription act, the *Springfield Republican* emphasized news about its implementation, publishing a regular column of "Items about the Draft" as well as lists of the drafted, grouped by their local communities; names of drafted men thus stood in columns where lists of the dead and wounded often appeared. In April 1863, *Harper's New Monthly* notes that "any person actually drafted may be discharged from the draft by furnishing an acceptable substitute or by paying a sum not exceeding 300 dollars"; the article also notes that there are some three million "able-bodied men between the ages of 20 and 45" who are "liable to be called into military service."[55] After summarizing the financial and the conscription measures and the suspension of *habeas corpus* passed by the Lincoln administration, the article observes that "power more ample was never assumed by or confided to any ruler."[56] Registering both the vast sums of money and the vast numbers of lives at stake, Dickinson's poem calls into question the printing and spending of money, the buying of soldiers and slaves, and the killing of men that the war machine requires. While the *Atlantic Monthly* essay argues that "whatever has a worth also has a cost," Dickinson counters "The price is great – Sublimely paid."[57]

Cristanne Miller notes that the poem takes on directly the moral dilemmas inherent in Northern white men hiring substitutes for the draft, as Dickinson's brother Austin would later do in May 1864; many scholars have noted that Austin's decision to pay for a substitute may have been a particularly difficult one in view of his friendship with Stearns.[58] Dickinson examines this complex array of wartime economic developments, weighing the slave's "Liberty" against the body of the fallen Union soldier; weighing the "Liberty" of the wealthy Union draftee against the body of his working-class substitute; weighing Northern ideals of "Liberty" against Southern ones, with dead bodies marking the difference between them.[59] In this poem, Dickinson suggests that all noncombatants—a group she describes with the collective first-person plural "we that wait"—have effectively bought substitutes for themselves, but at a terrible price. It seems no accident that Dickinson uses a rare "we" (presumably a reference to noncombatant Northerners, but possibly including all civilians) in a poem in which she also dissects the moral hypocrisy of the noncombatant's position. Stanza four juxtaposes the uniqueness and individuality of the life that has been lost—"such Enormous Pearl"—with the anonymous interchangeability of the many lives that have been "piled" like "Dollars" on the battlefield. Though the poem concludes with the speaker's assertion that the men who die "Present Divinity," she also represents them as "unsustained – Saviors," suggesting that the support—financial or otherwise—provided by those who do not fight is insufficient or inappropriate to the soldiers' sustenance. Like "When I was small, a Woman died," which represents a soldier's heroism as an ascent to heaven, "It feels a shame to be Alive –" represents fallen soldiers as divine. Unlike the former poem, however, "It feels a shame to be Alive" offers a scathing critique of the moral complacency and blindness of those who have remained at home—suggesting that "we that wait" achieve the ideal of "Liberty," or for that matter our own "Renown," only by pawning off the lives of soldiers. "Are we that wait – sufficient worth –?" asks the speaker. The poem refuses its readers the comforts and security of an affirmative answer.

While several of Dickinson's war poems reflect on the experience of noncombatant survivors, meditating on the meaning of Civil War deaths, in still other poems she explores the soldier's experience of the pleasures of combat, the intensity of the emotion and the comradery that accompany war's violence. The much-anthologized "My Life had stood – a Loaded Gun –" (F 764) is seen as a paradigmatic Dickinson poem and has become a touchstone for feminist readings of her work.[60] With elliptical syntax and focus on the pleasures of violence, to twenty-first-century eyes the poem seems far removed from the genteel rhymed verse of Dickinson's nineteenth-century contemporaries—Whittier, Bryant, or Longfellow, for example. Yet the poem signals the strength of Dickinson's connections to nineteenth-century discourses: first because it strongly echoes a popular war poem from the same era and second because it arguably responds to the narrative of Stearns's Christian conversion and his martyrdom in battle.

On July 4, 1863, *Harper's Weekly* published an anonymously authored 17-stanza poem titled "The Gun"; the poem offers a first-person description of a battlefield scene in the voice of an artillery piece. Since Austin and Susan Dickinson regularly received *Harper's Weekly* and since magazines were often exchanged between the two households, it is possible Dickinson saw the poem. At the very least, the parallels between the two texts suggest that Dickinson had read many accounts of combat and many popular poems representing it. While the longer, more conventional poem reminds a reader that the Dickinson poem is a tour de force of compression and paradox, the parallels between the two poems are nonetheless striking; that both poems present the gun as their speaker is just one of several similarities between the two. Tropes that personify guns are not uncommon in Civil War–era poetry, though such tropes are not usually sustained for the length of the poem; the sustaining of the trope is thus another parallel.[61]

Like the Dickinson poem, "The Gun" emphasizes the pleasures of violence or combat, using imagery of sexual release to represent both killing and the emotional and physical intimacy that develops among comrades in arms. Both poems sidestep the shock effect of the human pleasure of participating in violence by making the gun the first-person speaker. The intimacy of comradery comes clearly to the fore in the first three stanzas of "The Gun," which describe the making of the gun, a light artillery piece:

From my bed, quick! roll me out,
  I am choked with this hot sand;
And my throat swells with a shout,
  Gathering that shall shake the land.

Clear me with your twisted probes,
  Smooth me round with biting steel,
Fit me with your iron globes,
  Set me up on oaken wheel.

Ho! I am the conquering gun,
 Iron son of fire and noise;
Through my frame already run
 Thrills obscure of coming joys.

Like the Dickinson poem, "The Gun" moves briskly from peace to wartime. Just as the speaker in "The Gun" is forged for the war effort, so too does the speaker in the Dickinson poem find an identity with the outbreak of war ("The Owner passed – identified – / And carried Me away –" [F 764]). The *Harper's Weekly* poem, however, relies on frequent use of the imperative to voice a rousing call to arms; the poem also positions itself clearly on the side of the Union, arguing that lives must be lost in order to preserve the nation. The next two stanzas make this allegiance explicit, identifying soldiers both as factory workers and farmers and making clear whose flag they are dying to defend:

Come ye men from forge and farm—
 Men of might in arm and knee;
He whose blood takes quick alarm
 Better not companion me.

Wheel me Southward: are those graves
 On the slope of yonder hill?
Yes, but o'er them proudly waves
 The old starry banner still.

The next six stanzas then go on to describe a scene of combat, using imagery that figures the shooting of the gun both in terms of its eye and in terms of its voice, images that have direct parallels in Dickinson's evocation of the gun's voice ("And every time I speak for Him – / The Mountains straight reply –") and the gun's eye ("None stir the second time – / On whom I lay a Yellow Eye –"):

Rest me now upon this height:
 What is that before the rim
Of the forest? Look! My sight
 Is a little blurred and dim.

Ah! I see—quick with a shell
In my throat—boom—there it goes

Though the poem justifies the conflict as having the aim of preserving the Union, it does move in a darker direction in its last five stanzas, where so many soldiers seem to have died that there are few left for the speaker to address: "Are too many voices drowned / In the silence of the slain?" The "you" addressed narrows over the course of the poem until the speaker seems to address a solitary soldier in the final stanzas.

The last three stanzas of the poem briskly reiterate its central arguments, portraying the gun as an inanimate object without feeling ("Iron sense is rather coarse— / I am but a callous gun"), and then emphasizing the heroic martyrdom of the fallen soldiers ("While above the angels greet / Patriot souls with sweet All Hail!") before returning to the intense pleasures of combat. The poem concludes:

But for me is only joy—
Iron joy at victory won;
I was fashioned to destroy—
Ho! I am the conquering gun.

While the writer of "The Gun" reiterates the idea of the gun's fatal power in the poem's penultimate line ("I was fashioned to destroy"), Dickinson places a similar statement in the same key position in her final stanza: "For I have but the power to kill." While the Dickinson poem ends with the riddling paradox of the gun's immortality ("For I have but the power to kill, / Without – the power to die –"), "The Gun" ends by returning to the pleasures of combat, emphatically repeating the word "joy" in the final stanza's first two lines.

Dickinson's decision to avoid the clarity of ideological context provided by "The Gun" enables her to suggest multiple possibilities for the speaker's identity within the opaque narrative of the poem. Sidestepping the issue of Northern or Southern allegiances also allows Dickinson to heighten the intensity of the pleasure the speaker feels, by focusing on the individual's emotional experience of intimacy or comradery with a solitary other—instead of with a nationalist collective. The poem immediately emphasizes the pleasure that the speaker finds in his or her newly assumed identity:

My Life had stood – a Loaded Gun –
In Corners – till a Day
The Owner passed – identified –
And carried Me away –

And now We roam in Sovreign Woods –
And now We hunt the Doe –
And every time I speak for Him –
The Mountains straight reply – (F 764)

If we read the poem's allegorical characters in relation to nineteenth-century American culture, then the tensions and the intimacy between the "Gun" and the "Owner" in the poem's narrative suggest that the pair of figures might represent a young wife and her new husband, a slave who feels a mixture of affection and anger toward his or her "Owner" or "Master," a convert who finds a new self in his or her devotion to Christ, or a young soldier who finds a new self in combat and in a close relationship with his commanding officer. The "We" that the poem establishes results from an intimacy established through violence, the violence of hunting, possibly the violence of slavery, or the violence of combat. Though none of these interpretive possibilities can be wholly sustained throughout the poem, each brings a new layer of meaning to our understanding both of the piece and of the cultural context in which Dickinson produced it. In this sense, the "we" in Dickinson's poem is analogous to the multilayered "we" of Howe's "Battle Hymn": the affectionate intimacy of the "we" that Dickinson establishes here takes it power from these multiple interpretive possibilities. For twenty-first-century readers, schooled by New Critical reading methods to enjoy the modernist pleasures of ambiguity and indeterminacy, "My Life had stood – a Loaded Gun –" offers a rich and suggestive textual field for interpretive work.

Repositioning the poem in relation to both popular war poetry and soldiers' narratives illuminates the boldness of Dickinson's experiment in imagining the pleasures of military violence from a first-person perspective. Here at last she offers both a confident "I" and a unified "we" in a war-related poem, softening the implications of the gender identity of the poem's speaker by making that first-person speaker a gun. Reading the poem in relation to the narratives of Frazar Stearns's life offered by his friends and relatives suggests the possibility that the speaker might be both a soldier *and* a Christian believer, finding a vital purpose and a renewed sense of self in the war, as Stearns himself clearly did. While I do not mean to suggest that all roads in Dickinson's Civil War–era poems lead back to Frazar Stearns, parallels between the Stearns texts and the poem bring some of the gestures and details in the latter text into sharper focus. And while Dickinson would have read many other accounts of battles and soldiers' deaths in the newspapers, the story of Stearns's military service clearly had particularly strong resonances for her. The pleasure of having good weapons and the thrill of the fight are recurring themes in the Stearns letters his father included in the memorial volume. In a letter from November 17, 1861, Stearns describes the mood in his regiment when new weapons arrived: "Gen. Burnside is a splendid man, and I can go anywhere with him; we are to have *rifles* and everything which heart could desire. In fine we are to be admirably accoutred in every respect, and are all of us wild with delight."[62] On February 8, 1862, Stearns took part in a charge at the battle of Roanoke Island, later describing its intensity in a letter to his family:

> At about 1 1/2 A.M., Major Clark came up with the rest of the regiment, and Gen. Reno ordered us to charge bayonets. We did so, crossing over one hundred yards of exposed ground. It was here the bullets poured in like rain. We were ordered to halt, fire, and lying down behind a little natural elevation to load. Then we were ordered to charge bayonets, and rising up, we could see the enemy running. I never in my life saw a sight so magnificent. I never was so thrilled. As our noble men advanced with bayonets fixed, at a short quick step, a low involuntary cry burst from their lips. It was no war-cry; it was a cry of exultation, of joy, which came leaping from a thousand hearts, swelling into a perfect storm of cheers as we entered the battery . . .[63]

Stearns's stirring account of the assault on the battery may be echoed in the visual effects Dickinson relies on in her poem, as she describes a valley lit up both by gunfire and by the speaker's adrenalin-charged perspective:

> And do I smile, such cordial light
> Opon the Valley glow –
> It is as a Vesuvian face
> Had let it's pleasure through – (F 764)

Dickinson's description of the sounds of combat ("And every time I speak for Him –/The Mountains straight reply –") may respond to Stearns's experience of the military command structure as well. In January 1862, Stearns was promoted to the rank of acting adjutant, a position that would have entailed speaking for senior officers both by transcribing and relaying their orders.

If the poem is a Christian parable, the final stanzas describe both the bonds of loyalty within a combat unit and the immortality that Christian soldiers believe they find on the Civil War battlefield. The deep affection the foot soldier feels for his commander and the love the Christian soldier feels for Christ is palpable:

> And when at Night – Our good Day done –
> I guard My Master's Head –
> 'Tis better than the Eider Duck's
> Deep Pillow – to have shared –
>
> To foe of His – I'm deadly foe –
> None stir the second time –
> On whom I lay a Yellow Eye –
> Or an emphatic Thumb – (F 764)

In one letter, Stearns describes God as "our best Major-General," noting that "*He* seems to be doing the work now, and I must hope *He* will achieve the victory for us."[64] The strength of the bond between Stearns and Colonel Clark was widely reported in the newspapers; a *Hampshire and Franklin Express* piece from March 1862 notes that when Stearns was shot, Colonel Clark "was affected to tears and was almost unable to proceed in his charge."[65] Dickinson probably draws on this account of the battle when she writes to her Norcross cousins in late March 1862: "They tell that Colonel Clark cried like a little child when he missed his pet" (JL 255). The paradox that closes the poem suggests that the Christian soldier who dies on the battlefield may achieve an immortality that the surviving members of his unit cannot yet experience:

> Though I than He – may longer live
> He longer must – than I –
> For I have but the power to kill,
> Without – the power to die – (F 764)

Read in the context of Frazar Stearns's death, the poem's riddling last stanza may suggest that Dickinson reached out toward belief in the idea of Stearns achieving Christian immortality through his heroism. At the very least, the stanza would seem to affirm that both Stearns and his family believed that a devout soldier could achieve that immortality by dying for the cause of the Union.

In explaining the reasons for his son's decisions to go to war, William Stearns, like many Northern writers of this era, stresses the importance of preserving the Union, mentioning the problem of slavery only rarely. The letters he cites from Stearns in the memorial volume also make only occasional reference to the need for abolition. With the Emancipation Proclamation of January 1863, however, Lincoln links the cause of the Union to the abolition of slavery and authorizes the enlistment of black soldiers. After 1863, then, even writers with Whig commitments begin to address the challenges of abolition, emancipation, and the position of blacks in the military.[66] Dickinson turns to the subject of race occasionally, though she only rarely seems to evoke both the war and race in the same poem.[67] Beginning in the summer of 1863, the first in which black units were placed in combat positions, Northern newspapers and magazines began to praise with increasing frequency the bravery and accomplishments of black soldiers. Dickinson would have followed news of Higginson's work with his black soldiers in local papers and magazines, and Higginson's frequent editorials calling for equal pay for black soldiers were also carried widely in the Northern press. In reading "Color – Caste – Denomination –" (F 836) in relation to newspaper and magazine articles about the abilities of blacks and their achievements in battle, I will suggest that Dickinson uses an oblique image of a battlefield covered with bodies of different races to examine the hierarchies of race and class in American society and to reflect on the position of black soldiers in the Civil War.[68]

In "Color – Caste – Denomination –," Dickinson argues that systems of racial and class hierarchy are human and earthly constructs, "Time's Affair." Death, she suggests, will not recognize such categories:

Color – Caste – Denomination
These – are Time's Affair –
Death's diviner Classifying
Does not know they are –

As in sleep – all Hue forgotten –
Tenets – put behind –
Death's large – Democratic fingers
Rub away the Brand –

If Circassian – He is careless –
If He put away
Chrysalis of Blonde – or Umber –
Equal Butterfly –

They emerge from His Obscuring –
What Death – knows so well –
Our minuter intuitions –
Deem unplausible – (F 836)

In 1863 and 1864, Northern newspapers and magazines published a growing list of articles not only on the achievements of blacks in the Union army, but also on leading African American thinkers and speakers. In January 1863, the *Atlantic Monthly* published an article on Benjamin Banneker and then in April of that year, an article by Stowe offering a textual portrait of Sojourner Truth.[69] An illustration from *Harper's Weekly* on February 28, 1863 shows a group of African American officers from the First Louisiana Native Guards (fig. 8). After noting the range of different skin tones among the men, the article connected with the image observes: "These officers all long to prove their loyalty and assert their manhood in the field" (143). By the summer of 1863, the Northern press began to praise frequently the combat service of black regiments. Essays in the *Atlantic* that offered high praise for blacks' military abilities included a June piece on the rebellion at San Domingo, a September essay entitled "The Freedmen at Port Royal." and in December, a "Letter to a Peace Democrat."[70] Even the more staid *Harper's New Monthly*, whose editors usually aimed for a detached tone in responding to political events, offered repeated praise for black soldiers. Describing the June 14th siege of Port Hudson, the editor notes that the siege was "signalized by the great bravery on the part of a colored regiment, being the first instance in which our troops of this class have been brought under severe fire."[71] Also responding to events at Port Hudson, a writer for the *Springfield Republican* notes: "The negroes have fought most bravely in every instance, as everyone who knew their nature predicted."[72] Praise for black troops would

8. "Our Colored Troops—The Line Officers of the First Louisiana Native Guards," magazine illustration, 1863

be repeated both in these columns and elsewhere in the months to come.

In July 1863, two significant events brought issues of "Color," "Caste," and "Denomination" to the forefront in debates about conscription and the Union army. Growing tensions between black laborers and striking Irish Catholic dock workers in New York City eventually led to four days of riots in response to the draft, resulting in the deaths of more than one hundred people; Irish immigrants were particularly outraged by the substitute provision which allowed wealthier men to avoid military service. Blacks and white supporters of abolition made up a majority of the riot's victims while Irish immigrants played a leading role in the violence. The *Springfield Republican* offered thorough coverage of the riots, condemning the acts of violence as "horrible barbarities" and emphasizing the plight of the many African American women and children who were among the victims.[73] Just one day after the riots were finally suppressed and order restored on July 17, Colonel Robert Gould Shaw and the black soldiers of the Fifty-Fourth Massachusetts Infantry walked onto the stage of history when they led an unsuccessful assault on a well-fortified Confederate battery at Fort Wagner in Charleston. Massachusetts newspapers were particularly eager to cover the accomplishments of Shaw's Fifty-Fourth. Even before Fort Wagner, images that positively evoked the mingling of black and white blood on Civil War battlefields had already begun to appear in Northern articles and editorials. The June *Atlantic* article "The Horrors of San Domingo" closes with an impassioned plea that the black man should be allowed to fight: "he will not ennoble the republic till his heart's core is the war's core, and the colors of the two races run into one."[74] Such imagery was made concrete, of course, with the widely publicized death of Shaw in the battle of Fort Wagner. When Shaw fell behind enemy lines, Confederate soldiers did not return his body—though this was a custom often observed in the case of officers' deaths—burying him instead in a mass grave with a group of his black soldiers. The Northern press ran prominent coverage of the circumstances of Shaw's burial, quoting reports that a Confederate soldier had said "We have buried him with his niggers!" Reprinting a story from the *Charleston Courier*, the *Springfield Republican* confirmed the circumstances of Shaw's burial: "The body of Col Shaw, of the negro 54th Massachusetts regiment, was also sent for during Sunday, but he had been buried in a pit, under a layer of two of his own dead negroes."[75] On July 27, 1863, the *Springfield Republican* ran an obituary that praised Shaw as "a brave and noble-hearted gentleman and a tried and skillful soldier."[76] Immediately beneath Shaw's obituary, the editors noted that a subscription campaign in New York to raise funds for blacks "robbed and abused" in the recent draft riots had succeeded in raising twenty-four thousand dollars.[77] As this juxtaposition suggests, the bravery and heroism of Shaw's black troops and the horrifying acts of violence committed against blacks in New York were often linked in the Northern press; by late July 1863, the tide of Northern public opinion had largely swung in favor of blacks' military service. Responding to reports of Confederate mistreatment of captured black Union soldiers, Lincoln ordered strong retaliatory measures on July 30, 1863, dictating that for every black Union prisoner executed, a Confederate prisoner would be executed. Published in the *Springfield Republican* in early August, the phrasing of the order—particularly in the first few sentences—offers striking parallels to the opening stanza of "Color – Caste – Denomination –": "It is the duty of every government to give protection to its citizens of whatever class, color or condition, and especially to those who are duly organized as soldiers in the public service."[78]

In the first months of 1864, still other events might have brought the image of black and white soldiers on a battlefield to the forefront of Dickinson's thoughts. In January, the question of equal pay for black soldiers—still another debate about "Color" and "Denomination"—was again brought to public attention with the execution of Sergeant William Walker of the Twenty-First U.S. Colored Infantry. Protesting the unequal pay, Walker was convicted of inciting mutiny and was executed before Lincoln had had the opportunity to consider his case. In late January, the *Springfield Republican* printed Charles Graham Halpine's "Miles O'Reilly on the 'Naygurs'," a poem in the voice of a working-class Irish soldier who begrudgingly admits the ability of black soldiers under fire, even as he hopes that a black soldier will die in his stead.[79] Also in January, the *Atlantic* published a poem by James Russell Lowell that celebrated Shaw as a hero of the war and of the cause of abolition, signaling the start of a long line of glowing tributes to Shaw. While Lowell's poem offers a dazzling image of Shaw's courage—"Cleared at a bound, he flashes o'er the fight, / A saintly shape of fame, to cheer the right"—Dickinson's poem offers a careful weighing of bodies of different races.[80] Though Dickinson's poem may or may not be a response to the battle of Fort Wagner and the circumstances of Shaw's burial with his soldiers, it does point implicitly toward a mingling of different kinds of bodies in the grave, arguing very strongly for the erasure of difference after death. Rejecting the distinction between the "Chrysalis of Blonde – or Umber –," the poem ends by imagining a collective "They" whose souls, figured as butterflies, ascend: "They emerge from His Obscuring –." Implicitly criticizing racial and class hierarchies in this temporal world as fictional constructs, the poem emphasizes that "Death's large – Democratic fingers" will erase the physical markers or "the Brand" of difference. Beyond "Death's diviner Classifying," the afterlife will offer equality: "If He put away / Chrysalis of Blonde – or Umber – / Equal Butterfly –" The poem concludes by reiterating the limitations—the blinders, in effect—of the human perception of difference: "What Death – knows so well – / Our minuter intuitions – / Deem unplausible –".

The opening line's key word "Denomination" suggests in general the naming and classifying of categories, but also more specifically categories of money or currency and the categories of religious sects and differences, categories that were vitally at stake in wartime decisions about who might be exempted and who might be drafted. Like "It feels a shame to be Alive –," "Color – Caste – Denomination –" points toward the linking of money with the value of individual human lives and the weighing of different lives in terms of currency. The reference to "Denomination" suggests the counting that took place at regional draft offices, as local leaders attempted to meet their mandated quotas with lists of African American, Irish, and German soldiers, as well as whites with more distant European origins. Laden with multiple layers of association, the word "Denomination" points in compressed fashion toward all of the wartime arguments about race, economic class, and religion that would have been most vital and pressing at the time Dickinson wrote the poem. The word "nation" also hovers within the larger word, designating this act of naming or classifying and underlining the ways that acts of naming, counting, or designating inevitably resonate with ideological force. Shaped by Dickinson's characteristically precise diction, the poem suggests that the language of public policy and the language of poetry both work to determine the fate of the nation. The word "denomination" underlines the splitting of the nation that must inevitably occur when politicians—or indeed poets—seek to name or "denominate" its constituents.

Resituated in their nineteenth-century discursive contexts, Dickinson's poetic responses to wartime ideologies are not always as skeptical, liminal, or oblique as they have sometimes seemed. Freed from the pressures of print publication, Dickinson can experiment more broadly in her work than Julia Ward Howe, Frances Harper, or even Walt Whitman, and the flexibility of the stances of poetic voice in the war years means that poetry is particularly well suited to her exploration of conflicting aesthetic and ideological positions. Just as Whitman's anxious apostrophes to the nation ultimately foreground the inevitable breakdown of national unity, so too does Dickinson emphasize the inefficacy of poetry's attempts to unify the nation. Deeply suspicious of the dramatic posture of the address to the nation, in "This is my letter to the World," Dickinson shows how the unified nation of her "sweet countrymen" fractures into individuated discrete readers just as it is addressed by the feminine lyric "I." Imagining the carnage of the battlefield, Dickinson emphasizes that women too are inevitably touched by the war's violence; her artful battlefield landscapes reveal the limitations of the romantic vocabulary for representing war even as they also implicitly suggest that women writers can and should respond to the war.

Like Julia Ward Howe, Dickinson writes a poem that imagines the thrill of combat from the first-person perspective; Dickinson sidesteps the issue of gender identity, however, by writing the poem in the dramatic persona of not a soldier but rather a gun. While Howe uses the collective "we" to unify Northerners in her "Battle Hymn," Dickinson uses the collective "we" to indict the hypocrisy of Northern noncombatants in "It feels a shame to be Alive –." Like Frances Harper and also like Walt Whitman, Dickinson uses an authoritative voice (in "Color – Caste – Denomination," for example, or "It feels a shame to be Alive –") to address the nation on the subject of ideologies central to the war. While Harper uses her reputation as a successful abolitionist orator to shore up the authority of her speaker's voice, Whitman roots the authority of his speaker in his direct contact with soldiers through his work in the military hospitals. In Dickinson's case, however, both her reclusiveness and her refusal to publish in print free her to establish rhetorical authority through the textual positing of an impersonal speaker. Yet while Dickinson's work signals the beginnings of a modernist poetics that will use fractured language to question the ideologies of both the nation and the military, her work also echoes popular song and poetry in its engagement with sentimental and nationalist stances. And while Dickinson may be deeply suspicious about the efficacy of a poetics that seeks to establish a nationalist "we," she nonetheless writes poems mourning the deaths of soldiers, addressing her family, her Amherst community, and by extension also the Union. Just as the nation she addresses is divided then, so too is Dickinson herself subject to deeply divided aesthetic and political loyalties: even as she suggests that poetry can never work to reunite the nation, so too does she also write poems that celebrate the thrill of combat and the bravery of men under fire, poems that impute heroic and nationalist meaning to soldiers' deaths in battle.[81]

CHAPTER FIVE

ROMANTIC VISIONS AND SOUTHERN STANCES

Henry Timrod, Sarah Piatt, and George Moses Horton

While Northern poets like Whitman and Dickinson find in romantic landscape description an important topos for representation of battlefield violence, for Southern poets representation of the natural world becomes still more central, all but essential to the poetics of war. For Southern writers, as this group is usually understood—white Confederate men—the construct of the Confederate nation is inseparable from the Southern natural world: Southern writers represent the new nation through the prism of nature, including images of the Southern flora and climate that foreground the South's iconic status as an Edenic paradise, a land of natural harmony and plenitude. Antebellum poems such as Samuel Henry Dickson's "I Sigh for the Land of the Cypress and Pine" or William Gilmore Simms's "Song of the South" become models for Confederate wartime celebrations of Southern landscapes; as I noted in chapter two, Confederate soldier George Washington Hall's "When the War Is Over" follows these models by linking the warmth and plenitude of a Southern natural world to Southern ideals of femininity. Moreover, as I suggested in my reading of Dan Emmett's "I Wish I Was in Dixie's Land," Edenic images of the South figured largely in Northern and Southern imaginations both immediately before the war and during the war years. For women writers in both the North and the South, the stances of romantic landscape depiction make possible an oblique approach to representation of battlefield violence: like Emily Dickinson, the Kentucky-born poet Sarah Piatt uses aestheticized images of landscapes, flowers, and the changing seasons to represent soldiers dying in vast numbers on battlefields. Again like Dickinson, Piatt sometimes addresses the American nation by means of an oblique stance, a stance that offers a pointed critique of the ways in which war and wartime writing excludes and limits the participation of women.

For the Southern writer, questions about what kind of audience one might reach and what kind of collective "we" one might establish in one's work become vexed and vexing immediately before, during, and after the war since the centers of literary power and reputation were located in the Northeast.[1] For Southern writers who did not support the Confederacy the task of establishing a collective "we" with readers becomes still more complex as they seek to imagine a readership who will understand their conflicted relationship to the Southern nation. Though white Confederate writers responded to the founding of the Confederacy with an outpouring of literary creativity, both before and after the war placing a book with a major Northeastern publisher was considered *the* measure of literary success for Southern writers. In this chapter, then, I will offer analysis of two Southern poets who opposed the Confederacy and who also achieved professional success by publishing in the Northeast: Sarah Piatt and George Moses Horton. The Kentucky-born Piatt published eighteen volumes of poetry in addition to publishing in the leading Northern literary magazines of her day; in terms of her ability to place collections with major Northern publishing houses and to place poems in prestigious Northern magazines, she was the most successful Southern poet—of either sex—of her generation. George Moses Horton, who described himself as "the black bard of North Carolina," was published in both Northern and Southern newspapers and magazines while he was still a slave, and Northern presses reprinted their own editions of his first volume of poems, *The Hope of Liberty*. An analysis of the full spectrum of Confederate poetry—a compelling and complex topic in its own right—lies beyond the scope of this book; my aim in reading a small but representative selection of Henry Timrod's poems is rather to contextualize the liminal Southern examples of Sarah Piatt and George Moses Horton in relation to the normative Confederate example of Timrod. A brief analysis of Timrod's staunchly Confederate poetics will serve to illuminate the critiques that both Sarah Piatt and George Moses Horton offer of Southern culture, Southern racial hierarchies, and Edenic images of a Southern natural world. While white Confederate writers like Timrod seek to invent and unify a white Confederate readership, both

Piatt and Horton position themselves in relation to multiple colliding audiences, audiences with conflicting understandings of the construct of the nation. Pronoun positions will prove to be particularly complex and nuanced in Piatt's and Horton's work then, as each poet resists the Confederate nationalist "we," proposing both alternative collective models and first-person stances in its stead. In rejecting the Confederate nationalist "we," both Piatt and Horton will offer critical rejoinders to Confederate versions of romanticism.

Addressing and Creating the Confederate Nation: The Romantic Stances of Henry Timrod

The arc of Henry Timrod's life and his brief but much acclaimed career as a poet were indelibly shaped by the rise of Southern romanticism and by the rise and fall of the Confederate nation. Born in 1828 in Charleston, South Carolina, to a family with a long history of military service, Timrod began publishing poetry in his twenties. While working as a private tutor, he moved in the most distinguished of Charleston's literary circles and was friends with the group who launched *Russell's Magazine*, a publication that aimed to rival Northern magazines by presenting the very best of Southern literary talent. Based on the success of the pieces he placed in *Russell's*, Timrod published a volume with the prestigious Boston publisher Ticknor and Fields on the eve of the war in 1859; the collection received positive reviews in both the North and the South. Deterred by ill health from serving in the Confederate army, Timrod worked as a war correspondent for the *Charleston Mercury* before becoming an editor of the *South Carolinian*. When the Union army arrived in Columbia in February 1865, Timrod went into hiding. He reemerged to find a devastated city; his infant son died in the autumn of that year. The defeat of the Confederacy accelerated Timrod's descent into tuberculosis and poverty, and he died just two years after the war's end. Often called the "Poet Laureate of the Confederacy," Timrod was considered by his peers—and later on by scholars—to be one of the most gifted Southern writers of his generation.

The central aim of Henry Timrod's wartime poetry is to address—and thus to forge—a unified white community within the newly created Confederate nation. To this end, Timrod will establish a Confederate nationalist "we" in his body of work; distinguishing himself as more than just a popular poet, however, Timrod will also rely extensively on the solitary lyric "I" of romanticism. Indeed Timrod's versatile use of both pronoun positions signals his success as both a popular and a literary poet in his day. Timrod uses high romantic images of a Southern paradise as a foundation for his vision of the exalted Confederate nation. Like the Confederate soldier-poet George Washington Hall, Timrod foregrounds the argument that white Southern women—the human embodiment of nature—perform the essential work of sustaining the new nation: the Southern women in Timrod's war poems appear as a unified bloc of Confederate loyalists, inspiring men to acts of battlefield heroism. The crisis of the foundering of the Confederacy sends powerful shock waves through Timrod's work, shaking the confidence of the solitary romantic speaker. In the poems he wrote in the middle years of the war, the representation of military setbacks is pervaded by an elegiac recognition of nature's betrayal of the human world: the Southern paradise cannot guarantee the stability of the Confederacy. Analyzing Timrod's work, I will examine the relationship between the nationalist "we" and the solitary lyric "I," the way he uses romantic landscapes to represent the birth of the Confederacy, his account of Southern women's crucial role in that birth, and his elegiac use of romantic landscapes to mourn the Confederate nation's setbacks and failures.

In two poems that proclaim and celebrate the birth of the Southern nation, Timrod argues that nature herself endorses the cause of the Confederacy. In both "Ethnogenesis" and "The Cotton Boll," he relies on a metaphor of global climate regions to insist that the traditional cultural and economic superiority of icy Northern regions to balmy Southern ones will be upended by the founding of the Confederacy. Composed in February 1861 during the first meeting of the Confederate Congress and widely republished both in the nineteenth and the twentieth centuries, "Ethnogenesis" begins by claiming that all of the elements of nature are aligned in support of the Confederacy. Establishing the poem's political foundations, Timrod boldly posits a collective nationalist "we" in the poem's opening lines: "At last, we are/A nation among nations . . ."[2] Inseparable from that nationalist "we" is the Southern natural world, strongly gendered as feminine. The poem's first section offers a proliferating array of Nature-based feminine figures who embody natural harmony and plenitude: the Year's "gentle daughters" bear "long spears of golden grain," while "June flings her azure banner" and "her sisters"—presumably bearing a range of different kinds of crops—pass by (92–93).The sequence of harvest images builds to a climax with the mention of cotton. Offering a utopian vision of all that cotton will do for the new nation, Timrod calls cotton "THE SNOW OF SOUTHERN SUMMERS," arguing that its "endless sheets" will protect the South from the ravages of Northern competition and hostility (93). Likening "the very soil" of the South to "the heart of woman," the poem suggests that both the soil and woman will "fight beside" Confederate warriors on a battleground where God himself will serve as a Southern ally (93). The poem concludes by arguing that Southern labor practices are more humane than Northern ones and will result in peace and prosperity that will flow from the South to the rest of the continent, like a gulf stream warming "the cold, untempered ocean" of the North (95).

In "The Cotton Boll," first published in September 1861 and widely republished in both the nineteenth and twentieth centuries, Timrod develops still further the idea of cotton's almost limitless capacity for supporting and expanding Southern prosperity. Moreover, "The Cotton Boll" presents the solitary romantic speaker-poet who contemplates—and indeed helps to create—the new nation: beginning with the solitary contemplative I, the poem builds to a collective nationalist "we" in the closing lines, where the speaker calls on God to assist the new nation ("Oh help us, Lord!" [99]). The poem represents cotton as a mystical substance that contains whole worlds within its strands and that will weave the continent together in pastoral peace and natural plenitude. Timrod again inverts traditional hierarchies of North and South, arguing that the "tropic day" of the South will illuminate the "Polar lands" thanks to the success of cotton (96). Moreover, the poem also claims that a great poetry will spring forth from the Edenic loveliness of the South and compares the poet-speaker's solitary work to the weaving of cloth. The poem's final lines swerve abruptly toward a call to arms, asking God to help "roll the crimson flood / Back on its course," striking at the heart of the North and bringing about the decline of Northern civilization (99). Though the poem includes no explicitly feminine nature metaphors, it otherwise extends and elaborates on the nationalist nature imagery of "Ethnogenesis"; collectively the two poems forge a Confederate "we" and offer a celebratory rallying cry for Confederate loyalists.

In articulating rallying cries for the Confederate cause, Timrod foregrounds images of feminine loyalty and patriotism in many of his poems.[3] In "A Cry to Arms," first published in March 1862, stanza four argues that men who hesitate need only look to the example of women in order to be strengthened in their military resolve:

> Does any falter? let him turn
>   To some brave maiden's eyes,
> And catch the holy fires that burn
>   In those sublunar skies.
> Oh! could you like your women feel,
>   And in their spirit march,
> A day might see your lines of steel
>   Beneath the victor's arch. (108)

Drawing on nineteenth-century ideologies that emphasize women's capacity for emotion, Timrod here links female patriotic ardor—"the holy fires"—with male bravery on the battlefield. Rhyming "feel" with "steel," the stanza reverses the formula that would argue that women's emotion makes them the weaker sex; rather, Timrod argues that quavering men should follow women's passionately and patriotically superior example. "A Cry to Arms" seeks to unify white Confederate society by suggesting that women are an essential base of moral support for the efforts of men; Timrod thus unifies the Confederate nation by forging a close alliance between white Southern women and men. The dominant pronoun in the poem is the collective "you" of the rallying address to white male soldiers; following the inclusion of the third-person reference to female supporters in stanza four, the poem builds to a climax with a collective "we" in its final stanza: "We battle for our Country's right" (109).

Timrod makes the alliance between male soldiers and female supporters the central thematic focus of a poem entitled "The Two Armies," first published in May 1863. Likening women's dedication and bravery to that of men, the poem argues that the work that women do in the hospitals, in sewing supplies for the troops, and in supporting their husbands and lovers emotionally is equal in importance to the work men do on the battlefield. In its final stanza, the poem argues that when the peace has been won at the war's end, both the male and female armies "may claim the victor's crest," a unified collective the poem represents with a third-person plural (126). Each army, like each man and woman in it, "shall see its dearest prize / Gleam softly from the other's eyes" (126). This closing image of reciprocal gazes superimposes an image of unity between husband and wife or lover and beloved onto an image of Confederate national unity: in "Two Armies," Timrod symbolically creates a unified Confederate nation by replacing the two opposing armies of Northern and Southern men with the two allied and mutually supportive armies of Southern men and women.

Inevitably, however, this harmonious vision of men and women serving as mutual supports to one another is disrupted in other poems; though Timrod writes no poems that represent wartime discord between the sexes explicitly, he does write poems in which nature's betrayal of human interests is figured as a fickle woman's betrayal of her lover. Because Timrod mingles images of Southern femininity with images of an Edenic Southern landscape, the pain his speakers feel in response to nature's detachment from human affairs is deeply personal. Like Dickinson, Whitman, and Piatt, Timrod uses romantic imagery to represent battlefield scenes that foreground the terrible cost of the war. In Timrod's poetics, however, the representation of the war's traumatic losses through nature imagery takes on a wrenchingly elegiac quality because Timrod has founded his utopian vision of the Southern nation on images of nature's plenitude. In his poetics, when nature does not work in support of the Confederate cause, the speaker's pain at nature's betrayal is acute: nature's betrayal of the Confederacy is a betrayal of love.

In the sonnet "I know not why, but all this weary day," first published in October 1861, Timrod layers a stance of mourning for the Civil War dead over the conventional romantic posture of the speaker's contemplation of melancholy in nature. The shift from the collective nationalist "we" of many of Timrod's other war poems toward the solitary lyric "I" signals the speaker's detachment from the collective of the nation. If we read the poem autobiographically, the elegiac lyric "I" may also signal a sense of guilt and sadness on Timrod's part that he was not able to serve as a soldier:

> I know not why, but all this weary day,
> Suggested by no definite grief or pain,
> Sad fancies have been flitting through my brain;
> Now it has been a vessel losing way,
> Rounding a stormy headland; now a gray
> Dull waste of clouds above a wintry main;
> And then, a banner, drooping in the rain,
> And meadows beaten into bloody clay.
> Strolling at random with this shadowy woe

At heart, I chanced to wander hither! Lo!
A league of desolate marsh-land, with its lush,
Hot grasses in a noisome, tide-left bed,
And faint, warm airs, that rustle in the hush,
Like whispers round the body of the dead! (100)

In "I know not why," the powerful influence of Wordsworth on Timrod's poetics is apparent both in the choice of the sonnet form and in the conjoining of political and natural contexts. The poem offers no specific wartime scene; rather the speaker voices a generalized feeling of dread, sorrow, and mourning. Throughout the octave, nature seems to oppose human efforts in general and military efforts in particular, as in the images of the "vessel losing way" against the storm and the "banner, drooping in the rain." The violence of combat is implied obliquely in the description of the "meadows beaten into bloody clay," an image that is at once indirect and shockingly graphic, suggesting a violence so brutal that it has driven human flesh into the soil. The landscape is thus inscribed by violence, but apart from the solitary speaker, no human agents appear in the poem; the image of the "bloody clay" transposes the impact of the war's violence from human beings to the natural world. Since Southerners had much more limited access than Northerners to visual images of the war, it is unlikely that Timrod is responding to the horror of the graphic images taken by photographers on Civil War battlefields; he may well be responding to his own brief experience of serving in the military, however.[4]

In the sestet, the speaker stumbles upon a body that may or may not be literal. He may have come across a corpse left behind after a recent battle or he may have stumbled inwardly on the realization of the war's terrible toll in dead bodies or on the realization that nature is utterly indifferent to the sufferings of human beings. The insistent use of exclamation points underlines his sense of shock: "Strolling at random with this shadowy woe/At heart, I chanced to wander hither! Lo!" (100). In the poem's last four lines, the "lush/Hot grasses" and the "faint warm, airs" evoke both bodies in the throes of passion and corpses bloating and decaying in the summer heat; the "noisome tide-left bed" suggests the stench of decaying flesh. The image of the "tide-left bed" underlines the idea of nature's fickleness: the potential for decay that lurks beneath its beauty and its impassivity in the face of human suffering. The image of rotting corpses on the battlefield is grotesquely sexualized; Nature's generative plenitude has here been transformed into degenerative decay. Moreover, Timrod here uses romantic imagery to emphasize the omnipresence of the dead: the speaker stumbles over them while on a seaside ramble. Timrod's "I know not why" thus hovers on the margins between a lush Wordsworthian romanticism and the graphic realism to come in the late nineteenth and early twentieth centuries. The corpse that Timrod's speaker stumbles on in "I know not why" may well be the corpse of Southern romanticism itself: the speaker is shocked and deeply grieved by the discovery of nature's betrayal and by the unexpected discovery of the limitations of romanticism. The image of the "noisome, tide-left bed" that closes the poem implies that the speaker feels nature's betrayal and romanticism's betrayal as acutely as he would had he been betrayed in love. Nature's betrayal shatters the possibility of establishing the nationalist "we," leaving the speaker to wander and mourn alone.

In "The Unknown Dead," first published on July 4, 1863, just one day after the end of the three-day battle of Gettysburg, Timrod once again relies on romantic stances to mourn Civil War deaths. In this poem, however, that posture of mourning is made wholly explicit: contemplating a rain storm through his window, the speaker hears the church bell and thinks of "nameless graves on battle-plains" (126). His thoughts turn quickly away from "the chiefs," the war's great heroes and leaders whose every deed will be celebrated, toward "the true martyrs of the fight," namely "the unknown dead" of the poem's title. Though Timrod most likely composed the poem before the battle, its emphasis on the graves of the unknown would have been particularly timely in the immediate aftermath of Gettysburg. In addition to stressing the contributions of nameless footsoldiers, however, the poem also offers a powerful argument about how nature should respond to the war's losses. In the poem's first ten lines, the speaker describes how nature's mood—the dreary storm—shapes his own: it is the "streaming window-pane" that has turned his thoughts to the dead. Here nature seems to mourn in company with human beings and to encourage their mourning. Yet even in these opening lines, Timrod already begins to suggest that nature may be out of joint with human purposes: the fog and rain conceal "the neighboring vane" of the church from the speaker (126). Symbolically God's will has been obscured. In the poem's last eight lines, the speaker laments the ways in which nature betrays the human world. Nature, he argues, should mourn for the dead but does not always do so:

Just such a sky as this should weep
Above them, always, where they sleep;
Yet, haply, at this very hour,
Their graves are like a lover's bower;
And Nature's self, with eyes unwet,
Oblivious of the crimson debt
To which she owes her April grace,
Laughs gaily o'er their burial-place. (127)

In these closing lines, the poem figures nature as a fickle, flirtatious woman, "oblivious" to her debts, decking herself out with spring flowers, laughing inappropriately over the soldiers' graves. The betrayal only obliquely implied at the end of "I know not why" is made explicit at the end of "The Unknown Dead": the Nature on which Timrod had founded his vision of Southern prosperity has become a fickle uncaring cheat. Nature's betrayal is signaled in the poem by the shift in the identity of the "we" the poem posits: the speaker laments that "we can only dimly guess" at the "worlds of all this world's distress" the war has brought to grieving families. The collective nationalist "we" has here been reduced not just to a "we" of white Southern noncombatants but more narrowly still to "we" of noncombatants who have not lost sons or fathers or husbands in the war—surely a very small group. This narrowly focused "we" signals both the speaker's detachment from the collective Confederate "we" and Timrod's ambivalence and guilt about his inability to serve in the Confederate army.

In his wartime poetry then, Henry Timrod relies on romantic stances to give symbolic birth to the Confederate nation. Superimposing images of a staunchly loyal Southern femininity onto images of strength and beauty in nature, Timrod invents and addresses a unified "we" of loyal white Confederate readers, both male and female, shifting adroitly between the solitary lyric "I" of romanticism and the celebratory "we" of Confederate patriotism. The very strength of Timrod's investment in romantic stances, however, ultimately reveals the instability of these stances: when nature betrays the Confederate cause, romanticism betrays Timrod's poetic and nationalist allegiances. In these poems, the lyric speaker grieves alone, lost in contemplation of nature's betrayal and detached from the utopian nationalist "we." Unlike Emily Dickinson and, as I will suggest, Sarah Piatt, Timrod cannot represent that betrayal in satiric or ironic terms; though his solitary speaker mourns nature's betrayal, Timrod continues to rely on the conventions of romanticism to represent that posture of mourning.

"The First Fierce Words of War": Dialogic Stances and Romantic Landscapes in the Work of Sarah Piatt

For Sarah Piatt, as for Henry Timrod, romanticism serves as an almost inexhaustible source of imagery for representations of the South. Yet while Timrod can interleave political and romantic stances without fear of his readers overemphasizing or overlooking either, Piatt's mingling of political and romantic stances is inevitably a more fraught procedure because of her sex. While Timrod uses both a Confederate nationalist "we" and a solitary romantic "I" in his body of work, the "we" of Piatt's poetics is usually the "we" of familial domesticity and the "I" is generally a genteel maternal speaker. Like Julia Ward Howe, Piatt is acutely aware that her educated middle-class readership will expect her to display a genteel feminine sensibility in her poems; in Piatt's case, such expectations would only have been heightened by her Southern origins. So Piatt, like Dickinson, decides to turn romantic stances to her own rhetorical advantage: she relies on an imagistic repertoire of flowers, gardens, landscapes, mothers, and children to offer oblique critiques of Southern nationalist ambitions, Southern racial hierarchies, and Southern gender norms. As Paula Bennett argues in her invaluable study of Piatt, this decision leads to Piatt's critical dismissal by twentieth-century scholars, who find in her body of work little more than the conventional array of poems about flowers, lovers, and the deaths of children.[5]

Offering a persuasive corrective to this dismissal, Bennett argues that Piatt's political poetry has until now received little attention since twentieth-century scholars focused primarily on the verse that she published in book form. By foregrounding the magazine poems in her edition of Piatt's work, Bennett offers compelling evidence to support her claim that "Piatt was a profoundly political poet for whom issues of social justice . . . were central."[6] Born in Kentucky in 1836 to a wealthy slave-owning family, Piatt moved to Washington, DC, with her husband not long after her marriage in June of 1861. Though she would never live in the South for an extended period of time again, she continued for the rest of her poetic career to meditate on the lost glories of the South of her childhood, the complex power relations between master and slave, and the relationship between the war's violence and the ideologies of Southern culture. Piatt and her husband spent the war years in Washington, where he worked for the Treasury Department. This geographical position—living on the boundary between North and South—is clearly reflected in Piatt's critical and aesthetic restlessness. As Bennett observes, Piatt writes from a position of double alienation: she can find refuge neither in the Kentucky of her childhood nor in the white Northern middle-class world she lives in after her marriage.[7] This double alienation results in Piatt's most interesting and challenging stylistic trademark: she frequently builds dialogic structures into her poems, imagining conversations between mothers and children, women and their lovers, and husbands and wives. These dialogic structures point up differences, overlap, and slippage in these characters' viewpoints and identities; Piatt uses pronoun ambiguity to imply unexpected shifts in her speakers' identities. Conjoined with her bitingly ironic use of romantic and Victorian imagery, Piatt's use of pronoun slippage and her dialogic structures underline the deeply conflicted perspectives of her female speakers. In her poems, circuits of address shift and proliferate: like Emily Dickinson, Piatt will use a variety of stances of address to soften or partially conceal her stances of address to the nation. Piatt's dialogic stances embed her genteel feminine speakers in domestic Victorian contexts—seemingly limiting both the scope of her audience and the political force of her statements—even as they also allow her to scrutinize and sharply critique the confining limitations of those contexts. Piatt underlines the impossibility of resolving the tension between the personal "I" and the nationalist "we" by foregrounding shifting dialogic circuits in her poems. In so doing she underlines the extent to which the dialogues of the domestic sphere inevitably shape the dialogues of nationalist ideologies.

In her war poems, Piatt uses the romantic conceit of the fairyland to evoke the memory of her Southern childhood. Framing those memories by means of dialogues between mothers and children and women and their lovers, she can both revel in nostalgia and expose the hypocrisy that underpins that nostalgia. For Piatt, memories of this fairyland are inseparable not only from the guilt she feels about her family's participation in slavery but also from her knowledge of the devastation of the South caused by the Civil War, a war that was waged to preserve her childhood world. In expressing this potent mix of nostalgia, guilt, and mourning, she turns again and again to a genteel Victorian aesthetic, using images of picturesque landscapes, gardens, flowers, lovers, and children. In relying on genteel Victorian imagery to respond to the war, Piatt has a number of political and aesthetic aims: she wants to use romantic landscape depiction to critique aestheticized and sentimental depictions of battlefield violence; she wants to reflect on the ways the war changed relationships between slaves and their former masters; she wants to consider white middle-class women's relationship to the war's violence; finally she wants to examine the ways that gender roles and heterosexual desire work to endorse military ideologies in general and a Southern code of masculine heroism in particular. Steeped in a Victorian domestic femininity, Piatt's poetry meditates on the consequences of the war through the lens of women's fascination with violence and the lens of romantic attachments between men and women. Piatt uses her genteel female speakers to offer a nuanced critique of the masculine code of military heroism, the code that underpins Confederate nationalism.

"Hearing the Battle," which appeared in print for the first time in 1864, is a representative example of Piatt using genteel imagery to offer a pointed critique of militarism. Here she responds to the First Battle of Bull Run, one of the first major engagements of Union and Confederate forces, a battle where Northern sightseers rode out from Washington to watch the proceedings and had to flee abruptly when Confederate forces overran Union positions. Piatt's choice of this battle reflects both her close geographic proximity to it and also her awareness of the irony of civilian-sightseers having to flee the field. In "Hearing the Battle," Piatt both adopts and undermines a frequent stance in popular poetry of this era: in *The Imagined Civil War*, Alice Fahs describes a scenario—ubiquitous in the literature of the early years of the war—in which a young woman urges her beloved to go join the fight, thereby demonstrating his valor, defending his country, and also proving his love for the young woman.[8] The Currier and Ives print "The Brave Wife" foregrounds the unity of husband and wife in their support for the Union cause (fig. 9). At first glance Piatt's poem seems to present just such a scene; closer examination, however, reveals that it includes no direct references to bravery, loyalty to the nation, or love. Rather, the poem foregrounds the shocking juxtaposition of a private scene of domestic tranquility with a scene of wartime carnage:

9. "The Brave Wife," lithograph, ca. 1861

One day in the dreamy summer,
  On the Sabbath hills, from afar
We heard the solemn echoes
  Of the first fierce words of war.

Ah, tell me, thou veilèd Watcher
  Of the storm and the calm to come,
How long by the sun or shadow
  Till these noises again are dumb.

And soon in a hush and glimmer
  We thought of the dark, strange fight,
Whose close in a ghastly quiet
  Lay dim in the beautiful night.

Then we talk'd of coldness and pallor,
  And of things with blinded eyes
That stared at the golden stillness
  Of the moon in those lighted skies;

And of souls, at morning wrestling
  In the dust with passion and moan,
So far away at evening
  In the silence of worlds unknown.

But a delicate wind beside us
  Was rustling the dusky hours,
 As it gather'd the dewy odors
  Of the snowy jessamine-flowers.

And I gave you a spray of the blossoms,
  And said: "I shall never know
How the hearts in the land are breaking,
  My dearest, unless you go."[9] (2–3)

The "we" that the poem establishes is not the "we" of patriotic nationalism, but rather the "we" of the husband and wife, sitting alone together at their beautiful country home. While "a delicate wind" rustles the "dewy odors" of the "jessamine-flowers" on this "beautiful night," corpses from a recent battle lie on a field nearby: "things with blinded eyes/That stared at the golden stillness/Of the moon in those lighted skies." Like Whitman in "Look Down Fair Moon," Piatt here offers a romantic landscape gone awry, with the moon casting its light on the gory aftermath of a battle. The phrase "blinded eyes" underlines the meaninglessness of the aestheticized perspective on the post-battle scene: while the poet or artist can offer a picturesque vista of a battlefield landscape to civilian readers and viewers, those who died in battle have been "blinded" forever to the beauty of the lunar "golden stillness" that surrounds them. When the speaker urges her beloved to go to war, this plea seems to result from the disparity between the "beautiful night" she sees around her and the "ghastly" violence she knows is taking place at the same time.[10] The poem's speaker longs to experience the collective "we" of the nationalist undertaking, but she can do so only by sending her husband off to war, thereby dissolving the "we" of marital unity.

The speaker's suggestion that her lover should head off to war follows just one stanza after the description of the dead in the poem, and the matter-of-fact tone in which the speaker makes this proposal would seem to suggest more that she's anxious to be free of his presence or that she's anxious to have the experience of loss rather than that she's eager for him to become a hero:

> And I gave you a spray of the blossoms,
>   And said: "I shall never know
> How the hearts in the land are breaking,
>   My dearest, unless you go."

In "Hearing the Battle," the lovers' quiet tête-à-tête is juxtaposed with the soldiers' death agonies, struggles the speaker describes in the sexualized language of stanza five as "a wrestling/In the dust with passion and moan." As in Timrod's "I know not why," Piatt here establishes a powerful and grotesque analogy between the aftermath of battle and the bed of love-making. Yet while there's "passion" on the battlefield in Piatt's poem, there doesn't seem to be much passion in the romance. The convention of the female speaker urging her beloved off to the fight is thus given an undertone of irony in a poem that offers no redemptive vision of war, but rather a pointed contrast between pastoral landscapes and the dying agonies of soldiers.

Moreover, in the poem's final stanza, the speaker also emphasizes that she can never know the experience of other women unless her lover joins the fight. In view of Piatt's divided geographic loyalties, it is not surprising that when she evokes this community of suffering women, she does so without separating North from South; indeed, the final stanza implicitly unifies the two groups into one. These lines also suggest that the knowledge of love can only result from the loss of it. Significantly, the poem does not reveal whether the man in question chooses to enlist or remains at home, an omission that means that the emotional dilemma of the poem's speaker remains unresolved at the poem's end.[11] Will she share the collective experience of other women—joining the "we" of the wives left behind—by undergoing the heartbreak of wartime loss? Or will she remain trapped in a domestic world of "delicate" winds and "dewy" flowers, the unified but complacent "we" of her marriage? Offering no answer to these questions, the poem leaves its speaker caught in that genteel world of isolation, living at a painful remove from both the "fierce words of war" and the "worlds unknown" of the battlefield; she is also cut off from the collective experience of women who have suffered wartime losses. Though it is far more oblique and ambiguous, the edge of irony in Piatt's "Hearing the Battle" is not unlike the more explicit ironic bitterness that shapes the speaker's voice in Julia Ward Howe's "The Jeweller's Shop in War-Time." The female speaker in each poem is caught in a stifling world of middle-class convention that dictates for her the very narrow range of wartime roles she can perform. In sharp contrast with Howe's "Battle Hymn," which implicitly unites Northern men and women into a unified "we" ("Let us die to make men free"), Piatt's "Hearing the Battle" emphasizes both the female speaker's separation from the men dying on the battlefield and also her separation from other women.

If we read Piatt's "Hearing the Battle" in relation to Dickinson's "The name – of it – is 'Autumn' –" (F 465), key parallels and contrasts become apparent in these two women poets' methods as well. Although both poems rely on the juxtaposition of a pastoral scene with a battlefield scene, Piatt creates her shock effect by alternating between the two, whereas Dickinson creates her shock effect by collapsing the two scenes into one. Thus Piatt's poem emphasizes the vast divide that separates civilians' experience of the war from soldiers' experience of it while Dickinson's poem emphasizes that no one remains untouched by the conflict. Dickinson plunges her speaker into the midst of the war's carnage, yet she does so in such an oblique manner that the kind of reader who might be unsettled by her representation of violence can read the poem as presenting nothing more than an autumnal scene. For her part, Piatt takes a risk in writing about battle, but she controls that risk by positioning her feminine speaker away from the front and by emphasizing her separation from it: for Piatt's speaker, the worlds of battle are "worlds unknown."

Like "Hearing the Battle," Piatt's "My Dead Fairies" evokes battlefield carnage by way of romantic landscape depiction and by way of contrast with a genteel Victorian domesticity. In "My Dead Fairies," Piatt stages a startling collision between a high Victorian image of fairies in a meadow and a battlefield covered with Civil War dead. Though the poem does not explicitly identify its location, Piatt's motific use of the "fairyland" seems to suggest a Southern context. Like many of Piatt's finest poems, "My Dead Fairies" is structured by a dialogic exchange between two voices, in this case a mother and child. The child's question about mortality prompts for the mother a vivid wave of awareness that her day-to-day life is unfolding in close proximity to Civil War battlefields where thousands lie dead:

MY DEAD FAIRIES

"Do the Fairies ever die?"
  Why, yes, they are always dying.
There, in the freezing dark close by,
  A thousand, dead, are lying.

Of the time they made so fair
  But the fading shadow lingers;
Oh, how the light gold of my hair
  Curled on their airy fingers!

I shall not see them again.
  They fell in the Sun's fierce bright'ning;
They were drowned in drops of – "Rain?"
  They were burned to death with lightning.

With bloom, as the bee-songs pass,
  Our sweet-briar keeps its promise;
The fireflies shine in the grass;
  Winds blow our butterflies from us!

Yet under that thin gray tree,
  With the moonrise in its stillness,
They keep hidden away from me,
  Forever, in dusty [ch]illness. (19)

Far from reassuring the child about the immortality of the fairies, the mother responds by suggesting that the dying and dead—the countless victims of the war—are everywhere present and always nearby. Stanza three evokes the violence of combat, a violence she figures first with a fierce sun, then with an image of drowning, and finally with scorching lightning. The reference to lightning evokes the destructive power of artillery fire as well as the torching of cities that became a central strategy of Sherman's campaign through the South. The reference to lightning also echoes Julia Ward Howe's "Battle Hymn" in which a God of righteous anger looses "the fateful lightning of his terrible swift sword" on a nation gone astray. What's missing in Piatt's response to Howe's image is a God who judges who shall live and who shall die. As represented in Piatt's poem, battlefield deaths are so numerous as to be depersonalized: they are swift and visually arresting, but without a redemptive Christian meaning.

Like Timrod's sonnet "I know not why," in which a romantic speaker out for a solitary walk stumbles on a symbolic corpse, Piatt's "My Dead Fairies" uses high Victorian fairy imagery to emphasize that the Civil War dead are always nearby. Yet while Timrod's poem is suspended between romanticism and a more graphic realism, Piatt's "My Dead Fairies" suggests that the thin veneer of Victorian imagery can only temporarily paper over the trauma of the war. Piatt's use of fairy imagery to evoke battlefields signals the exhaustion of the Victorian aesthetic and foregrounds her critique of sentimental visions of battlefield deaths. Like Dickinson's wartime landscape poems, Piatt's "My Dead Fairies" uses images of a pastoral world not to describe nature's recuperative cycles, but rather to point toward the violence inherent in nature and the arbitrary way that death and suffering are meted out in war. In "They dropped like Flakes" and "The name – of it – is 'Autumn' – ," Dickinson uses images of changing seasons, falling leaves, and falling snow to conjure up not only the speed and regularity with which death comes on the battlefield but also the vast scale of the destruction. By presenting battlefield carnage in the guise of decorative landscape depiction, Dickinson and Piatt both offer ironic commentary on the argument that genteel women should write about what they know best: namely children, the home, flowers, and nature. In these poems, Dickinson and Piatt suggest that their perspective on the American landscape has been irrevocably changed by the war, underlining the idea that even seemingly tranquil pastoral vistas were once scenes of suffering. Moreover, Piatt writes with an acute awareness that while the war happened elsewhere for Northern civilians, for many Southerners battlefields were not remote. Unlike many of her Northern counterparts then, Piatt explicitly addresses a dual audience, seeking to represent the proximity of Southern battlefields in a way that will be meaningful for both Northern and Southern readers. The possessive pronoun in the poem's title signals the immediate proximity of the dead; the poem implies they lie just beyond the speaker's garden. The singular possessive pronoun also emphasizes that the speaker's awareness of the dead isolates her in a posture of mourning; the poem offers no unified "we" of female mourners.

"My Dead Fairies" turns abruptly back to the genteel imagistic repertoire in stanza four, back to the poetic language of the garden, but the abruptness of that swerve implies not a confident closure of the earlier topic—war's destructive power—but rather a painful swerve away from unbearable knowledge. With its jarring juxtapositions of darkness and brightness, summer warmth and winter's chill, life and death, the poem underlines how closely these opposites are wedded to each other. Images of plenitude—swarms of bees and flowers and fireflies—implicitly evoke the vast numbers of the dead, and the field of flowers points toward the national rituals of Decoration Day; the meadow or garden becomes a cemetery.[12] One of the most arresting aspects of this poem is the way that it evokes the omnipresence and proximity of the dead who are nonetheless lost to the speaker, "hidden away" forever though they are always still dying and always "in the freezing dark close by" (19). The poem implies that there can be no temporal closure, no resolution, no letting go of the war's traumatic losses: "'Do the Fairies ever die?'/Why, yes, they are always dying." Because the poem is structured around a dialogue between mother and child, Piatt implies that the mother's inability to achieve closure on these losses will profoundly shape her relationship to the child: just as the mother can see only the carnage of battlefields when she looks out on the garden, so too will the child be irrevocably shaped by the mother's dark vision. The poem uses the maternal speaker's address to her child to critique sentimental and sanitized depictions of battlefield deaths. Piatt here seems both to literalize and to ironize the late nineteenth-century fascination with fairies, undermining the sentimental postures that would represent the dead as sleeping at peace or that would represent fairies as bloodless and benevolent immortal beings. She may also be suggesting that Americans' memories of the war and the war dead are more harrowing by far than any encounters with fairies and ghosts from poetry could be. In "My Dead Fairies," the genteel Victorian aesthetic proves to be nothing more than a thin veneer covering over but not containing the traumatic memory of war.

In representing the South of her childhood as a fairyland lost to the war's ravages, Piatt also reflects on her own conflicted relationship to slaves she knew as a child. In poems like "The Black Princess" and "A Child's Party," she examines the complex bonds of affection, racial hierarchy, and family loyalty that allied her with her African American nurse and with the enslaved black playmates of her childhood. "The Old Slave-Music" and "Over in Kentucky" both consider how the war irrevocably changed those bonds, upending the lives of black and white Southerners. In these two poems, Piatt imagines, from her position of white middle-class privilege, that slaves too might mourn the loss of some aspects of that earlier way of life; in both poems, she gives particular attention to the collective singing of the slaves and white and black characters' memories of it. While the white female speaker in "The Old Slave-Music" suggests that singing offered slaves a provisional form of freedom—a freedom that has now been forever lost because of the war—"Over in Kentucky" imagines a three-way conversation between a white mother, her daughter, and a black woman who was once enslaved, representing all three characters' visions of a lost Southern world. The former slave is most likely based on Piatt's African American nurse, who appears as a motific figure of wisdom and compassion in several of Piatt's poems. Like "Hearing the Battle" and "My Dead Fairies," "Over in Kentucky" relies on romantic landscape description to evoke the lost splendor of the South. In "Over in Kentucky," however, Piatt also offers a complex and multilayered analysis of the ways in which the bonds of slavery and family shape remembered and imaginary visions of the South for these three women.

Set in Cincinnati, Ohio, where its characters can look back with longing toward the state where the adult women used to live, "Over in

Kentucky" suggests that each woman's nostalgia and desire shapes the longing of the others. The poem opens with an unidentified speaker lamenting the industrialized grittiness of Cincinnati: "This is the smokiest city in the world" (36). This first speaker would seem to be the young daughter of the poem's main speaker, a middle-class white woman. In stanza one, the daughter wishes aloud that she might travel to the antebellum world her mother conjures up in her stories: "I'd like to have my prettiest hat and go / There were some violets had to stay, you said, / Before your torn-up butterflies were dead" (36). Even as the daughter longs to travel to the South, she acknowledges that the South of her mother's stories no longer exists.

As the poem's narrative unfolds, each of the three female characters in turn expresses this longing to return to the antebellum South. In stanzas two and three, the former slave recalls the world that has been lost and the white female speaker reflects on the black woman's nostalgia for that world:

> Then one, whose half-sad face still wore the hue
> The North Star loved to light and linger on,
> Before the war, looked slowly at me too,
> And darkly whispered: "What is gone is gone.
> Yet, though it may be better to be free,
> I'd rather have things as they used to be
> Over in Kentucky."
>
> Perhaps I thought how fierce the master's hold,
> Spite of all armies kept the slave within;
> How iron chains, when broken, turned to gold,
> In empty cabins where glad songs had been,
> Before the Southern sword knew blood and rust,
> Before wild cavalry sprang from the dust,
> Over in Kentucky. (37)

In these stanzas, both the freed slave and the white female speaker express a profound ambivalence about the end of the Southern way of life. In all of Piatt's poems about her relationship to slaves, her position of white middle-class privilege limits her ability to imagine the perspective of those slaves. What's remarkable about her representation of the former slave's nostalgia in "Over in Kentucky," however, is the extent to which she underlines that the former slave and her former mistress are allied by their shared ambivalence about the South. The former slave balances the view "it may be better to be free" against her nostalgia for the past: "I'd rather have things as they used to be." In symmetrical fashion, the white mother first imagines the counterargument—that the war rightfully ended the terrible wrong of slavery—before going on to express her own longing for the antebellum South. Advancing the counterargument, she declares that slavery had a "fierce" and terrible hold on the lives of the enslaved which "armies"—at least initially—could not end. Ultimately, however, the war's violence turns those "iron chains" into "gold," liberating the enslaved.

Yet even as she acknowledges that the war ended the "fierce" hold of masters over slaves, the white mother also feels nostalgic for the Southern world that has been lost. So she will conjure up the Southern fairyland as a story to tell her daughter, one which, the poem implies, she will also tell readers of her poetry: "I have a phantom pencil that can make / Shadows of moons, far back and faint, to rise" (stanza 4, p. 37). In these lines, the mother acknowledges that that world is the product of her own nostalgic imagination. She has shaped her child's longing for this world of the past, and the past that the child longs for is a past that never existed: a past of "unshaped steel, unfancied wars, / Unbuilded cities, and unbroken lands" (stanza 8, p. 37). The poem implies that the land was "broken" and that the war was fueled both by the industry of smoky Northern cities—cities where steel was shaped into munitions—and by the romantic military pride of the South with its "Southern sword," its "wild cavalry" (stanza 3, p. 37), and its "graves where legends hide" (stanza 5, p. 37). Though the white mother conjures up the utopia of an innocent Southern paradise, she knows that that paradise was built both by Southern slavery and, indirectly, by Northern industry. Ultimately, "Over in Kentucky" uses a dialogic exchange between a white female speaker and her former slave to establish a utopian bond of nostalgia between the two women. This is the unstated "we" of the poem: Piatt suggests that the white mother and her former slave are united by their shared understanding of their own ambivalent longing for the past, an understanding that excludes not only the speaker's daughter but also implicitly the Northern white readers whose position the speaker's daughter represents. For like the daughter's longing for the antebellum South, the

Northern white reader's affection for the Edenic South is shaped entirely by the white female speaker's stories; "Over in Kentucky" emphasizes that those stories are shaped by a profoundly ambivalent speaker who nonetheless seeks to enchant and to entertain.

While the female speaker in "Over in Kentucky" meditates briefly on her own and her daughter's relationship to the war's violence (the "unshaped steel" and "unfancied wars" of stanza six), in other poems Piatt gives still more extensive attention to white women's relationship to the violence of combat. In "Another War," which was first published in 1872, Piatt again offers a dialogue between a mother and a child that seems to implicate both in the longing for a return to war. In "The Palace-Burner" and "Paris," she uses French settings to explore white Southern women's relationship to Southern codes of military heroism. All three poems examine the ways in which white Southern women endorsed and supported a military ethos for white Southern men.

"Another War" opens with the maternal speaker viewing a parade of soldiers, seemingly through the eyes of her young son. In stanzas one through six, the speaker addresses the son with a reiterated "you," articulating what the boy sees and how she understands his response. The maternal speaker imagines that she gives voice to the son's thoughts. Stanza two reads:

> You think the captain looks so fine,
>   You like, I know, the long sharp flash,
> The fair silk flags above the line,
>   The pretty scarlet sash? (27)

The simplicity of meter and rhyme scheme echoes the simplicity of children's rhymes, suggesting that the speaker's son is a young child, easily dazzled by the sounds and sights of a parade of uniformed men. Already in this second stanza, however, Piatt begins to sow seeds of doubt about what the mother does and does not know about her son's desires. Details in the phrasing that underline that the poem is spoken to the son also undermine the idea that the mother understands her son's desires: the confident "I know" of line two is belied by the question mark that ends the stanza.

The poem next presents the expected contrast between the older wiser adult's perspective on the war and the boy's romantic visions of it. In stanza four, a superior-sounding maternal voice declares:

I wisely think the uniform
  Was made for skeletons to wear
But your young blood is quick and warm,
  And so—you do not care. (28)

Here the mother's experience of the traumatic losses of the war shapes her perspective on the passing soldiers: looking at living bodies in uniforms, she sees the skeletons they will become or the skeletons that their predecessors became. The reiterated "you" of the address to the son becomes gently accusatory as the maternal speaker declares "And so—you do not care." The central question of the poem is posed in its fifth stanza:

You lift your eager eyes and ask:
  "Could we not have another war?"
As I might give this fearful task
  To armies near and far. (28)

Almost immediately after hearing the question, however, the poem's maternal speaker has a startling revelation: it was not her child who posed this question—"Could we not have another war?"—but rather she herself. Here Piatt's dialogic technique yields a particularly interesting and unsettling turn. The child's voice calling for a return to war is revealed to have been the mother's voice, and the son who has been the addressee throughout the poem is abruptly supplanted by an unidentified "dear," presumably a double or split of the maternal self:

It was that restless, wavering child
  I call Myself. No other, dear.
Perhaps you knew it when you smiled
  Because none else was near.

The alternation of the reiterated "you" with the maternal "I" leads to an instability in the articulated "we": for the "we" of nostalgia for war would be an unspeakable "we," unimaginable from the perspective of adult maternal wisdom and experience. The maternal speaker sounds world-weary, bemused, and incredulous by turns, as she tries, in the poem's final stanzas, to make sense of her own longing for a return to war:

Then not my boy, it seems, but I
  Would wage another war?—to see

> The shining sights, to hear the cry
> Of ghastly victory? (28)

The reiterated question marks imply that the speaker does not know her own desires any more than she knew those of her son. The poem implies both that the desire for war is inevitable in the "warm" blood of the young and that that desire is handed down from mother to child.

Even as she calls herself a "restless, wavering child," however, the speaker also emphasizes her acutely adult awareness of the inevitability of loss. She insists that she does not long for war because of its romance; another war could bring "no second bloom to wither'd flowers,/No second song to birds that sing" (stanza 11, p. 28). Rather she argues in the poem's final stanza that life itself is so laden with loss that she can imagine no world beyond the war:

> But, friend, since time is full of pain,
> Whether men fall by field or hearth,
> I want the old war back again,
> And nothing new on earth! (29)

In the final stanza, the poem's addressee has again changed, this time to a generalized "friend," presumably another adult. The closing address to an unspecified "friend" would seem to be part of the speaker's crisis: she seeks an interlocutor or listener who will understand the tangle of her own conflicted responses to the war. It is precisely those aspects of the poem that make Piatt seem like a less skillful poet—the pronoun slippage, the shift in speakers—that make this poem particularly representative of Piatt's dilemmas as a poet: though she mainly addresses a white middle-class Northern audience with her work—as evidenced by her frequent placing of poems in prestigious Northeastern literary magazines—Piatt has an intimate knowledge of Southern culture, Southern codes of masculine heroism, and the racial hierarchies of the South that her Northern readers lack. The speaker's crisis of address is also therefore a crisis of identity: is she a mother who worries that her naïve and enthusiastic son will blindly march off to a war or a young woman who remembers the romantic power and glamour of military trappings? She is both and neither, and the polyvocality of the poem narrows Piatt's audience to a very limited group of readers, those who are willing to tease out the complexities of the ambivalent female speaker's positions. While the slippage between the son's desires and the female speaker's desires in Piatt's "Another War" suggests that women's desires play a crucial role in endorsing and sustaining the violence of combat, the more important form of slippage in the poem is the proliferation of unidentified addressees, as Piatt anxiously tries to imagine that there might be at least a few readers or listeners who could understand her speaker's position.

Ultimately, however, what "Another War" signals is Piatt's overriding conviction that such readers will be few and far between—and those few will be easily shocked by the speaker's nostalgia for the war. In "Another War," she uses the unexpected slippage between the son's and the mother's perspective on the passing parade of soldiers to soften the shock effect of a white American woman of a Southern background calling for a return to war's violence. In "The Palace-Burner" and "Paris," Piatt uses French settings to explore emotional stances that might have been still more shocking to American readers had she directly attributed them to an American woman of the South. Piatt turns to French settings because her ambivalence about Confederate nationalism prohibits her from positing a Confederate nationalist "we" in her poetry. In these two poems, Piatt takes as her subjects the fall of Paris to Prussian forces in January 1871 ("Paris") and the Paris Commune uprising of the spring of 1871 ("The Palace-Burner"). Though both poems respond to European violence, their urgency and vitality undoubtedly result from Piatt's emotional engagement with the American Civil War. In the palaces of Paris, Piatt finds an apt metaphor for the beauty, corruption, and aristocratic privilege on which American Southern society relied. "The Palace-Burner" points to the class tensions and reformist impulses that resulted in the creation of the Commune even as it also points obliquely toward the class hierarchy that underwrote Southern nationalism. The Commune also offers Piatt a particularly vivid example of a civil conflict that placed women in prominent leadership roles. "The Palace-Burner" thus examines the role that French women played in the violence of the uprising; it also reflects on the gentility and privilege of American Southern women, examining the relationship between white Southern femininity and the war's violence.

Like "Another War," which was also first published in 1872, "The Palace-Burner" takes the form of a dialogue between a mother and her son; again like "Another War," "The Palace-Burner" suggests that women play a key role in supporting the violence of combat. In July 1871, *Harper's Weekly* featured an illustration of a "pétroleuse" or "palace-burner" as she awaited execution for her participation in the Commune uprising, and it is this illustration that the American mother and son consider at the start of Piatt's poem.[13] The opening stanzas establish gender positions that the rest of the poem will then exaggerate and re-examine: the son's desire to commit acts of destruction is contrasted with the demure American mother's shocked response.

THE PALACE-BURNER
(A *Picture in a Newspaper*)

She has been burning palaces. "To see
The sparks look pretty in the wind?" Well, yes—
And something more. But women brave as she
Leave much for cowards such as I to guess.

But this is old, so old that everything
Is ashes here—the woman and the rest.
Two years are oh! so long. Now you may bring
Some newer pictures. You like this one best?

You wish that you had lived in Paris then?
You would have loved to burn a palace, too?
But they had guns in France, and Christian men
Shot wicked little Communists, like you.

You would have burned the palace? Just because
You did not live in it yourself! Oh! why?
Have I not taught you to respect the laws?
You would have burned the palace. Would not *I*?

Would I? Go to your play. Would I, indeed?
I? Does the boy not know my soul to be
Languid and worldly, with a dainty need
For light and music? Yet he questions me.

Can he have seen my soul more near than I?
Ah! in the dusk and distance sweet she seems,
With lips to kiss away a baby's cry,
Hands fit for flowers, and eyes for tears and dreams.

Can he have seen my soul? And could she wear
    Such utter life upon a dying face,
Such unappealing, beautiful despair,
    Such garments—soon to be a shroud—with grace?

Has she a charm so calm that it could breathe
    In damp, low places till some frightened hour;
Then start, like a fair, subtle snake, and wreathe
    A stinging poison with a shadowy power?

Would *I* burn palaces? The child has seen
    In this fierce creature of the Commune here,
So bright with bitterness and so serene,
    A being finer than my soul, I fear. (39–40)

In the poem's opening stanza, the seemingly innocent son, contemplating the picture, imagines the woman's action as a playful or mischievous gesture, asking his mother if the woman has burned palaces "To see/The sparks look pretty in the wind?." Piatt, however, swiftly undercuts the idea of the son's innocence by addressing the subject of his desire to take part in the violent drama his mother has described. In a tone of mild reproof, his shocked mother questions: "You wish that you had lived in Paris then?/You would have loved to burn a palace, too?" Responding to the picture before her, the female speaker contrasts the palace-burner's bravery with her own genteel cowardice. This contrast forms the central drama of the poem in stanzas five through eight, as the speaker questions the relationship between her own life and the life of the palace-burner. Dialogic shifts and pronoun ambiguities proliferate in this dense and multilayered section of the poem.

Like the female speaker of "Another War," the female speaker of "The Palace-Burner" embarks on a process of self-scrutiny. Pressed by her son to say whether or not she would have burned a palace herself, the speaker wonders, "Can he have seen my soul more near than I?" As in "Another War," the mother's dialogue with her son now becomes a dialogue with herself. As so often in Piatt's work, there are few collective pronouns and no collective "we"; instead the poem offers a shifting array of positions for the "I," the "you," and the "she." The speaker begins by describing herself as the genteel Victorian housewife, "languid and worldly, with a dainty need/For light and music," phrasing that also marks the difference in social class between the speaker and the working-class palace-burner. In stanzas six, seven, and eight, she extends this examination of her own genteel femininity. These three stanzas suggest multiple and mutually exclusive interpretive possibilities for the third-person feminine figure whom they describe, an ambiguity that becomes the crucial interpretive knot of the poem. One reading would see the maternal speaker as the "she" of these stanzas, a reading that interprets the pronoun shift from "I" to "she" as a splitting of the self, an experience of self-alienation in the process of self-scrutiny. Still another reading would read this "she" as describing the "palace-burner," a reading that would allow the third-person to function consistently throughout the poem. Piatt overlays one female character on top of the other in order to examine the genteel American mother's relationship to the working-class French woman's actions.

Stanza six represents motherhood in a series of idealized images, images that seem to support a reading of this "she" as the poem's genteel American speaker: "Ah! In the dusk and distance sweet she seems, / With lips to kiss away a baby's cry, / Hands fit for flowers, and eyes for tears and dreams." By stanza seven, however, the "she" the speaker refers to becomes more ambiguous:

> And could she wear
> Such utter life upon a dying face,
> Such unappealing beautiful despair,
> Such garments—soon to be a shroud—with grace? (40)

In this stanza, the image of the genteel mother facing her own death is superimposed on the image of the palace-burner who faces the execution squad so that the identity of the "she" becomes undecidable. One reading would suggest that the American speaker contemplates and admires the courage, "grace." and beauty with which the French palace-burner faces her death. Still another reading would suggest a comparison between the genteel American woman's death and that of the palace-burner, as the speaker wonders aloud if she could face death with the palace-burner's fearlessness and commitment. A third possible reading would suggest that the genteel Victorian mother is dying of her own languor and passivity, dying of her powerlessness in the world—"such unappealing beautiful despair"—and dying a glamorous and picturesque Victorian death, in the graceful "shroud" of her "garments." Like the female speaker in "Hearing the Battle," this version of the "she" is caught within the suffocating confines of Victorian domestic femininity. Stanza seven suggests all three possibilities without at this point obliging a reader to choose among them.

In the eighth stanza, the speaker imagines the stealth and deception that enabled the palace-burner to perpetrate acts of violence. She imagines the woman starting "like a fair, subtle snake" and wielding "a stinging poison." These lines, however, also seem to describe the kinds of social power that women may exercise without ever taking up weapons or torches—the kinds of power genteel middle-class women may exercise through stealth, wiles, and manipulation:

> Has she a charm so calm that it could breathe
> In damp low places till some frightened hour;
> Then start, like a fair, subtle snake, and wreathe
> A stinging poison with a shadowy power?

The stanza suggests the repressed rage that lurks beneath the surface of the genteel woman's languor—"the charm so calm that it could breathe / in damp low places." It also suggests the ways that female anger invisibly supports and sustains the anger that men express through physical violence: the woman's "charm" wreathes the "stinging power" of male violence with a "shadowy power." Read in this light, the stanza seems to suggest that women's pride and anger might serve as the fuel for wars fought by men; or read in the American Civil War context, this stanza implies that the Southern code of genteel femininity sustains the Southern code of masculine heroism in battle.

In its final stanza, however, the poem abruptly closes off the multiple possibilities that stanzas six through eight propose by responding to the accumulated list of unanswered questions: the speaker suggests that her son's prying questions have exposed her own hypocrisy and impotence. She returns to her earlier position, suggesting that the woman of the Commune represents "a being finer than my soul, I fear." Yet while the poem's conclusion once again emphasizes the contrast between the palace-burner's violent acts and the genteel Victorian mother's passivity, in establishing this contrast the poem as a whole has reflected on what connects the two women. And at the very least, the multiple reading possibilities suggest multiple possible avenues for expression of female anger. In her analysis of the poem, Bennett reads the genteel Victorian mother's passivity as evidence of her "apolitical narcissism," her failure to act in response to the social injustice that surrounds her.[14] Yet while the poem bears out this reading, I would argue that the poem's shift from mother-son dialogue to internal dialogue within the mother, its pronoun slippage, and its polyvocality all work to accomplish still more than offering a critique of genteel feminine passivity. As I have suggested, the poem also implicitly explores the ways that genteel femininity invisibly endorses male violence. Both the speaker's internal dialogue and the insistent use of unanswered questions in stanzas five through eight work to unsettle any easy opposition between the palace-burner and the speaker, by emphasizing a capacity for motherhood, a capacity for rage, and a capacity for violence that both women share.

While "The Palace-Burner" characterizes genteel femininity as sheltered and secure, still another Piatt poem on political upheaval in France suggests that the violence of war touches even the most sheltered women—that no veneer of gentility can be sustained in the face of war's onslaught. In the poem "Paris," which first appeared in 1871, Piatt invents a female speaker who speaks either from beyond the grave or from beyond innocence about the ravages of war:

PARIS

(January, 1871)

Speak! Dying, that never can be dead!
Speak! O wounded, and wan, and wasted!
"Blood is better than wine," she said—
"Famine the sweetest food I have tasted.

"Pallor is brighter than bloom, and scars
Than my old jewels have made me fairer.
When the Vapor put out my lamps, the stars
Gave me a surer light and a rarer.

"My flowers were false, my glory was shame,
My Life was Death, in my years of pleasure.
Divine from my sorrow my Beauty came—
Safe in my ashes shall shine my treasure." (16–17)

The poem opens with an unidentified speaker addressing a dying woman—"Speak! Dying, that never can be dead!"—in terms that glorify the cause for which she has suffered. In answer to this call, the main female speaker replies with a list of comparisons, taking the measure of her life before and after the war: "'Blood is better than wine,' she said/Famine the sweetest food I have tasted." Since the poem's title situates the main female speaker in the four-month-long siege of Paris that ended the Franco-Prussian war, the dialogue between the unidentified first speaker and the main female speaker in the rest of the poem suggests an American woman calling on a French woman to describe her experience of this siege. Read in relation to the American Civil War, this exchange implies that the American woman reflects on the ways that war has ravaged the lives not only of Parisian women, but also of American women, particularly Southern women whose lives and homes were most immediately upended by the conflict. The poem thus layers the experience of the Southern belle over the experience of the aristocratic French woman. Read from this angle, the main speaker is not just a French aristocrat but also a Southern belle who still expresses loyalty to the South, even as she describes her former life of luxury as a life of sham-glories. Moreover, the poem also points to the numbers of Southern women who suffered injury and deprivation during the war years; famine cut across all social classes in the South. Speaking of the pleasures of her aristocratic past, the woman declares that the sufferings of war are a more dazzling ornament than her former blushes and jewels. The third and final stanza suggests that the speaker sees her antebellum life as a kind of hypocrisy, a kind of Death-in-life: "My flowers were false, my glory was shame,/My Life was Death, in my years of pleasure" (17). By contrast then, the suffering she has endured in the aftermath of war has granted her a more legitimate beauty: "Divine from my sorrow my Beauty came—/Safe in my ashes shall shine my treasure." In the poem's closing lines, the speaker at once memorializes and repudiates the luxurious life she led in the antebellum years. While the speaker of "The Palace-Burner" remains trapped beneath a genteel veneer that prevents her from taking direct and violent action, the female speaker in "Paris" emphasizes that her sufferings testify to her direct involvement with the war. Setting these two poems in a French context allows Piatt to explore contradictory arguments about women's relationship to violence by inventing multiple positions for her female speakers; setting the poems in a French context also allows her the freedom to write with great emotional intensity, exploring genteel feminine passivity and powerlessness even as she also explores the ways that white Southern women were ravaged by the Civil War.

Ultimately what links all of Piatt's Civil War–related poems is their focus on the ways that social and gender roles support a Southern code of masculine heroism; again and again, Piatt uses her female speakers to offer critical scrutiny of the ways that men and women endorse that code. While "The Palace-Burner" and "Paris" explore Southern women's relationship to violence, in "A Ghost at the Opera," Piatt calls forth the motivic figure of her Southern warrior-lover, a character who appears in some of her most accomplished and widely anthologized poems, including "Giving Back the Flower" and "Mock Diamonds." In all three of these poems, Piatt attends to the ways that romantic desire between men and women sustains the ideologies that fuel the war. If the "fairyland" is Piatt's code word for the South, then the central human figure in that "fairyland" is the Southern soldier. Piatt uses the figure of a Confederate officer—gallant but morally corrupt, handsome but visibly scarred, a figure who often appears in the guise of a former lover—to embody the South and the fate of the Confederacy. Her decision to use the gallant Southern soldier as her central symbol for the Confederacy is particularly striking when read in relation to Civil War poems by male writers from both North and South. In poems by writers as varied as William Gilmore Simms, Confederate footsoldier George Washington Hall, Sidney Lanier, and Oliver Wendell Holmes, the South is inevitably figured as a woman—a voluptuous beauty, a bride-to-be, a ravaged mother, or a capricious but lovable sister. In the context of this tradition, Piatt's decision to make the Southern soldier her central figure is clearly highly self-conscious.

In "A Ghost at the Opera," first published in 1873, Piatt uses a theatrical setting to focus on the idea that wartime gender roles are performed, not innate. "A Ghost at the Opera" links the illusions of theater with the illusory splendors of the antebellum South, tying the performance of emotion in the theater with the performance of emotion on the battlefield.

A GHOST AT THE OPERA

It was, I think, the Lover of the play:
  He, from stage-incantations, turned his head,
And one remembered motion shook away
  The whole mock fairyland and raised the dead.

I, in an instant, saw the scenery change.
    Old trees before me by enchantment grew.
Late roses shivered, beautiful and strange.
    One red geranium scented all the dew.

A sudden comet flung its awful vail
    Around the frightened stars. A sudden light
Stood, moon-shaped, in the East. A sudden wail
    From troubled music smote the spectral night.

Then blue sweet shadows fell from flower-like eyes,
    And purplish darkness drooped on careless hair,
And lips most lovely—ah, what empty sighs,
    Breathed to the air, for something less than air!

Oh, beauty such as no man ever wore
    In this wan world outside of Eden's shine,
Save he who vanished from the sun before
    Youth learned that youth itself was not divine!

I might have touched that fair and real ghost,
    He laughed so lightly, looked so bright and brave—
So all unlike that thin and wavering host
    Who walk unquiet from the quiet grave.

Myself another ghost as vain and young,
    And nearer Heaven than now by years and years,
My heart, like some quick bird of morning, sung
    On fluttering wings above all dust and tears.

But some great lightning made a long red glare:
    Black-plumed and brigand-like I saw him stand—
What ghastly sights, what noises in the air!
    How sharp the sword seemed in his lifted hand!

He looked at me across the fading field.
    The South was in his blood, his soul, his face.
Imperious despair, too lost to yield,
    Gave a quick glory to a desperate grace.

I saw him fall! I saw the deadly stain
    Upon his breast—he cared not what was won.
The ghost was in the land of ghosts again.
    The curtain fell, the phantom play was done. (43–44)

Offering a history in miniature of the Civil War, this poem exposes both the artifice and the ideologies that underwrite Southern nationalism by juxtaposing the history of the war with the unfolding of a drama on the stage. Piatt develops this critique through four stages of analysis: first she considers the construct of the South as an Edenic paradise; next she considers the Godlike beauty of the opera's gallant young hero; she then turns to her female speaker's participation in the drama and the ways that the performance engages her; lastly she turns to the battlefield itself, evoking scenes of combat through a series of stylized stage postures. Nowhere does the poem establish a collective "we," refusing both the collective stance of Confederate nationalism and also the collective stance of the audience witnessing the opera; again Piatt presents a solitary female speaker who contemplates the war's terrible costs in genteel isolation from others.

In stanzas two and three, Piatt carefully disassembles the "mock fairyland" of the Southern natural paradise. Underlining the extent to which that romantic paradise was a construct of human imagination and human labor, she describes how clever stagecraft can make the garden come to life in the theater: "Old trees before me by enchantment grew. / Late roses shivered, beautiful and strange. / One red geranium scented all the dew" (43). These lines also point obliquely toward the unseen slave labor that maintained the Southern garden paradise. Stanza three begins by alluding to the comet of 1861, a comet first visible in the northern hemisphere in June of that year. Steeped in the Protestant faith in signs, Northerners and Southerners alike interpreted the comet as a sign of God's intervention in human affairs: "A sudden comet flung its awful vail / Around the frightened stars" (44). Piatt undermines the Protestant faith in signs, however, by reminding her readers that this particular heavenly phenomenon is produced not by God, but rather by the theater's lighting designer. And the lighting designer's decisions are supported by the music from the orchestra: "A sudden light stood moon-shaped in the East. A sudden wail / From troubled music smote the spectral night" (44). The insistent repetition of the word "sudden" underlines that the astonishment of the audience is carefully controlled by the decisions of the opera's director and designer. Piatt here implies a link between stagecraft and the nationalist and romantic ideologies of the Confederacy.

In stanzas four through seven, Piatt turns from the staging of that garden paradise to the studied performance of the central hero, the young lover, considering also the presumably female speaker's enraptured response as a member of the audience. Like the garden setting in which he appears, the hero is figured in Edenic terms: his divine beauty, closely allied with that of nature, makes him seem like a young Adam. Here too, however, Piatt scatters numerous clues about the artifice that makes the Southern hero's beauty seem natural. The "blue sweet shadows" around his eyes and the "purplish darkness" on his "careless hair" point to the role that lighting, makeup, and hairstyle play in the theater. The actor plays the role of the "careless" nonchalant, but his appearance has been carefully staged. The romantic "empty sighs" that he "breath[es] to the air" underline the role of breath control in the singer's or actor's performance; these sighs, which stir such strong emotion in the audience, are artful rather than involuntary. And yet, as Piatt suggests again and again, the illusions of the hero's performance are wholly persuasive and compelling: "I might have touched that fair and real ghost, / He laughed so lightly, looked so bright and brave." Sitting in the audience, the speaker is so thoroughly drawn into the performance that she imagines that she herself is participating in it by breaking into song: "My heart, like some quick bird of morning, sung / On fluttering wings above all dust and tears." These lines imply that Southern women's romantic adoration sustains the performance of Southern masculine chivalry, that women's performances sustain the leading roles played by men. The speaker declares that she herself was "another ghost as vain and young" as the hero on the stage.

It is this engagement on the part of the audience—their faith in the illusion of the performance—that implicates Southern women in the battlefield violence that the last three stanzas of the poem describe. Stanzas nine and ten emphasize the intensity of the exchange of gazes between the hero and the speaker with the lines "He looked at me across the fading field" and "I saw him fall. I saw the deadly stain" (44). It is not the deadly wound that the speaker sees, but rather the "stain" of the artificial blood used for the performance. These lines also suggest a "stain" on the character of Southern masculinity as well: in a series of images that suggest the outsized gestures and postures of the opera, the last three stanzas present the solitary soldier as a symbol of wasted Southern male pride and courage. It is that waste that turns the godlike hero into a "brigand." These stanzas argue that the excesses of pride and an overly zealous performance of masculine heroism led to the South's downfall: "The South was in his blood, his soul, his face. / Imperious despair, too lost to yield. / Gave a quick glory to a desperate grace." The war, Piatt suggests, was one of quick performances, "quick glory" and quick deaths, deaths that effectively erase the meaning of victory. Indeed the poem's final stanza equates death with the loss of the ability to care about victory: "I saw him fall. I saw the deadly stain / Upon his breast—he cared not what was won." Here Piatt reads strongly against the literary and ideological tradition that interprets battlefield deaths as heavily laden with symbolic meaning; she clearly rejects the argument that a Civil War battlefield death is a form of Christian martyrdom. In the poem's final stanza, the soldier's performance of glory is emptied of meaning by his death—and by the actor's fall to the stage. The line "he cared not what was won" seems to suggest not only that the soldier has died, but also that the actor has finished his performance and that the emotions of the character he has played have ceased to matter to him. He has stepped out of his role with the drama's end: "The ghost was in the land of ghosts again. / The curtain fell, the phantom play was done." With this closing, Piatt indicts both the masculine player and the female audience member, suggesting that, in performing their respective roles, both have become complicit in the senseless waste of war, a war that she here dismisses as a stage show, a series of brief though visually arresting stage postures. Significantly Piatt focuses the poem not on the collective experience of soldiers but rather on the postures and gestures of an individual soldier and the emotional responses of an individual woman in the audience.

In her analysis of Piatt's work, Paula Bennett suggests that Piatt wrote herself out of an audience by positioning herself on the boundary between "the outmoded practices of an antebellum high sentimentalism and its emerging aesthetic and political antithesis, the irony-based modernism to come."[15] In her body of Civil War poetry, Piatt uses irony to undermine the beauty and tranquility of romantic landscapes and Victorian domestic scenes, foregrounding the horror of battlefield carnage and the trauma of wartime loss. In her insistent use of individual and often maternal female speakers, she marks her intended audience as a genteel and literary one. Her work addresses a genteel white Northern audience even as it also implies that a vast divide separates Northern readers from the experience of a white Southerner; she addresses a genteel Southern audience—the society into which she was born—even as she also critiques the gender roles and racial hierarchies on which Southern society was founded. In the shifting array of speakers and addressees whom Piatt creates for her poems, her anxiety about the challenges of finding an audience who might understand the complexity of her relationship to the South—to the slaves she knew as child, to genteel white Southern women, and to the figure of the heroic Confederate soldier—is writ large. Dialogic structures and pronoun ambiguities foreground the restlessness of her female speakers, who often assume stances only to abandon them for opposing or contradictory ones. Dialogues between mothers and children emphasize that enthusiasm for war is passed down from mother to child; at the same time, Piatt uses dialogues between mothers and children to offer a scathing critique of sentimental, sanitized visions of battlefield suffering. Shifts from mother-child dialogues to internal dialogues within maternal speakers probe at women's ambivalent relationship to the violence that ravages their homes. For Sarah Piatt, addressing the divided nation is a particularly fraught process since the splitting of the nation is deeply inscribed into her own life experience and indeed into the psyche that produces her poems. As the shifting array of speakers and addressees in her war poems makes clear, Piatt cannot imagine a unified American community in the war's aftermath; she cannot imagine a "we" that would work to reconstitute that nation. Nor can she imagine the collective "we" of genteel middle-class women enduring the trauma of war's losses: rather her female speakers are almost invariably solitary figures, isolated from one another in domestic settings where conversations with children and occasionally with husbands or lovers make up their daily round of events. Indeed so conflicted is Piatt by her Northern and Southern allegiances and by her awareness of the limitations of late nineteenth-century gender roles that she can scarcely imagine a unified "I" or self for any one of her female speakers. For Sarah Piatt, the traumatic dividing of the nation is reproduced in the traumatic dividing of the feminine poetic "I".

"The Southern Refugee": Romantic, Heroic, and Sentimental Stances in George Moses Horton

While Piatt's shifting pronouns and conflicted dialogic structures signal the challenges she faces as a white Southern woman addressing a split

Northern and Southern readership, the broad range of George Moses Horton's experiments with stances of address and pronoun positions underlines his eagerness to accommodate the tastes of as wide an array of readers as he can hope to reach with his work. As a successful white literary poet, Piatt has the luxury of displaying more frustration and more bitterness in her work than Horton does; both Horton and Piatt, however, use the flexibility of their poetic speakers' rhetorical stances to suggest indirectly their deeper frustrations with Confederate nationalism. Like Piatt, Horton finds himself in the position of being unable to use a collective Southern "we" as the foundation for his poetics because his loyalties are divided. A lifelong resident of the South, Horton expresses deep affection for the Southern natural world even as he also condemns the slavery that shaped Southern life and the Confederacy.

While Henry Timrod and Sarah Piatt both make literary romantic stances central to their wartime poetry, for George Moses Horton romanticism is just one of the range of postures he uses to try to maximize his appeal to multiple audiences, both Northern and Southern, white and black, military and civilian. Whereas Timrod relies for the most part on high literary stances to create and address a cultured white Southern readership, Horton echoes contemporary Southern romanticism, heroic classical verse, contemporary abolitionist poetry, popular sentimental stances, soldiers' marching songs, and patriotic verse in order to draw in a broader audience. Across the range of these poetic experiments, Horton uses a shifting network of pronouns to address and include his multiple readers. Like Julia Ward Howe, Horton will turn again and again to dramatic voice effects—using an apostrophe to slavery, to liberty, or to his fellow poets, for example, or speaking in the first person in the voice of Union or Confederate soldiers. Like Julia Ward Howe, Horton will use such voice effects both to establish his literary credentials as a poet and also to shore up the authority of his poet-speakers. In chapter three, I argued that Howe's reliance on voice-effects results from her exclusion, as a genteel middle-class woman, from the public platform of the lecture hall. In analogous fashion, Horton's commitment to using dramatic voice-effects results from the many ways in which he is restricted, as an enslaved black man, from writing and speaking. His ingenuity at resisting these restrictions—both in his life and in his poetry—is truly remarkable; his ability to work in multiple literary styles is central to this resistance.

Not surprisingly, Horton's work was initially dismissed by twentieth-century scholars both because of its imitative eclecticism and because some of the poems lack polish.[16] The critical assessment of Horton's work as stylistically eclectic is certainly apt as applied to *Naked Genius*, the group of poems that he published in the immediate aftermath of the war, many of which he wrote while on the march with the Ninth Michigan Cavalry; the volume also appears to have been edited in haste. Yet as Leon Jackson's incisive study of Horton's relationship to the literary marketplace suggests, Horton's work offers readers an important test case for understanding nineteenth-century American poets' strategic positioning of themselves in relation to their audiences.[17]

For George Moses Horton, an enslaved African American who gains his independence only when the Union Army reaches his home state, the lyric I of romanticism, the collective address to his fellow poets, the impersonal authoritative speaker, the accusatory "you" of the abolitionist's address to the slaveholder, and the collective "we" of soldiers returning home are all pronoun positions fraught with extraordinary challenges. A brief sketch of Horton's life will serve to illuminate the complexity of his relationship to these pronoun positions.[18] Born into slavery in North Carolina in the late 1790s, George Moses Horton began as a young man to make regular trips to Chapel Hill where he worked as a jack-of-all-trades for the white male students and faculty of the university, selling fruit, running errands, giving speeches on demand, and composing love poems made-to-order for students. Often writing these poems in the first person, Horton quickly became acquainted with the dramatic flexibility offered by poetic voice in particular and the genre of poetry more broadly. His frequent reliance on dramatic voice-effects including the apostrophe and dramatic personae in his poetry may result from his extensive experience at giving speeches on demand for assembled groups of students; the ability to mimic the rhetorical styles of other speakers would have stood Horton in good stead in this context.[19] So adept did he prove at writing poetry, giving speeches, and performing odd jobs that by the 1830s, Horton had succeeded in persuading his master to let him hire his own time. Though Horton learned to read in the 1810s, he did not learn to write until the 1830s; initially he composed his poems in his head and dictated them to his paying customers. Horton was thus well known as a poet in the state even before he had the ability to write; his strong commitment to regular rhyme and meter may well result from these early composition methods. In the late 1820s, the assistance of a white Northern-born female sponsor, Caroline Hentz, enabled Horton to publish poems in Northern newspapers; reprinting practices meant that Horton's work appeared in Northern papers read by both white and black audiences.[20] Meanwhile, white Southern supporters aimed to raise funds to buy Horton's freedom with the publication of his first collection, *The Hope of Liberty* (1829); though the fundraising attempt was unsuccessful, *The Hope of Liberty* was nonetheless the first book published by an African American living in the South. His second collection, *The Poetical Works of George M. Horton, the Colored Bard of North Carolina* (1845), shows the impact of the tightening restrictions on slaves in antebellum North Carolina: none of the forty-five poems Horton included in this collection is an anti-slavery poem, though the *Hope of Liberty* had foregrounded such pieces.

When the Union army arrived in North Carolina in April 1865, Horton—who was by this time in his late sixties—attached himself to the Ninth Michigan Cavalry Volunteers, traveling for some months with this unit and once again writing love poems made-to-order for young white men, in this case Union soldiers. Horton published his third and final collection of poems, *Naked Genius*, in the summer of 1865 with the help of William Banks, the captain of the Ninth Michigan; Joan Sherman notes that Horton composed ninety new poems for this volume during his summer of travel with the Michigan soldiers, a remarkable rate of productivity for any writer and particularly for one who was on the march as he worked.[21] In its generic versatility, Horton's *Naked Genius* shows the influence of this period of travel with the Michigan unit: many of the poems Horton includes in this collection offer specific addresses to groups of soldiers and echo the conventions of the songs and poems popular in the military camps. The eclectic collection also includes poems in praise of Union generals; poems mourning the death of Lincoln; temperance poems; comic ballads; many poems about romantic love; poems of complaint about being unhappily married; patriotic poems celebrating the reuniting of the nation; poems that criticize the Confederacy; many poems mourning a separation from home; and a few abolitionist pieces. Horton's long history of writing and delivering poems to University of North Carolina students clearly shapes the stances of *Naked Genius*: many of the romantic love poems in the volume could be written or spoken in the voice of a soldier who has left his beloved behind, and in several poems he writes in the first person in the voice of a soldier. Horton may have read or performed some of his poems for the soldiers he traveled with during the summer when he completed the editing of the volume. It is believed that he moved from Chapel Hill to Philadelphia about a year after *Naked Genius* appeared. Historian Reginald Pitts traces Horton's further periodical publications and his unsuccessful attempt to publish a fourth collection of poems following his move North. Pitts finds compelling evidence to suggest that Horton, disillusioned by Northern racism, emigrated to Liberia about a year after his arrival in Philadelphia. It is unclear whether he lived out the remainder of his days in Liberia or whether he eventually returned to the United States.[22]

Horton's postwar departure from the South becomes one of the crucial argumentative threads of *Naked Genius*, as Horton, like Piatt, meditates on the war's long-term impact on Southern society. He uses the stances of Southern romanticism to express a nostalgic longing for the landscapes of the Southern paradise. In exploring the workings and the limits of Southern romanticism, however, Horton, like Timrod, also works with explicitly political stances, thereby both endorsing and also destabilizing the linkage between a natural paradise and the Confederate South. His intimate acquaintance with the tastes and preferences of the white Southern readers who had enabled him to make a living as a writer is much in evidence on the pages of *Naked Genius:* Horton recognizes that paeans to the Southern homeland will strike a deep chord of recognition with a wide array of readers. Echoing the trope of the displaced Southerner that brought Dan Emmett great success in both the North and the South with "Dixie," several poems in *Naked Genius* present speakers who either explicitly or implicitly speak of their nostalgia for a Southern paradise. In the immediate aftermath of the war, of course, that nostalgia was felt by whites and blacks alike, as vast numbers of people of both races were displaced. Horton thus uses romantic stances to express the emotions both of white Southerners and of black Southerners—who would more fully understand the complexity of his ambivalent relationship to the South. In these pieces, Horton participates in a tradition of postbellum writings by Southern blacks that express a nostalgia for antebellum life in the South.[23] In expressing this nostalgia, Horton layers many different emotional stances on top of one another in a performance of masking that both conceals and reveals his own emotions; this performance seems to talk back to the stereotyped racism of blackface minstrelsy even as it also offers a forerunner to Paul Laurence Dunbar's strategic use of masking in his dialect poems. In Horton's treatment of it, the vision of a Southern paradise is always inflected by a melancholy that seems to point silently toward the ways that the violence of the slavery system has sustained the Southern way of life.

In "The Southern Refugee," Horton uses the conventional romantic posture of the solitary speaker's sorrow at parting to speak to the specific situation of the Southerner's farewell to his home. He uses a first-person romantic speaker to maximize possibilities for identification among his readers. In a way analogous to Julia Ward Howe's layering of her "Battle Hymn of the Republic" onto "John Brown's Body," Horton here offers a more literary rewriting of Emmett's "Dixie," elevating the speaker's diction and stance both to erase the racism of Emmett's blackface portrait and to offer a wider array of readers—white and black, Southern and Northern—a means of identification with the exile's lament:

> What sudden ill the world await,
> From my dear residence I roam;
> I must deplore the bitter fate,
> To straggle from my native home.
>
> The verdant willow droops her head,
> And seems to bid a fare thee well;
> The flowers with tears their fragrance shed,
> Alas! their parting tale to tell.
>
> 'Tis like the loss of Paradise,
> Or Eden's garden left in gloom,
> Where grief affords us no device,
> Such is thy lot, my native home.
>
> I never, never shall forget,
> My sad departure far away,
> Until the sun of life is set,
> And leaves behind no beam of day.
>
> How can I from my seat remove
> And leave my ever devoted home,

And the dear garden which I love,
  The beauty of my native home.

Alas! sequestered, set aside,
  It is a mournful tale to tell;
'Tis like a lone deserted bride
  That bade her bridegroom fare thee well.

I trust I soon shall dry the tear
  And leave forever hence to roam,
Far from a residence so dear,
  The place of beauty—my native home.[24]

Horton experiments with a range of conventional romantic stances: in stanza two, nature mourns in harmony with the human world as the willow "droops her head" and the flowers weep. The speaker declares that his decision to leave the South will mean "the loss of Paradise" (22). Yet he also goes on to state that this paradise has been blighted. When he describes the South with the phrase "Eden's garden left in gloom," he implies that whether or not he departs, the beauty of the landscape has been irrevocably damaged; the South will never recover from the dual ravages of war and of slavery. He insists that there will be no relief from this unbearable loss, for "grief affords us no device."

Pointing toward the complex ties of power, fear, hate, and love that bound masters and slaves together in the South, he compares his departure to the end of a marriage, when the "lone deserted bride" bids her "bridegroom fare thee well" (23). The slippage in Horton's metaphors opens up multiple reading possibilities: in conventional Confederate romantic poems, the Southern paradise is figured as a woman, but here Horton seems to position the woman as the refugee who parts from her beloved South, figured as the groom. Heightening the slippage around this gender reversal is the fact that the bride's position seems to be both passive—she is the "lone deserted bride"—and active—she bids him "fare thee well." That there is pain at parting is clear, but the cause of the parting and the source of the pain are left ambiguous. The speaker's momentary identification with the feminine position is noteworthy since Horton's work is often disparaging on the subject of women.

While Horton wants his white readers to identify with the emotions of his first-person speaker, the poem also points implicitly to the possibility of its speaker being black: one of the first audiences for the piece—the men of the Ninth Michigan Cavalry—may well have understood the speaker as Horton himself, particularly since he left his home to travel with their unit. Moreover, nineteenth-century readers not personally acquainted with Horton were reminded of the author's race twice on the title page of *Naked Genius*.[25] The poem's seventh and final stanza in particular seems to gesture toward the possibility of the speaker being black. Here Horton offers his most pointed rejoinder to Dan Emmett's "Dixie." In sharp contrast to the speaker of "Dixie" who reiterates his homesickness for the South in every chorus, Horton's poem insists in its final stanza that the speaker will achieve emotional closure on this longing:

> I trust I soon shall dry the tear
>   And leave forever hence to roam,
> Far from a residence so dear,
>   The place of beauty—my native home. (23)

While the final two lines again evoke a beloved Southern home, the first two lines emphatically assert that the speaker's mourning will end. In "The Southern Refugee," Horton offers an eloquent reply to Emmett's "Dixie," puncturing the racist caricature of Emmett's blackface speaker by giving voice to the complex mix of emotions that Horton's speaker feels as he considers what he will lose by heading North. In "The Southern Refugee," Horton dismisses the fantasy of "old times" in "Dixie" as fantasy, implicitly suggesting that this is a white fantasy that blacks can never share. At the same time, he uses the convention of the romantic speaker's grief at parting to lend authenticity and dignity to the experience of a grieving black Southern speaker; Horton's opaque and multilayered poem thus breathes depth and complexity into the African American's speaker's voice, as he mourns the prospect of his impending exile from the land where he was born and raised.

In still another poem that relies on romantic nature imagery, the speaker again meditates on his relationship to a lost homeland. In "My Native Home," however, the ambiguous metaphoric status of the poem's "native land" in combination with the emphatically reiterated possessive pronoun "my" signals the speaker's deeply conflicted relationship with that "land" (126–27). Drawing on the Revolutionary-era rhetoric about liberty that was central to both Union and Confederate ideologies, Horton uses the first person to speak for white and black Americans, both

Northerners and Southerners in this poem. Like Timrod, Horton invests a natural landscape with powerful political resonance. Yet while Timrod emphatically links an idyllic Southern natural paradise with the present and future glories of the Confederate nation, Horton uses a shifting sequence of associations to align both North and South with the elusive "liberty." Structuring the poem around a series of dramatic apostrophes to the ideal of "liberty" and to his "native home," Horton uses the slippage built into the figure of address to propose a series of conflicting ideas about the location of this "native home." The sequence of apostrophes may have made the poem a particular favorite for oral performance; the abstract quality of the apostrophes would have enabled multiple listeners or readers to identify with the speaker's expressed sentiments.

In "My Native Home" as in "The Southern Refugee," Horton uses the versatile position of the first-person speaker to sidestep the impossibility of constructing a collective "we" that will work for the multiple readers he hopes to reach. The first-person speaker also pushes the poem more firmly into the realm of high literary poetry and away from the collective postures of explicitly abolitionist poetry:

> Oh! liberty my native land,
> From thee how can I bear to roam,
> Or leave thy patriotic band,
> A stranger to my native home.
>
> The distant isles aspire to thee,
> And plough the ocean's brackish foam,
> A land from despotism free,
> My birthright and my native home.
>
> No, let me die upon thy shore,
> And freedom flourish o'er my tomb,
> Heaven grant me seraph's wings to soar,
> And leave in peace my native home.
>
> Should I sail to some distant plain,
> Where pleasures laurels fail to bloom,
> Oh! fortune o'er the stormy main,
> Back waft me to my native home.

Tho' gold and pearls abundant shine,
And fortune crown the flowery dome,
But fair Columbia thou art mine,
The lot of peace my native home.

When smoke from mortars vein the sky,
With thunders from the shattering bomb,
Oh! let me then with safety fly,
For shelter to my native home.

Let this be chased in my breast,
Through this and future years to come,
My last abode, my final rest,
Be lodged with thee my native home. (126–27)

The poem begins with the speaker's emphatic address to "liberty" his "native land," a statement that superimposes the position of the African American slave in the summer of 1865 onto a more generic romantic posture that links liberty, nature, and homeland. In the summer of 1865, Southern African Americans who had been slaves had freedom for the first time in the land of their birth. As the poem develops, however, the status of this addressed and much-praised "native land" seems to keep changing in ways that expand the poem's meaning beyond the issues of slavery and abolition to include the broader impact of the war's violence on the whole population and the postwar status of the American nation.

The impossibility of pinning down the identity of the poem's speaker also encourages a proliferating array of different meanings for the addressed "native land." In stanza one, for example, the speaker is forced to leave his "native land" for reasons not explained, and this stanza seems to imply that the native land is not liberty but rather the South, if the speaker is a refugee traveling in the aftermath of war. Stanzas two, three, and four all emphasize the speaker's exile from his home, again suggesting the speaker is a Southern refugee. In stanza five, however, the speaker makes explicit the idea that "Columbia" is this "native home," and that it is also now a land of "peace"; here Horton seems to refer to the reunited nation. In stanza six, the speaker declares that when bombs threaten, he will "fly" to the "safety" of his "native home," a statement that points back toward the recent horrors of the war but that would seem to rule out the possibility of the South being the speaker's "native home," since the South was the scene of so much of the fighting. In the seventh stanza, the speaker ends the poem by hoping that this native home may be "chased" or engraved in his breast and—after a quick shift in the metaphor—that he might ultimately be buried in that peaceful land of liberty, his "native home." The poem thus seems to switch off between addressing the native home as liberty, as the South, and as the reunited nation, consistently representing that "native home" as a utopian state not yet achieved or attainable, sometimes representing it as spatially remote from the speaker and other times emphasizing its close connection with the speaker's body, as in the final stanza. The speaker's persistent repetition of the poem's refrain phrase—"my native home"—is ironically at odds with the proliferating array of possible meanings for the phrase.

If we read the speaker of the poem as a Southern black—reading the poem in relation to Horton's decision to move North at the war's end—then the poem certainly seems to unsettle all easy equations of the North with freedom and the South with racist oppression. Indeed the narrative of the poem seems to fall into shape much more smoothly if we read its speaker as a white Southern refugee, one who laments the fall of the Southern nation with the war's end and one who might represent the principle of states rights by means of the word "liberty," as many Southern writers did. What's arresting about "My Native Home" then is the way in which it conjoins these two narratives into one poem: the narrative of the white Southern refugee whose dreams of a Southern nation have been destroyed by the war's end and the narrative of the black Southern refugee who knows that "liberty" may not be so easy to find either in the North or in the South. The seemingly contradictory linkage of "liberty" and the "native home" in the narrative of the black speaker suggests that Horton was fully aware that leaving the South would not necessarily lead him to a land of freedom; the pain of losing his home might never be compensated for by the kinds of freedom he might find in the North. While the shifting grounds of the poem's central figure of address could be seen as the mark of Horton's amateurism as a writer, these shifting grounds also reflect the ways that the geopolitical ground is literally shifting under Horton's feet as he travels across North Carolina with the conquering Union Army in the summer of 1865, and as he, later on, makes his way from the South of his enslaved experience to the North. Shifts in the poem's addressee also foreground Horton's attempts to shift his stance as a writer from addressing the young white Southern men he served in Chapel Hill to addressing the young white Northern men he travels with in the summer of 1865. In "My Native Home," Horton uses the dramatic romantic apostrophe to the homeland to underline the idea that the Southerner's "native home" is changing in shape and form even as the poem is being published.

While Horton relies on romantic postures to represent his ambivalent relationship with the South, when he turns his hand to representing battlefield combat he takes European classical and heroic verse as his models. Like many American poets of the Civil War era, including Julia Ward Howe and Herman Melville, Horton self-consciously seeks to legitimate his work—and U.S. history—by echoing European models for war poems as he writes about events taking place on American battlefields. "The Spectator of the Battle of Belmont" is an interesting case in point since it offers not only a sequence of literary images of combat but also a self-conscious commentary on the ways that poetry makes soldiers into heroes. When one reads "The Spectator of the Battle of Belmont," it is not hard to understand why twentieth-century scholars might have dismissed Horton's work as unpolished and derivative: the poem offers a patchwork of literary postures and exclamations without presenting a cohesive account of any one battle or a unified argument about its significance. Horton commits himself to a metrical scheme of anapests, a galloping meter used in Greek martial verse and also by the English Romantics, perhaps most famously by Byron in "The Destruction of Sennacherib" (1815). This metrical scheme seems at times to test the limits of his abilities as a poet, pointing to the haste with which he had to compose and edit many of the pieces in *Naked Genius*.[26] In its contradictory mix of high literary postures, the poem seems to endorse poetic accounts of military heroism and to exalt the position of the war poet even as it also suggests that literary representations of war do not correspond to the experience of combat.

Already in the title and in the poem's first few stanzas, questions about literary representation come to the fore. The title suggests that the poem will explore not the position of the soldier but rather the position of "the spectator." The poem opens with the speaker calling out "O brother spectators," a high literary apostrophe that is also an oddly unheroic reference (50). Neither the soldiers in the field nor the loved ones at home, but rather noncombatant observers are addressed. The poem implies that these observers would be the poets who try to write about what they have seen ("What mortal, the fate of this combat shall tell?"); in Horton's poetics, this address to a collective of fellow poets is highly unusual. At the same time, however, this apostrophe also obliquely suggests the exclusion of African American men from military service: blacks were only officially authorized to fight in the Union Army in January 1863, and even then they had to contend with the racism of white Union officers and the discrimination of unequal pay. In addressing his "brother spectators" then, Horton may be obliquely addressing Southern black men or black men of both the North and the South, an extremely unusual stance of address in his body of work. This unexpected stance points toward a question that is an urgent one for Horton's project in *Naked Genius:* how does a Southern black man write about a war that he has been forbidden to observe or take part in? In foregrounding the position of the "spectator" instead of the "soldier," Horton writes a war poem that is in the first person in the poet's voice, a poem that is about the dilemmas he faces in trying to write a literary poem about the war. If the poem threatens to collapse under the weight of its own inconsistencies, that collapse would seem to result in part from the liminal historical position that Horton found himself in: writing about a war that he could not directly observe, that he could not take part in, but that would determine his future. By traveling with the Ninth Michigan and by composing the poems in *Naked Genius*, Horton could make his own observations about the war; he could also make his own contribution to the Union war effort.

Horton does not specify the race of his speaker within "The Spectator at the Battle of Belmont," an omission that is characteristic throughout *Naked Genius* with the exception of a few abolitionist pieces. Yet he nonetheless scatters throughout the poem a trail of linguistic markers that point—sometimes obliquely, sometimes more directly—to the position of blacks in relation to the war. These markers are particularly densely concentrated in the poem's fourth stanza:

> Blood breaks from its vein like a stream from its fountain;
>   Spectators the pain of the conflict explore;
> The fugitives fly to the cave on the mountain,
>   Betrayed by the vestige of blood in their gore. (50)

The image of gushing blood in the first line may point toward the politics of race and racialized blood that fueled the Civil War. The "fugitives" might be wounded white soldiers attempting to conceal themselves from the foe, or they might be fugitive slaves, seeking freedom before or in the midst of the war, as Horton himself may have done in April 1865. The reference to fugitives being "betrayed by the vestige of blood in their gore" refers obliquely to nineteenth-century discourses of racial purity, discourses that frequently figure race in terms of drops of blood; the reference to "fugitives" thus also blurs the line between black and white soldiers, implicitly underlining that wounded men of both races have the same color blood. Fleetingly and obliquely the poem gestures toward the black men and women who shed blood both under the institution of slavery and in the context of the war. As I suggested in reading the work of soldier-poets in chapter two, shifts and inconsistencies in the foreground of a hastily written poem can reveal as much about the poet's resistance to wartime ideologies as those fissures that lie beneath the surface of a more metaphorically complex or aesthetically pleasing poem. If Horton's "The Spectator at the Battle of Belmont" does not offer a smoothly polished surface or a unified political argument, its collage of colliding stances nonetheless reminds readers of Horton's position as a previously enslaved black Southern poet; stanza four in particular suggests that the blood shed by African Americans will be erased in literary accounts of the Civil War.

If "The Spectator of the Battle of Belmont" evokes slavery only indirectly, in other war poems based on European classical and heroic models Horton avoids the topics of race and slavery altogether. In "The Terrors of War," he puts the Civil War in the context of the great military conflicts of the western world even as he also laments the terrible ravages of war. Here Horton sidesteps the problematic issue of the presence of the first-person speaker, relying instead on an authoritative impersonal voice to describe the arc of war through human history. Like his contemporary Frances Harper, Horton forges a voice that establishes its own authority by taking the long view of time in human history. Personifying war as a masculine figure, "The Terrors of War" focuses intently on depicting War's ambitions, caprices, and pride, and the senseless slaughter of soldiers that results. While the poem may include some references to the Civil War—the comet mentioned in the first line, the reference to the "imperial powers" in line five—in general the poem avoids specifying any particular conflict (68). The one exception to this rule is the strong link the poem establishes between its masculine god of war and the figure of Napoleon who appears in stanza two. Stanza three opens with an address to a second-person figure—"Ye breathe a doleful strain—a momentary address to the poet or poets who must lament the war's losses. The poem's emphatic rhyme scheme foregrounds the driving compulsion of military and imperial ambition. By situating his poem in a European context and by sidestepping use of the first-person speaker, Horton can lament war's ravages without immediately having to address the issue of slavery—or the particular war that resulted in his own emancipation. Indeed "The Terrors of War" reads like an anti-war piece, a position that he will develop more fully in other poems in the volume.

While Horton uses an authoritative impersonal voice to condemn war in "The Terrors of War," in a few poems in *Naked Genius* he uses the authoritative impersonal voice of the abolitionist tradition in order to condemn slavery. Like Frances Harper, Horton uses biblical arguments to bolster the authority of this speaker's voice. In the abolitionist poems in his first collection, *The Hope of Liberty,* Horton staked his claim for the right to freedom on his individual gifts as a poet: offering a series of arguments for his own emancipation, he relied on a strategic first-person pronoun, avoiding the more rhetorically assertive "we" of Northern abolitionist stances, a stance that would have made his work unacceptable to many white Southern readers. When he writes as a slave in the late 1820s then, Horton focuses on presenting himself as a solitary poet whose talents have been widely recognized in his community and whose exceptional gifts warrant his emancipation. Writing forty years later in *Naked Genius,* however, he allows himself to use bolder collective pronouns in a few poems both because of the war's end and because of the sympathetic Northern audience he found in the Ninth Michigan Cavalry. In a poem titled "Slavery" for example, he opens with an accusatory apostrophe to slavery and a collective "we" that might include both newly emancipated slaves and also white supporters of abolition: "Slavery, thou peace-disturbing thief, / We can't but look with frowns on thee" (66). By stanza six, he builds to a rhetorical climax, positing a "we" for the collective of slaves and juxtaposing that "we" with a critical "they" for white Southerners: "Are we not men as well as they / Born to enjoy the good of earth" (67). Horton has narrowed the broader "we" of abolitionists from stanza one to the crucial "we" of African American slaves, a collective stance he uses only rarely in *Naked Genius;* his decision to use only occasionally the collective "we" of African Americans signals his awareness of how unsettling such a pronoun position might be for whites from both the North and the South.

In another abolitionist poem, one that advances a still more ambitious sequence of biblically based arguments, Horton builds to a more boldly accusatory "you" for white Southern supporters of slavery. In "The Slave," Horton layers a Northern abolitionist argument about the African American's right to liberty over the conventional white Southern argument about liberty and states' rights. In this complex and multilayered poem, he traces the ideological threads that bind these two opposing arguments inseparably to each other, like the two conjoined bodies of the topsy-turvy doll. This is one of the few poems in Horton's body of work that addresses white Southerners with an accusatory "you," a posture of address that forms the poem's dramatic climax in its sixth stanza. An initial accusatory "you" in stanza three builds eventually to the climactic accusation in stanza six—"you've your consanguine brother slain"—followed by three more stanzas that reiterate this accusatory "you" and a tenth stanza calling for an end to slavery:

> What right divine has mortal man received,
> To domineer with uncontroll'd command?
> What philosophic wight has thus believed
> That Heaven entailed on him the weaker band?
>
> If Africa was fraught with weaker light,
> Whilst to the tribes of Europe more was given,
> Does this impart to them a lawful right
> To counterfeit the golden rule of Heaven?
>
> Did sovereign justice give to robbery birth,
> And bid the fools to theft their rights betray,
> To spread the seeds of slavery o'er the earth,
> That you should hold them as your lawful prey?
>
> Why did the Almighty God the land divide,
> And bid each nation to maintain her own,
> Rolling between the deep, and wind, and tide,
> With all their rage to make his order known?

The sad phylactery bound on rebel Cain,
  For killing Abel is in blood reveal'd,
For which the soldier falls among the slain,
  A victim on the sanguinary field.

Thus, in the cause of vile and sordid gain;
  To gratify their lust is all the plea;
Like Cain you've your consanguine brother slain,
  And robbed him of his birthright—Liberty.

Why do ye not the Ishmealites enslave,
  Or artful red man in his rude attire,
As well as with the Black man, split the wave,
  And to his progeny with rage aspire.

Because the brood-sow's left side pigs were black,
  Whose sable tincture was by nature struck,
Are you by justice bound to pull them back
  And leave the sandy colored pigs to suck?

Or can you deem that God does not intend
  His kingdom through creation to display,
The sacred right of nature to defend,
  And show to mortals who shall bear the sway?

Then suffer Heaven to vindicate the cause;
  The wrong abolish and the right restore;
To make a sacrifice of cruel laws,
  And slavish murmurs will be heard no more. (23–24)

In stanzas five and six, Horton uses the Cain and Abel story to remarkable effect, comparing the white Southerner to Cain both in his slaying of the African American—the violence of slavery—and in his slaying of his white Northern "brother"—the violence of the Civil War battlefield. Pronoun ambiguity in stanza five means that the fallen soldier—"a victim on the sanguinary field"—might be either the white Southerner who must die because of his support of slavery or the white Northerner who dies trying to support the cause of abolition.

By stanza six, however, the "consanguine brother" who has been slain is the African American slave. Horton's extraordinary position as a black writer from the South gives him an intimate intellectual relationship with the Southern states' rights argument; moreover, his intimate and ambivalent relationship with Southern audiences is signaled in "The Slave" by the speaker's oscillation between referring to white Southerners in the third-person plural and addressing white Southerners with a forceful accusatory "you." From stanza six onward, white Southerners are addressed only in the second person or by means of imperatives. While ambiguity about the racial and regional identity of the "consanguine brother" persists through stanza five, by stanza six Horton has narrowed and focused his personal references, limiting the "consanguine brother" to the African American slave and limiting white Southern supporters of slavery to an accusatory "you." Like Frances Harper, Horton carefully layers pronouns to build up to that accusatory address. In "The Slave," he strategically avoids a collective "we" for abolitionists or for slaves, even as he also avoids the limitations of the personal "I." Rather, he relies on the high literary commitments of iambic pentameter and some of the most sophisticated diction in this volume to heighten the authority of his impersonal speaker's stance. Though tempered by the poet's high literary stance, this is probably the angriest and most forceful denunciation of slavery in *Naked Genius*. In the sequence of poems in the volume, however, Horton surrounds this abolitionist poem with others that would be more palatable to white Southern readers and to white readers who were not opponents of slavery: the poem is preceded by "The Southern Refugee" and followed by two other poems about departing from one's homeland. While it's clear that *Naked Genius* was edited in haste, the placement of the abolitionist poem "The Slave" in the midst of a group of poems with much broader appeal to white readers seems strategic.

In reading the abolitionist poems that Horton includes in *Naked Genius*, I have suggested that he only rarely uses a "we" to speak for opponents of slavery and/or emancipated slaves. If he usually avoids the "we" of abolition, however, he uses collective first-person stances repeatedly and enthusiastically when writing in the voice of Union—and even Confederate—soldiers. In "The Soldier on His Way Home," for example, Horton offers a popularly styled, readily singable upbeat piece in the voice of soldiers now headed home. In the first stanza, the speaker declares:

> Soon, soon we shall depart,
> Like light ascending out of gloom;

> We now are ready to depart,
> To our dear native home. (87)

Horton's decision not to include any specific regional markers makes the poem applicable to the situation of either the Union or the Confederate soldier, though its cheerful tone would have been more appropriate for a Northern reader. In "The Dying Soldier's Message," Horton uses a singular first-person speaker, working with the sentimental convention of the dying soldier's parting words to his family. Addressing in turn the mother, the father, the brother, and the sister, the poem echoes many popular songs and poems of its day, focusing particularly intently on the soldier's relationship to his mother. In its refusal to impute a patriotic meaning to the soldier's death, the poem may be offering an implicit anti-war message, contributing to this undercurrent that runs throughout Naked Genius.

Horton's strategic use of the soldier's voice and collective pronouns is still more remarkable in two poems that celebrate the reunification of the nation. Indeed both "Like Brothers We Meet" and "The Union of Parties" seek to perform rhetorically the national reunification they call for. Horton dedicates "Like Brothers We Meet" to "the Federal and Late Confederate Soldiers" (47). Between his many years of work in the university community of Chapel Hill and his months of travel with the Ninth Michigan, Horton would have known many soldiers on both sides of the conflict. In the first stanza, Horton uses a celebratory "we," including his unnamed speaker in the imaginary throng of former enemies now reconciled:

> Like heart-loving brothers we meet,
> And still the loud thunders of strife,
> The blaze of fraternity kindles most sweet,
> There's nothing more pleasing in life. (47)

Only in the fourth stanza does he slip in the word "union," a subtle reminder of who won the war:

> The union of brothers is sweet,
> Whose wives and children do come,
> Their sons and fair daughters with pleasure they greet,
> When long absent fathers come home.

Horton here uses an image of nationwide familial reunion to offset the risks of the word "union." The poem closes with an image of earth and

Heaven reuniting, a celebratory finish that nonetheless subtly implies that the ideal of nationwide reconciliation may be a utopia. The poem includes no specific reference to race or to the debate about slavery that fueled the war; rather the "we" would seem to be the collective "we" of the Union and Confederate soldiers to whom the poem is dedicated.

"Like Brothers We Meet" treads lightly around the word "union," using it only twice in six stanzas. In "The Union of Parties," on the other hand, Horton uses the word as an emphatic refrain, underlining at the end of each verse the name of the victorious army. With its strong rhyme scheme and long metrically regular lines, "The Union of Parties" reads like a marching song, one that might be particularly popular with Union troops on their way home. Stanza one represents a reunion in nature that coincides with the reunion among men who were once enemies:

> Like rivers in conflux, let parties now blend,
> Who e'er was a foe, let him now be a friend;
> In one tide of glory, together all mix,
> The system of concord completely to fix;
> Let us all come together, and all sing together—
> In the Union. (132)

The poem includes no specific references to race nor any explicit reference to former masters' reconciling with former slaves. Remarkably, however, the poem's fourth stanza does include a celebratory reference to future possibilities for intermarriage:

> We'll mingle in wedlock, we'll mingle in prayer,
> To interdict marriage what mortal shall dare;
> No longer divided the nation shall be,
> Let us all go together, by land and by sea;
> Let us all go together and all stick together—
> In the Union. (133)

Though the explicit reference here would be to new possibilities for intermarriage between Northern and Southern whites, given the centrality of fears about miscegenation to the white cultural imagination in both the North and the South, Horton seems to be offering a satirical alternative suggestion, reminding white Americans of forms of cultural mixing that are still highly taboo. "We'll mingle in wedlock, we'll mingle in prayer," the speaker proclaims, boldly using an inclusive "we" that would have reminded Horton's readers of the race of the author, of the fear of miscegenation, and of the racial segregation of American churches. "No longer divided the nation shall be," Horton's speaker declares. But beneath the crowd-pleasing and celebratory imagery of this marching song, Horton underlines also that the "we" he has posited is still a utopian one, still hypothetical. In the great national reconciliation to come, Horton suggests, blacks may well prove to be the forgotten and excluded party. For the nation is surely still divided into white and black—as evidenced by George Moses Horton's reluctance to use a collective "we" more than once or twice in his expansive volume of poetry.

The tone of the intermarriage stanza is difficult to read; I have been suggesting that the threat of miscegenation might be read as a satirical undercurrent beneath the celebratory sentiments of the poem's surface. Though Horton includes in *Naked Genius* several conventional love poems and several that represent the soldier's pain at being away from his beloved, at least a half dozen poems in the volume represent marriage itself as fraught with frustrations, quarrels, and misunderstandings. This wider textual context makes it possible to read the intermarriage stanza in "The Union of Parties" as bitingly satirical, even as it is also comically tongue-in-cheek. For example, a poem called "The Treacherous Woman" begins: "Woman, thou bloom of every danger, / From whose charms my sorrows rise, / To thee I'd live and die a stranger; / He who shuns thee must be wise" (49). In the poem "The Use of Liberty," Horton represents marriage as an impediment to freedom. Using a jangling meter and rhyme scheme that read like sly doggerel, Horton writes: "But man in a nation without a true wife, / Had better continue without one, / To live in contention forever in strife, / Why should I be crazy about one?" (92). In the vivid and comical "Snaps for Dinner, Snaps for Breakfas[t], and Snaps for Supper," Horton represents married life as an unending and exhausting quarrel (142); though the wife seems the more shrewish and snappish party of the two, the husband doesn't come off particularly well either. Thus when "The Union of Parties" represents harmony in marriage as central to reestablishing national harmony, Horton is clearly enjoying a joke that he hopes at least some of his readers will catch; for members of the Ninth Michigan who were familiar with Horton's laments about marriage, the celebration of intermarriage in stanza four would have seemed more than a little ironic. The nation is irrevocably divided not only by Northern and Southern allegiances and by racial difference but also by gender difference, Horton's poem implies.

In the poems he writes in the first person in the soldier's voice, Horton draws on his months of travel and his friendships with the Ninth Michigan Cavalry to write poems that represent aspects of the Union soldiers' experience: their pain at being parted from their loved ones, their excitement about the end of the war and their impending return home, their hopes for the future of the newly reunited nation. As I have suggested, Horton is otherwise reluctant to use first-person collective stances in *Naked Genius*. He does, however, write two poems that address the fallen Confederate nation in particular as well as the reunited Union more broadly. In this interconnected pair of poems, "Weep" and "Negro Speculation," he again uses the impersonal authoritative voice that he relies on in his abolitionist pieces, offering a damning indictment of the pride that led to the Confederacy's downfall and of the senseless bloodshed caused by that national pride. In the second poem of the pair, "Negro Speculation," he laments the damage done by slavery. "Weep" is the most powerful anti-war poem in the collection; "Negro Speculation" is the darkest and most despondent meditation on the terrible long-term costs of slavery. Horton's liminal status as a previously enslaved black man who is now finally able to write and speak freely allows him extraordinary freedoms in this volume: unlike Frances Harper who has to maintain political consistency in her positions because of her position of influence in the abolition movement, Horton can include in his postwar collection poems that condemn the waste of war and that lament slavery's losses; his outsider status enables him to mingle these elegiac poems with much lighter poems that celebrate national reunification. Writing in the immediate aftermath of the war, in the immediate aftermath of Lincoln's assassination, and on the eve of his departure from the South where he had spent his whole life, Horton chooses not to include a poem that joyously celebrates the end of slavery; though the last poem in the volume acknowledges the end of slavery, the overall tone of this piece—and of the two Lincoln elegies that precede it—is one of mourning.

The remarkable anti-war poem "Weep" includes no reference to slavery. Instead the poem focuses intently on the downfall of the Confederate nation and the terrible bloodshed of the war; rather than representing war as an evil necessary to end the outrage of slavery, Horton dwells at length on the senselessness of the killing. In stanzas one, two and three, Horton's speaker calls on his fellow Americans not to celebrate the war's end but rather to lament its terrible costs and to tremble before the uncertain future. The speaker seems to address not only supporters of the defeated Confederacy, but also the reunited nation as a whole, reminding Americans that a long period of mourning for the war's losses is in order:

> Weep for the country in its present state,
> And of the gloom which still the future wait;
> The proud confederate eagle heard the sound,
> And with her flight fell prostrate to the ground!
>
> Weep for the loss the country has sustained,
> By which her now depe[n]dent is in jail;
> The grief of him who now the war survived,
> The conscript husbands and the weeping wives!
>
> Weep for the seas of blood the battle cost,
> And souls that ever hope forever lost!
> The ravage of the field with no recruit,
> Trees by vengeance blasted to the root! (113–14)

In its three final stanzas, the poem condemns the pride of the Confederate leadership in general and of Jefferson Davis in particular. Horton's discomfort with accusing Confederate readers even as he mourns their losses is evident in the poem's uneasy switching between the collectives "you," "they," and "our" in these stanzas. His pronoun choices become particularly slippery in the opening lines of the last stanza: "Weep o'er peculiar swelling coffers swelling, / Our treasures left, and all their banks destroyed" (114). Now the addressee of "weep" has narrowed to exclude white Confederates who have been shifted to a third-person reference. With the phrase "Our treasures left," Horton points toward the fact that the North remains on economically secure footing; the phrase may also point obliquely to the "treasure" of African American freedom, linking emancipated slaves and white Northern opponents of slavery as one community. The poem closes by prophesying—with some accuracy—that the South may never recover from the financial blow of the fall of the Confederacy.

Immediately following "Weep" Horton includes "Negro Speculation" whose title picks up on the argument about the Confederacy's financial ruin that closed the earlier poem. Opening with a "we" that would presumably include all Americans—not just the opponents of slavery—the poem's first stanza laments the horrors of the Middle Passage:

> We think of the shackles and fetters,
> And traverse to countries of pain;
> 'Tis written in blood-dripping letters,
> Whilst struggling, but fast in the chain!
> Weep humanity, weep! (114)

By taking the first line of each stanza of the poem "Weep" as a closing refrain for each stanza in "Negro Speculation," Horton interlinks the two poems, underlining the ways that the importation of slaves, the slave market, and the institution of slavery were all integral to the rise and eventual fall of the Confederacy. In stanza two, he laments the shattering of the African American family under slavery. This stanza seems both to look backward toward the separation of families under slavery (both through sales and escapes) and to look forward toward the painful future separation of families with the Great Migration:

> Oh! Where is my sister and brother?
> Gone, hopeless, the land to explore;
> And, stationed afar from each other,
> To see their dear kindred no more!
> Weep, humanity, weep. (115)

In calling on all of humanity to mourn the pain and the losses of slavery, Horton boldly addresses the American nation, reminding his readers that the nation was originally founded on the violence of slavery and that that legacy of violence must inevitably shape the future of the now-reunited country. He calls on Americans, both white and black, Northern and Southern, to mourn for the terrible damage done.

By treating the damage done by the war and the damage done by slavery in two discrete but closely connected poems, Horton adroitly engages more potential readers in his call for national mourning; but by placing the poems together in the volume and by taking the refrain of the second from the first, he underlines the hand-in-glove relationship between the Confederacy and the institution of slavery. "Weep" and "Negro Speculation" are two of the most powerful and politically impassioned poems in *Naked Genius;* Horton positions them not at the very end, however, but rather about two-thirds of the way into the 160-page volume, thereby taking some of the rhetorical weight off these two crucial pieces. By closing the collection with two Lincoln elegies and a first-person poem mourning his years of slavery, Horton softens the edge of his anti-war and anti-slavery arguments and aims to engage a broader array of readers.

In *Naked Genius*, George Moses Horton alternates in his use of a romantic first-person speaker, authoritative impersonal stances that condemn war and slavery, stances that accuse a Southern collective in the second-person plural, and celebratory first-person plural stances representing soldiers' perspectives, with particular attention to the position of Union soldiers on their way home. Though Horton is extremely cautious in his use of the first-person plural for abolitionist stances, he does address his fellow Americans, urging them to grieve the war's terrible losses and to remember the legacy of the war's violence and slavery's violence amidst the celebrations of the war's end. The proliferating array of pronoun positions and stylistic commitments in Horton's *Naked Genius* signals his extraordinarily nuanced awareness of how fragmented that reunited nation is, as he includes groups of poems within the volume that address a range of different constituencies. When he posits a "we" in these poems, that "we" is most frequently the "we" of the Union soldiers who were the immediate audience for his wartime collection; remarkably, however, Horton also writes poems in which the "we" includes both Northerners and Southerners, again focusing particularly on the soldiers whom he would have known both from his years of work at the University of North Carolina and from his months of travel with the Ninth Michigan Cavalry.

Both the eclecticism of Horton's aesthetic commitments and the versatile range of his pronoun stances underline that American poetry, like the American nation, is in a state of transition. Echoing both nationalist patriotic verse and heroic classical poetry, Horton shows himself to be a skillful reader of American popular and literary tastes in the nineteenth century, underlining the diversity of poetic stances that were appealing to readers in this era. Like his contemporary Henry Timrod, Horton makes the lyric I of romanticism a central stance in his poetics; yet while Timrod's dependence on Southern romanticism ultimately marks his project as a nostalgic and retrospective one, Horton's decision to appropriate literary Southern romantic postures for a poetic speaker who may be African American signals an important development in American poetry. Like Sarah Piatt, Horton uses Southern identity as a kind of masking in his poems. While Piatt revises the conventions of genteel Victorian domesticity with her ironic dialogues between mothers and children about war, Horton revises the conventions of Southern literary romanticism, claiming the power of those elite white stances to represent the Southern African American experience.[27] The conventional romantic postures of the longing for one's homeland or the longing for freedom assume a new urgency when the writer is a former slave who decides to move North in the aftermath of the war. Horton demonstrates extraordinary skill as a poet by creating solitary romantic speakers who offer possibilities for identification to displaced American readers both white and black, Northern and Southern, in the war's aftermath.

CHAPTER SIX

"THEY ANSWERED HIM ALOUD"

Popular Voice and Nationalist Allegiances in Herman Melville's Battle-Pieces

Like his contemporary George Moses Horton, Herman Melville produces a body of war poetry that is remarkable for the range of aesthetic stances it includes. Like all of the writers examined here, Melville uses his wartime poetry to examine the possibilities that poetic voice offers for speaking to and for the divided nation; in the boldness of its experimentation with both traditional and innovative poetic stances, however, Melville's *Battle-Pieces* foregrounds with particular clarity questions about how poetry might work to fracture, to unify, and to redefine the nation. While scholars who have analyzed Melville's war poems have often approached them thematically, focusing on his engagement with postwar ideologies of reconciliation, in this chapter I will suggest that Melville is as interested in exploring the discursive functions and formal properties of poetry as he is in intervening in postwar debates about Unionism.[1] The volume's title *Battle-Pieces and Aspects of the War* already points toward the splitting of the nation, evoking a proliferation of vantage points on the conflict; scholars often comment on this restlessness of perspective, arguing that Melville's speakers can find no stable position from which to observe the war.[2] Like Julia Ward Howe, Melville will experiment extensively with voice-effects in his wartime poetry. Yet while Howe's experimentation with voice-effects signals her frustration at the limitations placed on middle-class women's lives, Melville's wide-ranging voice-effects emphasize above all the extent to which American poetry is in a state of transition, as diverse in its aesthetic stances and commitments as the many Americans who read and write it. More than any other writer in this study, Melville embraces the full range of possibilities the genre of poetry offers for experimentation with voice. Remarkably, Melville will use both the "we" and the "I" only sparingly in this collection; he will replace the rhetorical authority of first-person stances with the rhetorical intensity of voice-effects.

The wide range of voice-effects Melville works with includes the apostrophe, the exclamation, the refrain, dialogue, and the use of multiple speakers within one poem, all effects that emphasize the illusion that the poem is not a written text but rather a voice calling out.[3] While scholars of the volume invariably comment on its high literary devices—its lofty apostrophes and its elaborate metrical and rhyme patterns, for example, or its extensive network of classical allusions—I contend that Melville mixes high literary and more popularly oriented voice-effects in the collection, not only to broaden his audience but also because he is torn between a desire to critique nationalist poetry and a desire for the consolations that a nationalist poetry might offer.[4] While New Criticism has taught scholars to value the syntactic compression and elliptical ambiguities of some of the most innovative of these poems ("The Portent," for example, or "Shiloh"), it has also led scholars to neglect those poems that respond most directly to popular and nationalist strains in Civil War–era poetry.[5]

Melville's poetry pleased neither nineteenth-century reviewers nor twentieth-century scholars: many of the former lamented the seeming detachment of the poems, while the latter have tended to anthologize and celebrate only the terse proto-modernist pieces.[6] If Melville's collection baffled two centuries worth of readers, this response results in part from the ways that the volume marks the transition between nineteenth- and twentieth-century poetry, signaling the beginning of the decline of patriotic nationalist verse and a turn toward the compression and fragmentation of modernist poetry; in Melville's *Battle-Pieces*, as in poems by Union soldier Lyman Holford, Emily Dickinson, and Walt Whitman, the turn toward linguistic compression is accompanied by a commitment to using graphic realism to represent the violence of war. Rather than aligning himself wholly with either patriotic nationalism or realist compression, however, Melville works extensively with both, trusting that the capaciousness of the genre of poetry will allow him this freedom. The range of work in the volume makes clear that Melville was keenly aware of the central role that poetry had played in wartime discourses and of the role it would continue to play in reuniting the nation in the war's aftermath. Reading the transition from Melville's work as a novelist to his work as a poet, Robert Milder argues that Melville shifted from "a popular, mimetic art (narrative) to a formal, largely private one (poetry)."[7] I will counter that Melville is acutely aware of the ways in which poetry is both a popular and public art in the Civil War era. Thus in shaping *Battle-Pieces* into what Milder calls "a vehicle for persuasion," Melville enters into a lively debate about what role poetry might play in defining national identity in the war's aftermath.[8] In order to understand Melville's contribution to this debate, we need to consider both the full range of poetry the volume includes and the many ways in which he responds to the work of his contemporaries.

There are in *Battle-Pieces* only relatively few evocations of private domestic spaces, no poems representing letters to or from soldiers, and few poems focused on one individual's personal sorrow; Melville's primary investment in this volume is in the poetic voice of collective recollection. Four contexts that are of particular interest to him in this collection include the public-oriented discourses of popular song, journalism, battlefield landscape depictions, and battlefield monuments. The battle hymns sung at parades of departing or returning soldiers, articles or bulletins by war correspondents, visual or textual depictions of battlefield vistas, and inscriptions on battlefield monuments: Melville responds to these kinds of discourses with a particular sense of urgency. In its alternation between a patriotic nationalism and more skeptical elegiac stances, Melville's work shows strong affinities with Emily Dickinson's wartime project. While Melville seems in some *Battle-Pieces* poems to argue for the powers of poetic voice—suggesting that a well-crafted poem might work to reunite the divided nation—other poems reveal a deep-seated suspicion of the illusions of community and presence that poetic voice can create. These poems acknowledge that poetry worked to fuel the divisive nationalist passions that caused the war.

Certain refrain-driven poems in *Battle-Pieces*, including both the seemingly conventional and the more experimental, strongly echo popular Civil War poetry. Melville's decision to mix hero-making poems such as "Lyon" or "The Victor at Antietam" in the same volume with more innovative pieces like "The Portent" reflects his ambivalent relationship to the stances of popular nationalist poetry. In the poems that engage with popular poetry, Melville seems particularly interested in exploring the rhetorical effect of the repetition of names.[9] "Lyon," "The Victor of Antietam," and the two elegies for Stonewall Jackson all echo the conventional use of heroes' names in marching songs and recruitment poems; name-centered refrains conjure up the collective voices of community that might read such poems at public gatherings to persuasive effect. In a recruitment poem first published in July 1862 that soon also circulated as a popular song, James Sloan Gibbons responds to Lincoln's call for voluntary enlistments with the refrain "We are coming, Father Abraham, three hundred thousand more!" Evoking images of an American landscape filled with columns of brave volunteers, the poem uses Lincoln's name to reiterate Northern obedience to Lincoln's authority, an authority figured in both paternal and biblical terms; Lincoln's name thus becomes a rallying cry for Union loyalty.[10] John Williamson Palmer's "Stonewall Jackson's Way," first published in September 1862, works with Jackson's name in an analogous fashion, using the refrain "That's 'Stonewall Jackson's way,'" to punctuate a series of verses praising Jackson's bravery and piety and urging all Confederate soldiers on to future victories under Jackson's symbolic leadership.[11] What separates Melville's use of the name-centered refrain from that of Gibbons and Palmer is Melville's decision to use the refrain in an elegiac context instead of the more frequent wartime context of the rallying cry or recruitment poem. His decision to use this technique in elegies for fallen generals may well reflect his ambivalence about the nationalist positions such name-centered refrains often promoted.

A poem called "The Cumberland" presents a particularly striking example of Melville's exploration of the nationalist implications of the refrain. In "The Cumberland," Melville reflects explicitly on the incantatory power of names, examining the possibility that names might become aural monuments to war's losses. The first in a four-poem sequence on the naval battles of March 1862, "The Cumberland" describes the sinking of the wooden Union ship the *Cumberland* by the ironclad C.S.S. *Virginia* (now better known by its earlier name, the *Merrimack*).[12] Meditating on the memorializing powers of poetry, the speaker in "The Cumberland" insists that poetic voice makes possible the timeless preservation of heroic names, deeds, and battles. The poem's opening stanza argues that the sounds of names may ring out into an infinite future:

> Some names there are of telling sound,
> Whose voweled syllables free
> Are pledge that they shall ever live renowned[13]

The writer's task then is to create poems that celebrate and commemorate such storied names, the kinds of poems that nineteenth-century Americans might read aloud at a community gathering. Though the *Cumberland* was defeated in battle, its name will persist in a poetic present tense created through the musical reiteration of the ship's name in the refrain:

> Long as hearts shall share the flame
> Which burned in that brave crew,
> Her fame shall live—outlive the victor's name;
> For this is due.
> Your flag and flag-staff shall in story stand—
> Cumberland! (54)

Drawing on a detail of the battle, Melville links the enduring power of the sound of the ship's name to the Union flag on the mainmast which still fluttered above water even after the ship had sunk.[14] In poems like "The Cumberland," Melville demonstrates the possibilities that poetry offers for forging a nationalist collective voice, a voice whose chanting ensures that the name of the *Cumberland* will "outlive" that of its foe. His decision to publish "The Cumberland" in *Harper's New Monthly Magazine* a few months before the appearance of *Battle-Pieces* suggests that he may have thought this poem would be particularly effective with a broader audience.[15]

But even as Melville uses elegiac poses to try to create a collective voice, other poems in *Battle-Pieces* foreground the ways that dissonance inevitably works to undermine the unified voice of the community. If we read Melville's "The Cumberland" in relation to Longfellow's more widely circulated poem of the same title, Melville's ambivalence about the commitments of nationalist poetic voice comes still more clearly into view. Longfellow's "The Cumberland" relies on conversational language and the confident authority of a speaker who is one of the Union sailors on board the doomed ship. In Longfellow's version of events, those Union sailors form a bravely united "we" in the poem's climactic stanza. Emphasizing that "we," stanza five describes a verbal sparring match between the Confederate and Union commanders in the engagement:

> "Strike your flag!" the rebel cries,
> In his arrogant old plantation strain.
> "Never!" our gallant Morris replies:
> "It is better to sink than to yield!"
> And the whole air pealed
> With the cheers of our men.[16]

By contrast, Melville uses a more distant "they" to refer to the Union sailors and addresses the sunken ship with a dramatic "you" only in his poem's penultimate stanza. Like Melville, Longfellow also dwells on the detail of the Union flag floating above the sunken ship: "Next morn, as the sun rose over the bay, / Still floated our flag at the mainmast-head." For Longfellow, however, the persistence of the flag points symbolically toward the national reunification that will follow the conflict's end, a future that the speaker confidently foretells in an apostrophe to the nation:

> Ho! brave land! with hearts like these,
> Thy flag that is rent in twain,
> Shall be one again,
> And without a seam. (217)

Although Melville's poem ends with a declaration that the glory of the sunken ship will endure ("Your flag and flag-staff shall in story stand / Cumberland!"), his apostrophe addresses only the ship itself, and his prediction for the future remains narrowly focused on the ship's persistence in "story," that is, literature and history. Melville's poem echoes neither Longfellow's confident apostrophe to the nation ("brave land") nor his assertion that the Union will be reestablished "without a seam." His insistent and elegiac reiteration of the ship's name—"Cumberland! Cumberland!"—gestures toward the nation (with the final syllable "land") even as it points to the ways that the nation is "encumbered" or burdened, threatened with overthrow by the divisive forces of regional loyalties.[17] The now obsolete and defeated wooden sailing ship becomes a ghostly stand-in for the foundering nation; the reiterated name of the

"Cumberland" becomes an alternative for the apostrophe to the Union that Melville's speaker cannot utter.

By examining how poetry might work to forge a nationalist collective voice in an elegiac poem about the sinking of a wooden Union ship, Melville may also be questioning the risks of such nationalist poetic projects and pointing implicitly toward future developments in the stances of war poetry. If we read as a group the four poems that reflect on the battles of the ironclads ("The Cumberland," "In the Turret," "The Temeraire," and "A Utilitarian View of the Monitor's Fight"), the sequence as a whole unfolds the argument that poetry must adopt a grittier, more realistic stance to correspond to the developing technologies of modern war. The speaker of "The Temeraire" declares:

> [. . .] Splendors wane. The sea-fight yields
> No front of old display;
> The garniture, emblazonment,
> And heraldry all decay. (58)

"A Utilitarian View of the Monitor's Fight" links this argument about the end of "heraldry" directly to poetry, calling for a language that suits the "anvil-din" of the combat of the ironclads (62). The "flowing, rolling" musicality of "The Cumberland" (53), which is figured in relation to the human voice ("flowing, rolling on the tongue"), must give way to a poetry that echoes the metallic clang of the modern machinery of war, "the ringing of those plates on plates" (62). Though the speaker of "A Utilitarian View of the Monitor's Fight" does not anticipate that this new kind of poetry will prevent future wars ("War shall yet be, and to the end"), he expects it to reflect the changed position of the human subject in military conflict. Heroic depictions of the brave warrior must give way to accounts of the workings of "crank / Pivot, and screw," to the calculations of military engineers and gunners: "War yet shall be, but warriors / Are now but operatives" (62). Through the range of poems in *Battle-Pieces*, Melville calls for a poetry whose "plain" and "ponderous" language will reflect the dispassionate technologies of modern war, even as he also considers how popular refrain-driven poems work to fan the flames of nationalist passions.

In his own refrain-driven poems—"The Cumberland," "The Victor at Antietam," and the elegies for Stonewall Jackson, for example—Melville controls the nationalist force of the construct of collective voice both by means of temporal perspective and through his choice of pronouns. Battles in this group of poems are generally represented in an elegiac if sometimes celebratory past tense. *Battle-Pieces* includes no fiery call to arms comparable to Julia Ward Howe's "Battle Hymn of the Republic," to Whitman's "Beat! Beat! Drums!" or to Henry Timrod's "A Cry to Arms," though Melville would have read many examples of such calls to arms, and though Howe, Whitman, and other poets chose to include such poems even in collections published after the war's end.[18] While Howe's "Battle Hymn" builds to a climactic collective imperative in its final stanza ("Let us die to make men free"), Melville's war poems generally avoid both the imperative and the collective first person. When Melville does include a present-tense imperative in a *Battle-Pieces* poem, that imperative is most often calling for an act of commemoration, not a turn toward the violence of the battlefield. In "Sheridan at Cedar Creek," for example, the sequence of imperatives in the first line of each stanza ("Shoe the steed with silver," "House the horse in ermine," etc. [116–17]) calls for a ritual honoring of the horse's (and rider's) courage in a battle that the poem represents in the past tense.[19]

Melville's reluctance to use the present tense in describing scenes of battle corresponds to his limited use of the pronoun "we." Though Melville uses the second person to address specific military leaders (Worden in "In the Turret," for example, or McClellan in "The Victor of Antietam"), in "The Cumberland" as in many other *Battle-Pieces* poems, he relies on a distanced "they" to describe Union soldiers or sailors. These pronoun choices have the effect of keeping the poems focused on specific engagements and specific groups of soldiers, often resisting extrapolation from that group to the Union as a whole. By contrast, the poem "Lyon," laden with ungainly rhymes and inversions, uses an unusual "we" and an equally unusual first-person standpoint in describing combat, as for example, in stanza six: "We fought on the grass, we bled in the corn—" (25). Yet a jangling rhyme scheme that links a fictive "Corporal Tryon" to the glorious "Lyon" (in stanza 11 [26]) betrays Melville's discomfort with the poem's hero-making rhetoric and its collective first-person plural perspective. And though Melville uses both a Northern and a Southern "we" in the pair of elegies for Stonewall Jackson, these pronoun choices are calculated to foreground the conflicting ideological positions of North and South, with the first poem spoken in the voice of a Northern soldier and the second in the voice of a Virginian. The two distinct "we's" in this pair of poems then do not so much endorse nationalist allegiances as they underline the ways in which nationalism fueled the war and will impede reunification.

While the repetition of proper names works to emphasize nationalist fervor in the poems I have been discussing, in still other poems Melville uses name repetition to achieve far more ambiguous effects. In "The Portent," for example, the alternating repetition of the names "Shenandoah" and "John Brown," both of which appear as exclamations within the poem, sets the two terms against each other in dialogic opposition. And the symbolic significance of each name remains indeterminate: the Shenandoah river valley is the site both of Brown's unsuccessful raid and of his execution; the valley is a scene of great pastoral beauty and it is also—again and again over the four years of the war—the scene of some of its bloodiest fighting. With its focus on the symbolic meaning of Brown's hanged corpse, "The Portent" clearly responds to the lyrics of the popular song "John Brown's Body." While the song uses repetition of Brown's name to suggest that he was a Christian martyr in a holy war ("John Brown's body lies a mould'ring in the grave,/His soul is marching on!"), the repetition of Brown's name in Melville's poem refuses such ideological certainties; the swinging body—formally evoked through the repetition of Brown's name—instead becomes a figure of hovering ambivalence.[20] Melville's phrase the "cut is on the crown" likens Brown to a crucified Christ, yet the phrase "the stabs shall heal no more" argues against a redemptive or recuperative vision of the war's violence (11). The popular song separates Brown's soul from his body in order to argue that his death is a form of Christian martyrdom, insisting "He's gone to be a soldier in the army of the Lord." Melville's poem, on the other hand, focuses on the unreadability of Brown's body, the refusal of the "portent" to assume a fixed ideological meaning:

> *Hidden in the cap*
> *Is the anguish none can draw;*
> *So your future veils its face,*
> *Shenandoah!* (11)

The popular song reads natural signs as evidence that God supports the

Union position in the war ("The stars of Heaven are looking kindly down"), but while Melville's poem also points toward natural signs ("the meteor of the war" which is symbolically linked to "the streaming beard"), "the meteor" in Melville's poem points only to the inevitability of the war, without disclosing whose side God supports. Given the great popularity of "John Brown's Body," many of the Union soldiers who sang it in camp or on the march very likely did not particularly endorse the cause of abolition or the idea that the war was being fought to free the slaves. The hovering ambiguity of the symbolism in Melville's "The Portent" reflects his keen awareness of this contradiction. As I mentioned in chapter one, in the *Rebellion Record,* Frank Moore cites an instance early on in the war in which Massachusetts soldiers marched down Broadway in New York singing "John Brown's Body"; many of Melville's fellow New Yorkers were so moved by the soldiers' fervor that they began to sing along, a development that the journalist describes with astonishment. In light of the brutal acts of violence committed by white New Yorkers against blacks and abolitionists in the 1863 draft riots, Melville would have fully recognized the irony of New Yorkers singing "John Brown's Body." In "The Portent," he signals this recognition by rewriting the popular song, replacing the narrative of Brown's martyrdom with a poem that refuses to reify Brown as either a martyr or a traitor. Melville suggests that the bonds forged by such collective singing may do little more than temporarily smooth over profound underlying differences.

In the poems I have been discussing thus far, Melville uses repetition of names to explore the ways that popular song and popular poetry can work both to fuel nationalism and to reestablish community in the war's aftermath. These poems rely on exclamatory voice effects, foregrounding the fluid boundary between popular song and poetry in this era and offering oral models for communal or collective poetic voice. In the long poem "Donelson," Melville makes explicit his interest in the ways that wartime texts work to divide and to build communities; "Donelson" examines how Northern civilians receive war news, representing both the journalists and editors who produce the texts and the readers and listeners to whom they are addressed. Through its proliferation of readerly and writerly voices, newspaper headlines and poetic cries, the poem also offers an extended meditation on the relationship between the written text and poetic voice. More than any other poem in *Battle-Pieces*, "Donelson" takes up quite directly the question of how journalists represented the war and the related question of how poets use journalism to create poetry.

Melville's insistent linking of poetry and journalism underlines the fact that most Civil War poets relied on newspapers for descriptions of battlefield tactics and events. As Timothy Sweet points out, "Donelson" also offers a critique of the ways that Civil War journalism sometimes romanticized and aestheticized the violence of combat.[21] In "Donelson," Melville stages scene after scene of reading aloud. Because scenes of speech invariably refer to scenes of writing, the poem suggests that there is no access to the war—for any Northern civilian—outside the mediation of the written text. And yet the poem repeatedly presents newspaper texts as fallible and misleading: Melville thus implies that neither poetry nor journalism can accurately depict the horrors of war. While it may seem surprising that Melville places such a formally and thematically innovative poem toward the start of the collection, "Donelson" offers arguments that are key to our understanding of some of the more conventional poems that follow it. For example, the many footnotes that Melville attaches to the poems in *Battle-Pieces* remind readers again and again of his reliance on Frank Moore's *Rebellion Record*.[22] Even as the footnotes remind us of Melville's journalistic sources, however, "Donelson" urges us to understand these journalistic sources as being neither more nor less reliable than the poetry that the war produces.

In "Donelson," Melville stages the interplay of a group of wartime voices, including those of the poet-speaker, journalists, newspaper editors, and the crowd who reads from and hears the bulletins posted outside the newspaper office. The poem thus takes up quite directly the question of how journalism and poetry circulate, emphasizing the ways that partisan writing can forge a community, eliding differences of perspective and allegiance. The structure of the poem consists of the alternation of two writerly voices, an alternation that Melville represents typographically by means of a shift from plain to italicized type: there is the poet-speaker who presents the frame story about the group of people in a Northern community reacting to the news, and there are the journalists and editors who present that news to the community in writing, texts that Melville presents in italics. Linking the stanzas of the poet-speaker and the stanzas of journalistic text is the voice of a Reader in the crowd who delivers the posted bulletins aloud.

The Reader's voice underscores the public and private reading of both journalism and poetry that took place throughout the war. By rendering journalistic prose in meter and rhyme and by emphasizing the Reader's voice, Melville signals poetry's dual status as a voiced performance and a text. In place of John Stuart Mill's paradigm of the solitary reader eavesdropping on the solitary soliloquizing poet, Melville offers a historically accurate nineteenth-century American scene in which one man reads news bulletins to a waiting crowd. He thus presents an American response to the romantic ideal of the solitary poet who seeks to represent "emotion recollected in tranquility."[23] In "Donelson," journalism, like poetry, presents a cacophony of voices—simultaneously textual and oral—conflicting and colliding in the public square through assertion, contradiction, and revision. With its colliding voices and conflicting mix of ideological and aesthetic commitments, "Donelson" offers a microcosm of the structure of *Battle-Pieces* as a whole.

In addition to refusing to represent the soldier's perspective in the first person, "Donelson" further destabilizes its own narrative authority through the *mise-en-abîme* of its story-within-a-story structure in which a poet-speaker describes a series of anonymous readers and listeners reading and responding to a succession of anonymously authored and edited texts. These scenes of public reading initially portray Northerner listeners as a unified bloc of Union supporters, as for example in a section of the poem that renders newspaper headlines about a Union advance in the battle in emphatic capital letters and in meter and rhyme:

> GLORIOUS VICTORY OF THE FLEET!
> FRIDAY'S GREAT EVENT!
> THE ENEMY'S WATER BATTERIES BEAT!
> WE SILENCED EVERY GUN!
> THE OLD COMMODORE'S COMPLIMENTS SENT
> PLUMP INTO DONELSON! (40–41)

The steady meter of these phrases mimics the tapping of the telegraph, the technology used to transmit bulletins from the front. This is the only section of the text that presents dramatic headlines, a fact that heightens their effect as spoken phrases. Experimenting with typography, Melville uses capital letters to represent the typeface of newspaper headlines; the capitals also point toward the voicing of the lines, suggesting both the cries of newspaper vendors, who call out headlines to sell papers, and also the exultant shout of the Reader reading to the crowd. Stirred up by partisan journalism or poetry, the crowd answers the dramatic headlines and their enthusiastic Reader with a resounding "hip, hurrah!," an exclamation that is itself a textual rendering of the unrepresentable sound of the crowd's collective cheer (41). Moreover, both the voice of the Reader and the exclamatory quality of the headlines underline the idea that in "Donelson" voices are always already textual voices; the poem thus emphasizes that the voice that poetry creates is nothing more than an illusion of presence.

The power of partisan poetry or partisan journalism to mislead and deceive is driven home when moments after heralding these headlines, the newspaper issues a subsequent bulletin that retracts the earlier news. The editors present their retraction with a parenthetical note: "*(Our own reporter a dispatch compiles, / As best he may from varied sources)*"(41). The aside exposes the illusion of the war correspondent's presence on the battlefield, suggesting that all the journalist can do is "compile" a report, using other writers and speakers as sources. It is a self-referential gesture insofar as it describes the work that Melville and other poets do in assembling war poems from a mix of sources. More radically still, the stanza suggests that the chaos of battle may be such that no eyewitness can accurately represent battlefield events.[24]

Having suggested that even a witness to the war may be unable to represent it, Melville then goes on to emphasize the temporal gap that divides readers and listeners from soldiers on the battlefield. By introducing a mid-sentence interruption in the telegraph service on the eve of the Union victory, Melville insists that readers and listeners are denied access to the soldiers' present-tense experiences, no matter how vivid or realistic the journalists' texts might be. Melville here comments on the use of technologies that writers and newspaper editors more typically choose to conceal from their readers. A brief article in *Harper's Weekly* from January 24, 1863 describes the installation and use of telegraph equipment at the front and includes an unusual illustration showing a telegraph line being set up during combat (fig. 10); the illustration underlines not only the possibility of rapid installation but also the potential precariousness of this means of communication. In these lines from "Donelson" then, Melville uses both enjambment and caesurae to underline the tentative

10. "The Army Telegraph—Setting up the Wire during an Action," magazine illustration, 1863

and fragmentary quality of the news received, reproducing syntactically and formally the gap that divides soldiers from civilians:

> *Lew Wallace, moving to retake*
> *The heights late lost—*
> *(Herewith a break.*
> *Storms at the West derange the wires.*
> *Doubtless, ere morning we shall hear*
> *The end; we look for news to cheer—* (49)

The instantaneous news that the telegraph provides—the reader's feeling that he or she might be present on the battlefield—is exposed as an illusion; at the same time, the community of the Union—linking soldiers at the front with civilians at home—is revealed to be a theoretical construct created by wartime discourses.

For while "Donelson" represents the fanning of nationalist ardor in a public square with partisan journalism read by an eager Reader, the poem also foregrounds the differences and factions within the Union, first by representing a dispute between the crowd and a passing Copperhead and ultimately by contrasting the collective victory celebration with the silent individual weeping after the posting of the list of the dead. Midway through the poem, when a Copperhead heaps scorn on Union supporters who are attempting a cheer in spite of recent setbacks at the front, he points to the ways in which journalism and poetry can stir up a patriotic crowd and blind them to the war's costs:

> "Win or lose," he pausing said,
> "Caps fly the same; all boys, mere boys;
> Any thing to make a noise.
> Like to see the list of the dead" (39)

And it is this list that ultimately divides Northern civilians again in a later section of the poem that separates the cheering crowd celebrating the Union victory from the women who later seek out the death list on the following day. The Reader's exultant shout at the news of the final Union victory is echoed by an eager responding shout from the crowd, presumably a crowd of men and boys:

> The man who read this to the crowd
> Shouted as the end he gained;
> And though the unflagging tempest rained,
> They answered him aloud. (51)

A group of voices answers the Reader's single voice, and the exultation of voices postpones the work of mourning that the next day's text will require; "the frequent shout" throughout the night defers the reading of the "lists of killed and wounded," a text that is promised as part of "the morrow's dispatch" (51).

The death list is the one newspaper item that is neither represented directly nor read aloud in the poem. Its description coincides with the first reference to women in the poem, who, we learn, read the list silently; these feminine seekers constitute a divide in the Union along gender lines. The speaker of the poem's frame story reappears to narrate how the women read:

> But others were who wakeful laid
> In midnight beds, and early rose,

And, feverish in the foggy snows,
Snatched the damp paper—wife and maid.
The death-list like a river flows
Down the pale sheet,
And there the whelming waters meet. (52)

The conjoined image of flowing paper and flowing water recalls Melville's description of the machine that converts pulp to paper in "The Tartarus of Maids": "when, suddenly, I saw a sort of paper-fall, not wholly unlike a water-fall."[25] In "Donelson" as in "The Tartarus of Maids," Melville likens the deathly pallor of women's skin to the whiteness of paper, here the "pale sheet" streaming with tears. The death list image in "Donelson" also connects the paper of this final bulletin to the bridal sheets of "wife and maid" and the funeral shrouds of the fallen soldiers. Linking the death list to the Cumberland River, which played such a crucial role in the assault on the fort, the passage suggests that the list is ever-flowing, can never cease. If we keep "The Tartarus of Maids" in mind, the growing death list still wet from the press recalls the new technologies for paper milling and newspaper printing, technologies that made the circulation of newspapers with their lists of the dead cheaper, faster, and more efficient in the Civil War era. "Donelson" thus suggests that the war machine will keep spilling out lists of the dead inexorably. While the voices cheering the victory can sustain the illusion of a unified Union only temporarily, the printed list of the dead—with its power to divide Copperheads from Unionists and cheering boys from weeping mothers—will keep growing indefinitely.

The poem's final stanza offers a somewhat unexpected swerve to the high literary stance of the romantic apostrophe, as if the speaker sought to arrest the inexorable machinery of the war effort, the paper mill, and the printing press by means of a nostalgic and time-stalling poetic stance. The tumult of the Northern victory celebration is altogether silenced by the solitary poet-speaker's performative cry of anguish. The speaker calls on God and Time to "bring wail and triumph to a waste," to tear down "battle flag-staff" and "bastion" (52). In this final stanza, the end of war is figured as the erasure or obliteration of a landscape that has been deeply marked by partisan flags, opposing military positions, death, and suffering. The contrast between the raucous victory celebrations, the women's silent mourning, and the poet-speaker's cry of despair foregrounds the rift—"the curs'd ravine"—that separates soldier from civilian, North from South, and men from women in the blighted postwar landscape. As if to emphasize the limits of his rhetorical power—the inefficacy of the poet's apostrophe to God—the speaker paradoxically calls for the obliteration of a landscape that has already been deeply scarred by the several days of intense combat that took place there. The poem offers no guarantee that the speaker's cry of despair will be in any way answered by God or the passage of Time. The final stanzas of "Donelson" suggest both that no one authoritative voice can speak for the nation in time of war and that there is no recuperative possibility for collective grief through nationalist poetic voice.

Like Whitman and like Dickinson, Melville uses the vocabulary of romantic landscape depiction to explore the limits of that vocabulary for representing wartime violence. As Timothy Sweet suggests in his insightful study of *Battle-Pieces*, the pastoral is a central mode of representation in Melville's war poetry, and Melville's use of the pastoral is fundamentally skeptical: while Whitman and some contemporary photographers often offer redemptive visions of nature's capacity for healing human loss in the aftermath of war, Melville's war poems propose a darker and more detached vision of the natural world. In reading the poems I discussed in the first section of this chapter, I suggested that repetition of names offers both elegiac and critical commentary on the relationship between hero-making rhetorical stances and nationalist ideologies. By contrast, the repetition of place names in a number of Melville's battlefield landscape poems seems to underline nature's immutable indifference to human actions in general and to the violence of war in particular. While Melville echoes the hero-making repetition of personal names in order to question the nationalist ideologies that underwrite these rhetorical gestures, he repeats place names in romantic landscape poems in order to contrast the impassive unity of nature with the discord and division of the human world.

As Sweet emphasizes in *Traces of War*, Melville's battlefield landscapes "demonstrate the incongruities between the pastoral mode of representation and the realities of war."[26] "Malvern Hill" presents a particularly striking example of the ways that Melville combines traditional literary devices with contemporary and innovative representations of violence.

He here mixes a high literary apostrophe to the elm trees—including dramatic repetition of the battle's place name—with a description that clearly responds to the graphic depictions of battlefield corpses in wartime photography:

> Ye elms that wave on Malvern Hill
> In prime of morn and May,
> Recall ye how McClellan's men
> Here stood at bay?
> While deep within yon forest dim
> Our rigid comrades lay—
> Some with the cartridge in their mouth,
> Others with fixed arms lifted South—
> Invoking so
> The cypress glades? Ah wilds of woe! (67)

With its image of an army unit in fixed postures, the opening stanza of the poem describes both bodies reified by rigor mortis and a photograph of those bodies, underlining the idea that photography arrests time. The phrase "the cartridge in their mouth" suggests the way that soldiers would tear open with their teeth the paper wrappings on cartridges prior to loading their rifles; at the same time, the phrase also evokes the graphic sight of soldiers shot through and bleeding from their mouths, a reading that is confirmed by stanza two's reference to the "beards of blood." Either reading of "the cartridge in their mouth" suggests awkwardly gaping mouths: stanza one seems simultaneously to capture the scene in the moments just before battle and in the moments just after. The frozen gaping mouths are echoed by the "fixed arms," a phrase that simultaneously suggests soldiers taking aim with their rifles or bayonets prior to an assault, the ungainly post-battle postures of rigor mortis, and also a theatrical gesture of supplication or longing, "invoking so/The cypress glades." The theatrical and poetic gesture of "invoking" the "cypress glades" is further heightened by the dramatic alliteration of "Ah wilds of woe!," a phrase in which the speaker's excess of emotion spills over into high literary exclamation. In contrast with the fixed postures of the dead men, the elms "wave" in an eternal literary present, a suspended present tense captured in the literary cry of the speaker's apostrophe. The juxtaposition of the high literary apostrophe and the implied reference to post-battle photography—both time-stalling modes of representation—signals Melville's desire to forge a new kind of poetry, a poetry that would fuse the stances of high literary tradition with a new graphic realism.

The poem as a whole is structured as a dialogue between a human voice and the voice of nature: in each of the poem's first three stanzas, the human speaker calls out to the elms, asking if they remember the scene of human suffering that took place on Malvern Hill. The battle's place name also appears three times in the poem: in the apostrophe to the elms in first stanza, in a variant version of this apostrophe ("Malvern Wood") in stanza three, and finally in the elms' concluding response, a voice represented typographically by means of italics. This repetition of the battle's place name serves to remind readers both of the violence that occurred in this pastoral setting and of nature's unchanging aspect.[27] Describing the battle, the speaker points to lines of regional loyalty that divide Northern from Southern soldiers—contrasting "our strength" with "their yell," for example, in stanza three; in "Malvern Hill," Melville experiments with an unusual first-person plural for the perspective of the Union soldiers. Yet while the poem establishes a collective "we" of Union soldiers, Melville's ultimate goal is not to establish that collective "we" but rather to contrast the deeply divided human community of the nation with the impassive and wholly unified natural world. The closing lines in the poem underline nature's indifference to divisions and violence within the nation:

> *We elms of Malvern Hill*
> *Remember every thing;*
> *But sap the twig will fill:*
> *Wag the world how it will,*
> *Leaves must be green in spring.* (68)

The brevity of these closing lines, the monosyllabic and full rhyme scheme, and the insistent meter all serve strongly to differentiate the elms' collective voice from the voice of the poem's Union speaker; the formal elements of this closing stanza also underline the imperturbable and final authority of nature. The voice of the elms is detached, remote from the world of human struggles. Human dramas will unfold as they must, but nature's cycles will inevitably continue. The authority of the elms' collective "we" thus trumps the heroic "we" of the Union soldiers in stanza three ("Reverse we proved was not defeat"). Three times the poem's speaker has called out to the elms, asking if they remember the battle. When the elms finally reply in the poem's final stanza, their response is far from consoling. Like the conclusion of "Donelson" then, "Malvern Hill" emphasizes the inefficacy of the literary apostrophe. In "Malvern Hill," the speaker's dialogue with nature is not a dialogue; rather the exchange underlines the unbridgeable divide that separates the natural and the human worlds. In "The Cumberland," Melville suggests that poetic voice might work to unify communities by allowing for timeless preservation of heroic names and deeds; in "Malvern Hill," by contrast, the repetition of place names signals the irrelevance of human events to nature, where time continues to unfold in its inevitable and imperturbable cycles.

Like "Malvern Hill," the much anthologized poem "Shiloh" offers a romantically inflected description of a blighted post-battle landscape; again like "Malvern Hill," "Shiloh" reiterates the battle's place name three times in incantatory and elegiac fashion. Yet while "Malvern Hill" uses an opening apostrophe to the elms, an exclamation of grief, and a closing stanza that offers a dialogic reply—all dramatically heightened voice-effects—"Shiloh" is a much quieter, more understated poem, more in keeping with the tastes and sensibilities of New Critically trained scholars. "Malvern Hill" uses the dramatic gesture of the apostrophe to suspend time ("Ye elms that wave on Malvern Hill"[67]), while "Shiloh" uses verb tenses ("Skimming lightly, wheeling still, / The swallows fly low" [63]) to achieve its time-stalling effects. While "Malvern Hill" experiments with a collective "we" for the Union soldier-speaker, "Shiloh" relies on Melville's more usual distanced "they" for the soldiers. "Malvern Hill" ends with nature itself speaking, marking its distance and detachment from human affairs; at the end of "Shiloh," nature remains silent. "Malvern Hill" typifies the ungainliness of Melville's improbable combinations of traditional and contemporary aesthetic elements; "Shiloh," on the other hand, seems to typify the spare understated nuance that mid-twentieth-century critics admired and haled as proto-modernist. Like Whitman's and Dickinson's poems, Melville's *Battle-Pieces* are often read forward in relation to the poetry of the twentieth century. Yet like "The Portent," another widely anthologized and much admired poem, "Shiloh" is very much rooted in its nineteenth-century context. Just as "The Portent" offers an aesthetically innovative and philosophically ambivalent response to "John Brown's Body," so too does "Shiloh" respond to a contemporary popular song, in this case "The Drummer Boy of Shiloh."

Written and composed by the Kentuckian Will Hays, "The Drummer Boy of Shiloh" endorses a number of ideologies that circulated widely in both the Union and the Confederacy: it focuses on a child's heroism, piety, and patriotism, suggesting that adult soldiers might be brought to heroism, piety, and patriotism themselves by following the child's example. Mourning the many deaths at Shiloh, the song offers assurance that soldiers who die in battle will have died as Christian martyrs. The song also relies on the widely used trope of the child-soldier who is reunited in heaven with a pious mother.

1) On Shiloh's dark and bloody ground,
   The dead and wounded lay,
Amongst them was a drummer boy
   Who beat the drum that day.
A wounded soldier held him up
   His drum was by his side;
He clasp'd his hands, then rais'd his eyes,
   And prayed before he died.
He clasp'd his hands, then rais'd his eyes,
   And prayed before he died.

2) "Look down upon the battle field
   Oh, Thou our Heavenly Friend!
Have mercy on our sinful souls!"
   The soldiers cried "Amen!"
For gathered 'round a little group,
   Each brave man knelt and cried;
They list'ned to the drummer boy,
   Who prayed before he died,
They list'ned to the drummer boy,
   Who prayed before he died.

3) "Oh, Mother," said the dying boy,
   Look down from heaven on me,
Receive me to thy fond embrace—

Oh, take me home to thee.
I've loved my country as my God;
To serve them both I've tried,"
He smiled, shook hands—death seized the boy
Who prayed before he died.
He smiled, shook hands—death seized the boy
Who prayed before he died.

4) Each soldier wept, then, like a child—
Stout hearts were they and brave;
The flag his winding sheet—God's Book
The key upon his grave.
They wrote upon a simple board
These words: This is a guide
To those who'd mourn the drummer boy
Who prayed before he died.
To those who'd mourn the drummer boy
Who prayed before he died.

5) Ye angels round the Throne of Grace,
Look down upon the braves,
Who fought and died on Shiloh's plain,
Now slumb'ring in their graves!
How many homes made desolate—
How many hearts have sighed—
How many like the drummer boy,
Who prayed before they died!
How many like the drummer boy,
Who prayed before they died![28]

The song's refrain ("Who prayed before he died . . .") emphasizes the child's piety, linking that piety directly both to Christian redemption and to patriotism. Praying on his deathbed, the child-soldier addresses first God and then his mother. The weeping soldiers who dig the boy's grave model appropriate Christian and patriotic mourning practices by burying him with both a flag and a Bible; the poem's final stanza calls on God to consecrate the field where so many were slain and suggests that many men emulated the drummer boy's loyal and prayerful death.

Like Will Hays, Melville makes Christianity a central element in his poem. Yet while Hays uses the sentimental image of the individual pious boy soldier, Melville focuses instead on the geographical and impersonal detail of the church's position in the heart of some of the battle's fiercest fighting.[29] The poem describes a collective gathering of the nameless wounded and dead rather than focusing on one individual's death. The only individuated image in the poem is that of the church building.

Skimming lightly, wheeling still,
    The swallows fly low
Over the field in clouded days,
    The forest-field of Shiloh—
Over the field where April rain
Solaced the parched ones stretched in pain
Through the pause of night
That followed the Sunday fight
    Around the church of Shiloh—
The church so lone, the log-built one,
That echoed to many a parting groan
      And natural prayer
    Of dying foemen mingled there—
Foeman at morn, but friends at eve—
    Fame or country least their care:
(What like a bullet can undeceive!)
    But now they lie low,
While over them the swallows skim,
      And all is hushed at Shiloh. (63)

In Hays's "Drummer Boy," the figure of the boy-soldier is in the lyrics' foreground, while the landscape receives only passing mention (verse one: "On Shiloh's dark and bloody ground"). Melville's poem, by contrast, places the pastoral setting of the battle in the foreground, a strategy that widens the poem's lens to embrace the whole sweep of the landscape, including the many bodies of the dead and wounded.[30] Moreover, while Hays's poem insists that soldiers' deaths are meaningful both for Christian and for nationalist reasons, Melville's poem treats nature's impassivity in such a way as to suggest the meaninglessness of war's carnage. Though the "April rain" may have "solaced the parched ones stretched in pain," it cannot ease the shock of the realization that accompanies the soldiers' deaths. Enemies have become friends and the cause of nationalism has lost importance: "Foeman at morn, but friends at eve—/Fame or country least their care:/(What like a bullet can undeceive!)." Though the church has echoed with "many a parting groan/And natural prayer," the poem refuses to offer its readers the consolation of seeing the soldiers' deaths as having either Christian or patriotic meaning. Rejecting the naïve piety of Hays's "Drummer Boy," Melville's "Shiloh" offers instead a post-battle scene in which adult men are compelled to contemplate the possibility that their deaths are tragically without meaning. The swallows are "skimming" and "wheeling still," as if no battle had ever taken place.

The shock of this revelation registers particularly in the poem's insistence on the present-day quiet, an insistence that the poem articulates formally as well as thematically: the reiteration of the battle's name—"Shiloh"—repeats a "sh" sound that is ultimately made explicit in the poem's final line: "And all is hushed at Shiloh." The repetition of the "low" sound also implies quiet, as does the opening reference to the swallows "wheeling still." The repetition of the battle's place name signals the temporal shift that takes place within the poem from the pastoral present ("the forest-field of Shiloh"), to the past-tense tumult and suffering of battle ("the church of Shiloh/[. . .] That echoed to many a parting groan"), and back to the quiet of a pastoral present ("all is hushed at Shiloh"). The repetition of the place name underlines the inevitable continuation of nature's cycles and the insignificance of the human suffering that took place in this landscape ("But now they lie low"). In contrast to "Malvern Hill," which is structured around dramatic voice-effects and a dialogue between man and nature, the spare understated voice of "Shiloh" seems to imply that poetic language itself must fall silent in the face of such suffering; in the poem's closing lines, nature's silence is figured as an imperturbable indifference. Implicitly, the poem enjoins its readers to contemplate the pastoral setting where the battle took place in silence as well.

In "Malvern Hill," Melville uses the traditional romantic apostrophe to nature to underline the gap that separates the natural world from the world of human warfare; "Shiloh" asks human observers to emulate nature's quiet when contemplating the pastoral scene where a battle took place. In "An uninscribed Monument," Melville combines these two approaches, paradoxically using an apostrophe to the reader to call for silent contemplation of a battlefield scene. Melville's investment in high literary gestures is everywhere evident in the sixteen poems entitled "verses inscriptive and memorial" that he includes in *Battle-Pieces*. In this group, Melville responds to the discourse of the battlefield monument even as he also responds to the conventions of the romantic lyric. In "Donelson," he uses a high literary apostrophe to end a poem about popular reception of wartime journalism; in the "verses inscriptive and memorial," he uses the stances of the romantic lyric to reflect on the speeches, commemorations, and inscriptions that would soon fill American cemeteries in the war's aftermath. Contrasting the ephemeral quality of poetic voice with the permanence of monument inscription, the group works through a range of rhetorical stances for these inscriptions, foretelling the floodtide of monument building yet to come. Echoing the classical epitaph with its injunction of "Stay, Traveler!," the group also responds to the "Inscriptions" of both Southey and Wordsworth. In "An uninscribed Monument," Melville uses prosopopeia—the trope in which an inanimate object or an absent or dead person speaks—to invent a speaker who addresses his readers with an intimate—if high literary—"thou." As in the closing stanza of "Donelson," Melville here seems to rely on a high literary poetic stance to silence the tumult of popular American Civil War discourse, even as he also uses a collision of high literary and popular commitments to suggest how inadequate both discourses are to the task of mourning.

AN UNINSCRIBED MONUMENT
ON ONE OF THE BATTLE-FIELDS OF THE WILDERNESS

Silence and solitude may hint
(Whose home is in yon piny wood)
What I, though tableted, could never tell—
The din which here befell,
And striving of the multitude.
The iron cones and spheres of death
Set round me in their rust,
These, too, if just,
Shall speak with more than animated breath.
Thou who beholdest, if thy thought,
Not narrowed down to personal cheer,

> Take in the import of the quiet here—
>   The after-quiet—the calm full fraught;
> Thou too wilt silent stand—
> Silent as I, and lonesome as the land. (173)

Melville here uses the word "Wilderness" to point both to a specific battle and more broadly to the horrors of war. In May 1864, the Battle of the Wilderness marked the start of Grant's relentless Overland Campaign, which would engage vast numbers of troops and result in a staggering increase in the casualty rates for both sides. The terrain on which the battle was fought was so densely wooded that soldiers often could not see their opponents, and the rate of gun-fire was so intense that thousands of pounds of lead were later removed from the woods for recasting. Melville may have visited the site in the spring of 1864. Even if he did not, however, he very likely saw John Trowbridge's description of it in an essay that appeared in the *Atlantic Monthly* in January 1866; a piece on Trowbridge's tour of the Gettysburg battlefields had appeared two months earlier.

In contrast with the noise and the crowds of the Battle of the Wilderness, Melville's poem foregrounds the silent desolation of the site, echoing Trowbridge's emphasis on the silence of battlefields. Yet while Trowbridge presents himself as an urbane and eloquent Northern writer who will offer readers a window onto the recently ended war, Melville's "uninscribed Monument" presents a speaker who is impersonal, terse, abstracted from individual experience. The speaker is either the personified uninscribed Monument or perhaps the fallen soldier who lies beneath it. The undecidability of the speaker's identity is crucial to Melville's strategy since he is resistant to speaking in the first person in the voice of a soldier. Like its English romantic models, Melville's poem addresses a traveler—in this case a visitor to the battlefield—and urges that traveler to contemplate the landscape, the fate of the dead, and a text—paradoxically an absent text: the blank tablet. The poem thus presents the relationship between text and voice as a paradox: in the poem, the uninscribed Monument speaks.

And yet the poem represents noise itself as violence: battle is evoked through the phrase "the din which here befell" and the possibility that the spent munitions might "speak with more than animated breath" ominously suggests a possible resumption of the clamor of the fight. The resumption of that fighting would, of course, threaten the safety of the poem's addressee. As Paul de Man suggests in reading Wordsworth's "Essays upon Epitaphs," when death speaks in the figure of prosopopeia, the symmetry of the trope threatens the poem's addressee with entry into the silent world of the dead, a world evoked in Melville's poem with the phrase "the after-quiet—the calm full fraught."[31] In "An uninscribed Monument," only a confrontation with mortality can shock the battlefield tourist into silent contemplation of war's unknowable horror.

In its last six lines, the poem suggests that language itself fails when faced with the task of representing battle. Commenting on the proliferation of poems, speeches, journalism, and inscriptions, the speaker of "An uninscribed Monument" observes that silence is the only fitting response for a battlefield visitor. Urging the visitor not to "narrow[]" his thought "down to personal cheer," the speaker suggests that the visitor, like the poem's speaker, must not limit his experience to the personal; the speaker thus points toward the impossibility of knowing the war from any one position. Melville may well be lamenting the conversational tone of battlefield essays like Trowbridge's, which mixes humorous portraits of rural farmers with descriptions of desolate battlefields. Melville's poem suggests that neither monument inscriptions, nor touristic essays can rebuild what the "din" of war has destroyed. The speaker admonishes the traveler to "take in the import of the quiet here," and with that admonition, the speaker himself returns to the inanimate and silent state of the uninscribed tablet: "Thou too will silent stand—/Silent as I, and lonesome as the land" (173). The poem closes with a direct address to a would-be citizen of the reunited nation, yet that citizen is presented as a solitary and isolated figure, "lonesome as the land," a phrase that suggests that no national community can be reconstituted in the war's aftermath.

With its blank stone and its silent speaker, "An uninscribed Monument" presents both a failed scene of writing and a failed scene of speaking. What communicates in this poem is the failure of metaphor. Calling into question both the poetic text and the gravestone inscription as possibilities for memorializing the dead, "An uninscribed Monument" urges writers to proceed with caution as they seek to rebuild communities, lives, and a sense of national identity. For like the "din" of battle which might "speak with more than animated breath," Melville argues that poetry has the capacity both to rebuild and to destroy the nation. Perceptive poets and historians will, he suggests, stand "silent," acknowledging the impossibility of representing or understanding the war.

Both the ungainly structure of the volume *Battle-Pieces* and the prose Supplement Melville adds at the end of the collection attest to the poet's ambivalence about the response of silence he himself calls for. The volume as a whole refuses any logical or clear-cut argumentative trajectories: it does not begin with nationalist anthems and end with skeptical and understated proto-modernist lyrics. Rather it includes an eclectic array of postures and experiments, with innovative and ambivalent poems like "Donelson" positioned early on and far more conventional poems like the hero-making "Sheridan at Cedar Creek" positioned toward the middle of the collection. The inclusion of multiple concluding gestures—the "Verses Inscriptive and Memorial," "Lee in the Capitol," "A Meditation," the Notes and then the prose Supplement—underlines Melville's aesthetic and political discomfort with this mix of material. Poems like "The Portent" and "Shiloh" examine and critique the military and nationalist ambitions that tore the nation apart; poems like "The Cumberland" and "Sheridan at Cedar Creek" seem at least partially to endorse those same military and nationalist ambitions. Melville is keenly aware of the ways that patriotic poetry can work to fan the flames of nationalist ardor, the ways that poetry read and spoken aloud can unify communities. Yet he also turns to prose in his Supplement in order to make an explicit call both for national reunification and for white Northern forgiveness of white Southern aggression.

As many scholars have noted, the prose Supplement flattens the nuance, complexity, and ambivalence of the arguments that the collection of poems advances about national conflict and reunification.[32] As if unsettled by this ambivalence and perhaps also by the generic instability of his poetic innovations, Melville lapses into prose to try to fix and reify those arguments. His nervousness is writ large in the Supplement's opening paragraph: "Were I fastidiously anxious for the symmetry of this book, it would close with the notes. But the times are such that patriotism—not free from solicitude—urges a claim overriding all literary scruples" (259). Still another passage reveals his anxiety about the reactions some of the poems may prompt from some readers:

> it will hardly occasion surprise that, in looking over the battle-pieces in the foregoing collection, I have been tempted to withdraw

> or modify some of them, fearful lest in presenting, though but dramatically and by way of a poetic record, the passions and epithets of civil war, I might be contributing to a bitterness which every sensible American must wish at an end. (263)

Melville's misgivings about the overall composition of the volume were, of course, matched by those of contemporary critics who found the collection's eclectic generic and political stances unsettling at best and baffling at worst. For twenty-first-century readers, however, *Battle-Pieces* offers an extraordinary example of American poetry in a transitional state, suspended between the romantic apostrophes of Wordsworth's poetics and the more graphic and plainspoken language of the unknown soldier-poet Lyman Holford or of the soon-to-be canonical Walt Whitman. Melville's *Battle-Pieces* looks back with longing at the sentimental and patriotic pieties of popular songs like "The Drummer Boy of Shiloh" or "The Vacant Chair" even as it also looks forward—with both dread and relief—to the newly developed printing and photographic technologies that will forever change the ways that Americans respond to war.[33]

In *Battle-Pieces*, Melville draws on representational techniques from popular song, journalism, landscape depiction, and monument inscription to consider how poetry can work to constitute nationalist communities even as it also blinds readers and listeners to the costs of a brutal modern war. Many of these poems evoke either directly or indirectly images of group celebrations or commemorations, pointing toward the ways that Civil War poetry was read, sung, and recited aloud. In the sequence of poems about the ironclad battles as in the long poem "Donelson," Melville begins by proposing a model for a collective voice of nationalist pride, only to have that voice disrupted by the cacophonous noise of the machinery of modern war. The nostalgic pride the speaker feels when he repeats the "flowing, rolling" name of the "Cumberland" will be replaced by the mechanical "anvil-din" of a new kind of combat. The joyous cheers of a celebrating Northern crowd will give way to the weeping of mothers and wives, as they read the ever growing list of the dead that is sped across the country by the clatter of the telegraph, the railway, and newly efficient paper mills and printing presses. The dramatic dialogue with nature that "Malvern Hill" proposes is ultimately not a dialogue; the silence that ends "Shiloh" is nature's indifferent response to the war. In compiling these poems into a collection, however, Melville does not present a developmental trajectory, beginning for example with poems that endorse nationalist stances or poems that endorse a redemptive view of nature's response to the war and moving on to a radical critique of those stances. Rather he presents a collection that oscillates between these conflicting commitments. In his elegies for generals and for the sailing war-ship, Melville longs for the consolations of patriotic voice. Though it is a profoundly skeptical and elegiac poem, "Malvern Hill" expresses a nostalgic longing for a dialogue with a redemptive and consoling nature. Still other poems, however, reveal a deep suspicion of the illusions of community, presence, and union with nature on which those consolations depend. These poems acknowledge that poetry worked to fuel the divisive nationalist passions that caused the war. Staging repeated encounters between the sounds of poetic voice and the page of the written text, poems like "Donelson" and "An uninscribed Monument" suggest that neither voice nor text can bring about the desired reunion of the nation.

Such poems, however, leave Melville and his grieving American readers with little comfort. Like the nation he seeks to address, Melville has deeply divided allegiances: he expresses both a nostalgic faith in the powers of nationalist poetic voice and a profound skepticism about the ways that poetry might work to reunite a divided nation. Melville's work thus serves as a forerunner not only to the graphic realism and political disillusionment of the British poets of World War I but also to the aesthetic fragmentation, formal innovation, and moral ambivalence of American modernist poets such as Mina Loy, H.D., and Ezra Pound. Yet, as I have suggested, while the beginnings of these changes are particularly evident in the wartime poetry of Herman Melville, they are also apparent across a wide range of Civil War poetry by American writers: in soldier-poet Lyman Holford's bitter denunciation of the nationalist ideologies that are used to encourage young men to become soldiers; in Howe's shifting and conflicted pronoun choices; in Dickinson's experimentation with both patriotic and skeptical stances; in Piatt's ironic wartime rewriting of the stances of genteel Victorian femininity; in Horton's reclaiming of the stances of Southern romanticism for a black speaker departing from his Southern home. American poetry of the Civil War era thus signals some of the crucial aesthetic and political fault lines that will shape twentieth-century American poets' responses to war.

EPILOGUE

Civil War Poetry in the Twentieth and Twenty-First Centuries

On September 14, 2001, a nationally televised memorial service for the victims of the September 11 attacks was held at the National Cathedral in Washington, DC. Called "A Day of Prayer and Remembrance," the service included a performance by the U.S. Navy Sea Chanters of Julia Ward Howe's "Battle Hymn of the Republic." The congregation, which included former presidents and other political leaders, rose and joined in the singing. "Mine eyes have seen the glory of the coming of the Lord," the song begins, linking individual singers and listeners together through an imaginatively shared experience of prophetic vision. Though Howe would go on to become an activist for the cause of peace after the Civil War and though her full body of Civil War–era poetry reflects a profound ambivalence about nationalist stances, her "Battle Hymn" remains a defining anthem for American identity in the post-9/11 era. With its stirring martial tune, its religious imagery, and its dramatic forging of a collective national "we," Howe's song seemed an appropriate choice to the organizers of the service. Evoking a God of wrath who descends to earth to save the American nation, the song clearly also signaled the U.S. military response that would follow the attacks. More broadly, the choice of this song underlines the centrality of the American Civil War to contemporary definitions of American identity: when performed in twenty-first-century settings, Howe's song emphasizes that a divided American nation was reunified through the Civil War.

Yet because the Civil War–era song that has earned this towering cultural status is in fact a Northern-authored Union anthem, the song's ironic persistence as a statement of American national unity also underlines the fault lines of region, race, and history that continue to divide Americans into multiple divergent political constituencies. A quick glance at the comments posted in response to the YouTube clip showing ABC's coverage of the song's performance at the 9/11 memorial reveals a broad (if highly polarized) spectrum of political views, ranging from paeans to the greatness of the American nation (of which there are many), to calls for vengeance on the terrorists, to reminders about the Northern origins of the song and the history of its composition.[1] Pasted in in full by the YouTube user who uploaded the video clip, Howe's lyrics clearly still resonate with many viewers and readers. The example of this television clip and Howe's lyrics being uploaded to YouTube—and the wealth of responses to them—underlines the proliferation and specialization of audience communities in the age of globalization and Internet connectivity, a reminder of the proliferation and fragmentation of audience communities that occurred in the United States during the American Civil War. Though the poetry of the Civil War has for the most part fallen out of favor with contemporary readers, Howe's "Battle Hymn" persists, a remaining trace of the culturally central position that poetry held in the Civil War era.

I have suggested that tensions built into the poetics of many Civil War–era poets signal the changes to come in American poetry in the twentieth century: a move away from formal regularity toward disjunctive and colliding sound-effects; a refusal of patriotic confidence in favor of skepticism and ambivalence; a rejection of aesthetic unity in favor of fragmentation and decentered perspectives. Like their nineteenth-century predecessors, in responding to two World Wars many modernist writers would turn to poetry to represent the horrors of war and to question the patriotic ideologies that fueled military conflicts. For twentieth- and twenty-first-century American poets, the Civil War remains extraordinarily influential, shaping many writers' negotiations with the complex balance between personal and political stances in their work. Indeed one way to read through the developmental trajectory of twentieth- and twenty-first-century American poetry would be to focus on poems that look back again to violence of the Civil War, many of which offer defining moments for that developmental trajectory, even as they also respond dialogically to one another. In contemporary American poetry in particular, reading for responses to the Civil War showcases the extraordinary versatility of the genre, as writers with a wide range of aesthetic and formal commitments reflect on the present-day legacy of nineteenth-century history. Focusing on the relationship between the lyric I and the first-person collectives posited by these poems also foregrounds the diversity of aesthetic commitments in contemporary work.

Some twentieth-century writers clearly look back to nineteenth-century poets in responding to the Civil War. Both in its commitment to form and in its romantic evocation of a Southern pastoral world, Allen Tate's "Ode to the Confederate Dead" harkens back nostalgically to the work of the Confederate Poet Laureate Henry Timrod, echoing most directly Timrod's 1866 "Ode Sung on the Occasion of Decorating the Graves of the Confederate Dead." With its focus on unmarked graves and a silent onlooker, Tate's poem may also be echoing Herman Melville's "An Uninscribed Monument on one of the Battle-Fields of the Wilderness." First published in 1928, the same year in which he published a hero-making biography of Confederate General Stonewall Jackson, Tate's ode became a manifesto for the group of twentieth-century white Southern male poets known as the Fugitives. Yet while Tate's prose and his body of poetry offer a staunch defense of the Southern agrarian past, his ode's depiction of a Confederate cemetery is shot through with ambivalence—both about the mourner's detachment from the fate of the slain Confederate soldiers and about nature's indifference to human affairs. While Tate relies on the romantic stances that were so crucial to his predecessor Henry Timrod, the romantic Southern world Tate's ode calls into being is permeated by both despair and decay.

While Tate looks back to nineteenth-century poets, many later twentieth-century poets respond explicitly to Tate. This is clearly the case with Robert Lowell's "For the Union Dead." A student and admirer of Tate's, Lowell first read the poem at the Boston Arts Festival in 1960. More explicitly angry and far more immediately rooted in the contemporary political realm than Tate's poem, "For the Union Dead" also marked a turn in Lowell's work toward a looser, less formally structured poetics and a reliance on more personal stances; the poem is widely seen by scholars as signaling the shift toward confessional speakers that would dominate American poetry in the final decades of the twentieth century. While Tate's poem is shaped by a unified repertoire of aestheticized images of nature, Lowell's poem hooks together a disparate set of scenes and descriptions, underlining the psychic detachment and fragmentation of the lyric self in the 1960s.

Moreover, the towering influence of Tate's and Lowell's poems extends into the contemporary era as well, as is evident in the work of the African American poets Kevin Young and Natasha Trethewey. The title poem of Kevin Young's 2007 collection *For the Confederate Dead* responds to Whitman, Tate, and Lowell in representing the speaker's ambivalent reaction to a Southern Civil War monument and to a recently uncovered mural depicting plantation life in the Old South. Natasha Trethewey won a Pulitzer Prize for her 2007 collection *Native Guard*, a group of poems that mingle stories of Trethewey's childhood in a mixed-race family in the South with stories of the black soldiers from Louisiana who formed the first black regiment in the Union Army, the Native Guard of the collection's title. In awarding Trethewey the Pulitzer, the prize committee was in part recognizing a mixed-race Southern writer's response not only to Tate and the Fugitives, but also more broadly to the legacy of the Civil War. Underlining the shaping influence of Lowell in particular, both Young and Trethewey rely on confessional speakers in these collections even as they also offer biting critiques of American political hypocrisy.

If we trace the pronoun stances used throughout these four poets' responses to the Civil War, lines of influence and rejoinder come into still sharper focus. Tate's long and formally intricate ode presents a speaker who is torn between a desire to celebrate the heroism of the fallen Confederate soldiers and a looming awareness of the meaninglessness of so much carnage. The poem's first four stanzas focus on a solitary mourner, addressed by means of the pronoun "you," a pronoun choice that seems to pinpoint its addressee in a posture of passivity and ambivalence. In stanzas six and seven, however, the poem posits an embattled but nonetheless collective "we" of white Southern mourners. Stanza six makes explicit the unanswerable questions that these white mourners must face:

> What shall we who count our days and bow
> Our heads with a commemorial woe
> In the ribboned coats of grim felicity,
> What shall we say of the bones, unclean,
> Whose verdurous anonymity will grow?[2]

In its persistent emphasis on the rotting and anonymous bodies of the dead Confederate soldiers, Tate's poem seems also to offer a high literary rejoinder to the gallows humor of the soldiers' marching song "John Brown's Body." Unlike the marching song, however, Tate's poem proposes no possibilities for redemption either for the fallen soldiers or for the mourners who come to their graves: the "we" that Tate's poem builds to is a collective that must recognize the rotting of the bones of the dead, the near-futility of the work of memorialization, and the risk of being suspended forever in a deadening posture of mourning at the "ravenous grave" (22). The Edenic paradise of the South has been transformed into a landscape whose verdure is dependent on the imperturbable turning of the seasons and the all-but-meaningless rotting of corpses. The poem closes by exhorting the mourner or mourners to leave the cemetery and reminding them of their shared mortality:

> Leave now
> The shut gate and the decomposing wall:
> The gentle serpent, green in the mulberry bush,
> Riots with his tongue through the hush—
> Sentinel of the grave who counts us all. (23)

While Tate's poem is certainly a nostalgic celebration of the Lost Cause of the South—stanza four, for example, invokes Stonewall Jackson and a list of famous battle names—in its depiction of a mourner who is suspended in a posture of perpetual irresolvable mourning, it is surely also an angry and deeply conflicted celebration. The "us" that closes the poem unites the Southern mourners, but unites them primarily through a shared mortality.

While Tate's ode carefully avoids the first-person singular, Lowell's "For the Union Dead" is centered on the observations of an angry and alienated first-person speaker who laments the gutting of Boston, as the city succumbs to the pressures of development and commerce. Contemplating the construction site of a parking lot being built beneath Boston Common, Lowell's speaker is brought up short by Saint-Gaudens's powerful monument to Robert Gould Shaw and the Massachusetts Fifty-Fourth. In the speaker's reckoning of the scene, the figure of Shaw stands like a monument to a kind of courage and conviction now lost to humanity:

Their monument sticks like a fishbone
in the city's throat.
Its Colonel is as lean
as a compass-needle.

He has an angry wrenlike vigilance,
A greyhound's gentle tautness;
he seems to wince at pleasure,
and suffocate for privacy.[3]

Lowell's poem contrasts the power and beauty of Saint-Gaudens's monument with the appalling commercialism of a billboard advertisement that features a safe surviving the blast at Hiroshima. Images of present-day commercialism and detachment from the suffering of others contrast with images of the bravery and moral engagement of Shaw and his men. The poem is framed by two images of the first-person speaker. It opens with the speaker as a child, wistfully observing the fish on the other side of the glass at the now torn-down aquarium. Toward the end of the poem, the adult speaker is transfixed by televised images of young black children in the South, images of the struggle for civil rights: "When I crouch to my television set,/the drained faces of Negro school-children rise like balloons" (179). The speaker's posture of crouching passivity, echoed by the "servility" of the poem's penultimate line, contrasts with the "tautness" and "vigilance" of the figure of Shaw in the monument (180, 179). While Tate's poem builds to a collective of white Southern mourners for the Confederacy, Lowell's poem suggests that no unified collective is possible in the current political climate. The image of Shaw being buried in a mass grave with his black soldiers serves as a counterweight to Lowell's solitary, disillusioned, and passive speaker and to the crass commercialism that destroys any possibility for community in the Boston of the 1960s.

Kevin Young opens his "For the Confederate Dead" where Lowell ends his poem: with a first-person speaker transfixed by a television. The poem begins with an apocalyptic weather forecast, gesturing toward the turbulence of global climate change: "These are the last days/my television says."[4] Focused intently on the observations of its speaker, the poem uses short heavily enjambed lines to unfold a series of terse descriptive statements occasionally disrupted by an emotion-laden statement: "I do not/trust weathermen"; "only/the milk makes sense" (97). The speaker's gaze shifts from a Confederate war monument to a mural on the walls of the café where he sits. Following the lead of the epigraph from Whitman—"I go with the team also"—the speaker observes the depiction of slave labor in the mural: slaves picking cotton or driving carriages (97). The third and final scene is an imagined glimpse of a battlefield, with soldiers retreating and other soldiers bayoneting prone bodies. Invoking both past and present, the speaker forges a collective "we" that is inescapably haunted by war: "We prepare/for wars no longer/there" (98). In its closing stanzas, the poem offers further commentary on these disparate scenes, noting the tumult both in the weather and in the world: "if I did not know/better, I would think/we were living all along/a fault" (99). The "we" that the poem proposes is thus both meteorologically and geographically unsettled, a nation still divided by the markers of race, region, and history. The poem closes with the speaker exhorting this "we" to take action: "Race/instead against the almost/rain" (99). But they struggle in the humidity which engulfs them like inertia: "till we strike/water, sweat/fighting the sleepwalking air." The first-person speaker allies himself with a collective "we," but that "we" seems as unsettled and troubled as the speaker himself, burdened by memories of violence and racism, memories that are inseparable from American national identity.

In the title poem of *Native Guard,* Natasha Trethewey offers a narrative retelling of the history of this regiment, as seen through the eyes of one black soldier, the poem's first-person speaker. A tightly structured sequence of sonnets with the first line of each new sonnet reiterating the last line of the preceding one, the poem traces the development of the regiment into a cohesive military unit, linking the individual soldier's "I" with the "we" of the collective. The poem emphasizes the layering of different individual stories—both white- and black-authored—into a collective history, a layering that is made metaphorically explicit when the poem's speaker describes how he writes in a journal taken from a Confederate home, writing his own story at right angles, cross-hatched, to that of the white Confederate writer. The discipline of the poem's form shapes the quiet understatement of the speaker's voice, and that formal discipline echoes both the earlier restrictions of slavery and the rules of the military. Trethewey here gives voice to a collective of black soldiers whose experience of the war was for the most part excluded from white-authored histories—and indeed from much white-authored poetry about the war; the poem reminds readers of the widespread anti-black racism of white Union officers. While "Native Guard" talks back to Tate only implicitly, Trethewey makes her response to the Fugitives explicit in "Pastoral," a poem that stages her imaginary encounter with these poets. The poem concludes "My *father's white*, I tell them, *and rural. / You don't hate the South?* they ask. *You don't hate it?*"[5] The collection *Native Guard* offers Trethewey's complex and nuanced answer to this question. In the closing lines of "Pastoral," the proliferation of personal pronouns traces the fault lines of race and family history that intersect in the Southern landscape.

While Young and Trethewey offer twenty-first-century lyric speakers in response to Tate's and Lowell's Civil War poems, two contemporary experimental women poets propose alternatives to the lyric self in their Civil War–focused projects. Both Jena Osman and Janet Holmes turn back strongly to nineteenth-century sources in their engagement with the Civil War, meditating on the inseparable connection between nineteenth- and twenty-first-century forms of violence. In her multimedia project "Public Figures," poet Jena Osman juxtaposes photographs of Civil War monuments with twentieth- and twenty-first-century journalistic photography from war zones.[6] First delivered as a Powerpoint presentation at the Penn Humanities Forum in 2006 and now available through the on-line journal *How2*, Osman's piece mixes essayistic writing with hypnotic and contemplative repetition of key phrases; Osman meditates on the invisibility of war monuments in public space and on the iconography of weapons in both monuments and journalistic photography.[7] She opens the project by considering what can be seen from the vantage point of the human figures in these Civil War statues before moving on to consider the history of the funding and site choice for specific monuments. By shooting images of public plazas from the unexpected vantage-point of the statues that look out over them, Osman underlines the decentering and unsettling of the individual human perspective that must necessarily take place when heroes are made and monuments are erected. While the opening chapters of "Public Figures" narrate Osman's work on the project from a first-person perspective, by the third chapter she represents the questions she is considering by means of a more distanced—but also more inclusive—"you." Osman moves away from the personal "I" in this project in order to put more pressure on her readers and viewers to respond—and be responsive—to the war monuments that surround them. In chapter four, she traces the complex colonial history that lies behind the use of the Zouave costume in the Civil War; turning briefly to contemporary reenactor culture, she notes that a group specializing in Zouave reenacting describes their work as "a living monument."[8] Clearly signaled by the juxtaposition of Civil War monuments and twentieth-century wartime photography throughout the piece is the argument that Civil War military culture continues to shape American identity in ways that have become invisible to Americans going about the business of their everyday lives. Pairing a journalist's photo of a soldier peering along the sights of his gun with a war monument of a soldier carrying a gun, Osman asks "How can a weapon and the body that carries it become so neutralized—to the point where I no longer take it in? [. . .] Is there a way to wake myself up?"[9] Osman uses a multimedia, mixed-genre piece and shifting pronoun stances to compel her readers and viewers to attend to the war imagery that all-but-saturates the culture around them.

While Osman uses a multimedia collage to unfold her inquiry about war monuments and memory, poet Janet Holmes turns back to the work of Emily Dickinson, generating her own poems by performing erasures of a group of Dickinson pieces from 1861 and 1862. Allowing herself only to eliminate words from a poem or group of poems, not to add or rearrange any, Holmes titles her project *The Ms of My Kin*, a title which is itself an erasure of *The Poems of Emily Dickinson*.[10] Bringing military and political diction into the forefront in her poems, Holmes's erasure project makes clear that Dickinson was deeply engaged in responding to the Civil War in her work. By using Dickinson texts as her palimpsest, Holmes underlines the ways that Civil War culture continues to shape American identity; at the same time, she foregrounds the inseparability of the categories of military and American identity. Published in 2009, Holmes's *The Ms of My Kin* also reminds readers that the United States has been at war in Afghanistan and Iraq for almost a decade now.

Holmes closes the project with a note listing all of the speakers, soldiers, politicians, reporters, and contemporary incidents to which her poems allude, allusions all made possible by Dickinson's language. Holmes's deftness in generating contemporary topical pieces with Dickinson's language is frequently remarkable. A piece drawn from Dickinson's "The lamp burns sure – within –" (F 247) has just three terse lines: "It matters / that the oil / is gone."[11] Still another poem critiques the deception and manipulation of military decisions made at the highest level:

or a lesser

superior

qualified for

our new
Tactics

should have been
blamed— (44)

The ample white space used in this erasure suggests both the censoring of language from intelligence reports and the judicious choosing of words by a diplomat or military leader in the midst of a tense negotiation. Moving sometimes slowly, sometimes swiftly through the chosen poem or poems, Holmes demonstrates the procedure of erasure on the page, using white space to mark omitted text and retaining Dickinson's punctuation. From some poems she will select several words, from others just a single one. Dickinson's idiosyncratic and slightly archaic diction is preserved, but in their spareness and quiet compression, these poems make Dickinson's originals seem loquacious, almost chatty, by contrast. The erasure has the effect of removing all but the faintest traces of Dickinson's formal commitments, another reason why the Holmes poems seem so much quieter of voice than the originals.

The poems only occasionally turn to first-person pronouns and do not seem to be centered on a solitary lyric self, yet they are nonetheless colored by the personal emotion of lyric voice. By frequently eliding the first person in this erasure project, Holmes plays with our expectations about authorial originality: readers who know Dickinson's corpus well will certainly recognize traces of Dickinsonian rhetoric and diction, but the poems in *The Ms of My Kin* are unmistakably their own project. While the first-person speaker is already fragmentary and elusive in Dickinson's original poems, the further disintegration of a centralized lyric speaker in Holmes's erasures signals the obliteration of the lyric self in the face of 150 years of violent conflicts fought by American soldiers. A one-page section of one poem reads:

awful
to

live to know
such a day (83)

The violence and political maneuvering that Holmes finds in Dickinson's meditations on the Civil War reflects the violence and political hypocrisy of our own times, as Americans contemplate the repeated U.S. military interventions in the Middle East in the late twentieth and early twenty-first centuries. Where Holmes posits a collective first person, that first person is often united through a shared complicity or guilt in the prosecution of wars being fought for reasons other than those publicly stated. Again and again Holmes confronts her readers with the horror of this discovery:

the fair Ideal,
we discover

a lie— (106)

In the same poem, she follows these lines with an argument about how hero worship sustains the military endeavor:

We adored
Him—
Obedient to

command (106)

In the nineteenth-century Protestant rhetoric of Dickinson's poems, Holmes finds abundant continuity with the contemporary theological commitments that underpin U.S. foreign policy. In still another piece, a first-person collective longs for a God who might resolve the conflicting desires and commitments of the American people:

we hide our brave

dream

to the end—

Take us Lord— (17)

By turns skeptical, angry, elegiac, and philosophical, Janet Holmes's *The Ms of My Kin* finds in Dickinson's Civil War poetry a provocative response to twenty-first-century U.S. foreign policy and to contemporary models for American identity.

These recent projects by Kevin Young, Natasha Trethewey, Jena Osman, and Janet Holmes make clear that many American writers still turn to poetry as their preferred genre for responding to the violence of war. Though some readers may lament the passing of an era when poetry enjoyed a remarkable cultural centrality, as it did in the nineteenth century, to do so is to misunderstand the fracturing and specialization of poetry's proportionally smaller but nonetheless devoted audiences in the late twentieth and early twenty-first centuries. The fracturing of aesthetic commitments in contemporary poetry's audiences mirrors the political fault lines that run throughout contemporary American society. It would be a mistake to say that contemporary American poets do not engage with their political context or that they write exclusively for academic audiences. All four of these writers respond powerfully and provocatively both to American history and to present-day policies shaped by nineteenth-century legacies; each also seeks a readership that is skeptical of patriotic and conventional pieties both about the nineteenth century and about contemporary models for nationalism. Young and Trethewey reclaim lyric stances for the twenty-first century, relying on lyric speakers to serve as the moral centers for their pieces, a decision that likely broadens their readership. Osman and Holmes probably reach smaller audiences—though also intensely loyal ones—given their decisions to unsettle the stability and established conventions of the lyric speaker. Osman's commitment to generic hybridity—like Holmes's erasure project—works to unsettle our received notions about the relationship between the author and the lyric speaker in the poetic text. For readers committed to experimental work, the shattering of the lyric speaker's moral authority corresponds to a disillusionment with the forms of moral authority offered by American political and military leaders, a correspondence that echoes the skepticism found in the work of Lyman Holford, Emily Dickinson, and Herman Melville, among other Civil War poets.

Contemporary poets return to the Civil War not only because it was a defining moment for American identity but also because it was a defining moment for American poetry: the proliferation of multiple specialized audiences that begins in the Civil War leads to the further specialization and fragmentation of poetry's audiences in the twentieth and twenty-first century. Yet in spite of the change in poetry's cultural status and in spite of the sometimes polarizing debates between confessional and experimental writers in contemporary poetry, for a wide range of American writers poetry continues to be a central site for discussion of the meaning of national identity and of the ethical dilemmas of representing war's violence. One commitment that Young, Trethewey, Osman, and Holmes clearly all share is this: all four of these writers find a legacy of nineteenth-century violence hidden in plain sight all around us in the twenty-first century. Their responses to the American Civil War remind us that contemporary poetry remains a vital and flexible literary genre, one that lends itself readily to dialogue and responsive debate, and one that is particularly well suited to the necessary work of examining the relationship between the individual and the nation in a time of war.

NOTES

INTRODUCTION

1. For representative selections from this broad range of work, see *"Words for the Hour": A New Anthology of American Civil War Poetry* (Amherst: University of Massachusetts Press, 2005), which I coedited with Cristanne Miller.
2. I refer to the title of chap. 5 of Fussell's *The Great War in Modern Memory* (New York: Oxford University Press, 1975): "Oh What a Literary War" (155–90). Though Fussell notes that the American Civil War was the first in which large numbers of literate men served as footsoldiers, he argues that British soldiers in World War I were not just literate but rather "vigorously literary" (157). Reading American writers of World War I, he argues that a lack of consciousness of "a national literary canon" makes American work about the war "spare and one-dimensional" (158). I would counter that it is precisely that lack of a national literary canon that allows American Civil War–era poets to draw freely from both English and American and from popular and literary traditions.
3. Edmund Wilson, *Patriotic Gore: Studies in the Literature of the American Civil War* (New York: Oxford University Press, 1962). Wilson uses this oft-cited phrase to dismiss Melville's *Battle-Pieces* in particular, though he applies the same criticism more broadly to much of the poetry produced during this era (479). For his discussion of Civil War poetry overall, see 466–507. Daniel Aaron devotes a book-length study to male Civil War writers both Northern and Southern, but like Wilson, he seems ambivalent about these writers' accomplishments. He writes: "One would expect writers to say something revealing about the meaning . . . of the War. This book argues implicitly throughout that, with a few notable exceptions, they did not" (*The Unwritten War: American Writers and the Civil War* [Madison: University of Wisconsin Press, 1987]) xxii.
4. All four of these studies proved invaluable to me in my approach to Civil War poetry: Paula Bennett's *Poets in the Public Sphere: The Emancipatory Project of American Women's Poetry, 1800–1900* (Princeton: Princeton University Press, 2003), Mary Loeffelholz's *From School to Salon: Reading Nineteenth-Century American Women's Poetry* (Princeton: Princeton University Press, 2004), Eliza Richards's *Gender and the Poetics of Reception in Poe's Circle* (Cambridge University Press, 2004), and Angela Sorby's *Schoolroom Poets: Childhood, Performance, and*

the *Place of American Poetry, 1865–1917* (Durham: University of New Hampshire Press, 2005). Joan Shelley Rubin's *Songs of Ourselves: The Uses of Poetry in America* (Cambridge: Belknap Press of Harvard University Press, 2007) offers a history of the cultural practices of reading poetry from the 1880s to the 1950s. The growing number of articles on Civil War poetry signals the increased interest in this body of work. A 2008 special issue of *ESQ: A Journal of the American Renaissance* focusing on poetry includes three important essays on Civil War poetry: Eliza Richards, "Correspondent Lines: Poetry, Journalism, and the US Civil War," *ESQ* 54: 145–69; Jessica Roberts, "A Poetic *E Pluribus Unum:* Conventions, Imperatives, and the Poetic Call-to-Arms in Frank Moore's *Rebellion Record,*" 171–97; and Mary Loeffelholz, "Anthology Form and the Field of Nineteenth-century American Poetry: The Civil War Sequences of Lowell, Longfellow, and Whittier," 217–39.

5. Timothy Sweet, *Traces of War: Poetry, Photography, and the Crisis of the Union* (Baltimore: Johns Hopkins University Press, 1990); Elizabeth Young, *Disarming the Nation: Women's Writing and the American Civil War* (Chicago: University of Chicago Press, 1999); Alice Fahs, *The Imagined Civil War: Popular Literature of the North & South, 1861–1865* (Chapel Hill: University of North Carolina Press, 2001); Lisa Long, *Rehabilitating Bodies: Health, History, and the American Civil War* (Philadelphia: University of Pennsylvania Press, 2004); Kathleen Diffley, *Where My Heart Is Turning Ever: Civil War Stories and Constitutional Reform, 1861–1876* (Athens: University of Georgia Press, 1992); and Shirley Samuels, *Facing America: Iconography and the Civil War* (Oxford: Oxford University Press, 2004). My analysis is particularly indebted to the work of Timothy Sweet. For a study that situates American Civil War writing in the theoretical context of trauma theory and human rights law, see James Dawes's *The Language of War: Literature and Culture in the U.S. from the Civil War through World War II* (Cambridge: Harvard University Press, 2002), especially chap. 1. Coleman Hutchison was working on his ground-breaking study of Confederate literature at the same time that I was writing this book. The questions he raises about war-time models for national identity and about the relationship between popular song and popular literature run parallel to the questions I pursue in this book. See his *Apples and Ashes: Literature, Nationalism, and the Confederate States of America* (Athens: University of Georgia Press, 2012).
6. Virginia Jackson, *Dickinson's Misery: A Theory of Lyric Reading* (Princeton: Princeton University Press, 2005).
7. Meredith McGill, *American Literature and the Culture of Reprinting, 1834–1853* (Philadelphia: University of Pennsylvania Press, 2003).
8. Milette Shamir, *Inexpressible Privacy: The Interior Life of Antebellum American Literature* (Philadelphia: University of Pennsylvania Press, 2006).
9. Christopher Castiglia, *Interior States: Institutional Consciousness and the Inner Life of Democracy in the Antebellum United States* (Durham, NC: Duke University Press, 2008).
10. Fahs, *The Imagined Civil War.* See especially chap. 1.
11. Ibid., 31; *Southern Field and Fireside*, March 6, 1864, 5.

12. Frank Luther Mott, *A History of American Magazines, 1850–1865* (Cambridge: Harvard University Press, 1938), 454 and 10. Mott is careful to emphasize that circulation numbers for nineteenth-century periodicals must be taken with a grain of salt since the only sources for these numbers are "the occasional boasts of successful publishers" (10). Still he observes that "the average circulation of American magazines appears to have increased" between 1850 and 1865 (9).
13. Ibid., 460.
14. Ibid., 475–76.
15. Fahs, *The Imagined Civil War,* 49.
16. On Southern broadsides in particular, see William Moss's *Confederate Broadside Poems: An Annotated Bibliography* (Westport, CT: Meckler, 1988).
17. As Fahs notes, literacy rates were significantly higher in the North than in the South: "Approximately 70 percent of the free male population in the South was literate, in contrast to some 90 percent in the more populous North" (*The Imagined Civil War,* 323, fn 10).
18. For analysis of the pedagogical centrality of poetry in the post–Civil War era, see Sorby's *Schoolroom Poets*.
19. For analysis of a poetry album from the antebellum era, see Mary Louise Kete's *Sentimental Collaborations: Mourning and Middle-Class Identity in Nineteenth-Century America* (Durham, NC: Duke University Press, 1999).
20. Nineteenth-century reprinting practices may have also spurred on Civil War era poets; at the very least, these practices speeded the pace of the circulation of poetry. For analysis of two Civil War poems' recirculation, see Ellen Gruber Garvey's "Anonymity, Authorship, and Recirculation: A Civil War Episode," *Book History* 9 (2006): 159–78. For discussion of antebellum reprinting practices, see McGill's *American Literature and the Culture of Reprinting*.
21. A significant difference between Northern and Southern publications is that the most widely read of the Northern periodicals—*Frank Leslie's* and *Harper's Weekly*—were lavishly illustrated with engravings of battlefield scenes, maps of battlefield topography and movements of troops, and portraits of military leaders. Few Southern publications were able to include illustrations, and those they did include were far less sophisticated than their Northern counterparts. On this issue, see Fahs, *The Imagined Civil War,* 35–37.
22. For a discussion of the relationship between elite and popular culture in nineteenth-century American, see Lawrence Levine's *Highbrow/Lowbrow: The Emergence of Cultural Hierarchy in America* (Cambridge: Harvard University Press, 1988).
23. Benedict Anderson, *Imagined Communities: Reflections on the Origin and Spread of Nationalism* (London: Verso, 1991).
24. For analysis of the Civil War era scrapbook Henry Ingersoll Bowditch assembled in memory of his soldier-son, see Garvey's "Anonymity, Authorship, and Recirculation," especially 171–75. Garvey notes that scrapbooking was practiced by both men and women in the Civil War era; she argues that Bowditch's carefully assembled collection of poems indicates that both male and female readers found solace in sentimental postures for mourning soldiers' deaths. For further analysis

of scrapbooking practices in the nineteenth century, see also Garvey's "Scissorizing and Scrapbooks: Nineteenth Century Reading, Remaking, and Circulating," in *New Media, 1740–1915*, ed. Lisa Gitelman and Geoffrey Pingree (Boston: MIT Press, 2004), 207–28, and "The Power of Recirculation: Scrapbooks and the Reception of the Nineteenth Century Press," *New Directions in American Reception Study*, ed. Philip Goldstein and James Machor (Oxford: Oxford University Press, 2008): 211–31.

25. For an insightful analysis of the important genre of the call-to-arms poem, as that genre was anthologized in *The Rebellion Record*, see Roberts's "A Poetic *E Pluribus Unum*." Roberts argues "*The Rebellion Record* and other anthologies capitalized on the rhetorical flexibility of popular genres—a flexibility born of the fact that their 'I's' and 'you's' did not suggest subjectivity but rather proffered patriotic subject positions—and thereby transformed individual (often regional) performances of citizenship into collective (and, therefore, national) displays of patriotism" (179). An example of a scrapbook volume that assembles clippings from Civil War era newspapers is Nathaniel Paine's *Poetry of the Rebellion: A collection of cuttings from the various newspapers of the day, both north and south* (Worcester, 1862) in the holdings of the American Antiquarian Society.

26. On the history of scrapbooking practices, see Susan Tucker, Katherine Ott, and Patricia Buckler, eds., *The Scrapbook in American Life* (Philadelphia: Temple University Press, 2006). In the introduction to the volume, the editors note that "commercial scrapbooks were marketed widely throughout the nineteenth century" (8).

27. Fahs, *The Imagined Civil War*, 52.

28. Commenting on the centrality of song to Northern and Southern soldiers' experience, historian Bell Irvin Wiley writes: "The men who wore the blue, and the butternut Rebs who opposed them, more than American fighters of any [other] period, deserve to be called singing soldiers." See Wiley's *The Life of Billy Yank, the Common Soldier of the Union* (Indianapolis: Bobbs-Merrill, 1952), 157. Wiley notes that Union soldiers sang "on the march, in the trenches, on fatigue, on the battlefield, and especially in bivouac" (158). He adds: "the urge to sing was so irrepressible that men on outpost duty sometimes had to be reprimanded for lifting their voices and giving away their positions" (158).

29. The genesis for this book was a dissertation I wrote on the lyric address in the work of Emily Dickinson in the Department of Comparative Literature at UC Berkeley. A few years ahead of me in the Comparative Literature program was William Waters, whose dissertation on the apostrophe in the work of Dickinson, Rilke, and other poets subsequently became an elegant and insightful book, *Poetry's Touch: On Lyric Address* (Ithaca: Cornell University Press, 2003). Like Waters, I am interested in the ways that tropes of address foreground the construct of poetic voice. Waters's comparative approach, embracing multiple periods and national literatures, leads him to attend with particular care to the apostrophe's hailing of the poem's reader; by situating Civil War poems in their historical and discursive contexts, I aim to examine the ways that American poets position themselves

in relation to the multiple audiences that the context of the war offered them.

30. Wilson, *Patriotic Gore*, 487–88.

31. For an account of the position of Mill's model in New Critical and post-structuralist theories of the lyric, see for example Jonathan Culler's "Changes in the Study of the Lyric," in *Lyric Poetry: Beyond New Criticism*, ed. Chaviva Hosek and Patricia Parker (Ithaca: Cornell University Press, 1985), 38–54, and also Herbert Tucker's "Dramatic Monologue and the Overhearing of Lyric," in the same volume, 226–46. Culler also emphasizes the centrality of Mill's model in his influential essay "Apostrophe," in *The Pursuit of Signs* (Ithaca: Cornell University Press, 1981), 135–54. For a critique of the shaping influence Mill's model of the scene of address has had on twentieth-century readings of the lyric in general and Dickinson's poetry in particular, see Jackson, *Dickinson's Misery*, especially 129–33. As Jackson rightly notes, "later critics of the lyric have often taken up Mill's influential metaphors for lyric address while ignoring both their generic complication and their concern about the relation between writing and voice" (132). Jackson's insightful analysis of this broader problem of misreading nineteenth-century poetry helped to shape my own critical approach to Civil War poetry.

32. John Stuart Mill, "What Is Poetry?" in *Essays on Poetry by John Stuart Mill*, ed. F. Parvin Sharpless (Columbia: University of South Carolina Press, 1976), 12.

33. William Wordsworth, Preface to *Lyrical Ballads* (1802), in *William Wordsworth*, ed. Stephen Gill (Oxford University Press, 1990), 611. For a study that reads the lyric as a time-suspending genre, see for example Sharon Cameron's *Lyric Time: Dickinson and the Limits of Genre* (Baltimore: Johns Hopkins University Press, 1981).

34. In recent decades many scholars of American culture have responded to Habermas's model for the print-mediated public sphere. While Michael Warner's *Letters of the Republic* adopts the Habermasian model for the American context, scholars such as Jay Fliegelman, Nancy Ruttenburg, and Christopher Looby emphasize the primacy of voice over print. Paula Bennett uses Nancy Fraser's feminist critique of Habermas's version of the public sphere as a foundation for her ground-breaking analysis of nineteenth-century American women poets' participation in print culture (See Bennett's *Poets in the Public Sphere*). Remarkably, however, the scholarly debate about the primacy of oral versus print culture in antebellum America has for the most part not focused on the genre of poetry. This omission is particularly surprising given how often poetry was read aloud, declaimed, recited, and sung in nineteenth-century America. In this historical context, poetry often offered audiences not only the metaphorical illusion of voice (i.e., the text presents the reader with the illusion that someone is speaking) but also a live oral performance. See Michael Warner's *The Letters of the Republic: Publication and the Public Sphere in Eighteenth-Century America* (Cambridge: Harvard University Press, 1990) and *Publics and Counterpublics* (New York: Zone Books, 2005). See also Jay Fliegelman, *Declaring Independence: Jefferson, Natural Language, and the Culture of Performance* (Stanford: Stanford University Press, 1993); Christopher Looby, *Voicing America: Language, Literary Form, and the Origins of the United States* (Chicago: University of

Chicago Press, 1996); and Nancy Ruttenburg, *Democratic Personality: Popular Voice and the Trial of American Authorship* (Stanford: Stanford University Press, 1997).

35. R. W. Franklin's dating of Dickinson's manuscripts would suggest that she wrote more than 900 poems between 1861 and 1865. See Franklin's *The Poems of Emily Dickinson* (Cambridge: Harvard University Press, Belknap Press, 1998).
36. The phrase comes from the first stanza of Piatt's "Hearing the Battle.—July 21, 1861." Cited from Paula Bernat Bennett, ed., *Palace-Burner: The Selected Poetry of Sarah Piatt* (Urbana: University of Illinois Press, 2001), 2.

CHAPTER ONE. SHAPING COMMUNITIES THROUGH POPULAR SONG

1. Benedict Anderson, *Imagined Communities: Reflections on the Origin and Spread of Nationalism* (London: Verso, 1991), 145.
2. Judith Sacks and Howard Sacks suggest that Emmett's songwriting—and the writing of "Dixie" in particular—may have been shaped by his contact with the Snowdens, a family of African American musicians who lived near Emmett's hometown of Mount Vernon, Ohio, and gave frequent performances in that part of the state. See Howard L. Sacks and Judith Rose Sacks, *Way Up North in Dixie: A Black Family's Claim to the Confederate Anthem* (Washington, DC: Smithsonian Institution Press, 1993).
3. Researchers offer a conflicting array of explanations for the etymological origin of the name "Dixie." One theory links the word to a benevolent white slave owner in New York City; another links the name to a ten-dollar note printed in Louisiana (from the French word "dix"); yet another argues for the link between "Dixie" and the Mason-Dixon line. According to the *OED*, the first appearance of the term in print is in Emmett's song; it seems likely that Emmett's song worked to increase use of "Dixie" as a name for the South throughout the United States.
4. For a discussion of the song's widespread popularity, see Hans Nathan's *Dan Emmett and the Rise of Early Negro Minstrelsy* (Norman: University of Oklahoma Press, 1962), 269–74. For an analysis of the competing visions of nationalism offered by the many Northern and Southern variant versions of "Dixie," see Coleman Hutchison, "Whistling 'Dixie' for the Union (Nation, Anthem, Revision)," *American Literary History* 19 (2007): 603–28. See also Hutchison's discussion of "Dixie" in chap. 4 of his *Apples and Ashes: Literature, Nationalism, and the Confederate States of America* (Athens: University of Georgia Press, 2012). Hutchison's concerns in many ways parallel my own.
5. Kenneth A. Bernard, *Lincoln and the Music of the Civil War* (Caldwell, ID: Caxton Printers, 1966), 298.
6. Nathan, *Dan Emmett*, 245.
7. Ibid., 243.
8. Daniel D. Emmett, "I Wish I Was in Dixie's Land" (New York: Firth Pond, 1860).
9. The reference to the "'forty-pound'er" is somewhat obscure, but it seems likely that Emmett here refers to an artillery piece. While nomenclature for sizing of

artillery was inconsistent in the nineteenth century, forty pounds was not a standard size. Emmett may have shortened the term "forty-two pounder" (the size of some seacoast guns) to fit the song's meter.

10. Bell Irvin Wiley, *The Life of Johnny Reb: The Common Soldier of the Confederacy* (New York: Bobbs-Merrill, 1943), 154.
11. William Shepperson, ed., *War Songs of the South* (Richmond, VA: West and Johnston, 1862), 17–19, cited from *Documenting the American South*, http://docsouth.unc.edu/imls/shepperson/shepperson.html.
12. See for example Irvin Silber, ed., *Songs of the Civil War* (New York: Columbia University Press, 1960), 51, and H. M. Wharton, *Songs and Poems of the Southern Confederacy, 1861–1865* (Winston, 1904), 29–30.
13. The persistence of Emmett's version of the lyrics in the South is also made evident by the song's postwar history: in 1903, at the height of the movement to celebrate the Lost Cause of the Confederacy, a group of women organizers for the United Daughters of the Confederacy published a call for a loftier, more noble version of the song's lyrics, a version in standard English that could be officially recognized and taught. The call for a revised version of the lyrics was ultimately defeated by strong support among Confederate army veterans for Emmett's original version. For a detailed account of this episode, see John A. Simpson's "Shall We Change the Words of 'Dixie'?" *Southern Folklore Quarterly* 45 (1981): 19–40.
14. For a groundbreaking analysis of the social history of "contraband songs," see Michael C. Cohen's insightful essay "Contraband Singing: Poems and Songs in Circulation during the Civil War," *American Literature* 82.2 (June 2010): 271–304. Cohen argues persuasively that it was the very flatness and simplicity of many popular song lyrics that made them so versatile and so potentially effective politically during the Civil War (271). He also offers analysis of specific historical contexts in which various songs—including "Let My People Go"—were performed before going on to study parodies and satirical rejoinders to the pro-abolitionist "contraband" songs, including broadsides and single-page songsheets.
15. Cohen notes that this song deploys "a rhetoric that could be invisible or legible, depending on the performance context" (ibid., 283). The lyrics' call for violence could be read as an allusion either to the Old Testament or to the contemporary situation of enslaved African Americans in the South. Cohen also examines poetic rejoinders to "Let My People Go" (284).
16. Dena Epstein, *Sinful Tunes and Spirituals: Black Folk Music to the Civil War* (Urbana: University of Illinois Press, 1977), 245, 247.
17. In his letter to the *New York Tribune*, Harwood Vernon, secretary of the YMCA, emphasizes that Lockwood transcribed the song "verbatim from the dictation of Carl Holloway, and other contrabands." I cite Vernon's account from its reprint in the *National Anti-Slavery Standard*, December 21, 1861.
18. The version of the song that appeared in the *National Anti-Slavery Standard* was published under the heading "The Contrabands' Freedom Hymn."
19. *National Anti-Slavery Standard*, December 21, 1861.
20. Epstein, *Sinful Tunes and Spirituals*, 248–49. "Let My People Go" was not included

in the influential 1867 collection *Slave Songs of the United States* (ed. Allen, Ware, and Garrison).

21. C. A. Browne, *The Story of Our National Ballads* (New York: Thomas Y. Crowell, 1919), 188.
22. For a discussion of the relationship between "Say, Brothers, Will You Meet Us?," "John Brown's Body," and Howe's "Battle Hymn" from the standpoint of a musicologist, see Annie Randall, "A Censorship of Forgetting," in *Music, Power, and Politics*, ed. Annie J. Randall (New York: Routledge, 2005), 5–24.
23. For a nuanced analysis of how "John Brown's Body" worked to shore up Union nationalism—even in the face of growing numbers of wartime deaths—see Franny Nudelman's *John Brown's Body: Slavery, Violence, and the Culture of War* (Chapel Hill: University of North Carolina Press, 2004), chap. 1. My reading of the song is indebted to Nudelman's; yet while Nudelman argues that the song represents violence as redemptive for the Union, my analysis emphasizes that the symbolism of the lyrics is loose enough that soldiers might identify with the song's pro-Union message without particularly endorsing the abolitionist John Brown's actions.
24. See Browne, *The Story of Our National Ballads*, 181–99, and also Boyd Stutler, "John Brown's Body," *Civil War History* 4 (1958): 251–61.
25. Emerson, "Courage," *New York Tribune*, November 8, 1859.
26. Wiley writes: "Some fought to free the slaves, but a polling of the rank and file through their letters and diaries indicates that those whose primary object was the liberation of the Negroes comprised only a small part of the fighting forces." See Bell Irvin Wiley, *The Life of Billy Yank: The Common Soldier of the Union* (Indianapolis: Bobbs-Merrill, 1951), 40. James McPherson traces developments in the Union soldiers' perspective on the question of emancipation in *For Cause and Comrades: Why Men Fought in the Civil War* (New York: Oxford University Press, 1997), chap. 9. He begins by noting that "relatively few Union volunteers mentioned the slavery issue when they enlisted" (19) but goes on to suggest that by the war's later years, many Union soldiers had begun to believe that eliminating slavery was essential if the South was to be defeated (128–29). McPherson's analysis nonetheless supports my claim that many of the Union soldiers who sang the song in the war's first two years would not have seen Brown as a hero.
27. Wiley, *The Life of Billy Yank*, 32, 159.
28. Frank Moore, *The Rebellion Record*, vol. 2 (New York: G. P. Putnam, 1862), "Rumors and Incidents," 39.
29. Julia Ward Howe, "Reminiscences," *Atlantic Monthly* 83 (May 1899): 704.
30. "The Battle Hymn of the Republic," *Atlantic Monthly* 9 (February 1862): 145–46. All references to Howe's "Battle Hymn" are cited from this version. The version of Howe's "Battle Hymn" that was included in her 1866 collection *Later Lyrics* is identical with the exception of minor differences in punctuation.
31. Franklin Sanborn, ed., *John Brown: Life and Letters* (Cedar Rapids, IA: Torch Press, 1910), 620.
32. The first published version of Howe's "Battle Hymn" (*Atlantic Monthly*, February

1862) did not include the chorus; nor did Howe include the chorus in the version she published in *Later Lyrics*. Other published versions, however, often included it.

33. Ellen Gruber Garvey discusses how anonymous publication and nineteenth-century reprinting practices supported the efforts of another female poet of the Civil War era, Mary Woolsey Howland, to speak in the first person in the soldier's voice. See Garvey's "Anonymity, Authorship, and Recirculation: A Civil War Episode," *Book History* 2006, 9, especially 159–71.
34. Howe, "Reminiscences," 707.
35. My reading of Howe's "Battle Hymn" thus differs from that of Eliza Richards. While Richards suggests that Howe "divorce[s] lyric utterance from personal expression" in her wartime poetry, I would counter that a personal "I" persists even in Howe's most publicly oriented poem, her "Battle Hymn" (160). See Richards "'How News Must Feel When Traveling': Dickinson and Civil War Media," in *A Companion to Emily Dickinson*, ed. Martha Nell Smith and Mary Loeffelholz (Oxford: Blackwell, 2008), 157–79.
36. For Howe's account of her composition of the poem, see her "Reminiscences," especially 706–8.
37. Ibid., 707.

CHAPTER TWO. "WE ARE HERE AT OUR COUNTRY'S CALL"

1. I cite from the George Bryant Woods Papers at the American Antiquarian Society. Woods left typeset page proofs of this speech among his papers.
2. Bell Irwin Wiley notes that a wave of patriotic fervor swept through many Northern classrooms following the attack on Fort Sumter, spurring waves of enlistment from schools, colleges, and universities. See Wiley's *The Life of Billy Yank, the Common Soldier of the Union* (Indianapolis: Bobbs-Merrill, 1952), 18–19. For an insightful analysis of the ways in which the poetry of the schoolroom worked to build institutional and national communities in the post-bellum era, see Angela Sorby, *Schoolroom Poets: Childhood, Performance, and the Place of American Poetry, 1865–1917* (Durham: University of New Hampshire Press, 2005).
3. The fact that volunteers for the Union and Confederate armies were recruited and organized by town makes this example particularly pertinent. Reid Mitchell argues that town-based rituals of community worked to cement bonds of comradeship and loyalty for both armies, bonds that might well have been weaker had recruiting been centralized. Describing the community spirit of Union soldiers in particular, Mitchell writes: "this voluntary organization of small communities into a national army, the amalgamation of civic pride and national patriotism, serves as an example of how the volunteers imagined the Union should function" (22). Mitchell goes on to argue that "localism" was central to Northern patriotism and that "small-unit cohesion" played a crucial role in the Union victory (37, 158–60). Mitchell, *The Vacant Chair* (New York: Oxford University

Press, 1993). James McPherson discusses the ways that pressures from the home community worked to motivate units of soldiers in *For Cause and Comrades: Why Men Fought in the Civil War* (New York: Oxford University Press, 1997), 80–81.

4. Reading American responses to "The Charge of the Light Brigade," Charles Royster suggests that American readers "did not usually read it as a lament for men who had died unnecessarily"; he suggests rather that "Americans made the suicidal cavalry assault an inspiring example of courage," favorably comparing the bravery of fallen American troops at First Bull Run, Gettysburg, Vicksburg, and other battles with that of the Light Brigade at Balaklava. See Royster, *The Destructive War: William Tecumseh Sherman, Stonewall Jackson, and the Americans* (New York: Alfred A. Knopf, 1991), 257. Wiley mentions two Union soldiers who had verses from Tennyson's "Charge of the Light Brigade" flashing through their minds as they went into battle (*The Life of Billy Yank*, 73).

5. For an overview of representations of the soldier in American popular literature of the Civil War era, see Alice Fahs, *The Imagined Civil War: Popular Literature of the North & South, 1861–1865* (Chapel Hill: University of North Carolina Press, 2001), chap. 3, 93–119. While acknowledging the enormous popularity of Tennyson's poem with Civil War–era readers, Fahs argues that the most popular American poems of this era turned away from representations of battlefield heroics to focus on "the thoughts of individual soldiers" (103). I would counter that enormously popular song-poems such as "The Battle Hymn of the Republic" and "Battle Cry of Freedom" offered American readers and listeners images of collective battlefield heroics. Sentimentalized depictions of solitary soldiers were certainly also central to the popular imagination at this time, however.

6. Wiley notes that newspapers were widely available in the Union Army, though much harder to come by for Confederate soldiers (*The Life of Billy Yank*, 153). He also emphasizes the ready availability in the Union camps of cheap pocket songbooks and pamphlets brought out by Beadle and other publishers (159).

7. For an analysis that focuses in particular on the network of family and nationalist motivations that impelled Union and Confederate soldiers to enlist and to keep fighting, see Mitchell's *The Vacant Chair*. For broader analyses of the ideals, motivations, and experience of Northern and Southern soldiers, see Bell Irwin Wiley, *The Life of Johnny Reb, the Common Soldier of the Confederacy* (Indianapolis: Bobbs-Merrill, 1943); Wiley's *The Life of Billy Yank*; Randall C. Jimerson, *The Private Civil War: Popular Thought during the Sectional Conflict* (Baton Rouge: Louisiana State University Press, 1988); Reid Mitchell, *Civil War Soldiers* (New York: Viking Press, 1988); and McPherson, *For Cause and Comrades*.

8. Emphasizing the centrality of oral culture to the circulation of poetry in this era, Fahs also underlines the close ties between the war and poetry: "Such public war poetry was part of a wider understanding of the war as a literary event: far from literature being separate from the war, it was accepted as an appropriate, expected, and often deeply felt part of that experience" (*The Imagined Civil War*, 4).

9. In his Introduction, Edmund Wilson is particularly complimentary about the non-

fiction forms of writing that the war produced (letters, diaries, journals, speeches, and journalism) while he is more disparaging about the imaginative literature of this era. See his *Patriotic Gore: Studies in the Literature of the American Civil War* (New York: Oxford University Press, 1962), ix.

10. Ibid., 470.
11. In researching soldier-poets, I examined closely the poetry of thirteen Union and three Confederate soldiers. While I studied a broader sample of soldiers' letters and journals, this figure includes only those soldiers whose papers included poetry. This tally also includes only those cases where I could determine with some certainty that the poetry included in the soldier's papers was written by a soldier; in other words, I am not including soldiers' scrapbooks or poetry albums in this count. My archival work favors Northern soldier-poets since I had readier access to archives in the North and Midwest. The higher rates of literacy in the North may also have translated to higher rates of poetic production among Union soldiers, but unfortunately I had only limited opportunity to do archival work with Southern soldiers' writings.
12. I cite from the Jasper Jay Stone Papers, Manuscript Division, Library of Congress, Washington, DC. Stone, Letter to President Theodore Roosevelt, March 1, 1908. Stone titles his unpublished poetry manuscript "Polemeters."
13. *Southern Literary Messenger*, "Editor's Table," "How many young men will follow my example?," January 1863, 63.
14. William G Shepperson, ed., *War Songs of the South* (Richmond, VA: West and Johnston, 1862). Cited from *Documenting the American South*, http://docsouth.unc.edu/imls/shepperson/shepperson.html.
15. General William H. Hayward, *Camp Songs for the Soldier and Poems of Leisure Moments* (Baltimore: H. Robinson, 1864).
16. *Soldiers' and Sailors' Patriotic Songs* (New York: Loyal Publication Society, 1864).
17. Rev. J. W. Dadmun and Rev. Arthur B. Fuller, eds., *Army and Navy Melodies*, 10th ed. (Boston: Magee and Russell, 1862).
18. *Southern Zion's Songster* (Raleigh, NC: North Carolina Christian Advocate, 1864). Cited from *Documenting the American South*, http://docsouth.unc.edu/imls/zion/menu.html.
19. Francis J. Child, ed., *War Songs for Freemen*, 4th ed. (Boston, 1862).
20. The three-stanza poem is entitled "To an Absent Wife." All citations from Baker's poetry and prose are reproduced by permission of the Huntington Library, San Marino, CA.
21. Twenty-three at the time of his enlistment, Baker was older than many of his fellow soldiers. Gerald Linderman observes that for both Union and Confederate forces, "eighteen-year-olds constituted the single largest age group the first year of the war." See Linderman, *Embattled Courage: The Experience of Combat in the American Civil War* (New York: Free Press, 1987), 26. For a discussion of military service as a coming-of-age ritual and an affirmation of masculinity, see Mitchell's *The Vacant Chair*, chap. 1, 3–18.

22. Baker titles the poem "Do you."
23. I am grateful to Elizabeth Young for her helpful responses to my reading of this poem.
24. Baker's investment in reconciliation in this poem points toward the national commitment to reconciliation of Union and Confederate veterans that will become particularly pronounced starting in the 1880s. For a discussion of this era of reconciliation and the ways in which it erased race, slavery, and emancipation from narratives of the war, see David Blight's *Race and Reunion: The Civil War in American Memory* (Cambridge: Belknap Press of Harvard University, 2001).
25. The Civil War journals of Obadiah Ethelbert Baker, October 5, 1862.
26. Shepperson, ed., *War Songs of the South.*
27. Wiley notes that distribution of Christian literature was widespread and systematic among the Confederate ranks by the start of 1863; he adds that the spring of 1863 saw the start of revivals that swept through the Confederate army, culminating in the conversion of several prominent Confederate leaders (*The Life of Johnny Reb,* 180–82). James McPherson reminds us that "Civil War armies were, arguably, the most religious in American history," since the war followed the Second Great Awakening. He adds "many men who were at best nominal Christians before they enlisted experienced conversion to the genuine article by their baptism of fire" (*For Cause and Comrades,* 63).
28. I cite from the George Washington Hall Papers, Manuscript Division, Library of Congress, Washington, DC.
29. McPherson notes that Northern invasion of Southern territory provided a particularly strong motivation for Confederate soldiers: "a more concrete, visceral, and more powerful motive also came into play: defense of home and hearth against an invading enemy" (*For Cause and Comrades,* 21). For a discussion of Southern women's perspectives on the Union invasion of their homeland, see Drew Gilpin Faust's *Mothers of Invention: Women of the Slaveholding South in the American Civil War* (Chapel Hill: University of North Carolina Press, 1996), especially chap. 9.
30. In both North and South, the public may have also perceived Southern women as more actively engaged in promoting and supporting the cause of war. An 1863 pamphlet published by the pro-Union Loyal Publication Society staunchly defends Northern women against the accusation that they lag behind their Southern sisters in supporting the war. See "A few words in behalf of the loyal women of the United States, by one of themselves" (New York: Loyal Publication Society, W. C. Bryant, 1863). Drew Gilpin Faust argues, however, that Southern women's actual support for the war began to wane in the war's middle years: "The patriotism women had so enthusiastically embraced in 1861 began to erode before the seemingly endless—and increasingly purposeless—demands for sacrifice." See Faust's *Mothers of Invention,* 208. See also Faust's "Confederate Women and Narratives of War," in *Divided Houses: Gender and the Civil War,* ed. Catherine Clinton and Nina Silber (New York: Oxford University Press, 1992), 171–99.
31. "The Vacant Chair," words by Henry S. Washburn, music by George F. Root (Chicago: Root and Cady, 1861), 3–4.

32. Wiley argues: "the overwhelming majority of Confederates remained firm to the end in the conviction that the majority of Yankees were lacking in the stuff that it takes to make good soldiers" (*The Life of Johnny Reb*, 314).
33. For poems by Southerners that figure the South or individual Southern states as feminine, see for example: William Gilmore Simms, "Song of the South," in *Words for the Hour: A New Anthology of American Civil War Poetry*, ed. Faith Barrett and Cristanne Miller (Amherst: University of Massachusetts Press, 2005), 35–36; James Randall's "My Maryland" (*Words for the Hour*, 49–51), and Jane T. H. Cross's "The Confederacy" (*Words for the Hour*, 157–58).
34. See in particular McPherson's *For Cause and Comrades*, Mitchell's *The Vacant Chair*, and Wiley's *The Life of Johnny Reb* and *The Life of Billy Yank*.
35. I cite from the Lyman Holford Papers, Manuscript Division, Library of Congress, Washington, DC, Lyman Holford's diaries, volume 2.
36. Reading Holford's journal, Mitchell notes that Holford seems particularly unsettled by the ways in which war dehumanizes men, turning them into animals. Mitchell comments on a passage in which Holford observes, with disgust, a group of newly arrived Michigan soldiers cutting meat off a cow that had been dead for several days. See Mitchell, *Civil War Soldiers*, 69.
37. Fahs suggests that scenes of dying soldiers build on already well developed antebellum sentimental conventions for messages given to witnesses of the deathbed scene (*The Imagined Civil War*, 95).
38. Ibid., 101.
39. Blight, *Race and Reunion*. On the question of veterans' memoir-writing, see especially chap. 6, 171–210. In this chapter, Blight offers an extended analysis of an influential series of soldiers' accounts of the war published by *Century* magazine between 1884 and 1887. Describing the flood-tide of writing produced by white veterans, Blight writes: "The Civil War produced a democratic, vernacular form of autobiography. Much of this flood of writing never made it into print. But the sheer volume of such material that was published, the variety of people yearning to be heard, demonstrates a vast reservoir of stories from the war era by people from across the economic and social spectrum who wanted to be counted as participants in this epic event" (179).
40. In Stone's "Polemeters," see "Reminiscentia" (48–52), "The Old Sergeant" (54–66), and "The Vetran's [*sic*] Qualifications for Civil Service" (76–87).
41. Stone, Letter to Roosevelt.
42. Ibid.
43. Describing veterans' nostalgia for an earlier era in American society, Blight writes: "Old soldiers tended to measure each other as preservers of an older, more wholesome society, one uncorrupted by materialism" (*Race and Reunion*, 201).
44. Stone, "Polemeters," "Prologue," 142–44.
45. Ibid., 139.
46. Stone, "Polemeters," "Bequeathment," ii.
47. Ibid.

48. Ibid., iii. Describing the veteran's desire for public recognition of his military service, Blight writes: "The worst fate for old soldiers in the revival of popular fascination with the war was to go unrecognized. When that did occur, veterans had their interior battlefields to fall back into; but in a culture where memory had become such a desired and negotiable commodity, public recognition—on maps, monuments, and in books—was the more valuable possession" (*Race and Reunion*, 189).
49. "After the Battle," 21–23.
50. Ethelinda Beers's "The Picket-Guard" first appeared in *Harper's Weekly* on November 30, 1861, under the initials "E.B." The poem was widely reprinted and credited to both Northern and Southern authors. Many poets of this era followed Beers's example in imagining the death of an isolated sentry. "The Picket-Guard" is included in Barrett and Miller, eds., *Words for the Hour*, 65–66.
51. Beers's poem also foregrounds an argument about the military hierarchy, emphasizing that the death of the sentry—who is only a private—will receive little notice in the newspapers. Though Stone does not address the military hierarchy in "Relief at Last," he strongly emphasizes his commitment to representing the heroism of privates, particularly in the Prologue to a section of the volume called "Moon Runes" (see especially 140).
52. "Relief at Last," 41.
53. Ibid., 39–40.
54. Ibid., 40.
55. Ibid.
56. Ibid., 41.
57. Ibid., 42.
58. Ibid., 43.
59. Stone, "Moon Runes or the Sentry's Vision," 112.
60. Ibid., 107.
61. Ibid., 109.
62. Ibid.
63. Ibid., 128.
64. Ibid.
65. Stone, "Prologue," 134.
66. Stone, "Bequeathment," ii.
67. Stone, "Prologue," 134.
68. Blight writes "During Reconstruction, many Americans increasingly realized that remembering the war, even the hatreds and deaths on a hundred battlefields—facing all those graves on Memorial Day—became, with time, easier than struggling over the enduring ideas for which those battles were fought" (*Race and Reunion*, 31). See also chap. 6, 171–210.
69. McPherson, *For Cause and Comrades*, 19.
70. Stone, "Farewell," 16–17.

CHAPTER THREE. THE LYRIC I AND THE POETICS OF PROTEST

1. For analysis of the early stages of Howe's literary career and her conflicted relationship with her husband, see Gary Williams's groundbreaking *Hungry Heart: The Literary Emergence of Julia Ward Howe* (Amherst: University of Massachusetts Press, 1999).
2. For analysis of Howe's positing of a female poetic identity, see Shira Wolosky, *The Cambridge History of American Literature,* vol. 4: *Nineteenth-Century Poetry* (Cambridge: Cambridge University Press, 2004), 179–84.
3. I am grateful to Monica Rico for suggesting this connection.
4. The two poems for Florence Nightingale included in Howe's *Words for the Hour* further underline the urgency of her pursuit of this question.
5. Julia Ward Howe, *Words for the Hour* (Boston: Ticknor and Fields, 1856), 5–6. References to this collection are hereafter cited in the body of the chapter with the abbreviation "*WH*" followed by the page number.
6. For analysis of Samuel Gridley Howe's relationship to Charles Sumner, see Gary Williams's *Hungry Heart.*
7. Julia Ward Howe, *Later Lyrics* (Boston: J. E. Tilton, 1866), 22–23. References to this collection are hereafter cited in the body of the chapter with the abbreviation "*LL*" followed by the page number.
8. Julia Ward Howe, "Reminiscences," *Atlantic Monthly* 83 (May 1899): 707.
9. Further evidence of Howe's radical skepticism about socially prescribed gender roles for both women and men can be found in her remarkable unfinished novel, recently published under the title *The Hermaphrodite,* ed. Gary Williams (Lincoln: University of Nebraska Press, 2009).
10. For analysis of Harper's Reconstruction-era poetry, especially Moses and the Aunt Chloe sequence, see Mary Loeffolholz's *From School to Salon: Reading Nineteenth-Century American Women's Poetry* (Princeton: Princeton University Press, 2004), chap. 4, 94–127. See also Elizabeth Petrino's "'We Are Rising as a People': Frances Harper's Radical Views on Class and Racial Equality in Sketches of Southern Life," *American Transcendental Quarterly* 19 (2005): 133–53.
11. Frances Foster, ed., *A Brighter Coming Day: A Frances Ellen Watkins Harper Reader* (New York: The Feminist Press at CUNY, 1990), 54–55.
12. For analyses that foreground arguments for the recovery of Harper's work, see Patricia Liggins Hill, "'Let Me Make Songs for the People': A Study of Frances Watkins Harper's Poetry," *Black American Literature Forum* 15 (Summer 1981): 60–65; Elizabeth Ammons, "*Legacy* Profile: Frances Ellen Watkins Harper," *Legacy* 2 (Fall 1985): 61–66; Paul Lauter, "Is Frances Ellen Watkins Harper Good Enough to Teach?" *Legacy* 5 (Spring 1988): 27–32; Maryemma Graham, "Introduction," *Complete Poems of Frances E. W. Harper* (New York: Oxford University Press, 1988), xxxiii–lvii; Jana Knittel, "Songs for the People: Politics and Poetry in the Career of Frances Harper," *Mid-Atlantic Writers Association Review* 12 (June 1997): 30–43; and Sarah Elizabeth Bennison, "The Poetry and Activism of Frances Ellen Watkins Harper," *Journal x* 6 (Spring 2002): 203–23.

13. Foster, *A Brighter Coming Day*, 190. All quotations from Harper's poetry are taken from Foster's *A Brighter Coming Day* and are hereafter cited in the body of the chapter.
14. Carla Peterson, *"Doers of the Word": African-American Women Speakers and Writers in the North (1830–1880)* (New Brunswick, NJ: Rutgers University Press, 1998), 124–25. My analysis of Harper's poetics is deeply indebted to Peterson's insightful work.
15. Peterson notes: "Watkins Harper relied on highly conventional poetic forms just as she utilized highly traditional rhetorical modes in her public speaking; it was perhaps the very traditionalism of her verse that made publication with a main-stream press possible" (ibid., 128).
16. For an analysis of representations of the body in Harper's antebellum ballads, see Carolyn Sorisio's *Fleshing Out America: Race, Gender, and the Politics of the Body in American Literature, 1833–1879* (Athens: University of Georgia Press, 2002), 83–91.
17. William Still, *The Underground Railroad* (New York: Arno Press and the New York Times, 1968), 760.
18. Ibid., 775.
19. Cited ibid., 779.
20. Peterson, *"Doers of the Word,"* 122.
21. Ibid., 124.
22. I am grateful to Jason Siroky for suggesting this reading of the poem's final stanza.
23. Toni Morrison draws on these events in writing *Beloved.*
24. Paula Bennett, *Poets in the Public Sphere: The Emancipatory Project of American Women's Poetry, 1800–1900* (Princeton: Princeton University Press, 2003), 88.
25. Michael Bennett, *Democratic Discourses: The Radical Abolition Movement and Antebellum Literature* (New Brunswick, NJ: Rutgers University Press, 2005), 51, 53. Reading Harper's poetry in relation to the African American bardic tradition, Keith Leonard makes a similar point about Harper's abolitionist poems. Leonard writes: "Sentimentality was for Harper the substance of the moral heroism of black female selfhood, of the moral character women were bringing to the public sphere and national life, and thus the terms by which abolitionists should move to end slavery and all people should embrace female sensibility as the foundation of the nation." See Leonard's *Fettered Genius: The African American Bardic Poet from Slavery to Civil Rights* (Charlottesville: University Press of Virginia, 2006), 47.
26. Katherine Bassard, *Spiritual Interrogations: Culture, Gender, and Community in Early African American Women's Writing* (Princeton: Princeton University Press, 1999), 9. For a detailed account of this argument, see chap. 7.
27. Borrowing a phrase from Lawrence Buell, Peterson suggests that Harper's poetry relies on an "aesthetics of restraint" (*"Doers of the Word,"* 128); Harper prefers narrative stances to lyric ones, Peterson suggests, because of the ways in which narrative modes allow her to speak to and for the black community. Simultaneously, however, Peterson suggests that Harper uses "contemporary public poetic

conventions to portray her own private emotions" (127). Throughout this reading of Harper, I am drawing on Peterson's insightful argument in order to analyze the relationship between different pronoun positions in Harper's work.

CHAPTER FOUR. ADDRESSES TO A DIVIDED NATION

1. All references to Dickinson's letters are cited from Thomas H. Johnson and Theodora Ward, eds., *The Letters of Emily Dickinson* (Cambridge: Harvard University Press, Belknap Press, 1958). Letters are hereafter cited in the body of the text as JL, using the numbers assigned by Johnson and Ward.
2. John Lynen's position, while strongly stated, is nonetheless largely representative of this first wave of Dickinson criticism. Lynen writes: "Emily Dickinson is a baffling poet because she seems to bear little or no relation to the historical period within which she worked. She stands apart, as indifferent to the literary movements of her day as to its great events." See his "The Uses of the Present: The Historian's, the Critic's, and Emily Dickinson's," *College English* 28 (1966): 126. Jay Leyda offered an alternative view in his biography of the poet, suggesting that Dickinson "wrote more in time, that she was much more involved in the conflicts and tensions of her community than we have thought." See his *The Years and Hours of Emily Dickinson* (New Haven: Yale University Press, 1960), 1: xix–xx.
3. Sewall, *The Life of Emily Dickinson*, 536.
4. My analysis of Dickinson's war poetry is deeply indebted to Shira Wolosky's *Emily Dickinson: A Voice of War* (New Haven: Yale University Press, 1984). Wolosky was one of the first scholars to argue that Dickinson's extraordinary rate of productivity during the war years might signal the strength of her response to the war; R. W. Franklin's dating of Dickinson's manuscripts would suggest that she wrote more than 900 poems between 1861 and 1865. The growing body of scholarship on Dickinson and the war also includes the following: Wolosky's "Public and Private in Dickinson's War Poetry," in *A Historical Guide to Emily Dickinson*, ed. Vivian Pollak (New York: Oxford University Press, 2004), 103–31; Maurice Lee's "Writing through the War: Melville and Dickinson after the Renaissance," *PMLA* 115 (2000): 1124–28; Barton Levi St. Armand, *Emily Dickinson and Her Culture: The Soul's Society* (Cambridge: Cambridge University Press, 1984), especially chap. 3; Ed Folsom and Kenneth Price's *Dickinson, Slavery, and the San Domingo Moment*, www.unl.edu/Price/dickinson/; Martha Nell Smith, "The Civil War, Class, and the Dickinsons," www.classroomelectric.org/volume2/smith/; Marta Werner, Katie Chaple, Dave Higginbotham, Michelle Newcome, and Rebecca Harrison, eds., *A Nosegay to Take to Battle: The Civil War Wounding of Emily Dickinson*, www3.iath.virginia.edu/fdw/volume2/werner/WF1.html; Betsy Erkkila, "Dickinson and the Art of Politics," in *A Historical Guide to Emily Dickinson;* Coleman Hutchison, "'Eastern Exiles': Dickinson, Whiggery, and War," *Emily Dickinson Journal* 13.2 (2004): 1–26; Leigh-Anne Urbanowicz Marcellin, "'Singing Off the Charnel Steps': Soldiers and Mourners in Emily Dickinson's War Poetry," *Emily*

Dickinson Journal 9.2 (2000): 64–74; Cristanne Miller, "Pondering 'Liberty': Emily Dickinson and the Civil War," in *American Vistas and Beyond: A Festschrift for Roland Hagenbüchle*, ed. Marietta Messmer and Josef Raab (Trier: Wissenschaftlicher Verlag Trier, 2002), 30–50; Renée Bergland, "The Eagle's Eye: Dickinson's View of Battle," in, *A Companion to Emily Dickinson*, ed. Martha Nell Smith and Mary Loeffelholz (Oxford: Blackwell, 2008), 133–56; Eliza Richards, "'How News Must Feel When Traveling': Dickinson and Civil War Media," also in *A Companion to Emily Dickinson*, 157–79; Eliza Richards, "'Death's Surprise, Stamped Visible': Emily Dickinson, Oliver Wendell Holmes, and Civil War Photography," *Amerikastudien* 54.1 (2009): 13–33; and Benjamin Friedlander, "Emily Dickinson and the Battle of Ball's Bluff," *PMLA* 124.5 (2009): 1582–99.

5. For studies that read Dickinson's war poems in relation to modernist skepticism, see for example Wolosky's "Public and Private in Dickinson's War Poetry" and her *Emily Dickinson: A Voice of War*, as well as Maurice Lee's "Writing through the War." Wolosky points to Dickinson's fractured syntax and ambivalent imagery, linking her skepticism and her aesthetic commitments to those of early twentieth-century modernists. David Porter's analysis of Dickinson's relationship to modernism clearly influenced Wolosky and other scholars. See Porter's *Dickinson: The Modern Idiom* (Cambridge: Harvard University Press, 1981).
6. Two important studies of Whitman offer detailed analyses of the rhetoric of address in his work. Kerry Larson examines the relationship between Whitman's poetics of address and his political commitments in *Whitman's Drama of Consensus* (Chicago: University of Chicago Press, 1988). Tenney Nathanson offers a reading of the relationship between voice, writing, and lyric address in *Whitman's Presence: Body, Voice, and Writing in* Leaves of Grass (New York: New York University Press, 1992). My approach to address in Whitman is indebted to both of these studies.
7. John Stuart Mill, "What Is Poetry?" in *Essays on Poetry by John Stuart Mill*, ed. F. Parvin Sharpless (Columbia: University of South Carolina Press, 1976), 12.
8. Responding to Michael Fried's *Absorption and Theatricality*, Charles Bernstein considers the differences between the "absorptive text" and the "antiabsorptive" one, suggesting that "both require artifice, but the former may hide/this while the latter may flaunt/it." See Bernstein's "Artifice of Absorption," in *Artifice & Indeterminacy: An Anthology of New Poetics*, ed. Christopher Beach (Tuscaloosa: University of Alabama Press, 1998), 20. Bernstein also notes that "absorption may be a quality that characterizes specifically Romantic works" (13). In the poems in which they address America, Dickinson and Whitman both foreground the artifice of address in ways that disrupt the possibility of an absorptive reading.
9. Whitman's interest in public speaking is often mentioned in critical studies of his work, and his frequent use of dramatic apostrophes lends itself to comparative analyses between poetry and oratory. By contrast, Dickinson rarely uses any apostrophes and uses the apostrophe to a reading public only ironically. Dickinson's work, however, clearly responds to a range of nineteenth-century oratorical modes. Benjamin Lease and Beth Maclay Doriani both examine the relation-

ship between Dickinson's poetics and nineteenth-century sermon rhetoric. See Lease's *Emily Dickinson's Readings of Men and Books: Sacred Soundings* (New York: St. Martin's, 1990) and Doriani's *Emily Dickinson, Daughter of Prophecy* (Amherst: University of Massachusetts Press, 1996). Even before she began in her thirties to keep increasingly to her home, Dickinson would have had the opportunity to hear countless sermons, talks, and discussions at civic and university events in Amherst and South Hadley, at church services, and in her father's and brother's homes. Doriani calculates that Dickinson would have heard "well over fifteen hundred sermons during her period of regular attendance at church" (45).

10. Kerry Larson claims that Whitman's work provides a radical and innovative exception to Mill's definition insofar as the poetry makes plain its demands on the reader (*Whitman's Drama of Consensus*, 5–6). I would counter, however, that much of the popular and reform-minded poetry of nineteenth-century America makes its persuasive demands on the reader explicit. Moreover, in the high literary tradition of the nineteenth-century lyric poem, poets frequently turn to the gesture of the apostrophe, a figure that points insistently to the circuit of communication that links the speaker and the reader. Whitman draws from both popular and high literary poetic traditions in inventing his poetic speakers' stances of address. It is not only Whitman's poetics then that disrupts Mill's scheme, but rather broader cultural practices in nineteenth-century poetry.
11. References to Dickinson's poems are cited from R. W. Franklin's *The Poems of Emily Dickinson* (Cambridge: Belknap Press of Harvard University Press, 1998). These are hereafter cited in text using the initial "F" and the numbers assigned by Franklin.
12. During the war years, of course, the phrase "Sweet – countrymen –" would have made a collective whole out of what was in fact a divided nation. Moreover, the line breaks and spacing in the handwritten manuscript version of this poem work to heighten the gender divide in this stanza. In the manuscript version, the word "men" appears on a line by itself between the last two lines of the poem. While Franklin decides that Dickinson likely intended "men" to be the final syllable in the final word of the penultimate line, the position of the word on the manuscript page points toward still another possible reading of these lines: "For love of her [i.e., nature], sweet country, men judge tenderly of me. In this variant reading, Dickinson's speaker addresses not her "countrymen" but her "sweet country," and her male readers "judge" her "tenderly" because of their love for nature. See R. W. Franklin's *The Manuscript Books of Emily Dickinson* (Cambridge: Belknap Press of Harvard University Press, 1981), 1:548.
13. As Karen Dandurand notes, the three poems that appeared in the *Drum Beat* are: "Blazing in Gold and quenching in Purple" (F 321), "Flowers – well, if anybody" (F 95), and "These are the days when Birds come back –" (F 122). See Dandurand's "New Dickinson Civil War Publications," *American Literature* 56 (1984): 17–27.
14. Franklin notes that Dickinson sent poems to more than 40 people. He estimates that she sent 250 to Susan Gilbert Dickinson, 100 to Higginson, 71 to Louise

and Frances Norcross, and 40 to Samuel Bowles (*The Poems of Emily Dickinson*, 3:1547).

15. All references to Whitman's poetry are cited from *Leaves of Grass: A Textual Variorium of the Printed Poems*, ed. Sculley Bradley, Harold W. Blodgett, Arthur Golden, and William White (New York: New York University Press, 1980) and are hereafter cited in text by volume and page number. 2:290–92.
16. In his suggestive analysis of the rhetoric of address in Whitman, Tenney Nathanson writes: "Performative declarations that suggest the magical efficacy of the word abound in Whitman's early work. At their most dramatic, Whitman's performatives claim to produce actual presences, disposing creatures and objects by intoning their names as easily as the poet conjures up his own presence by declaring it" (*Whitman's Presence*, 7).
17. Pointing to the connection between Whitman's development of the open line and his commitment to the ideal of freedom, Allan Grossman suggests that Whitman's work calls for the rejection of symbolic hierarchies: "The rewriting of hierarchies—soul/body, collective/individual, nation/state—as equalities, and the rewriting of identities as conventional dualities, above all the self and the other, is the task of the 'translator,' whose goal is union as the fraternalization of the community." See Grossman's "The Poetics of Union in Whitman and Lincoln: An Inquiry toward the Relationship of Art and Policy" in *The American Renaissance Reconsidered*, ed. Walter Benn Michaels and Donald Pease (Baltimore: Johns Hopkins University Press, 1985), 194.
18. I am drawing here on David S. Reynolds's insightful work on Whitman's relationship to the cultures of popular performance. For a discussion of Whitman's interest in theater and oratory, see Reynolds's *Walt Whitman's America: A Cultural Biography* (New York: Vintage Books, 1995), especially chap. 6. For a discussion of the influence of evangelical preaching on Whitman's poetics, see Reynolds's *Beneath the American Renaissance: The Subversive Imagination in the Age of Emerson and Melville* (Cambridge: Harvard University Press, 1988), especially 15–27.
19. While such divisions prove anxious ones for the speaker in Whitman's poems, they also of course prove to be tremendously productive for his poetic imagination. Responding to both Larson's and Betsy Erkkila's accounts of the importance of union to Whitman's poetics, Mark Maslan notes that "these critics hesitate to express what their opinions effectively assume: that division is a vital principle of Whitman's poetics" (136). Maslan goes on to suggest, "Rethinking division in this manner—as enabling rather than debilitating—would involve reexamining a whole series of relationships in Whitman in which critics have seen union as the organizing principle" (136). See Maslan's "Whitman and His Doubles: Division and Union in *Leaves of Grass* and Its Critics," *American Literary History* 6 (1994): 119–39. See also Erkkila's *Whitman: The Political Poet* (New York: Oxford University Press, 1989). Mitchell Breitwieser makes a similar claim in arguing that Whitman's poems present a dialogue between two speakers, "one timid, gentle, frequently disconsolate, the other large, all-inclusive" (121). Breitwieser contends that "Whitman's great poems [. . .] are crisis poems that concern themselves with

being between these possibilities" (142). See Breitwieser's "Who Speaks in Whitman's Poems?" in *Bucknell Review* 28. *The American Renaissance: New Dimensions*, ed. Harry Garvin and Peter Carafiol (Lewisburg, PA: Bucknell University Press, 1983), 121–43. Focusing on Whitman's work in Civil War hospitals, Robert Leigh Davis suggests that the poet-nurse in Whitman's wartime writings is able to occupy a liminal position, hovering on the boundary between the living and the dead and thereby "proposing an alternative concept of Union," one that resists "the binary deadlock of secession and civil war." See Davis's *Whitman and the Romance of Medicine* (Berkeley: University of California Press, 1997), 6–7.

20. Two analyses argue that the poetry Whitman wrote during and after the Civil War takes a more complex perspective on the poetics of presence than some of the earlier poems. Michael Moon describes how later editions of *Leaves of Grass* complicate the first edition's account of the relationship between the world of the body and the discourses of the body. See Moon's *Disseminating Whitman: Revision and Corporeality in* Leaves of Grass (Cambridge: Harvard University Press, 1991). In a reading of "Come up from the fields Father," Mark Maslan argues that "the identification of text and body in Whitman requires that the body [itself] become representational." See Maslan's "Whitman's 'Strange Hand': Body as Text in *Drum-Taps*," *ELH* 58 (1991): 938.

21. Pointing to the power of the apostrophe in Whitman's work, Donald Pease argues: "Whitman experiences language not as a deprivation but as a plenipotential force" (155). "Living apostrophaically," Pease writes, "entails living for the sake of the activity which the apostrophe calls forth. An apostrophe has no existence apart from the activity it motivates. Hence death can have no dominion over it" (153). I would counter that the frenzied list of apostrophes in this poem reveals the speaker's fear of death, his terror at the prospect of the splitting of the nation, and his awareness that neither the language of poetry nor the language of political oratory can prevent that splitting. See Pease's *Visionary Compacts: American Renaissance Writings in Cultural Context* (Madison: University of Wisconsin Press, 1987).

22. Wolosky points to the ways in which Dickinson's demurrals are part of a deliberate stance: "Dickinson is an assertive and determined poet [. . .] whose retirement is a stance of attack, whose timidity is aggressive" (*Emily Dickinson: A Voice of War*, xiii).

23. Timothy Sweet's insightful study broke new ground in positioning Whitman in relation to nineteenth-century photography. See Sweet's *Traces of War: Poetry, Photography, and the Crisis of the Union* (Baltimore: Johns Hopkins University Press, 1990). Three other analyses of Whitman also read his work in relation to the discourses of visual art. James Dougherty examines the ways in which Whitman uses a visual vocabulary to "serve as the base of communion" between the poet and his readers (xiv). Drawing on Martin Buber's formulation of the "I–Thou" relationship, Dougherty argues that Whitman's poetics of the visual enables the poet and his citizen readers to share "a common space" (xvi). See Dougherty's *Walt Whitman and the Citizen's Eye* (Baton Rouge: Louisiana State

University Press, 1993). Dougherty's argument thus relies on a belief in the bond between poet and reader that my argument aims to unsettle. Ed Folsom examines the relationship between Whitman's poetics and the development of photography. Folsom argues that Civil War photographs by Matthew Brady and Alexander Gardner shape Whitman's poetic depiction of the conflict by encouraging him to focus on the aftermath of battle rather than the heroic deeds traditionally chosen as the subject of war poems and paintings. See Folsom's *Walt Whitman's Native Representations* (New York: Cambridge University Press, 1994), chap. 4. For an insightful overview of Whitman's relationship to contemporary painting and photography, see Reynolds's *Walt Whitman's America*, especially chap. 9. Reynolds argues persuasively that Whitman's desire to reach a broad audience with his poetry was influenced by his awareness of the ways in which photographers and painters made work that successfully appealed to a wide range of Americans. Renée Bergland reads Dickinson's Civil War poetry in relation to romantic landscape painting and photographic technologies of the war era in "The Eagle's Eye," and Eliza Richards examines Dickinson's relationship to photography in "'Death's Surprise Stamped Visible.'" Two other studies read Dickinson's work in relation to nineteenth-century painting, though neither of these focuses on Civil War–era images in particular. Judith Farr examines Dickinson's painterly interest in the sublime, and Barton Levi St. Armand reads Dickinson's work in relation to both the Victorian painterly aesthetic of the sublime and popular forms of folk art. See St. Armand's *Emily Dickinson and Her Culture* and Farr's *The Passion of Emily Dickinson* (Cambridge: Harvard University Press, 1992).

24. Just as the war threatens the stability of the poetic self, so too did it threaten Whitman's own psychic stability, as Daniel Aaron argues: "Given his personal expectations and his prophecies of American promise, [Whitman] had to insist on the providentiality of the War and to wring optimistic conclusions from its horrors" (68). See Aaron's *The Unwritten War: American Writers and the Civil War* (Madison: University of Wisconsin, 1987). The profound impact his nursing work had on Whitman's life and writing is clearly registered in both *Memoranda during the War*, an edited volume of journals and wartime letters that Whitman had privately published in 1876, and *Specimen Days*, a longer prose memoir published in 1882 that included substantial excerpts from the earlier, shorter volume. These prose works have recently begun to receive fuller scholarly attention. Mark Maslan's analysis of sexuality in Whitman's poetics attends with particular care to his wartime prose. See Maslan's *Whitman Possessed: Poetry, Sexuality, and Popular Authority* (Baltimore: Johns Hopkins University Press, 2001). Robert Leigh Davis's insightful analysis also offers an extended discussion of Whitman's wartime prose (*Whitman and the Romance of Medicine*). Roy Morris Jr. offers an excellent biographical account of Whitman's hospital work. See his *The Better Angel: Walt Whitman in the Civil War* (New York: Oxford University Press, 2000).

25. My reading of the recuperative force of the pastoral in Whitman's war poems is deeply indebted to Timothy Sweet's nuanced and persuasive analysis (*Traces of War*).

26. For a discussion of how Americans—both Northern and Southern—attempted to make sense of and respond to the vast numbers of dead during the war and in its aftermath, see Drew Gilpin Faust's *This Republic of Suffering: Death and the American Civil War* (New York: Alfred A. Knopf, 2008).
27. I would thus disagree with the emphasis Shira Wolosky places, in her reading of this poem, on the violence inherent in Dickinson's vision of nature. Wolosky writes: "The comparison of battle to snow and wind, far from making the death of the soldiers seem more natural, makes nature seem sudden and frightening" (*Emily Dickinson: A Voice of War,* 37). As I will suggest in the next section of my argument, I would instead offer the poem "The name – of it – is 'Autumn' – " (F 465) as an instance of Dickinson's reckoning with the violence of nature.
28. David Cody reads "The name – of it – is 'Autumn' –" in relation to the Civil War, juxtaposing the poem with possible source texts both from contemporary travel literature and poetry and from the Bible. See Cody's "Blood in the Basin: The Civil War in Emily Dickinson's 'The Name – of it – is – 'Autumn'," *Emily Dickinson Journal* 12 (2003): 25–52. See also Eliza Richards's insightful reading of the poem, which positions its imagery in relation to the limitations of photographic technology at this time ("'Death's Surprise, Stamped Visible,'" 27).
29. Howe's "Battle Hymn" first appeared in the *Atlantic Monthly* in February 1862; the Whittier poem was published in the *Atlantic* in October 1862; Gage's poem appeared in the *Springfield Republican* on October 18, 1862.
30. Sweet, *Traces of War,* 77.
31. Ibid.
32. *Drum-Taps* first appeared as a separate volume in 1865, and this edition included fifty-three poems; these poems were subsequently incorporated as an annex into the 1867 version of *Leaves of Grass*. In reading *Drum-Taps* in its historical context, it is, however, important to keep in mind, as Roger Asselineau notes, that many of the poems that first appeared in this volume were most likely written before the start of the war or during its first few months; more specifically, many of the poems may have been written before Whitman began his work as a nurse in the war military hospitals. See Asselineau's *The Evolution of Walt Whitman: The Creation of a Personality*. (Cambridge: Harvard University Press, 1960), 308–9. See also chap. 5 in Michael Moon's *Disseminating Whitman*.
33. Folsom, *Walt Whitman's Native Representations*, 119.
34. For an analysis of Civil War photography by Brady, Gardner, and others, see Alan Trachtenberg's "Albums of War: On Reading Civil War Photographs," *Representations* 9 (Winter 1985): 1–32.
35. Sweet agrees with Wilson's characterization of this poem as a realistic "sketch from life" (Wilson, *Patriotic Gore*, 482; Sweet, *Traces of War,* 209). I would counter, however, that this poem is as deliberately artful in its presentation of detail as any of the poems in *Drum-Taps*.
36. Betsy Erkkila notes that the relaxed and casual postures of the soldiers "contradict traditional notions of military order, discipline, and hierarchy, thereby projecting the figure of a democratic army" (*Whitman: The Political Poet*, 215). The

artfully casual posture of the soldiers corresponds to the artfully conversational voice of the poet-speaker.

37. The illustration fills two facing pages of the magazine: 200–201.

38. Waud's "Rebel Raid into Pennsylvania" appeared in *Harper's Weekly* on November 1, 1862.

39. Folsom, *Walt Whitman's Native Representations*, 119–20.

40. Justin Kaplan, *Walt Whitman: A Life* (New York: Simon and Schuster, 1980), 309–10.

41. "O Captain! My Captain!" first appeared in print in the *New York Saturday Press*, November 4, 1865 and was included in the *Sequel to Drum-Taps* of 1865.

42. In describing Dickinson's reaction to Stearns's death, Sewall qualifies his earlier comment that she had relatively little to say about the war: "When Frazar Stearns was killed the following March (1862), she described the circumstances for [her cousins] the Norcrosses with a detail and an intensity of feeling that should lay to rest the notion of her indifference to such matters" (*The Life of Emily Dickinson*, 631). Barton Levi St. Armand offers an extended analysis of Dickinson's relationship to Stearns's death, arguing that Dickinson strongly identified with Stearns's spiritual struggles and his martyrdom. See his *Emily Dickinson and Her Culture*, chap. 4.

43. Dickinson first wrote to Thomas Wentworth Higginson, enclosing some of her poems and asking for his opinion of them, about four weeks after Stearns's death. Clearly she was also in the midst of assessing her abilities and commitments as a writer during this time. For a discussion of the relationship between Stearns's death and Dickinson's decision to contact Higginson, see Werner et al., eds, *A Nosegay to Take to Battle: The Civil War Wounding of Emily Dickinson*.

44. See Thomas Johnson's note on this poem in his *Complete Poems of Emily Dickinson* (Cambridge: The Belknap Press of Harvard University Press, 1960). Johnson assigns the poem the number 426.

45. "Adjutant Frazier [*sic*] Stearns" in "Amherst Matters," *Hampshire and Franklin Express*, March 21, 1862.

46. "The Funeral of Adjutant Frazar A. Stearns" in "Amherst Matters," *Hampshire and Franklin Express*, March 28, 1862.

47. William Stearns, *Adjutant Stearns* (Boston: Massachusetts Sabbath School Society, 1862), 64.

48. Miller touches on this issue in analyzing Dickinson's lack of partisan vocabulary. See her "Pondering 'Liberty,'" 55.

49. Alice Fahs notes the centrality of the mother-son relationship in the popular literature of the war: "The reiteration of thoughts of mother reminds us that the Civil War occurred within a widespread maternalist culture that celebrated soldiers' connections to their mothers as an appropriate feminization of their characters" (*The Imagined Civil War: Popular Literature of the North & South, 1861–1865* [Chapel Hill: University of North Carolina Press, 2001], 105).

50. Though Johnson speculates that Francis Dickinson was the soldier represented in the poem, Franklin suggests that Dickinson may not have had one specific

soldier in mind. The representation may well be a composite of several soldiers Dickinson knew.

51. "Rifled Guns," *Atlantic Monthly* (October 1859), 448.
52. Lee argues that this poem's speaker "suspects that imagined reunions in heaven are only wishful thinking." See his "Writing through the War," 1127. In my view, such a reading pushes too skeptically against the grain of the poem, distorting the ways in which Dickinson here echoes more conventional Civil War elegies.
53. Benjamin Friedlander uses a reading of this poem to argue that "scholars must begin to take account of the fact that Dickinson's wartime writing encompasses multiple, contradictory forms of response [and] a diversity of representational strategies" ("Emily Dickinson and the Battle of Ball's Bluff," 1583). On this point, Friedlander's argument in this article in many ways runs closely parallel to my own. However, he seems to stop short of arguing that Dickinson might have actually endorsed some of the patriotic pieties of her neighbors, suggesting that "Dickinson expressed in her poems what she was willing and able to say about the war but not necessarily what she believed" (1583). My analysis leaves open the possibility that Dickinson might have held some of the beliefs about Christian martyrdom on the battlefield that she tests out in her soldier elegies. See also Eliza Richards's reading of this poem in "'How News Must Feel When Traveling,'" 167–69. While Richards reads the poem's refusal to align itself with the Union or Confederacy as part of Dickinson's dislocation from scenes of battle and her resistance to taking sides, I would counter that many Civil War era poems relied on context to make their regional and/or national allegiances plain (169).
54. D. A. Wilson, "The Law of Costs," *Atlantic Monthly* (February 1863), 242.
55. "Monthly Record of Current Events." *Harper's New Monthly Magazine* (April 1863), 701.
56. Ibid.
57. Wilson, "The Law of Costs," 242.
58. Miller, "Pondering Liberty," 57. See for example Sewall, *The Life of Emily Dickinson*, 536. and St. Armand, *Emily Dickinson and Her Culture*, 111.
59. I am relying here on Miller's insightful analysis of the word "Liberty" in this poem. While Miller notes that "nothing marks the 'Liberty' of this poem as referring to the emancipation of slaves," she also argues that "the poem's broad abstractions may suggest that 'Liberty,' like 'Life,' is an absolute: it cannot exist for one person or group in isolation from another" ("Pondering 'Liberty,'" 57). In an alternative account that emphasizes Dickinson's skepticism about the rhetoric of abolition, Karen Sánchez-Eppler argues that Dickinson offers a radical critique of the construct of "liberty." See her *Touching Liberty: Abolition, Feminism, and the Politics of the Body* (Berkeley: University of California Press, 1993).
60. For a representative selection of these feminist readings, see Vivian Pollak's *The Anxiety of Gender* (Ithaca: Cornell University Press, 1984), 150–54; Cristanne Miller's *Emily Dickinson: A Poet's Grammar* (Cambridge: Harvard University Press, 1987), 123–26; and Mary Loeffelholz's *Dickinson and the Boundaries of Feminist Theory* (Chicago: University of Illinois Press, 1991), 83–88.

61. See for example "The Voices of the Guns" in *Words for the Hour: A New Anthology of American Civil War Poetry*, ed. Faith Barrett and Cristanne Miller (Amherst: University of Massachusetts Press, 2005), 164–67, or Sarah Piatt's "Hearing the Battle—July 21, 1861," in *Palace-Burner: The Selected Poetry of Sarah Piatt*, ed. Paula Bernat Bennett (Urbana: University of Illinois Press, 2001), 2–3. "Voices of the Guns" sustains the trope of the gun as speaker throughout the whole poem; "Hearing the Battle" opens with an image that figures the sound of gun-fire as the "first fierce words of war" (2).
62. William Stearns, *Adjutant Stearns*, 80.
63. Ibid., 91–92.
64. Ibid., 96.
65. "The Battle of Newbern!" *Hampshire and Franklin Express*, March 21, 1862.
66. For an analysis of Dickinson's relationship to her father's Whig politics, see Erkkila's "Dickinson and the Art of Politics" and Hutchison's "'Eastern Exiles.'"
67. Several studies explore Dickinson's treatment of the racialized other, abolition, and whiteness. See Sánchez-Eppler's *Touching Liberty;* Benjamin Friedlander's "Auctions of the Mind: Emily Dickinson and Abolition." *Arizona Quarterly* 54 (1998): 1–25; Ed Folsom and Kenneth Price's *Dickinson, Slavery, and the San Domingo Moment;* Domhnall Mitchell's "Northern Lights: Class, Color, Culture, and Emily Dickinson," *Emily Dickinson Journal* 9.2 (2000): 75–83; Daneen Wardrop's "'That Minute Domingo': Dickinson's Cooptation of Abolitionist Diction and Franklin's Variorum Edition." *Emily Dickinson Journal* 8.2 (1999): 72–86; and Vivian Pollak's "Dickinson and the Poetics of Whiteness" *Emily Dickinson Journal* 9.2 (2000): 84–95.
68. I am grateful to Rixey Ruffin for his suggestion that this poem might be read in relation to the history of the Massachusetts Fifty-Fourth.
69. M. D. Conway, "Benjamin Banneker, the Negro Astronomer." *Atlantic Monthly* (January 1863), 79–84; Harriet Beecher Stowe. "Sojourner Truth, the Libyan Sibyl." *Atlantic Monthly* (April 1863), 473–82.
70. John Weiss, "The Horrors of San Domingo," *Atlantic Monthly* (June 1863), 768–86; Edward L Pierce, "The Freedmen at Port Royal," *Atlantic Monthly* (September 1863), 291–315; Francis Wayland Jr. "Letter to a Peace Democrat," *Atlantic Monthly* (December 1863), 776–89.
71. "Monthly Record of Current Events." *Harper's New Monthly Magazine* (August 1863), 415.
72. "From New Orleans," *Springfield Daily Republican*, July 27, 1863.
73. "The Riot in New York," *Springfield Daily Republican*, July 14, 1863.
74. Weiss, "The Horrors of San Domingo," 785.
75. "Barbarism of the Rebels at Charleston," *Springfield Daily Republican*, August 1, 1863.
76. "General News Summary," *Springfield Daily Republican*, July 27, 1863.
77. Ibid.
78. "The Protection of Colored Soldiers. An Order of Retaliation by the President," *Springfield Daily Republican*, August 3, 1863.

79. Charles Graham Halpine, "Miles O'Reilly on the 'Naygurs'," *Springfield Daily Republican*, January 27, 1864.
80. James Russell Lowell, "Memoriae Positum," *Atlantic Monthly* (January 1864), 88–90.
81. For analysis of the Dickinson family politics and also their connection to Southern relatives loyal to the Confederacy—still another way in which Dickinson's loyalties might be divided—see Martha Nell Smith, "The Civil War, Class, and the Dickinsons"; Erkkila, "Dickinson and the Art of Politics"; and Hutchinson, "'Eastern Exiles.'"

CHAPTER FIVE. ROMANTIC VISIONS AND SOUTHERN STANCES

1. For a fuller discussion of this issue, see Alice Fahs, *The Imagined Civil War: Popular Literature of the North & South, 1861–1865* (Chapel Hill: University of North Carolina Press, 2001), chap. 1. See also Coleman Hutchison's ground-breaking study of Confederate literature, especially chap. 3, which focuses on popular poetry of the Confederacy: *Apples and Ashes: Literature, Nationalism, and the Confederate States of America* (Athens: University of Georgia Press, 2012).
2. All references to Timrod's poetry are drawn from *The Collected Poems of Henry Timrod: A Variorum Edition*, ed. Edd Winfield Parks and Aileen Wells Parks (Athens: University of Georgia Press, 2007). This line from "Ethnogenesis" appears on 92. Hereafter I cite the poems in the body of the chapter.
3. For analysis of the role that Southern women played in supporting the Confederate nation, see Catherine Clinton and Nina Silber, eds., *Battle Scars: Gender and Sexuality in the American Civil War* (London: Oxford University Press, 2006); Drew Gilpin Faust, *Mothers of Invention: Women of the Slaveholding South in the American Civil War* (Durham: University of North Carolina Press, 2004); Catherine Clinton and Nina Silber, eds., *Divided Houses: Gender and the Civil War* (London: Oxford University Press, 1992); and George C. Rable, *Civil Wars: Women and the Crisis of Southern Nationalism* (Champaign: University of Illinois Press, 1991).
4. Fahs, *The Imagined Civil War*, 35–37.
5. My analysis of Piatt's war poetry is deeply indebted to Paula Bennett's scholarship. See her "Introduction" in *Palace-Burner: The Selected Poetry of Sarah Piatt*, ed. Paula Bernat Bennett (Urbana: University of Illinois Press, 2001). For an analysis that situates Piatt's critique of gender in her representation of the maternal, see Mary Wearns's "Subjection and Subversion in Sarah Piatt's Maternal Poetics," *Legacy: A Journal of American Women Writers* 23.2 (2006): 163–77. For an analysis of how periodical culture shaped Piatt's career in the years after the war, see Matthew Giordano's "'A Lesson from' the Magazines: Sarah Piatt and the Postbellum Periodical Poet," *American Periodicals* 16.1 (2006): 23–51.
6. Ibid., xli.
7. Ibid., especially xli–xlv.

8. Fahs, *The Imagined Civil War*. See chap. 4, especially 124–30.
9. Cited from *Palace-Burner*, ed. Bennett, 2–3. Hereafter I cite the poems from this source in the body of the chapter.
10. Paula Bennett reads Piatt's "Hearing the Battle" as an ironic response to her husband John James's poem "The First Fire," which imagines a domestic felicity so all-enveloping that the nearby Civil War scarcely intrudes upon it. See Bennett's *Poets in the Public Sphere: The Emancipatory Project of American Women's Poetry, 1800–1900* (Princeton: Princeton University Press, 2003), 144–46.
11. Biographical readings of Piatt's poems are particularly risky in view of her heavy reliance on personae and dialogic voices. Some biographical context may nonetheless be helpful as background for this poem: Piatt was twenty-five and her husband twenty-six at the outbreak of war. He held a political appointment in the Treasury Department from 1861 until 1867 and did not serve in the military, though he did encourage others to do so.
12. "My Dead Fairies" was first published in the magazine *The Independent* in 1871. David Blight notes that Southern Memorial Day commemorations began as early as the spring of 1866. In the North, Memorial Day commemorations were first observed in May of 1868 and 1869. Blight writes: "By the early 1870s [. . .], as late spring arrived and flowers were in full supply, one could not live in or near an American city or village, North or South, and remain unaware of the ritual of decorating the graves of the Civil War dead." See Blight's *Race and Reunion: The Civil War in American Memory* (Cambridge: Belknap Press of Harvard University Press, 2001), 71.
13. Recent historical work suggests that the figure of the "pétroleuse" was largely a fiction created by the conservative press in the aftermath of the Commune. See Gay Gullickson's *Unruly Women of Paris* (Ithaca: Cornell University Press, 1996).
14. Bennett, *Poets in the Public Sphere*, 138. Bennett writes: "Not the palace-burner's morality, but that of this genteel bourgeois woman is on trial in this poem. Her inactivity and moral indifference not only help perpetuate the status quo but encourage a similar passivity in her son" (138).
15. Ibid., 156.
16. Twentieth-century critics who dismiss Horton's work as imitative include Vernon Loggins and, more surprisingly, Richard Walser, author of the only book-length biography of Horton. See Loggins's chap. 3 in *The Negro Author: His Development in America to 1900* (New York: Columbia University Press, 1931), 107–17 and Walser's *The Black Poet* (New York: Philosophical Library, 1966), especially 25, 42, and 68,
17. Leon Jackson, *The Business of Letters: Authorial Economies in Antebellum America* (Stanford: Stanford University Press, 2008). Jackson reads Horton's relationship to the literary marketplace through the economies of the gift exchange and patronage, arguing insightfully that Horton's race limits him as an author to participation in a white-controlled paternalistic patronage system even though his texts often circulate through gift exchange. See Jackson's chapter 2, "The Black Bard and the Black Market."
18. I draw material for my biographical summary from Leon Jackson and also from

Joan Sherman's introduction in her groundbreaking edition of Horton's work, *The Black Bard of North Carolina: George Moses Horton and His Poetry* (Chapel Hill: University of North Carolina Press, 1997).

19. That Horton was well known among University of North Carolina students for giving speeches on demand is suggested by the fact that he was invited to give an oration to the freshman class at the University's Gerrard Hall in October 1857. Various students transcribed the talk in 29 pages; it mingles advice for young students with dramatic rhetorical flourishes, praise for the discipline of learning, political arguments, and literary allusions. Horton's profound sadness at being denied the privilege of education is abundantly evident in this remarkable document.
20. Though Hentz is now best known for the proslavery novels she wrote in the 1850s, she supported and promoted Horton's writing in a variety of ways. As Leon Jackson notes, "her opinions on racial servitude were significantly less conservative in the 1820's"; Jackson argues that Hentz initially saw blacks' intellectual inferiority as *result* of a slavery, not a justification for it (*The Business of Letters*, 62–63).
21. See Joan Sherman's "Introduction" in *The Black Bard of North Carolina*, 30. Though *Naked Genius* announces a forthcoming volume of poems by Horton, this later collection was apparently never published.
22. See Reginald Pitts's account of Horton's later life: "'Let Us Desert this Friendless Place': George Moses Horton in Philadelphia—1866," *Journal of Negro History* 80.4 (Autumn 1995): 145–56.
23. See for example Elizabeth Keckley's *Behind the Scenes, or, Thirty Years a Slave and Four Years in the White House* (1868). For analysis of these nostalgic stances, see William Andrews, "Reunion in the Postbellum Slave Narrative: Frederick Douglass and Elizabeth Keckley," *Black American Literature Forum* 23.1 (Spring 1989): 5–16.
24. All references to Horton's work are cited from *Naked Genius* (Raleigh, NC: William B Smith and Company, 1865), 22–23. Hereafter I cite the poems in the body of the chapter.
25. That title page reads: "Naked Genius: by George Moses Horton. The Colored Bard of North Carolina, Author of 'The Black Poet.'"
26. The Battle of Belmont took place in Missouri on November 7, 1861. Horton titles his poem "The Spectator of the Battle of Belmont, November 6, 1863." While it is possible that Horton or his printer may have mistaken the date, it seems more likely that Horton adjusted the date to fit the poem's formal scheme. Given the poem's lack of specificity about this particular battle, Horton may have chosen the title "the Battle of Belmont" at least in part because of the felicitous alliteration of the phrase and because its metrical pattern supports the grandly martial meter of the poem as a whole.
27. Reading Horton's poetry in relation to the African American bardic tradition, Keith Leonard argues that Horton's "construction of bardic genius was thus an elaboration of the artistic freedom of individual genius without a thoroughgoing examination of the connections between that freedom and the racial discourses of society" (41). Leonard goes on to say "By so successfully fulfilling the ideals of

romantic genius, Horton did not embrace fully the range of social and cultural ideals available to link literary culture to the nation's political life" (41). See his *Fettered Genius: The African American Bardic Poet from Slavery to Civil Rights* (Charlottesville: University Press of Virginia, 2006). While Leonard does not discuss Horton's Civil War–era poetry, I would counter that in this body of work Horton revises the conventions of Southern romanticism in a significant way, claiming the rhetorical power of a stance usually reserved for writers from the white literary elite. Horton's extraordinary position as a poet who wrote while enslaved leads him to articulate that revision in a nuanced and subtle fashion.

CHAPTER SIX. "THEY ANSWERED HIM ALOUD"

1. For articles that focus on Melville's intervention in postwar debates about reconciliation, see for example Andrew West, "Emersonian Pragmatism and Melville's *Battle-Pieces and Aspects of the War*," *Forum for Modern Language Studies* 46.3 (July 2010): 267–296; Deak Nabers "'Victory of LAW': Melville and Reconstruction," *American Literature* 75 (2003): 1–30; and Paul Dowling, "Melville's Quarrel with Poetry," in *Battle-Pieces and Aspects of the War*, ed. Richard H. Cox and Paul Dowling (Amherst, NY: Prometheus Books, 2001), 325–49. The growing interest in Melville's poetry is clearly signaled by several recent articles focusing on *Battle-Pieces* in particular. Maurice Lee reads the political commitments of *Battle-Pieces* in relation to the middle way of pragmatism in "Melville, Douglass, the Civil War, Pragmatism," in *Frederick Douglass and Herman Melville: Essays in Relation*, ed. Robert S. Levine and Samuel Otter (Chapel Hill: University of North Carolina Press, 2008), 396–415. In "White Fratricide, Black Liberation: Melville, Douglass, and Civil War Memory," Carolyn Karcher argues persuasively that "the overall tenor of *Battle-Pieces* reveals a shift in Melville's sympathies away from the slaves his antebellum fiction champions and toward their defeated masters" (*Frederick Douglass and Herman Melville*, 351). In "A Wayward Art: *Battle-Pieces* and Melville's Poetic Turn," Cody Marrs argues that "by occupying an aesthetic space that is at once inside and outside of history, these war lyrics are able to both reproduce time's destructive patterns and, in their own poetic structures, reconstitute and reimagine them" (*American Literature* 82.1 [March 2010]: 114). Ian Finseth argues that in *Battle-Pieces*, Melville "anticipated a long line of American cultural critics from Gertrude Stein to William Gaddis, who voiced a growing wariness about the manipulation of symbols for purposes of social cohesion and political consolidation." See his "On *Battle-Pieces*: The Ethics of Aesthetics in Melville's War Poetry," *Leviathan: A Journal of Melville Studies* 12.3 (October 2010): 89. Finseth's analysis of the tension between division and wholeness in Melville's vision of American national identity runs parallel to my own reading of *Battle-Pieces*. Reading the poems in relation to Unionist ideology, Timothy Sweet argues that Melville's *Battle-Pieces* is deeply skeptical of representations "that enlist nature in the service of legitimating [the war's] violence" (7). My analysis of *Battle-Pieces* is indebted to Sweet's insightful study, *Traces of*

War: Poetry, Photography, and the Crisis of the Union (Baltimore: Johns Hopkins University Press, 1990).

2. Hsuan Hsu examines the decentering of the observer's perspective and Melville's engagement with painterly aesthetics in "War, Ekphrasis, and Elliptical Form in Melville's *Battle-Pieces*," *Nineteenth-Century Studies* 16 (2002): 51–71.
3. For an analysis of Melville's development as a poet, see Hershel Parker's *Melville: The Making of the Poet* (Evanston, IL: Northwestern University Press, 2008). The growing interest in Melville's poetry is also signaled by the special issue of *Leviathan*, edited by Elizabeth Renker and Douglas Robillard, that focuses on this topic, *Leviathan* 9.3 (2007). For analysis of Melville's career as as a poet and past scholarly resistance to grappling with his poetry, see William Spengemann, "Melville the Poet," *American Literary History* 11 (Winter 1999): 569–609, and Elizabeth Renker, "Melville the Poet: A Response to William Spengemann," *American Literary History* 12.1–2 (Spring–Summer 2000): 348–54.
4. For a discussion of Melville's formal commitments, see for example Rosanna Warren's detailed analysis of meter and rhyme scheme in selected *Battle-Pieces* poems: "Dark Knowledge: Melville's Poems of the Civil War," in *Battle-Pieces and Aspects of the War*, ed. Cox and Dowling, 269–93. For a Bahktinian reading of dialogic voice in *Battle-Pieces*, see David Devries and Hugh Egan's "'Entangled Rhyme': A Dialogic Reading of Melville's *Battle-Pieces*," *Leviathan* 9.3 (2007): 17–33.
5. In *The Making of the Poet*, Parker suggests that Melville's *Battle-Pieces* was not much influenced by popular war poetry of the era (199); I would counter, however, that Melville is responding both to popular poetry and to popular song throughout this collection.
6. Of the contemporary reviewers who reacted negatively to Melville's *Battle-Pieces*, William Dean Howells is probably the most frequently cited. Writing in the influential *Atlantic Monthly*, Howells emphasizes the work's detachment from the war, asking "Is it possible . . . that there has really been a great war, with battles fought by men and bewailed by women? Or is it only that Mr. Melville's inner consciousness has been perturbed, and filled with phantasms of enlistments, marches, fights in the air, parenthetic bulletin boards, and tortured humanity shedding, not words and blood, but words alone?" William Dean Howells, *Atlantic Monthly* 29 (February 1867): 252.
7. Robert Milder, "The Rhetoric of Melville's *Battle-Pieces*," *Nineteenth-Century Literature* 44 (1989): 195.
8. Ibid., 196.
9. Helen Vendler discusses the "aura of names" in "Melville and the Lyric of History," in *Battle-Pieces and Aspects of the War*, ed. Cox and Dowling, 266.
10. Gibbons sang the song to Lincoln and other listeners following the Union defeat at Fredericksburg in December 1862.
11. Palmer's poem first appeared in the *Southern Literary Messenger* on September 17, 1862.
12. Stanton Garner suggests that Melville may have visited the Union ironclad the *Monitor* during the final stages of its construction since his cousin Guert Gansevoort was involved in the arming of the ship (131–32). For a discussion of Mel-

ville's knowledge of the ironclads and of this four-poem sequence, see Garner's *The Civil War World of Herman Melville* (Lawrence: University Press of Kansas, 1993), 131–37.

13. Herman Melville, *Battle-Pieces and Aspects of the War* (New York: Harper and Brothers, 1866), 53. All references to Melville's poetry are cited from this edition and are hereafter cited in the body of the chapter.

14. Garner links the musical sound of the ship's name to the grace of the sailing ships themselves: "The 'telling sound' of 'voweled syllables free' implies all of the other beauties of the old sailing ships, quiet swiftness, grace of carriage, gusting power and sunlit splendor" (*The Civil War World of Herman Melville*, 134).

15. "The Cumberland" appeared in *Harper's New Monthly* in March 1866 (vol. 32, p. 474). Other poems that appeared in *Harper's New Monthly* in the months leading up to the publication of *Battle-Pieces* include "The March to the Sea" (in February), "Sheridan at Cedar Creek" (under the title "Philip," in April), "Chattanooga" (in June), and "Gettysburg" (in July).

16. Henry Wadsworth Longfellow, "The Cumberland," *Tales of a Wayside Inn* (Boston: Ticknor and Fields, 1863), 216.

17. The *OED* reminds us of some now obsolete meanings of "cumber" that seem to resonate here. Beyond suggesting a "burden," "trouble," or "distress," verbal and noun forms of the word may denote "overthrow," "destruction," or "rout."

18. Though Melville's prefatory note suggests that most of the *Battle-Pieces* poems were written after the war's end, Hershel Parker observes that Melville began writing war poems "long before the fall of Richmond" (606). See Parker's *Herman Melville: A Biography*, vol. 2 (Baltimore: Johns Hopkins University Press, 2002), 606.

19. Thomas Buchanan Read's poem "Sheridan's Ride" first appeared in 1864 and quickly became a popular favorite. Melville is likely responding to Read's piece, as well as the many others written in response to this battle. For a nuanced reading of Melville's use of the imperative in this poem, see Jessica Roberts, "A Poetic *E Pluribus Unum:* Conventions, Imperatives, and the Poetic Call-to-Arms in Frank Moore's *Rebellion Record*," *ESQ: A Journal of the American Renaissance* 54 [1– 4] (2008): 171–97.

20. Though variant versions of the song proliferated throughout the war, I draw all of my citations from the first sheet music version published by Oliver Ditson in Boston in 1861 under the title "The popular refrain of Glory, Hallelujah as sung by the Federal Volunteers Throughout the Union."

21. Sweet points to "Donelson" as one of several poems in *Battle-Pieces* that versify journalism in order to "demonstrate the mystifying political effects of the prevalent journalistic and poetic tendencies to aestheticize the war" (*Traces of War*, 181). For another reading of this poem that also emphasizes its use of aestheticizing stances, see Eliza Richards, "'How News Must Feel When Traveling': Dickinson and Civil War Media," in *A Companion to Emily Dickinson*, ed. Martha Nell Smith and Mary Loeffelholz (Oxford: Blackwell, 2008), 160–62.

22. Hennig Cohen estimates that Melville relied on *The Rebellion Record* in composing at least twenty of the poems. Cohen's edition offers a thorough account of

Melville's work with this source. See Cohen's "Introduction," *The Battle-Pieces of Herman Melville*, ed. Hennig Cohen (New York: Thomas Yoseloff, 1963), especially 16 and 19.

23. William Wordsworth, "Preface to *Lyrical Ballads, with Pastoral and Other Poems*" 1802, in *William Wordsworth*, ed. Stephen Gill (Oxford: Oxford University Press, 1990), 611.
24. Examining the relationship between lyric and epic voice in Melville's *Battle-Pieces*, Vendler makes a similar point about erroneous newspaper reports in "Donelson": "The fallibility and interruptedness of the daily newspaper bulletin becomes, in Melville's hands, a symbol of the unknowability of war; modern battles are always too complex to be fully grasped. The successive headlines become a symbol of modern epic discontinuity" ("Melville and the Lyric of History," 263). For an analysis that reads "Donelson" in relation to the new technology of the telegraph, see Thomas D. Zlatic's "'Horned Perplexities': Melville's 'Donelson' and Media Environments," *Leviathan: A Journal of Melville Studies* 13.2 (June 2011): 38–53. My reading of the poem coincides with Zlatic's in emphasizing the ways that the telegraph both unites and divides the listeners waiting in the town square.
25. Herman Melville, "The Paradise of Bachelors, and the Tartarus of Maids," *The Piazza Tales and Other Prose Pieces, 1839–1860*, ed. Harrison Hayford, Alma A. MacDougall, G. Thomas Tanselle, and Merton Sealts (Evanston and Chicago: Northwestern University Press and The Newberry Library, 1987), 332. Reading the contrast between the jubilant public celebration of the victory and the private grieving of women the next day, Zlatic writes: "A principle motif of the poem, then, is the contrast between the residually oral community's vocal, public passion for the noble cause and a private silent recognition of the horrors of war" (49).
26. Sweet, *Traces of War*, 190.
27. Cohen suggests that Melville's depiction of the elms may have been influenced by the Grenada *Appeal*'s account of the battle, an account he could have seen in the *Rebellion Record* (*The Battle-Pieces of Herman Melville*, 231). Melville toured the site of the July 1862 battle two years later when he traveled to Washington to visit his cousin Henry Gansevoort, who was serving in the Union army.
28. Will S. Hays, "The Drummer Boy of Shiloh" (Louisville, KY: D. P. Faulds, 1863). I have silently corrected typographical errors in the lyrics.
29. For a reading that attends to the poem's representation of the theological underpinnings of state-sanctioned violence, see Michael Warner's "What Like a Bullet Can Undeceive?," *Public Culture* 15.1 (2003): 41–54.
30. The battle of Shiloh left more than twenty thousand soldiers dead or wounded. The high rate of casualties marked a turning point in public attitudes toward the war in both the North and the South: both sides began to realize that the war would be long and costly. Describing the aftermath of the battle, Grant noted that the field was "so covered with dead that it would have been possible to walk across the clearing, in any direction, stepping on dead bodies, without a foot touching the ground." Ulysses S. Grant, *Personal Memoirs* (New York: Penguin, 1999), 192.

31. Paul de Man, "Autobiography as Defacement," *The Rhetoric of Romanticism* (New York: Columbia University Press, 1984), 78.
32. As many scholars have also noted, Melville's Supplement also backs away from the radical critiques of racial hierarchies he offered in his earlier prose works; the Supplement suggests that white Northern forgiveness of white Southerners—"the communities who stand nearer to us in nature" (267)—must take priority over white Northern support for African American rights.
33. My reading of Melville's *Battle-Pieces* is thus at odds with Benjamin Friedlander's. Friedlander suggests that "one important difference between Dickinson's war poetry and Melville's is that hers resists a synthesizing narrative whereas his invites it." See Friedlander's "Emily Dickinson and the Battle of Ball's Bluff," *PMLA* 124.5 (2009): 1595. I would counter that the stylistic and political fragmentation of Melville's *Battle-Pieces* strongly resists any coherent synthesis—and that that fragmentation also results in the critical rejection of his collection in both the nineteenth and the twentieth centuries. I would further argue that this fracturing of stylistic and political commitments is evident in a broad range of Civil War–era poetry—not only in the work of Dickinson and Melville.

EPILOGUE

1. "Battle Hymn of the Republic, United States Navy," uploaded September 9, 2006 by Julius923, www.youtube.com/watch?v=IHVZK7nFYRQ.
2. All references to Tate's poem are from his *Collected Poems, 1919–1976* (New York: Farrar, Straus and Giroux, 1977) and are hereafter cited in text (22).
3. All references to Lowell's poem are from his *Selected Poems* (New York: Farrar, Straus and Giroux, 2006) and are hereafter cited in text (179).
4. All references are from Young's *For the Confederate Dead* (New York: Alfred A Knopf, 2008) and are hereafter cited in text (97).
5. Natasha Trethewey, *Native Guard* (Boston: Houghton Mifflin, 2007), 35.
6. A print version of "Public Figures" is forthcoming from Wesleyan University Press. I am grateful to Jennifer Geigel Mikulay for bringing Osman's "Public Figures" to my attention.
7. The multimedia version of the project available through *How2* includes Osman's recorded voice reading the full text, timed in relation to slides of the monuments and photographs, as well as text fragments layered over the images. See Osman's "Public Figures" at www.asu.edu/pipercwcenter/how2journal/vol_3_no_1/public_figures/
8. www.asu.edu/pipercwcenter/how2journal/vol_3_no_1/public_figures/ch4.html.
9. www.asu.edu/pipercwcenter/how2journal/vol_3_no_1/public_figures/ch2.html.
10. I am grateful to Elizabeth Robinson for bringing Janet Holmes's project to my attention.
11. All references to Holmes's work are from *The Ms of My Kin* (London: Shearsman, 2009) and are hereafter cited in text (24).

INDEX